THE
ADORNED
BODY

The Linda Schele Series
in Maya and Pre-Columbian Studies

THE
ADORNED
BODY

Mapping Ancient Maya Dress

EDITED BY
NICHOLAS CARTER,
STEPHEN D. HOUSTON,
AND FRANCO D. ROSSI

UNIVERSITY OF TEXAS PRESS ⬥ AUSTIN

This series was made possible through the generosity of William C.
Nowlin Jr. and Bettye H. Nowlin, the National Endowment for the
Humanities, and various individual donors.

♾ The paper used in this book meets the minimum requirements of
ANSI/NISO Z39.48-1992 (R1997) (Permanence of Paper).

LIBRARY OF CONGRESS CATALOGING-IN-PUBLICATION DATA

Names: Carter, Nicholas (Anthropologist), editor. | Houston, Stephen D.,
    editor. | Rossi, Franco (Anthropologist), editor.
Title: The adorned body : mapping ancient Maya dress / edited by
    Nicholas Carter, Stephen Houston, and Franco Rossi.
Description: Austin : University of Texas Press, 2020. | Includes
    bibliographical references and index.
Identifiers: LCCN 2019057919 | ISBN 978-1-4773-2070-9 (cloth) |
    ISBN 978-1-4773-2072-3 (ebook) | ISBN 978-1-4773-2071-6 (ebook
    other)
Subjects: LCSH: Mayas—Clothing. | Clothing and dress—Mexico. |
    Clothing and dress—Central America.
Classification: LCC F1435.3.C69 A43 2020 | DDC 391.00972/6—dc23
LC record available at https://lccn.loc.gov/2019057919

doi:10.7560/320709

Contents

THE
ADORNED
BODY

N

MAYAPAN ●   ● CHICHEN ITZA

COBA ●

JAINA ●   ● XCALUMKIN   TULUM ●

GULF OF MEXICO

DZIBANCHE ●   RÍO HONDO

CHETUMAL BAY

CALAKMUL ●   RÍO AZUL ●

EL MIRADOR ●   CARIBBEAN SEA

SAN BARTOLO ●

PALENQUE ●   EL ZOTZ   XULTUN ●   BELIZE RIVER
        UAXACTUN ●
        EL PERU ●   TIKAL ●

PIEDRAS NEGRAS ●   MOTUL DE   ● NARANJO
        SAN JOSE

TONINA ●   YAXCHILAN ●   UCANAL ●
        BONAMPAK ●   IXKUN ●   CARACOL ●
        CEIBAL ●   SACUL ●

DOS PILAS ●   NAJ TUNICH ●
        AGUATECA ●   NIM LI PUNIT ●
        MACHAQUILA ●
CHINKULTIC ●   CANCUEN ●   RÍO NEGRO

        SARSTOON RIVER

        MOTAGUA RIVER   QUIRIGUA ●

        ● COPAN

PACIFIC
OCEAN   KAMINALJUYU ●

USUMACINTA RIVER

0   100   200 km

FIGURE I.I. *The Maya region. Map outline courtesy of Clifford Brown and Walter Witschey.*

CHAPTER I

The Adorned Body

STEPHEN D. HOUSTON, NICHOLAS CARTER, AND FRANCO D. ROSSI

The human body is a key vehicle for expressing status and identity. Subject to external influence and internal motive, it declaims, moves, receives, and does. Yet the most flexible conduit of meaning is not the human frame itself—only so much can be done to physique. It is what the body wears, holds, and supports. By working through such projections of role and identity, this book offers a synthesis of dress in ancient Maya civilization, with special emphasis on the rich evidence from the Classic Maya who lived in or near the Yucatán Peninsula through much of the first millennium AD (fig. 1.1).

What is dress? To our view, it is the full array of objects, coverings, clothing, pelts, regalia, footwear, pectorals, headdresses, ear ornaments, belts, bracelets and anklets, body paint, and haircuts, as worn, held, or otherwise displayed on the human frame. These features are widely noted, excavated, and documented in images and archaeological corpora. Yet in the Maya case, there are thorough explorations of body concepts (e.g., Houston, Stuart, and Taube 2006), but relatively little is known about items of dress as separate things within ensembles (for useful if more broadly articulated exceptions, see R. Joyce 2001; and Orr and Looper 2014). There is little systematic literature on why these elements were worn, when, or by whom. Nor are there, outside of studies covering artifacts from particular cities, synthetic studies about such classes of objects, what they were

made of, or how they might be grouped and separated (for site-based artifact studies, see Kidder 1947; T. Lee 1969; Moholy-Nagy 2003, 2008; Sheets 1983; Taladoire 1990; Taschek 1994; Willey 1965, 1972, 1978; and Willey et al. 1994). There is insufficient understanding about how these features changed over time and how they varied from site to site. Other parts of the world seem more attentive to these matters (Callmer 2008; T. Martin and Weetch 2017), sometimes under the purview of "fashion," an intersection of aesthetic value, social competition, and personal caprice that continues to animate the walkways of Paris and elsewhere (Welch 2017). In Mesoamerica, the most comprehensive research comes from decades past (Anawalt 1990), with some strong additions in recent years (e.g., Olko 2005, 2014; Orr and Looper 2014).

To theorize dress, there is necessary guidance from comparative research (Hansen 2004). Influential sources suggest the following: (1) structures of power and the subjugation of individuals control the use of dress (Foucault 1995); (2) identity and boundary definition between self and society infuse ideas about what to wear (Strathern 1979; Turner 2012); (3) clothing and personal ornament bear complex, multivalent meanings, albeit with a foundation in basic themes such as gender, age, and so forth (Doniger 2017; Twigg 2015); (4) competition in royal courts and societies in elite contact tends to generate similarities and contrasts (Elias 1978); (5) dress, in the sense of body arts that modify human appearance, builds on historical practices that people must learn ("The body is man's first and most natural instrument" [Mauss 1973, 75]); (6) dress is always about wider change in relations of human inequality and unstable status—indeed, it "not only symbolized change but became a vehicle for change" (P. Martin 1994, 426); and (7) people copy others and enforce or self-enforce manners of behavior by "citing" or imitating those models (Butler 1990, 1993). Lurking behind these issues of choice and control is "sumptuary" law or tradition, by which certain dress or its coloration or material might be thought appropriate or not, depending on moral precepts and specified attributes of class or status (Anawalt 1980; Elliott 2008; Hunt 1996; Shively 1964–1965). Among the Maya, a jaguar pelt is known to have been worn by royalty, much as, for the Tudors of England, cloth of gold, an exceedingly expensive material, was intended for royalty, magnates, or prelates. Yet the ideal cedes to reality in most places. Much evidence suggests that sumptuary guidelines are often ignored and almost never enforceable. But such laws and rules do serve as ever-shifting projections of societies yearning for external tokens of social status (Hayward 2009, 27, 75).

Scholars such as Marcel Mauss, Michel Foucault, and Judith Butler are important influencers at this point, albeit with some reservations. In general, for all the many insights about how humans control one another through norms, subjugation, and mutual "citation," Mauss, Foucault, and Butler blunt the effects of personal preference and reduce the possibility of choices and whims unconditioned by the dictates of others (Houston 2018a, 7–13). This does not deny the centrality of their ideas to understanding dress or their ability to envision historical and cultural evidence in useful ways. Still, it may be that the way forward is less through broad theorizing than in the engrossing details of past and present arts of the body (e.g., for dance and gesture: Kaeppler 2011; McNiven 2000). These approaches have their own limitations. Of late, for example, "body arts" seem generally to coincide with studies of tattooing, masking, or altering the skin (e.g., N. Thomas 2014). Does this only reflect current aesthetic practices among the young today, or might we explore how physical adjustments send loud and even subversive messages in antiquity as well? Writing about such arts, Nicholas Thomas

looks with special intensity at the discontents, outliers, hybrids, liminal, and criminally variant (e.g., 2014, 139–173). In any human enterprise, absolute conformity, the desired aim of despots, is impossible to elicit or implement. Nonetheless, the royal imagery that grounds this book is by definition about a certain consistency of controlled representation. The work of official display is an earnest business, disinclined to capricious or insubordinate gestures.

Scholars often draw taut distinctions between this or that material (stone, textile, bone). They focus on separate technologies, potentials, and meanings, often, to be sure, in ways that greatly enhance Maya archaeology (e.g., Halperin 2016; Hruby 2007; Kovacevich 2016, 2017). The indirect result, however, is an atomization of objects by material. What may fall to the side is how such objects worked in unison, in what contexts, and with which kinds of people or beings. Specialist training often trumps any chance of finding cross-ties. Specific themes come to dominate, especially as they are related to the subject of gender, status, or, more recently, the discovery of masking and supernatural impersonation (Grube 1992; Houston and Stuart 1996; Looper 2009). Tatiana Proskouriakoff (1950) used some such features to study the temporal positioning of sculptures. For her, dress was less a final objective than a means of dating sculptures: clothing became an adjunct to seriation, an ordering of forms or features through time. On an otherwise eroded carving, a particular item of clothing might fix the monument to this or that twenty-year span, a standard unit for the Maya. To a surprising extent, this evidence has not been revisited in more than sixty years, offering clear rewards to future researchers.

For the ancient Maya, dress materialized in two guises: as actual objects, sometimes of quite ephemeral nature, or as items displayed in imagery, at times discussed in glyphic texts—glyphic nomenclature is retrievable, as the chapters in this book will show. First to actual objects. These may appear weightless in Maya imagery. Only Atlantean figures known as Itzam strive mightily to support heavy loads, and a few glyphs, shown in full-body form, toil with tumplines to carry freight (S. Martin 2015; Houston 2014b, 114). In practice, however, there is an unavoidable physics of dress. This includes features of weight, vector of motion, the responsiveness of certain items to rapid or slow movement, and the capabilities of varied human bodies, some slight, others muscular, short or tall. A perceptive study of a large piece of jade jewelry from Ucanal, Guatemala—the pectoral weighs in at 2.36 kilograms—gives some idea of how unwieldy such ornament might be (Halperin, Hruby, and Mongelluzzo 2018, 659). The authors analyze one stela at the city to estimate the weight of overall ornament carried by a royal dancer. At 11.43 kilograms, or 25.2 pounds, that dress seems heavy for most chair-bound academics, yet it lies well within the range of the weight of water (and its container) carried by young Maya girls, at least to judge from ethnographic information (Halperin, Hruby, and Mongelluzzo 2018, 766, 768).

The lessons from this study are revealing, but they may overlook two possibilities. The first is that the Classic Maya were known for inventiveness with pricey materials; for example, a set of hollow clay balls being daubed blue to reproduce jade (W. Coe 1959, fig. 58a). Clay is lighter than jade and far easier to wear, but the effect on viewers would be the same—an early example of "costume jewelry." In much the same way, a headdress of light, fibrous wood would not strain a neck, back, or legs, a real risk with hardwoods like mahogany (genus *Swietenia*) or guayacan (*Lignum vitae*). Second, some ponderous items of dress might not have been meant for humans. A Preclassic earspool from Pomona, now in the British Museum, is eighteen centimeters in diameter (Schele and M. Miller 1986, pl. 9). There is no published weight for this jade, but it is unlikely to have been worn by an ordinary person. Apparent "belt ornaments" also hang from images of palaces (Houston 2012b, pl. 56), and the Center Tablet of the Temple of the Inscriptions at Palenque, Mexico, may refer to the "collar" and "earflares" of local gods (M. Robertson 1983, fig. 96).

In fact, that same hieroglyphic text, still riddled with opaque passages, appears to establish an order for dressing deity effigies or, at least, offering or giving (*yak'aw*) ornaments to local gods. The process began with a skirt (*pih*) (also on La Corona Panel 1, a "back skirt" [*paat pih*] probably cued "backrack"; David Stuart, personal communication, 2011). It then referred to twenty-one "coverers" (*pixoom*), a possible reference to items of dress or to those doing the dressing. The passages go on to mention a royal diadem jewel (*sak hu'nal uuh*), an earflare (*tuup*), and a distinctive helmet (*ko'haw*) asso-

ciated with the city of Teotihuacan, Mexico (fig. 1.2a). On a Late Classic polychrome vase from the area of Naranjo (K1398), the dejected underworld deity God L complains of the theft of his apparel, naming items in nearly the reverse order: "The rabbit seized my jewels (*ni uuh*[?]), my clothing (*ni buhk*), my tribute (*ni patan*)" (fig. 1.2b). Jewels and ear ornaments are paired on another Late Classic vessel, this one from a royal burial at Tikal, with a scene in which a supplicant speaks to God L (fig. 1.2c). In Maya imagery, animals or insects might wear clothing or jewelry to signal that they could converse, participate in supernatural society, and play roles in mythic stories. In those contexts, to show dress on creatures was, in all likelihood, to equip them with near-human qualities.

In the Ucanal study, a divide exists between the measurements of two sorts of jade pendant (Halperin, Hruby, and Mongelluzzo 2018, fig. 5). That separation may accord precisely with whether they were worn by humans. A smaller set was feasibly an ornament, a larger set far too heavy for such use. Alongside the energy to wear and move with such costume—implying training, practice, and instruction in decorous movement—came other experiences. There would be the sound of percussive, high-toned clinking of jade against jade; the swish of cloth or feathers; the creaking of elaborate backracks; the squeaking of leathery footwear; and the rhythmic jangling of beads or shell pendants and their clappers. The visual effects of dress exist alongside the fact that they trigger other senses.

Yet if we are to be honest, concerns about depictive fidelity go to the core of how we view and interpret Maya representation. That is, what, precisely, was the nature of Classic "realism," its attention or commitment to close observation of things in their world? In part, there may be historical shifts at play in the Maya processes of looking and depicting. An urge toward an almost ocular precision, a fold shown as the eye sees it, not as the mind fixes it in orderly ways, is, perhaps, a distinct innovation during the later centuries of the Classic period (Houston 2018b). We return to this subject in the coda of this book. In a few instances, such precision can be evaluated directly. Elements of regalia or dress occur in imagery and also, by near miracle, happen to survive archaeologically. The list of such objects is not large, and an incomplete inventory includes an alabaster jewel re-

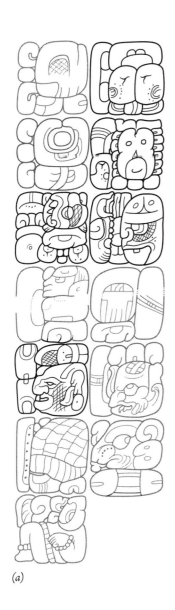

u pih
his skirts

pixoom
wrappers

u sak hu'nal uuh
his white paper diadem

u tuup
his ear ornaments

(a)

ni uuh, ni buhk, ni pat
my collar ornament,
my clothing, my tribute

(b)

ni tuup
my earspools

(c)

FIGURE I.2. *Hieroglyphic texts describing dress and ornament: (a) from Palenque, Temple of the Inscriptions, central panel, glyph blocks K3–K9; (b) on a Late Classic polychrome painted vessel from the area of Naranjo (K1398); and (c) on a Late Classic incised vessel from the Mundo Perdido Complex, Tikal. Drawings by Nicholas Carter, (b) after a photograph by Justin Kerr.*

covered from excavations at Aguateca, Guatemala, and also shown on Stelae 6, 7, and 19 at the site (Inomata and Eberl 2014, 92–94; see fig. 5.2). A jade from the cenote at Chichen Itza, Yucatán, may correspond to the belt ornament featuring an ancestor on Piedras Negras Stela 40 (Houston, Stuart, and Taube 2006, fig. 4.15a; Proskouriakoff 1974, 154, pl. 60, 1). A final example is the most decisive, a large jade pectoral in the shape of

the Ik', "wind," a sign excavated in a tomb at Nim Li Punit, Belize (Prager and Braswell 2016, figs. 6, 8, 9). The jade appears on several stelae at the site. As with some such objects, it is self-referential, the pectoral being recorded glyphically as a single polished stone suspended from a beaded collar—that is, one item of address connotes a set of related ornament (see also Źrałka, Hermes, and Koszkul 2018, fig. 14, for the same glyph on a jade pectoral at Nakum, Guatemala, after an observation by Simon Martin). These artifacts underscore the real chance that the portrayal of dress connects to tangible objects. Impressive heirlooms such as these may not have been the only examples, although others are more difficult to detect. A string of beads or a bracelet of jade or worked *Spondylus* shell could have been shown in imagery and also retrieved from a burial or cache. But their nondescript nature prevents any straightforward identification. What can be presumed is that rich stories informed all of these things (Hoskins 1998; R. Joyce 2000c) and even, as demonstrated for regalia, personal names for a certain dynastic treasure (Houston, Stuart, and Taube 2006, fig. 2.4).

There must have been some variance from tangible models, the objects seen or held by carvers or painters. A moment's glance at a quetzal plume, flimsy and narrow, shows a considerable departure from the massed plumage of headdresses on stelae or painted on pottery. (One of the few exceptions comes from graffiti at Tikal, where feathers appear in a convincingly scraggly manner [Źrałka 2014, pl. 69]). Even if real objects were on display—winnowed by artistic craft—regularization tends to suffuse Maya depiction via a removal of imperfections, a filling out, and an orderly presentation that enhances visual clarity but fails to exhibit the messiness of the original. In a sense, this is also the intention that informs that restorer's art in refurbishing Maya cities for tourists. Think of the results, which a moment's reflection exposes as a fantasy or a distortion: slumping of masonry, gone; uneven edges, leveled; indentations, smoothed and plastered to a perfection that was probably not there in the original. In a subtle way, images of Maya dress must have inflected later production of ornament, for their idealizations might be reproduced by makers some generations later or the objects themselves passed down as heirlooms (see the coda of this book).

In all such dress, there are social and aesthetic deliberations that are accessible but quite challenging to tease out from evidence (R. Joyce 2002). There may also be personal whims, the expressive personality of a particular ruler. David Cannadine (2001) and Paul Fussell (2002), observers of states, empires, and their indicators of uniform(ed) status and hierarchical distinction, revel in the opposite, the insistence that people look the same, if always with tokens of difference to leaven and subtly qualify systems of dress. Cannadine's mordant reflections on British imperial "ornamentalism" and Fussell's take on uniforms raise questions about what differed in Maya dress and what might have been, in a point noted before, an enforced sameness at royal courts. The plumed rulers in dance demonstrate a high degree of similarity, but so do their plainly attired courtiers.

The contrast between the two sorts of people was surely deliberate. The presence of the poor or underprivileged, a lively presence, say, in prints of Hanoverian England by William Hogarth, finds almost no visibility in Maya data—even slaves or captives pictured in imagery were likely to have been noble (the lone exception is, perhaps, a gray-garbed figure carrying a jar of atole at Calakmul, Guatemala [Carrasco Vargas and Cordeiro Baqueiro 2012, fig. 22]). A notable fixture of Maya dress is that complex assemblages cannot be brought together, positioned, or fastened by a single person. One attribute of social privilege is to wear clothing that requires assistance to drape over the body and, after use for particular occasions, some help in removing that dress. Moreover, the idea of a body that is covered and selectively exposed goes to the heart of that culturally laden term "nudity" (its classic positive distinction from mere nakedness occurs in K. Clark 1956; see also the cultural shifts and variant contextual meaning of such concepts [with magical or Freudian nuances imputed by some scholars] in Bonfante 1989, 544–545). Among the Maya and elsewhere, the state of being unclothed invoked, especially for the genitalia, a sense of shame and vulnerability, a relegation to the bestial and an acute feeling of contrasts between people (Houston, Stuart, and Taube 2006, 213–217; see also Bonfante 1989, 547–548, 560, 569–570). If animals and insects could be made human by wearing clothes and jewels, humans could be stripped of that status by the removal of dress.

Valuable items of dress must have been stored, their shape retained by lasts, and their security guaranteed by effective, monitored stowage. Bugs and mold needed to be kept at bay in the humid tropics. Several such lasts appear in Maya imagery, either for protective gear placed around the hip and torso of ballplayers (Houston 2012b, 318) or to maintain the dignified shape of royal crowns (Stuart 2005, fig. 87). In the area of the Usumacinta drainage and region of Palenque, Mexico, it is nobles who offer up regalia; sometimes this was done by the parents of a ruler (M. Miller and Brittenham 2013, figs. 285, 286, 297, 298). Perhaps they were responsible for the storage or curation of such precious objects, although the intention may have been figurative, if one or both of the parents were deceased. Others usually had to help with cumbersome gear, and not just among the Maya. A Victorian lady of distinction required a special maid for such needs, as did a French monarch at his levee; today, celebrities attending a gala have stylists and makeup artists to fuss over them (e.g., Beeton 1861, 1018; Elias 1983, 78–104).

Comfort was not always the objective, nor was ease of use. For women in many parts of the world, high heels prevent rapid movement, and the eroticized mutilations of "lotus feet" in China constrained and restricted freedom of movement, especially for females of higher rank or greater wealth (Craik 1994, 115; Ko 2007, 110). In the case of bound feet in China, it was concealment of an erotic feature that excited male imaginations and prompted "origin stories" about why certain practices had come into existence (Ko 2007, 110–114). John Berger famously excoriated Western art as the product of the male "surveyor" wishing to control women, and a male perspective may have shaped most of Maya imagery too (1972, 46–47; for Mayanist parallels, see Houston, Stuart, and Taube 2006, 51–56; Rossi 2018, 96–98).

Rare perfumes wafted from the body, in oils or potions concocted by specialists or by some home recipes prior to the advent of the "mass beauty industry" (Peiss 1998, 9). The Classical world had expensive ointments but many that were not so pricey. Housing such unguents led to other arts of the body: "Some inexpensive pyxides [receptacles for makeup] were made of wood, the blown glass used to hold unguents was cheap" (Olson 2009, 291). In fact, the ancillary crafts and means of storage are just as crucial to the adorned body and often accessible to archaeological study, although this topic is seldom pursued in New World archaeology. Moreover, the line between medicines and makeup can be thin or blurred and the costs of certain beauty agents, such as white lead or mercury sublimate, literally mortal to the wearer (Olson 2009, 306–308). Among the ancient Maya, tobacco may have been applied to the body, along with other substances that affected mood (Houston and Inomata 2009, fig. 8.4c).

Scenes of dressing highlight some Classic Maya images, always with consorts or underlings to help (K1524). At Bonampak, Mexico, figures surround princes to assist in their dressing and to hoist elaborate backracks of quetzal plumes that are mentioned in texts nearby (Houston 2018a, 150). Only a few people are named, suggesting that such service was not always carried out by close kin of royalty. Some of this activity was cross-gendered, women assisting men, especially in dynastic images (K2695 in the Justin Kerr database), but its model may have been supernatural. An essential part of preparing for dances by the Maize God was his dressing by young women, probably members of his harem (K3033). The Maya may also highlight a divine inversion of this act of clothing a god. As mentioned previously, a trickster rabbit was seemingly inclined to larceny, absconding with the hat and beaded collars of a deity connected to wealth (K1398). The abundance of goods implied a commensurate chance of theft (see K1560 for another example). Indeed, colonial-era sources from Yucatán stress the dire consequences of robbery if caught and prosecuted: enslavement or tattooing, if the crime were committed by nobles (Landa 1941, 60, 86, 90, 124). Societies that emphasized tangible wealth must have thought anxiously about its loss and, paradoxically, its greedy concentration in the hands of few. God L, a deity of traders, embodied that concern as a being who moved between and outside communities, a god of the night and furtive movement, perhaps the harbinger of, and spy for, violent raids or attacks. The many servants of Maya courts must have confronted their own temptations to lift an object or two . . . or been gifted dress by grateful masters and mistresses. In the Bonampak murals of Chiapas, Mexico, several depictions of clothing on courtiers reveal, with tantalizing omission of actual names, a set of painted texts. These designate dress as items of tribute or as personal possessions that might have come from others (Houston 2018a, 152). Yet, aside from these glimpses, the social "flow" of such ornament within and between kingdoms remains poorly understood.

In some contexts, ancient Maya dress was highly conservative, even fossilized, with certain garments or entire outfits, intended for certain settings, substantially unchanged from the Late Preclassic to the Late Classic period. Such was the case for some politically charged apparel connected with rulership: the white headband of kingship (see chapter 5 in this volume) or a headdress depicting the Principal Bird Deity (chapter 4). The violence of the ritual ball game imposed a certain functional stability on the kind of gear its players wore, albeit with some variations: one knee pad or two, and more or less elaborate headdresses to announce personal or team identity. Other suites of clothing and ornament appear to be conventional over wide distances and across political lines, but only for a few generations, as with the relatively standard assemblages depicted for sacrificers and sorcerers in the Late Classic period (chapter 2).

Yet within these broad categories and outside of them, what the ancient Maya wore and why they wore it are not reducible to tradition or ritual meaning. There must have been at least some judgments of beauty and taste, here, as in other places, dedicated in part to establishing contrasts between elites and less favored people (Bourdieu 1984). As Georg Simmel (1957, 542–543) showed long ago, fashion involves trendsetters and innovators, followed by an endless cycle of imitation and abandonment of that trend, leading on to new ways of distinguishing the bon ton from others. Metropoles played roles here, for they could establish "peripheries" of taste, in which provinces or marginal zones endeavored in turn to create their own standards (Bartlett 2011). Individual anxieties about choices operated in tandem with acts of reassurance or censure (Clarke and Miller 2002). That fashion is only a condition of modernity seems belied by numerous studies of shifting taste in the ancient world (e.g., Bartman 2001; compare with Belfanti 2009, 261, who situates "fashion" in the later Middle Ages and at the beginnings of industrialization). In some places, the need for finer distinctions of taste, conceived as "refinement," may be accurately tracked over time (Bushman 1993). Such processes must have existed among the Maya, too.

This book results from a seminar taught by Stephen D. Houston at Brown University in the spring of 2013. Years of writing and revision have passed; students have gone through their PhD ordeals, moved on to professional lives, worked on later projects. A few extra essays were also commissioned, from Mallory E. Matsumoto and Cara Grace Tremaine, to fill out the book. It is not the usual edited volume. All chapters were coordinated and laid out by Houston, with further suggestions from Nicholas Carter and Franco Rossi. The chapters follow a similar layout, a tandem arrangement of evidence, with topics leading toward an almost cartographic task: to map the Maya body, its alterations and accoutrements, over time. We were mindful of the need to find commonalities in evidence, but also to let divergent data

tell their own tales. The authors looked at manufacture (how were items made, what did material have to do with meaning, and who did that productive work?), possession and naming (who owned objects, and what terms applied to elements or ensembles of dress?), physicality (how were elements worn, how did they promote or obstruct movement, and what was the experience of using, seeing, and hearing them?), identity (what was worn by whom, when, and why, and was there evidence of individual preference or pattern?), meaning (what did such dress signify, what was it thought to accomplish when worn, and what were the referents of dress, be they dynastic or mythic?), and, the most elusive of all, variation (what shifted over time and through space, and what were the motivations for such variety?). All relevant evidence was entertained, with priority given to Classic-period evidence but with due accommodation of the more immediate leads from living or historic Maya.

In conceiving and helping to prepare this volume, Houston expresses gratitude for the resources of his Dupee Family Professorship at Brown University, which helped to defray costs. He is equally obliged for a leave of absence, in 2018 and 2019, from his teaching duties at Brown and for subsidies that academic year from the Kislak Chair, Kluge Center, Library of Congress, and the American Council of Learned Societies. Carter acknowledges the support of the Peabody Museum of Archaeology and Ethnology and the David Rockefeller Center for Latin American Studies at Harvard University, and especially the assistance and generosity of Barbara Fash and Cynthia Mackey. For his part, Rossi gives thanks to the Cora Du Bois Trust for its generous support during the writing of this manuscript, as well as Heather Hurst and the San Bartolo–Xultun Archaeological Project for overall help and encouragement. He also recognizes Boston University and Brandeis University for fostering a collegial and fruitful environment while preparing this manuscript. As editors, we are equally indebted to the University of Texas 2019 Maya Meeting and its contributors for their helpful comments and insights. All contributors give *abrazos* (hugs) to Justin Kerr for permitting the use of his superb photographs.

How is this "map" organized? The volume moves by logical arrangement from coverings and painting, the first chapters, and then addresses, in steady order, the top of the body all the way down to the feet. Chapters 10 and 11 step back to examine reasons for the variety in our evidence and the capacity of the adorned body to move, followed by a coda synthesizing the findings of the book. In all chapters, the fact that layerings existed came quickly to our collective view, along with a sense that this task required more than a single volume to map Maya ornament in all its splendor. More work is always needed. But a map begun is a map that promises further journeys on the *sak bih*, the high road to ancient Maya thought and life.

CHAPTER 2

The Clothed Body

NICHOLAS CARTER, ALYCE DE CARTERET, AND KATHARINE LUKACH

The Classic Mayan word for clothing was *buhk*, a term attested in a few hieroglyphic contexts and with cognates in Ch'olti' (*buk*) and Ch'orti' (*bujk*) (Boot 2004, 39; Hull 2005, 12). At least in the latter language, the closest living relative of Classic Mayan, the same root produces the verb *bujkse*, meaning "to adorn," including but not limited to the ornamentation of human bodies. A second Ch'orti' root, *pix*, means "to dress," "to cover," or "to wrap"—for instance, in the context of a headwrap or *pixol* (see chapter 4 in this volume). Most ancient Maya clothes were made of cloth, although some special garments were of hide or beaten bark, and modern Mayan languages are rich in terms related to spinning, weaving, and sewing. "To spin fibers" in Ch'orti' is *ch'ajna*, yielding *ch'ajnan* for spun fibers or anything made from them (Wisdom 1950), while "to sew" is *chuyi*. No verb for "to spin" is securely attested in the hieroglyphic corpus, but a term for sewing does appear in the Dresden Codex (*u chuy*, "his/her sewing," on page 2 of that manuscript). Ch'orti' *jar* is "to weave," applied to woven cloth but also to basketry and plaited hair (Wisdom 1950). A cognate Classic Mayan verb, *jal*, is known from the ancient inscriptions—notably in the names of the first month of the solar year, *K'anjalaw* or *K'anjalbu*, "Yellow Weaving," potentially a reference to weaving baskets or mats.

Another ancient term for working cloth with sharp instruments, *puutz'*, appears on some thin bone pins from a queenly deposit looted in or near the city of Naranjo, Guatemala (Houston and Stuart 2001, 64, 66, fig. 3.2). Hieroglyphic tags describe the objects as *u puutz' baak*, probably "the weaving-bone of" their queenly owner. A cognate term in Yukateko, *puts' baak*, denotes bone needles used for sewing (Barrera Vásquez et al. 1980, 678), but the objects from the Naranjo area are more likely picks for brocading or weaving. Another Yukateko term, *pechech*, refers to circular spindle whorls of the kind made from ceramic or stone by ancient Maya people; the word is cognate with Ch'olti' *petet*, "spindle" (Boot 2004, 26), and with Classic Mayan *pet*, "circle," "circular."

Words for animal skins in modern and historical Mayan languages include Ch'olti *tz'uhum* (leather), Ch'ol *tz'u'm* (skin, leather) and *pächij* (leather), Ch'orti' *k'ewer* (animal skin, leather), Yukateko *k'ewel* (leather), Ch'ol *nujkul* (hide, skin), Chontal *tz'u'm* (leather), and Tzeltal *nuhkul* (hide, skin) (Barrera Vásquez et al. 1980, 396; Boot 2004, 39; Hopkins, Josserand, and Cruz Guzmán 2011, 164, 176; Kaufman 2003, 373, 375). Of these, the last finds a known cognate in the hieroglyphs: Classic Mayan *nuk*, "skin," which can also apply to the plastered or painted walls of buildings. There is also a word sign, **K'EW**, that uses a partly prepared jaguar hide—its head missing but paws intact—to stand for "leather, skin, hide" (Zender, Beliaev, and Davletshin 2016b, 49–50, fig. 13). The most precious, high-value item seemingly served as the exemplar of a broader class that included, perhaps, pelts and hides of lesser worth.

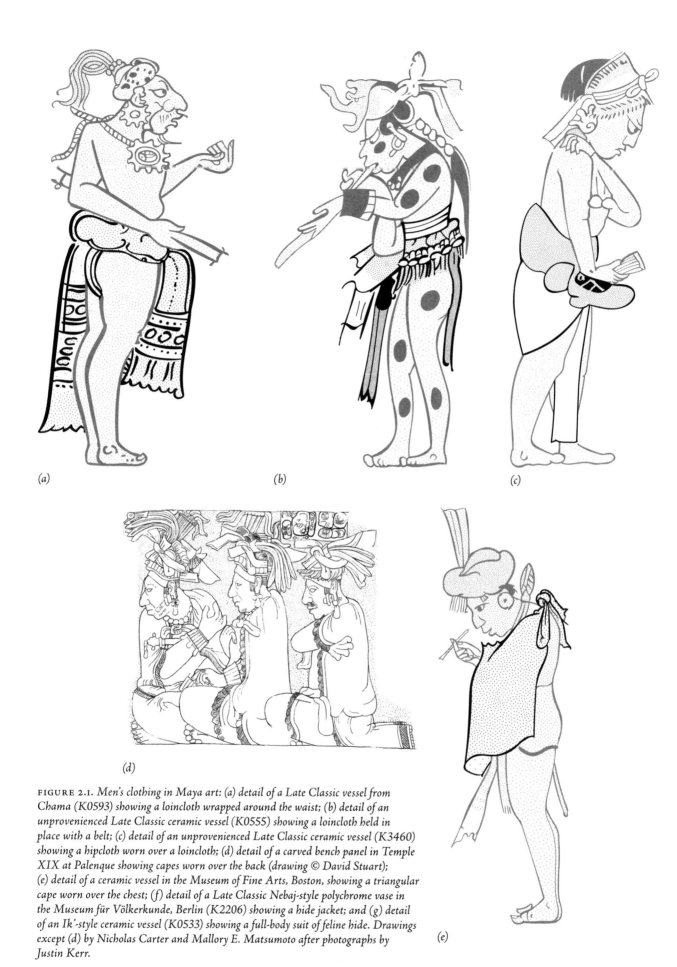

(a)

(b)

(c)

(d)

(e)

FIGURE 2.1. *Men's clothing in Maya art: (a) detail of a Late Classic vessel from Chama (K0593) showing a loincloth wrapped around the waist; (b) detail of an unprovenienced Late Classic ceramic vessel (K0555) showing a loincloth held in place with a belt; (c) detail of an unprovenienced Late Classic ceramic vessel (K3460) showing a hipcloth worn over a loincloth; (d) detail of a carved bench panel in Temple XIX at Palenque showing capes worn over the back (drawing © David Stuart); (e) detail of a ceramic vessel in the Museum of Fine Arts, Boston, showing a triangular cape worn over the chest; (f) detail of a Late Classic Nebaj-style polychrome vase in the Museum für Völkerkunde, Berlin (K2206) showing a hide jacket; and (g) detail of an Ik'-style ceramic vessel (K0533) showing a full-body suit of feline hide. Drawings except (d) by Nicholas Carter and Mallory E. Matsumoto after photographs by Justin Kerr.*

(f)   (g)

Cloth and hide could both be dyed or painted, techniques denoted by the root *bon* (color, paint, dye) in languages including Ch'ol, Ch'olti', Ch'orti' (*boni*, "to dye," and *bono*, "to paint"), Chontal, Tzotzil, Tzeltal, and Yukateko (Barrera Vásquez et al. 1980, 64; Boot 2004, 13; Hopkins, Josserand, and Cruz Guzmán 2011, 24; Hull 2005, 12; Kaufman 2003, 812). Canonically, there were five principal colors in the Maya palette—red, yellow, black, white, and blue/green—a concept expressed in Yukateko with the term *ho'bon* (five colors) for painting and colorwork in general (Barrera Vásquez et al. 1980, 64, 159, 215; this schema has obvious relations to Maya color-directional symbolism; Houston et al. 2009, 27). One Late Classic ceramic vessel (K6100, now housed in the collection of the Los Angeles County Museum of Art, M.2010.115.644) presents the idea visually, showing those colors in diagonal bands with a geometric band along the top, duplicating a blanket or mantle with a brocaded selvage.

TYPOLOGY

The fundamental articles of woven clothing and its analogues in other materials remained the same for both sexes from the earliest Maya representations of clothed human bodies until the Spanish Conquest. Royal and aristocratic costume involved elaborations of these basic elements, not their replacement with clothing radically different from that worn by farmers and craftspeople. For men, the most basic garment was the loincloth, a long strip of cloth wrapped around the waist, tied at the back, and then passed between the legs and pulled up behind the horizontal section at the waist, with one end allowed to hang down in front (fig. 2.1a). An alternative form used a separate belt or sash (fig. 2.1b). Loincloths of either kind could be elaborately decorated with a variety of techniques, discussed below.

Optionally, men could add a hipcloth or a woven or animal-hide kilt to their outfits, protecting their upper legs and permitting further displays of status or ornament (fig. 2.1c). Long or short capes or cloaks of various materials could be worn over the shoulder, fastened by knots or ties (fig. 2.1d). On occasion, capes—sometimes triangular—covered the front of the body instead of the back (fig. 2.1e). Men's vests and open jackets are attested on some Late and Terminal Classic figurines and in painted scenes (fig. 2.1f) (e.g., W. Morris 1985, 250; M. Miller and Brittenham 2013, fig. 125). Finally, full-

FIGURE 2.2. *Women's clothing in Maya art: (a) detail of a seventh-century mural from the Chiik Nahb complex at Calakmul showing a simple wrap with one end thrown over the shoulder (courtesy of Simon Martin and Ramón Carrasco Vargas); (b) detail of an unprovenienced Late Classic ceramic vessel (K6059) showing a sarong worn over the breasts; (c) detail of a codex-style ceramic vessel (K1339) showing a sarong worn below the breasts; (d) detail of an unprovenienced Late Classic ceramic vessel (K0554) showing an upper-body wrap worn over a skirt; (e) detail of an incised Late Classic alabaster vessel (K4340) showing a poncho; and (f) detail of an unprovenienced Late Classic ceramic vessel (K0764) showing a huipil decorated with a resist technique. (Drawings except (a) by Nicholas Carter and Mallory E. Matsumoto after photographs by Justin Kerr.)*

body suits, fitted to the arms and legs, are depicted in a variety of media, especially on Late Classic polychrome vases (fig. 2.1g). These garments were intended not for ordinary use but for ritually and politically potent performances in which the wearer performed the role of some animal or supernatural being.

Women's clothing emphasized draping and concealment of the body, with distinctions of status potentially indicated by different degrees of coverage. The simplest feminine garments were wide panels of cloth, wrapped around the body and legs and thrown over the shoulder (fig. 2.2a) or tied above or below the breasts in the manner of a sarong (figs. 2.2b, c). A variant of the sarong was a long skirt, either wrapped around the legs and tied at the waist or sewn into a tube from two pieces of cloth, and worn with or without a shorter wrap covering the chest (fig. 2.2d). Skirts and sarongs could also be combined with shawls or poncho-like garments, which covered the shoulders but did not extend far down the body (fig. 2.2e). Such clothing left the arms free, while restricting the movement and possible positions of the legs. Women also wore huipils: enveloping, tunic-like garments sewn shut on the sides, with holes for the head and hands (fig. 2.2f). Still used by many Maya women today, huipils could reach to the waist or lower legs and in both cases could be combined with sarongs or wrapped skirts.

SPATIAL AND TEMPORAL VARIATION

Unfavorable environmental conditions mean that archaeological textiles in the Maya region are rare and usually badly preserved. Early Classic fragments come, for instance, from tombs at Río Azul (Carlsen 1986, 1987) and El Zotz (Ordoñez 2015). For the Postclassic period, we have fragments of textiles from the Cenote of Sacrifice at Chichen Itza (J. Lothrop 1992) and Mayapan (Mahler 1965, 593), as well as from caves in the highlands of Chiapas (Johnson 1954). Nevertheless, evidence for the cultivation of fiber-yielding crops and their processing into textile clothing is sufficient to attribute those practices to the deep Mesoamerican past. Cotton grows well in a variety of soils, but requires a heavy rainy season followed by warm weather with ample sun (Berdan 1987, 237); such conditions obtain throughout Mesoamerica's lowland regions, especially

the Pacific, Gulf, and Caribbean coasts, but irrigation also allowed cotton to be grown in antiquity in river valleys in the interior. Domesticated varieties of cotton were being cultivated in the Tehuacan Valley of Central Mexico by 3500–2300 BC (C. Smith and Stephens 1971, 167) and in the southeastern Maya lowlands by 2210–1380 BC (Lohse 2010, 321). Plant fibers preserve poorly in the humid lowlands of eastern Mesoamerica and the Gulf Coast, but a ceramic sherd from the Middle Preclassic site of La Venta bears the impression of a woven material consistent with loom-made fabric, while Olmec figurines and monumental sculpture frequently depict both cordage and cloth (Follensbee 2008, 91; see, e.g., Guthrie and Benson 1995, 278–282; K. Taube 1995, fig. 6). Further evidence for cloth production in the form of brocade picks and weaving awls made from ceramic, greenstone, and perishable materials have been excavated from Middle Preclassic contexts throughout Mesoamerica, including at the Maya sites of Chacsinkin (Andrews 1986, 23–25), Edzna (Schmidt, de la Garza, and Nalda 1998, 578), Ceibal (A. Smith 1982, 243–244; Willey 1978, 97–98), and Tikal (Moholy-Nagy 1994, 84, 158–159).

Late Preclassic highland and lowland Maya monuments de-emphasize cloth in favor of other types of personal adornment. Textiles are certainly present, mainly in the form of loincloths, but the elite bodies such monuments depict tend to be bedecked in imperishable ornaments rather than cloth. The Late Preclassic mural paintings from San Bartolo are in line with this pattern. Few of the gods and supernatural beings they depict wear much cloth beyond loincloths or short skirts. At the same time, their scenes of coronation and ritual show that the elements of Classic-period elite dress were already in place by the third century BC, including jaguar-skin kilts, elaborate loincloths, and brocaded cloaks (fig. 2.3a). A depiction of the last of these is unique in Maya art: the cloak has sleeves covering the wearer's upper arms, while wide sections of weftless warp alternate with bands of brocade and twining or embroidery. In another scene, two of the Maize God's female attendants each wear a short skirt featuring a different geometric pattern (fig. 2.3b).

Early Classic monumental art in the Maya lowlands likewise shows little fabric. Early stelae and jadeite celts depict human figures, most of them divine kings en-

(a)

(b)

FIGURE 2.3. *Cloth garments in the San Bartolo murals:*
(a) coronation scene (San Bartolo Mural, illustration by Heather
Hurst, © 2005); and (b) female attendants (San Bartolo Mural,
illustration by Heather Hurst, © 2003. Both images courtesy of
Heather Hurst).

gaged in Long Count period-ending rituals, outfitted
in abundant quetzal feathers and greenstone jewelry.
What little skin-covering clothing they wear usually
consists of a jaguar-pelt kilt, often with a ritual apron
(see below) hanging down over it (fig. 2.4a). Early Classic celts portraying rulers duplicate both the format and
the costume conventions of the stelae, with hieroglyphic
texts incised on one side and the image of a bejeweled
but otherwise lightly clad ruler on the other. Yet other
Early Classic images, depicting other kinds of activities, suggest that cloth consumption was tied to social
status. For instance, male courtiers in the fifth-century
mural in Uaxactun Structure B-XIII wear long, bulky

skirts, incorporating multiple layers of differently colored cloth. Their headdresses, stiff cloth kerchiefs tied
with headbands, are the visual origin of a logogram potentially read **EBEET**, "messenger," an aristocratic title
(Houston 2018a, 104–105; Stuart 2005, 133–136; see
chapter 4 in this volume). The paucity of textiles in the
Preclassic and Early Classic visual records, then, may
simply be due to sampling bias: stone monuments and
celts, which preserve relatively well over centuries, tend
to present royal male bodies in ceremonial costumes
emphasizing ornaments over cloth. Women, nonroyal
elites, and activities other than calendrical ceremonies
are rarely portrayed in Early Classic lapidary work, and
the domestic and courtly scenes typical of some Late
Classic ceramic painting traditions are absent from the
earlier ceramic corpus.

Late Classic polychrome vessels constitute the larg-
est, most varied, and most detailed corpus of ancient
Maya depictions of cloth, but the Late Classic monuments of many Maya kingdoms also exhibit a concern

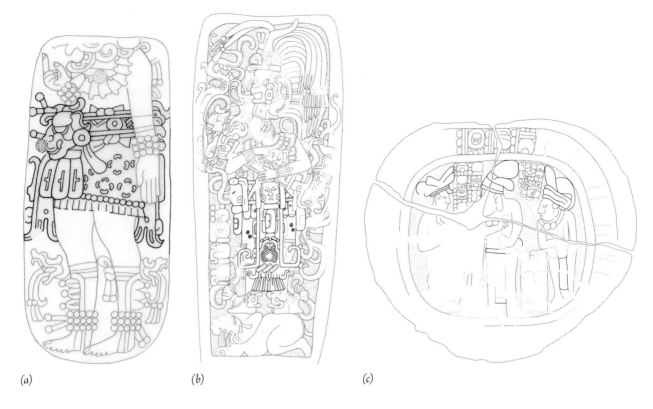

(a)   (b)   (c)

(d)   (e)

FIGURE 2.4. *Cloth and hide elements in royal costumes: (a) on an unprovenienced Early Classic belt plaque (drawing by Linda Schele, © David Schele, courtesy of Ancient Americas at LACMA [ancientamericas .org]); (b) on the Late Classic Naranjo Stela 12 (drawing by Ian Graham, © President and Fellows of Harvard College, PM2004.15.6.2.20); (c) on the Terminal Classic Caracol Altar 10 (drawing by Nicholas Carter); (d) on a Terminal Classic ceramic vessel (K6437) in the style of Señor del Petén (drawing by Nicholas Carter after a photograph by Justin Kerr); and (e) on the Terminal Classic Ceibal Stela 20 (drawing by Nicholas Carter).*

with representing cloth in stucco and stone. Textiles are most prominent in such works at sites in the western part of the Maya world—Palenque, Tonina, Yaxchilan, Piedras Negras, and Dos Pilas—the likely result of confluent factors. One of these may have been the greater importance of elite women, notably at Yaxchilan, in the roles of royal wives and mothers during that period. Especially in the eighth century AD, nonroyal nobles and junior members of royal families were likewise represented in the monumental art of that region to a greater extent than they had been anywhere in the Maya lowlands during the Early Classic era. Queens and subordinate nobles were depicted in a broad range of settings, calendrical rituals but also coronations and private bloodletting rites, affording sculptors the opportunity to record a variety of costumes corresponding to a wider range of statuses and roles.

With the political changes of the ninth century AD came a period of variation and innovation in the way cloth was depicted on monuments and in painted art. In northern Peten and southern Campeche, Terminal Classic stelae continued to portray rulers carrying out a limited range of ritual actions connected to period endings, wearing the same outfits—rich in jade, feathers, and jaguar skins, but with little woven cloth—that their forebears had worn on such occasions (fig. 2.4b). By contrast, Caracol's ninth-century monuments depict that site's kings wearing headscarves, loincloths, and thick cloth sashes, the same courtly attire shown on Late and Terminal Classic ceramic vessels (fig. 2.4c). A number of contemporary polychrome ceramics from the central lowlands carry the theme of restrained elite dress further, showing lords and kings wearing only minimal quantities of cloth and jewelry (fig. 2.4d). At Terminal Classic Ceibal, monumental records of royal clothing seem to shift with political connections between the Petexbatun region and other parts of the Maya world. Early-ninth-century rulers with ties to northern Peten and southern Belize favored elaborate variations on traditional sartorial themes for their period-ending monuments: elaborate headdresses, jade ornaments, and abundant feline pelts instead of fabric. Later monuments show figures of uncertain status wearing simpler costumes in which cloth played a more significant role (fig. 2.4e).

A number of Postclassic representations show gar-

ments hanging down over the wearer's chest, with the hanging end variously pointed or rounded and with or without fringed edges. Some of these garments resemble a *quechquemitl*: a kind of shawl made from two pieces of cloth sewn together so that one corner of each piece hangs down in the front and back, usually coming to a triangular point or, alternatively, being rounded by folding and sewing or by a special weaving technique (Anawalt 1981, 127; Lechuga 1982, 131; W. Morris 1985, 248–249). However, a paucity of images and sculptures showing the Postclassic Maya coverings from behind or in the round makes their identification as *quechquemiteh* problematic. Instead, some figurines from Mayapan suggest that they could have been capes worn over the chest, open in the back. More common in the Mayapan sculptural corpus, however, are short mantles that cover the body front and back but reach only to the upper arms; these are sometimes shown worn with cloth panels hung from stiff transverse bars of plaited cloth or mat-work, suspended from a cord around the neck, which take the place of the frontal cape (figs. 2.5a and b). Pointed frontal capes feature prominently in the mural paintings at Santa Rita Corozal (fig. 2.5c) and Tulum (fig. 2.5d), where they appear with selvages and stepped fringes.

The Dresden Codex depicts few different types of cloth or hide garments for each sex, although different deities are marked by certain clothes. Almost all goddesses appear in short or long skirts without upper garments (figs. 2.6a, b), although one woman wears a short cape with a fringe (fig. 2.6c). Male figures almost always wear loincloths, and when other garments appear at all, they are almost always capes or cloaks, usually with some iconographic significance. For instance, the death god Akan (God A') wears a rounded, fringed

FIGURE 2.5. *Postclassic cloth garments: (a) ceramic figurine from Mayapan showing a frontal cape (drawing by Nicholas Carter after R. E. Smith 1971, fig. 64c); (b) ceramic statuette from Mayapan showing a mantle worn with a cloth panel hung from a cord around the neck (drawing by Nicholas Carter after R. E. Smith 1971, fig. 32g); (c) detail of a mural painting on the west wall of Mound 1 at Santa Rita Corozal showing a pointed frontal cape and a rectangular cape worn over the back (drawing by Nicholas Carter after Gann 1900, pl. 31); and (d) detail of Tulum, Structure 5, Mural 1, showing a pointed frontal cape (drawing by Nicholas Carter after a painting by Felipe Dávalos G.).*

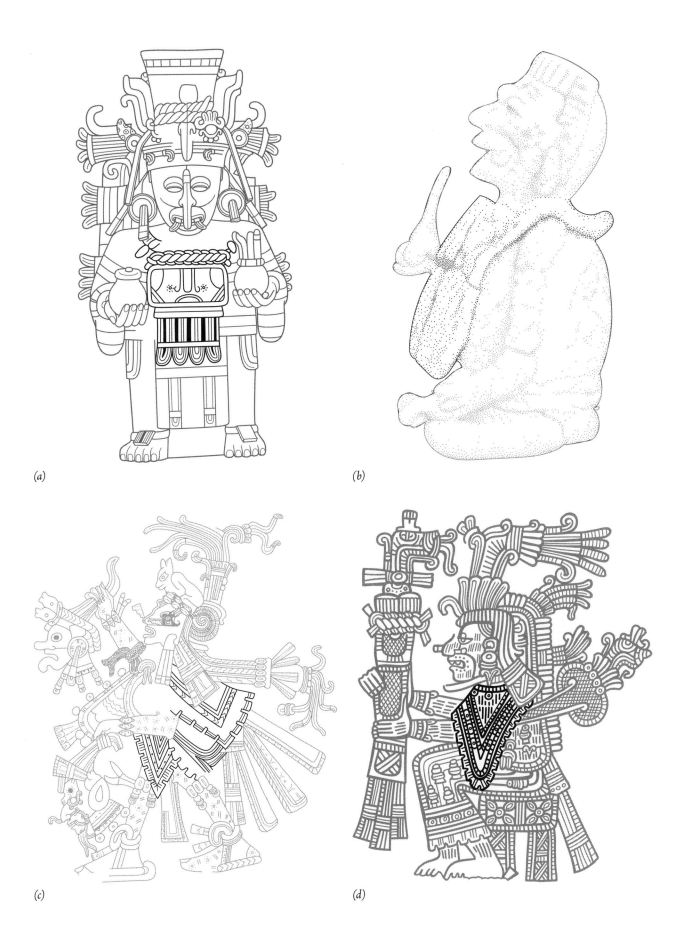

(a)

(b)

(c)

(d)

(a)   (b)   (c)

(d)   (e)   (f)

FIGURE 2.6. *Cloth and hide garments in the Dresden Codex: (a) Ix Chel wearing a short fringed skirt (p. 9); (b) death goddess wearing a long skirt (p. 9); (c) young goddess wearing a short fringed skirt and cape (p. 2); (d) Akan wearing a long fringed cape (p. 5); (e) death god wearing a long fringed cape (p. 12); (f) God D wearing a long fringed cape (p. 27); (g) God D wearing a frontal cape (p. 27); (h) opossum deity wearing a skirt made from strips of cloth (p. 27); and (i) Venus deity wearing a jaguar-hide skirt (p. 52). Drawings by Nicholas Carter and Mallory E. Matsumoto.*

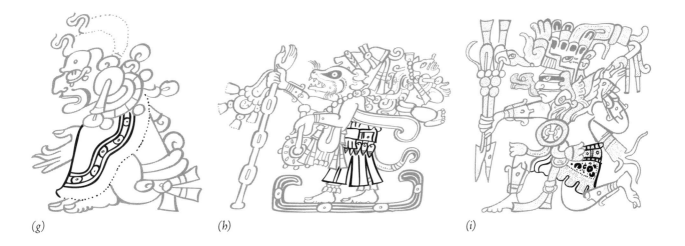

(g)   (h)   (i)

cape painted with crossed bones (fig. 2.6d), while another death god sports a longer cloak with similar decoration (fig. 2.6e). The celestial God D usually wears a
cape like Akan's, but without any underworld imagery
(fig. 2.6f); more rarely, he wears a frontal cape not unlike
the ones from Tulum and Santa Rita Corozal (fig. 2.6g;
see 2.5c for comparison). Among the few exceptions to
the standard loincloth in the Dresden is a skirt made
from strips of cloth hanging down the legs and bound at
the waist of an opossum deity carrying a fan and a traveler's staff (fig. 2.6h). An aspect of the planet Venus appears as a dart-throwing warrior wearing a skirt of feline
hide, the lower edge painted and fringed, continuing the
Classic association between spotted cats' pelts and martial prowess (fig. 2.6i).

PRODUCTION

The construction of ancient Maya textiles was constrained by the materials and technologies available,
given local ecologies and traditions. As elsewhere in
Mesoamerica, the major source of fiber for textiles for
the ancient Maya was cotton (*Gossypium hirsutum*); suc-
culent plants in the genus *Agave* were also used, but
were probably less important to the ancient Maya than
in Central Mexico (Baron 2018, 106). Other sources
would have included cattail reeds, and various species
of palms; even a kind of wild silklike material is attested
in Peten during the Spanish contact period (made from
the cocoons of caterpillars in the family *Saturniidae*),
though whether this material had pre-Columbian antecedents remains to be seen (Chase et al. 2008, 127–

128; Halperin 2008, 114). Yet, by the time of Spanish
contact, cotton was by far the most economically important fiber used in clothing in the Maya region, to the extent that one Spanish official thought it the principal
crop grown in the Audiencia de Guatemala (López de
Cogolludo 1957 [1688], 303; Quezada 2001, 73). Diego
de Landa recorded that two types of cotton—a small
annual variety and a larger variety that flowered every
year for five or six years—grew "in wonderful quantity"
throughout Yucatán (Tozzer 1966 [1941], 200).

To become cloth, fibers first had to be spun into yarn,
which Maya producers did by using handheld drop spin-
dles weighted with spindle whorls—perforated, disk-, or
bead-shaped weights stuck onto the spindle shaft to add
extra momentum to the rotating spindle, increasing the
speed of the process and helping ensure a tightly twisted
thread. The identification of spindle whorls in the archaeological record is surprisingly complicated: besides
obvious whorls crafted from stone or molded clay, that
record includes ceramic sherds taken from broken pots,
drilled through the middle, and shaped into rough circles. Some such objects were backings for ear ornaments
(Chase et al. 2008, 128), yet ethnographic parallels and
the close physical resemblance between perforated sherd
discs suggest that many or most were spindle whorls
(Baron 2018, 106).

The form of Maya garments was constrained by the
backstrap looms used for weaving cloth. Such looms,
still in use among indigenous people throughout Mesoamerica, are human scaled and indeed depend for their
functional existence on the presence of human bodies.
A backstrap loom has no permanent frame. In use, ei-

ther end consists of a horizontal stick or bar around which the warp threads are tied. First, the front loom bar, is tied to an upright support: a tree, a building post, or a stake in the ground. The weaver sits at a convenient distance from this support, the back loom bar held against her waist by a strap that passes around her body, the warp threads stretched between her and the support (fig. 2.7). In this position, she can control the tension of the warp threads, insert weft threads using a wooden shuttle and batten, and apply other decorative techniques like brocading. When a web of plainweave cloth thus produced is finished, its edges require a border of some kind: woven selvage made by adding extra warp threads along the edges (attested archaeologically at Chiptic Cave [Johnson 1954]), a separate hem (often brocaded), or a fringe made by tying off sections of warp or weft threads.

Because the weaver inserts the shuttle by hand from either side of the loom, she cannot produce a web of cloth wider than her own sideways reach. The finished section of cloth is kept rolled around the back loom bar, where its growing volume eventually impedes weaving. For this reason, resulting cloth pieces today generally do not exceed five yards in length (Hendon 2006, 362; Prechtel and Carlsen 1988, 125–126). The simplest Classic Maya cloth garments, like men's loincloths, would have been made from a single web of cloth; broader pieces of clothing, like skirts and sarongs, would have required two cloth sections stitched together, while larger huipils would have needed three (W. Morris 1985, 245–246). The seams from such joins, however, are rarely evident in monumental or painted art. They are present on some figurines from a Late Classic ritual deposit at Lagartero (Ekholm 1979), but typically not on Jaina-style figurines. Cutting is rare even in modern and historically attested Maya cloth production; in Classic times, it seems to have been limited to full-body costumes—virtually the only examples of ancient Maya tailored garments—as well as the necks of huipils and tunics and the cutaway motifs that characterize some high-status robes. The fact that Maya clothes makers were limited to single-edged cutting tools was likely one factor here, as was the superior strength of cloth woven to the desired shape rather than cut and sewn (W. Morris 1985, 251–252).

Sections of finished cloth, in varying shapes and sizes,

FIGURE 2.7. *Jaina-style figurine showing a woman using a backstrap loom. Drawing © Oswaldo Chinchilla Mazariegos.*

could be folded, wrapped, twisted, and tied into meaningful and aesthetically pleasing shapes. Such constructions could be stiffened with starch from corn or yucca (Bruhns 1986, 307) and pressed flat with hot stones. Torn into rags or perforated with holes, the plain-cloth garments in which Late Classic captives are sometimes shown signified their degraded status and perhaps the impending violation of their bodies (fig. 2.8a). The greatest variety of decorative techniques applied to cloth, however, affected its color or structure. Yarn or woven garments could be dyed, but whole garments are rarely shown dyed a single solid color. Instead, differently dyed yarns might be woven together into webs of cloth, yielding repeating multicolored patterns. The simplest such designs involved alternating bands of two colors in either the warp or the weft of the fabric (fig. 2.8b), but tartans incorporating two or more colors in both warp and weft are more common in the ceramic corpus (fig. 2.8c). More elaborate imagery could be produced by embroidering or brocading. In the latter technique, additional threads were incorporated into the cloth as it was woven, generating angular designs. Brocade is common in Late Classic imagery, particularly in selvage (fig. 2.8d),

(a)   (b)

FIGURE 2.8. (a) Detail of Piedras Negras Stela 8 showing a captive with torn clothing (drawing by David Stuart, © President and Fellows of Harvard College, PM2004.15.6.19.23); (b) detail of an unprovenienced Late Classic ceramic vessel (K7727) showing a striped garment (drawing by Mallory E. Matsumoto); (c) detail of a seventh-century mural at the Chiik Nahb complex, Calakmul, showing a tartan garment (courtesy of Simon Martin and Ramón Carrasco Vargas); and (d) detail of an unprovenienced Late Classic ceramic vessel (K2695) showing a netted huipil with brocaded selvage (drawing by Nicholas Carter after a photograph by Justin Kerr).

(c)

(d)

but both the technique and some Late Classic brocaded motifs date back to at least the Late Preclassic period.

Alternatively, cloth could be stamped with dye or painted freehand. Long cloaks, sarongs, and huipils offered the most spacious fields for painted designs (see figs. 2.2b and d). Garments of any size, including loincloths and sarongs, were decorated with resist techniques. Here, plain or dyed cloth was painted with wax (batik) and perhaps knotted (plangi), and then dyed with a darker color. The knots were then untied and the wax melted out of the fabric, leaving a variety of patterns in contrasting colors (fig. 2.2f) (Anawalt 1990). In a sanguinary twist on such methods, a late-eighth-century mural at Bonampak suggests that people responsible for ritual bloodletting—an official mutilating the fingers of war captives and a servant assisting royal ladies in bloodletting from their tongues—dyed their own clothing with spots of human blood (see Miller and Brittenham 2013, 83, fig. 160; 110, fig. 107).

Choices in textile adornment or elaboration produced an equally wide range of aesthetic variation. Besides brocaded or embroidered selvage, the hems of garments could be decorated with beads, fringes, or stepped or simple tabs of cloth. Ceramic vessels from northern Peten show loosely woven or netted huipils with brocade selvage and embroidered designs, a material sometimes deployed to erotic effect. A Late Classic mural painting from the Chiik Nahb complex at Calakmul shows a woman clad in another revealing garment (Carrasco Vargas, Vázquez López, and Martin 2009): a gauzy, translucent huipil dyed blue and painted with red glyphs. Light, gauzy fabrics, loosely woven from thin threads, are strongly but not exclusively associated with women in lowland Maya art (Halperin 2016); they were probably short-lived compared to heavier, more tightly woven clothing, but impressions of openwork cloth used for surface smoothing have survived on some ceramic objects (W. Morris 1985, 251), and fragments of gauzy textiles were recovered from the anoxic mud at the bottom of the Cenote of Sacrifice at Chichen Itza (J. Lothrop 1992, 33–39). As detailed renditions of royal costume at Yaxchilan and elsewhere make clear, brocade and embroidery were valued not just for polychromy but also for the layered, three-dimensional effects produced by contrasting depths and thicknesses of thread and fabric. One weaving technique in particular seems to have

been highly valued: yarn or cordage twined into a mat (**POHP**) motif, woven into a knotwork net or stretched across circular or quatrefoil holes cut in an expanse of cloth, to be worn over a background or interior garment of different design (fig. 2.9a).

The Maya had recourse to a variety of animal, vegetable, and mineral sources for dyes and paints (for a fuller treatment, see Houston et al. 2009, 59–61). Yellow dyes can be extracted from a wide range of indigenous plants, notably a tree called *k'ante'*, "yellow tree," in Yukateko (*Erythrina berteroana*; see Ciudad Real 2001 [1577], 326; Carter and Santini n.d.). A smaller number of native plants yield blue dyes, of which indigo (*Indigofera* spp.) is both the most economically important since the Spanish Conquest and the only one whose dye can readily be identified in laboratory analysis (Carlsen and Wenger 1991, 368). Dyes extracted from brazilwood, logwood, and cochineal can all be mordanted to produce shades of purple (Houston et al. 2009, 60); a marine mollusk native to the Pacific Coast of Mesoamerica, *Plicopurpura pansa*, is still "milked" for its deep-purple dye by indigenous craftspeople in Oaxaca, and textile fragments dyed with it were recovered from Chiptic Cave in Chiapas (Gerhard 1964, 30–31; Michel-Morfín, Chávez, and González 2002). Brazilwood can also dye cotton in pink and lavender tones; annatto, also a valued condiment, yields orange and orangey-red tones. True red dyes may have been harder to produce, since the carmine extracted from the cochineal insect—another important product under Spanish rule—does not set well in cotton cloth. Deep reds, well attested in ancient Maya art, may usually have been achieved using iron oxide–based paints, or even using the precious and highly toxic cinnabar, instead of being dyed in the yarn (Carlsen and Wenger 1991, 370; Houston et al. 2009, 64–65). The use of cinnabar as a fabric colorant is archaeologically attested for Early Classic funerary textiles at El Zotz (Ordoñez 2015, fig. V.4) and Río Azul (Carlsen 1986, 1987).

A second set of technologies dealt with the treatment of animal skins. Once stripped from the carcass, hides require processing to keep them from stiffening and decomposing. After being scraped clean of subcutaneous tissue and (when undesired) hair, skins would have been stretched and dried on a frame or on the ground, potentially leaving projecting tabs where the shrinking

(a)

(b)

FIGURE 2.9. (a) Detail of Yaxchilan Lintel 25 showing a long huipil with pohp motifs (drawing by Ian Graham, © President and Fellows of Harvard College, PM2004.15.6.5.22); and (b) detail of a Late Classic vessel from Chama (K0593) showing a cape of feline hide with the head and paws attached and with tabs of skin left from the drying process (drawing by Nicholas Carter after a photograph by Justin Kerr).

skin had been held by pegs or ties (fig. 2.9b). The hides of different animals were subject to varying degrees of processing. Stripped of their hair, deerskins could be used to make ties or thongs, worn as kilts or cloaks without further decoration, or dyed and painted, de-emphasizing the species of the animal. Some hides, especially those of cats, were worn with the head, paws, and tail still attached, typically hanging downward, with the rear of the animal at the shoulders, waist, or buttocks of the wearer.

Rare in all media, feathered cloaks are depicted on a few Late Classic monuments. In eastern Peten, they formed part of a ritual costume depicting the Jaguar God of the Underworld, worn by rulers to commemorate military victories (fig. 2.10a; Carter and Santini

n.d.). A pair of early-ninth-century monuments from Ceibal show a royal ball-playing costume including a feathered kilt (fig. 2.10b). Diego de Landa (1978, 44, 107) mentions that tunics, jackets, and other garments adorned with the feathers of birds wild and tame were worn for ritual occasions in Yucatán prior to the conquest, and Late Classic Jaina-style figurines show beautiful examples of the technique (fig. 2.10c). The contexts in which feathered clothing appear suggest not only the high value of such garments, but also an association between the flight of birds and the graceful movements of trained warriors and athletes.

SOCIAL ASPECTS OF TEXTILE PRODUCTION AND USE

Colonial sources indicate that cloth played a vital role in pre-Columbian economies (e.g., Sahagún 1959, 48; see Berdan 1975, 210–224). This is especially well attested in Central Mexico, where ethnohistoric documents such as the Codex Mendoza detail the advanced tributary system that extracted textiles in huge amounts from across the Aztec Empire. The Postclassic Maya

(a)   (b)   (c)

FIGURE 2.10. (a) *Sacul Stela 6 showing a feathered cloak as part of a martial costume (drawing by Nicholas Carter after a field sketch by Ian Graham); (b) detail of Ceibal Stela 7 showing a feathered hipcloth as part of a ball-game costume (drawing by Ian Graham, © President and Fellows of Harvard College, PM2004.15.6.17.7); and (c) Jaina-style figurine showing a feathered suit, possibly with protective padding (drawing by Nicholas Carter).*

world, especially the Yucatán Peninsula, seems to have participated in this "greater Mesoamerican commercial system," engaging in large-scale production and trade of textiles that tied the Maya region to areas as far away as Tenochtitlan to the west and Honduras to the south (Patch 1993, 16). In the Maya area, mold-made and stone spindle whorls appear in abundance much later than sherd discs in the archaeological record during the Late Classic period (Kidder 1947, 39, 68), a shift Joanne Baron (2018, 108) explains in terms of a changing role for cotton cloth in Maya economies. In Baron's model, purpose-made spindle whorls reflect a new concern with consistency in thread thickness and weight, as cotton

cloth became a more currency-like commodity that was standardized for tribute and exchange.

As with some other ancient Maya crafts (e.g., Kovacevich 2007, 2011), different stages of cloth production may have been carried out by people or households of different social status. For instance, at Motul de San José, spindle whorls were recovered in similar numbers from lower- and higher-status residential compounds, but the bone needles and picks used for embroidering and brocading were more abundant at higher-ranked residences (Halperin 2008). A potential implication is that most households engaged in the bulk production of thread, but that people with the time and skill to make highly valued works of textile art were better represented among the wealthier faction of the population. Nevertheless, there is little evidence for weaving as a full-time occupational specialty among the ancient Maya, as opposed to a widely but variably practiced form of household labor (Hendon 2006). Jaina-style figurines may reflect a similar status-based division of labor: according to a recent suggestion by Mary Miller

(2018), low-status women within that corpus, with simple clothing and often with exposed breasts, are represented engaging in a variety of activities, including spinning thread but not weaving cloth. This last activity appears largely restricted to women with more concealing clothing and richer ornamentation. A note of caution is in order here: Jaina-style figurines represent their makers' understandings of idealized or stereotyped social roles. That upper-class women were portrayed as weavers does not mean that they did all or even most of the weaving in ancient Maya society, only that that aspect of their domestic economic lives was highlighted in art.

For the ancient Maya, as for their modern descendants and for indigenous people across Mesoamerica, cloth production was traditionally centered on the home, practiced by people of varying socioeconomic status, and strongly but not exclusively associated with women and girls (Hendon 2006). Relevant knowledge and skills were transmitted through "home-based apprenticeship systems" that embedded cloth production within household economies: women, primarily, mastered this craft and trained their daughters in its techniques (Hendon 2006, 372; Inomata 2001, 323). Yukateko dictionaries compiled by Spanish clerics in the sixteenth century present the production of thread and cloth as the work of women, something echoed by modern ethnography (J. Clark and Houston 1998, 34; Pancake 1991). Indeed, textiles and associated implements had strong symbolic connections to women, childbirth, and healing in Mesoamerican mythology. A Late Classic vessel depicting a birth features the divine midwife, Goddess O, wearing a spool of cotton in her headdress (K. Taube 1992b, 103; K. Taube 1994, 657–658), and the modern Tzutujil Maya similarly associate the weaving of a textile with birth (Prechtel and Carlsen 1988). However, weaving might not have been completely exclusive to women, since spindle whorls have been recovered from male burials (Hendon 2006, 366). Men are likely to have been involved in certain kinds of textile decoration, especially painting hieroglyphic texts, since there is very little evidence for women as scribes (Houston 2011, 23).

Strong gender distinctions exist in the visual record of ancient Maya textiles and pelts. The use of animal hides of any kind, except perhaps in sandals or bindings (see chapter 9 in this volume) is virtually confined to men. A few exceptional images depict queens and supernatural women with jaguar-skin hair wraps (fig. 2.11a), but not with skirts or capes of that material. Deer were likely the usual source of leather and skins for men, but wealthy and powerful individuals—kings and war leaders above all—had access to the pelts of predatory cats. Jaguar and ocelot skins are the most frequently seen, recognizable pelts in Classic period images of dressed persons (fig. 2.11b), but the hides and heads of mountain lions would likely also have been worn.

In general, ancient Maya men probably wore less cloth, and exposed more of their bodies, than women did. Farmers and craftsmen would have worn loincloths, and optionally cloaks or hipcloths, leaving the arms free for work. For Classic Maya elite men, such practical concerns existed in tension with the need to signal wealth, status, and individual identity. This tension must have been especially acute for warriors on the field of battle, who seem to have resolved it by wearing elaborate and distinctive headgear while leaving their bodies as unencumbered as possible. Tight-fitting hide jackets afforded some warriors a measure of protection, but the quilted cotton armor favored by the Postclassic Mesoamericans is not widely attested in Classic Maya art. Exceptions come mainly from the corpus of Jaina-style figurines, some of which show warriors with padded vests.

By contrast, women tend to be depicted swathed in broad expanses of cloth, even in the Early Classic period when cloth appears less important to ritual display than in later times (see fig. 2.11c and chapter 4 in this volume). The connection between cloth and femininity was made early in life: the handful of young girls shown in Maya art, all members of the elite, wore huipils that stretched to their ankles—a rather limiting garment that helped inculcate proper deportment (fig. 2.11d; Miller and Brittenham 2013, 86, fig. 165 caption). Most adult women on Classic stone monuments likewise wear long, enveloping robes that both obscure the contours of their bodies and display their access to high-value textiles. Mural paintings and polychrome ceramics reveal the role that netted and translucent textiles played in creating an eroticized contrast between the concealment and the exhibition of the female form (fig. 2.11e). Decorum apparently called for elite ladies' shoulders to be covered with a cloak, mantle, or huipil in mon-

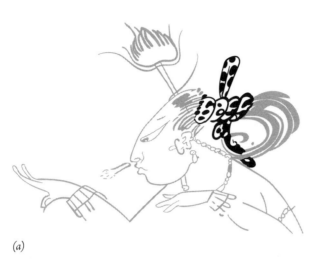

(a)

(b)

(c)

(d)

(e) (f)

FIGURE 2.11. *(a) Detail of a codex-style ceramic vessel (K2096)*
showing a woman with a feline-skin hair wrap (drawing by Mallory
E. Matsumoto after a photograph by Justin Kerr); (b) detail of
the mural painting in Room II at Bonampak showing a ruler with
feline-skin jacket, sandal uppers, headdress, and spear wrapper
(Gift of Bonampak Documentation Project, illustrations by
Heather Hurst and Leonard Ashby); (c) detail of the mural paint-
ing from Structure B-XIII at Uaxactun showing a woman with
a shawl and a long huipil or sarong (painting by Antonio Tejeda,
© President and Fellows of Harvard College, PM50-1-20/22982);
(d) detail of the mural painting in Room I at Bonampak showing
a royal girl in a long garment (Gift of Bonampak Documentation
Project, illustrations by Heather Hurst and Leonard Ashby);
(e) detail of an Ik'-style ceramic vessel (K2573) showing a royal
woman in netted garments (drawing by Nicholas Carter after a
photograph by Justin Kerr); and (f) detail of a mural painting from
the Chiik Nahb complex, Calakmul, showing a well-off lady in a
diaphanous blue huipil taking a jar from a servant in a simple wrap
(courtesy of Simon Martin and Ramón Carrasco Vargas).

umental art; in the scenes presented on Late Classic
polychrome vessels, the shoulders and breasts might be
covered in more formal contexts, or exposed in domestic settings, without bearing on the social status of the
women portrayed. Since women are less commonly depicted in Maya art, and nearly always members of the
elite class, we have less data on how details of clothing
might have signaled differences in their social station.
Distinctions of rank evident from other factors—gen-
erational differences, for instance—were at times flattened by uniform clothing, as in a scene of bloodletting
by palace ladies in the Bonampak murals (Miller and
Brittenham 2013, 141, fig. 279). Yet the examples from
the Jaina figurines, already discussed, suggest that enveloping textiles afforded higher-status women a greater
right to modesty than was available to poorer women
and slaves (M. Miller 2018). Further evidence comes
from the murals at Calakmul's Chiik Nahb complex
(S. Martin 2012): there, a woman in a translucent blue
huipil painted with bright-red medallions and a hieroglyphic text takes an olla of atole from the head of another woman wearing an opaque but likewise revealing
wrap of coarse, drab cloth. Elsewhere on the painted
platform, a similarly poor garment wraps an old woman
struggling under another giant ceramic vessel (fig. 2.11f;
see also fig. 2.2a). None of these women shows any indication of belonging to the elite, but the simple wrap
indexes hard, menial labor, while the more diaphanous
huipil apparently signals higher status.

(a)

(b)

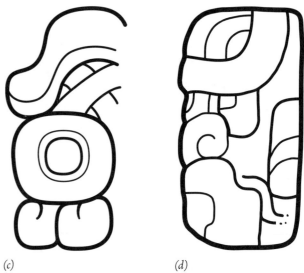

FIGURE 2.12. (a) Ritual apron or loincloth reinforced with wood on a Late Classic limestone panel in the Dumbarton Oaks collection (drawing © Alexandre Tokovinine, used with permission); (b) ritual apron with ʔLEM face on an unprovenienced ceramic vessel (K0787; drawing by Mallory E. Matsumoto after a photograph by Justin Kerr; (c) logogram **NUUN** (drawing by Nicholas Carter); and (d) animate form of the logogram ʔLEM (drawing by Franco D. Rossi).

(c)

(d)

For great kings no less than for poor farmers, loin-cloths were indispensable masculine garments. Rulers and other elite men wore outsize ritual aprons—false loincloths, in essence—and dance belts during public ritual performances. Ubiquitous in royal monumental portraits from the Early to the Terminal Classic period, these garments went together with a wide range of head-dresses and other costume elements worn for calendri-cal celebrations. Both the belt and the long frontal flap were made of cloth or paper reinforced with strips of bark or wood, which could curl out away from the hang-ing end (fig. 2.12a). Such a construction would not have been particularly flexible or easy to pass between the legs, so it was likely worn over a functional cloth under-garment. Further decoration was furnished by feathers, mat-work, or disks of shell or wood. The hanging flap might be painted or embroidered with the head variant of the logogram ?LEM (Stuart 2010, 293), which de-notes a glinting surface or objects with such a surface, like polished celts (figs. 2.12b, d). The apron itself is the graphic origin of another hieroglyph: syllabic **nu** and logographic **NUUN**, perhaps a ritual title (fig. 2.12c; Kettunen and Helmke 2014, 115).

Another ritual role, connected to mortuary rites, sor-cery, and infant sacrifice, had its own distinctive cos-tume. With extant representations confined to the Late Classic period in northern Peten and southern Campeche—Tikal Altar 5, the seventh-century Vase of the Initial Series from Uaxactun, and several un-provenienced painted vessels from the Mirador Basin and elsewhere—this office was distinguished by a long, brocaded cloak (fig. 2.13a) or a short mantle composed of strips of spotted cloth or bark paper (fig. 2.13b). A broad-brimmed hat covered with panels of cloth bound together at the crown completed the ensemble. The same garments characterize supernatural beings associ-ated with death, drunkenness, and the underworld, in-cluding Gods A' and L.

One garment in particular is associated with the life transitions of young elite males: a cloak of feathers or leaves affixed to a cloth backing, worn over the back and tied at the throat, or else hung over the chest from a cord around the neck. Disheveled compared to most feath-ered cloaks, the components of these garments are dif-ficult to identify, but they are marked with two or three dots and sometimes central lines—similar, but not iden-

tical, to the feathers of wild turkeys, but with a strong argument as well that these elements correspond to a penitential and quite painful garment of nettle leaves (figs. 2.13c, d, e, f; David Stuart, personal communica-tion, 2019). Such garments could be worn by young men or boys making their first blood offerings, as on Dos Pi-las Panel 19 (Houston 2009, 165); they also appear on youths presenting tribute to older men or receiving their benediction. The elder figures in such scenes hold ritual items, including aspergilla of feathers and painted pa-per with which they anoint the youths (see K1440). An avian headdress and a second type of distinctive cloak, made up of separate imbricated sections tied into knots, characterize the elder figures' costumes. This kind of costume of the elder who gives his blessings in such rites echoes the Late Preclassic murals at San Bartolo, where similar garments are worn by an old man presenting a royal diadem to a ruler (see fig. 2.3a). While uncommon in Classic imagery, the knotted cloak is not unique to this senior role, since a young prince is also shown wear-ing it on the main panel from the Temple of the Cross at Palenque (fig. 2.13g).

CONCLUSION

The study of clothing and textiles reveals a wealth of in-formation about ancient Maya society. Textiles, most obviously, clothed the body and constituted a rich sym-bolic system by which various aspects of an individual's identity were communicated. A loose sarong draped over one's shoulder indexes femininity; a feathered cloak highlights a young man's move through adoles-cence; a jaguar pelt announces the ferocity and valor of its wearer.

Although evidence for the domestication of cotton extends thousands of years into the past, early depictions of Maya dress feature little in the way of cloth. The lim-ited number of surviving monumental sculptures, mu-rals, and painted vessels from the Preclassic and Early Classic periods surely skews our perceptions of clothed Maya bodies during those times, but an emphasis on polished jade over cloth and hides is evident at least for ritual costumes. A shift toward greater abundance and variability in depictions of textiles and other clothing suggests a coincident shift in the way the clothed body was idealized and valued. Certainly, the image of the re-

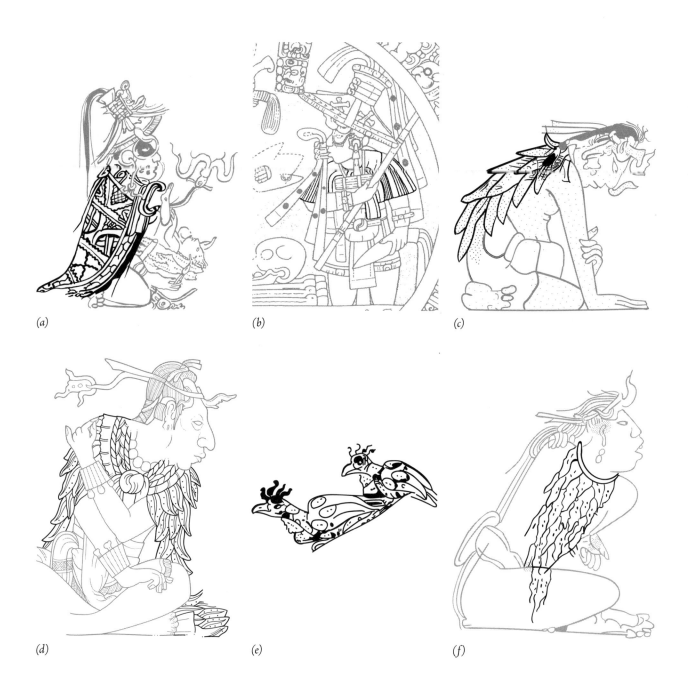

FIGURE 2.13. (a) Detail of a codex-style ceramic vessel (K1200) showing a sorcerer wearing a long, brocaded cloak (drawing by Nicholas Carter after a photograph by Justin Kerr); (b) detail of Tikal Altar 5 showing a ruler in a sorcerer's costume, including a short mantle of strips of cloth or bark paper (drawing by William Coe, image courtesy of the University of Pennsylvania Museum); (c) detail of an unprovenienced Late Classic ceramic vessel (K1440) showing a young man in a cloak of feathers or leaves (drawing by Mallory E. Matsumoto after a photograph by Justin Kerr); (d) detail of the bench panel from Temple XXI at Palenque showing a young prince in a cloak of nettles (drawing by Nicholas Carter after a photograph by Jorge Pérez de Lara); (e) detail of a codex-style ceramic vessel (K1247) showing wild turkeys with dotted feathers (drawing by Mallory E. Matsumoto after a photograph by Justin Kerr); (f) detail of a codex-style ceramic vessel (K1645) showing a young noble wearing a frontal cape of feathers or leaves (drawing by Mallory E. Matsumoto after a photograph by Justin Kerr); and (g) detail of the main panel from the Temple of the Cross at Palenque showing a prince wearing a knotted cloth cloak (drawing by Linda Schele, © David Schele, courtesy of Ancient Americas at LACMA [ancientamericas.org]).

(g)

gal male ruler, bedecked in jewels and an elaborate headdress but otherwise clad in little more than a loincloth, held primacy in the minds of early Maya artists. As figures of increasingly varied status began to be portrayed in elite art—an indication of the increasing importance of royal women and subordinate nobles to Maya political practice—so too did representations of clothing become more variable. Such variation permitted artists to convey, at a glance, the roles or identities of the people they rendered.

Concomitant with that Late Classic shift toward more representation of cloth garments, cloth as a commodity took on greater importance in Maya economies (Baron 2018). Wide networks of trade in all kinds of goods were supported at the domestic level by individual families producing standardized, easily exchangeable textiles. Cloth was key to the reproduction of Maya culture at every level. Its production and arrangement trained Maya women in proper decorum and marked differences in the respect culturally due to women in different roles. It facilitated political negotiations through tribute, redistribution, and marketing. It connected rural Maya households with larger communities and regions and the Maya area with the rest of the Mesoamerican world. Whatever an individual's social station, he or she was impacted by the production and consumption of cloth, the fabric of Maya life.

CHAPTER 3

The Painted Body

KATHARINE LUKACH AND JEFFREY DOBEREINER

Body paint appeared in some of the earliest Maya polychrome representations of humans and continued as a widespread and socially significant feature into historical times. Like scarification and tattooing, which also ornamented ancient Maya bodies, body painting projected information about roles and status. Unlike permanent skin modifications, however, painting permitted a shifting and wider-ranging set of such statements, because painted colors and designs could be washed off and replaced anew (Houston, Stuart, and Taube 2006, 15–16). In fact, the temporary nature of body paint required that it be reapplied. According to ethnohistorical accounts from the Colonial period (Tozzer 1966 [1941], 89), the Maya applied red pigments to their bodies to accentuate beauty, mark ritual periods and celebrations, and highlight status, age, or gender. Elucidating the exact meanings of specific motifs and colors of body paint in ancient Maya art is a difficult endeavor, yet some patterns do emerge from considerations of painted bodies on polychrome ceramics, murals, and codices.

Although the Classic Mayan language has a well-attested word for painting or writing (tz'ib), words for painting or coloring that apply to the skin in particular are absent from the hieroglyphic corpus. However, modern and historically attested Mayan languages do contain a number of such terms. In Yukateko, the verb yap means to shave or to apply makeup to the face. More specific to the skin are nab, to anoint or smear; kustab,

to paint oneself with achiote or other red colorants; and hots, whose primary values have to do with tattooing, branding, or scarification, but which can also apply to painting one's skin red (Barrera Vásquez et al. 1980, 234, 355, 546, 970). Skin can be colored with bon, a dye, coloring, or stain, in Yukateko and in Ch'ol (Aulie and Aulie 1978, 167; Barrera Vásquez et al. 1980, 64).

The primary colors applied to human bodies in ancient Maya societies, from the Late Preclassic period to contact with the Spanish, were red, white, and black, with brown also attested in some Late Classic representations. Blue body paint was used by Yukatek Maya priests at the time of the conquest (Tozzer 1966 [1941], 89), and blue-painted priests and deities appear in Postclassic codices, murals, and several Classic-period ceramic vessels. Painted designs tend to emphasize the division between the head and the rest of the body. On the postcranial body, color was generally applied to the shoulders or the full torso, but it sometimes covered the whole body down to the extremities. This paint was usually monochromatic, either applied in broad fields or used to draw designs that contrasted with the skin; the use of multiple colors on the same body is rare in Classic-period art, although it does sometimes occur. Paint could also accentuate the cheeks, eyes, or mouth, with swaths of pigment to cover those features or delicate patterns of line work to highlight them. In some instances, white paint was used as an undercoat for face decorations to make painted designs more visually striking. While multicolored face paint is still infrequent in ancient Maya art, there are still more examples of it than of two or more colors being used elsewhere on the body.

MATERIALS, PRODUCTION, AND APPLICATION

Body paint required at least two types of ingredients: a mineral or organic material to provide the color and a suspension—water or an oil, fat, or resin—to permit its application to the body (Houston et al. 2009, 61–62). According to Landa, Yukatek Maya men and women "had the custom of painting their faces and bodies red, and . . . thought it was very pleasing," and those with the economic means to do so mixed this paint with "a certain preparation of a gum, odoriferous and very sticky" (Tozzer 1966 [1941], 89).

Fortunately for the ancient Maya, Mesoamerica is rich in sources of red pigment. Suitable organic materials include annatto, obtained from the achiote tree (Caso Barrera and Aliphat Fernández 2006). Inorganic sources include red ochre, hematite, and cinnabar (Houston et al. 2009, 63); this last source, being poisonous, would have posed health risks as a body paint but may well still have been used. Cinnabar was sometimes used to coat the bodies of deceased royalty, a practice with religious significance that may also have protected the body from putrefaction for a time (Fitzsimmons 2009, 81–83). Black paint could readily have been made with ground carbon from burned resinous wood, while white paint was commonly produced from calcium carbonate in limestone or shells (Houston et al. 2009, 63).

Scenes of courtly life on Late Classic polychrome ceramics show several techniques for applying body paint. Broad swaths of paint were applied with a brush or cloth (fig. 3.1a). Finer details could be drawn on with a brush, as with facial paint (fig. 3.1b), or daubed or impressed with hands or fingers (fig. 3.1c). Although rulers appear in scenes being painted by their subordinates, the hieroglyphic corpus does not record a title for dedicated body painters or royal makeup artists. Instead, painting another person's body may have been a component of varying kinds of intimate relationships. In one such scene, a red-painted couple dance together, with a red-tipped paintbrush in the woman's headdress possibly indicating her role as the painter (fig. 3.1d). On a vessel depict-

ing a less romantic tableau, a hunter daubs camouflaging paint on the back of his companion in preparation for an excursion into the forest (fig. 3.1e).

SPATIAL AND TEMPORAL VARIATION

The Late Preclassic murals at San Bartolo provide an early and vivid glimpse into ancient Maya body painting (Saturno, Taube, and Stuart 2005). For example, in one of the two scenes on the north wall of Structure Sub 1A (fig. 3.2a), the Maize God (Individual 9), dynamically posed, looking backward over his shoulder, draws the eye of the viewer to the center of the composition. His face is painted red and white and his body daubed red with lighter outlines (as is one of his female consorts [Individual 10] floating on his upper right). This "reverse chiaroscuro" effect, noted by Michael Coe (1973, 71), creates an illusion of three-dimensionality, but also reveals a deep antiquity for using red body paint to mark agents of particular importance.

The other characters featured in the north-wall scene are also distinguishable by their distinct body and face paint. The Maize God's three male attendants' faces are painted black (Individuals 8, 13, and 14). The two farthest to the right (Individuals 13 and 14) carry offerings and are dressed as ballplayers; their bodies are covered in vertical stripes of red and black paint. Individual 8 kneels before the Maize God, holding up a gourd. His face is painted black, save for his cheek, which is red. His body paint is quite elaborate, featuring mostly alternating horizontal bands of red, gray, yellow, and black. Longer vertical bands painted in red (and one in gray) stretch along the front of his chest and appendages.

The four female figures each have different red-painted designs on their faces, contrasting with either their pale skin or white face paint. Their body and face colorings vary and hint that information about individual identities or roles in the narrative are encoded in the designs and colors. Individual 10 wears white face paint with a red rectangle on her cheek. She is painted red from the neck down, mirroring the Maize God's own body paint. Her lips are white, unlike the other female characters, whose lips are marked with a thin line of red paint. Below her, Individual 11 wears white face paint as well, with a diagonal streak of red paint covering her cheek and red paint over the septum of her

(a)

(b)

(c)

(d)

FIGURE 3.1. *Application of body paint on Late Classic polychrome painted vessels: (a) paint applied with a cloth (K0764); (b) an old god applying paint to his mouth with a brush as a young goddess with painted designs on her face holds up a mirror (K0530); (c) handprints in black paint (K2345); (d) a painted couple dancing together (K0554); and (e) one hunter applying paint to another (K1373). Photographs © Justin Kerr, used by permission. See plate 1.*

(e)

nose and onto her brow. She carries no body paint save for a horizontal band of red paint around her upper arm, which is outstretched toward the Maize God. To the right of these two women, Individual 13 has a small red design painted on her cheek, consisting of a straight vertical line and an upside-down *L* that hooks downward. Her neck and upper shoulders are painted red, and unlike the other women in the scene she wears a *Spondylus* shell over her pubis instead of a skirt—a custom marking virginity for the Maya of Yucatán, according to Bishop Diego de Landa (see Tozzer 1966 [1941], 106). Her body is outlined in a thin red line as well. Individual 7 is shown kneeling in a cave facing opposite the other women of the scene. She wears no body paint but does offer a vessel containing three tamales toward the Maize God. Her face paint consists of a diagonal band stretching from the bridge of the nose, over the eye to the ear, and an inverted version of the small red facial design of Individual 13 on her cheek. Individual 7's design vertically mirrors that of Individual 13, extending downward on her cheek from a horizontal red line that stretches from the corner of her mouth. Conceivably, then, body painting among women changed with their social roles and statuses over the course of their lives.

In some Early Classic portraits from the southern lowlands, the Maize God has a foliated, semicircular element surrounding his mouth. This design might correspond to tattooing or painting, a feature sometimes affecting human lords as well (fig. 3.2b; see Fields and Reents-Budet 2005, cat. nos. 21, 42, 53). Indeed, the element persisted into the Late Classic period in representations of the youthful gods who immolated the Jaguar God of the Underworld (fig. 3.2c; K4598). A figurine from the late-fourth- or early-fifth-century burial of a young woman at Yaxuna depicts a related design with red, blue, and white lines around the mouth (fig. 3.3a; Fields and Reents-Budet 2005, cat. no. 116). More extensive painting can be seen on the bodies of rulers depicted on an Early Classic lidded vessel (fig. 3.3b), emphasizing color contrasts between the face or shoulders and the rest of the body.

One productive Early Classic source for painted bodies is the now-destroyed mural from Structure B-XIII at Uaxactun (A. Smith 1950, 55–56), which shows several tableaux of individuals interacting with one another in courtly settings. In one scene, a warrior with red paint completely covering his body—possibly a local lord with connections to Teotihuacan, Mexico—confronts another man, who is painted fully in black and holds his arm across his chest in a respectful gesture of welcome (fig. 3.3c). To the right of this scene, two men and a woman confer within a roofed building (fig. 3.3d). The woman and one of the men, probably the hosts of the discussion, have red paint covering their faces and necks, except that the man displays a patch of black paint over his eyes and nose. Their interlocutor is painted black, except for his hands, and wears a contrasting plain white mantle and cloth headwrap. Another tableau in the same mural may show the beginnings of a bloodletting rite, in which mature male priests hold obsidian lancets to be used by adolescent boys (fig. 3.3e). The priests' bodies bear distinctive painted marks: horizontal stripes of red for one, fields of black for the other. The youths either are not painted or bear plain red paint on their faces and shoulders, as do all the participants in the final tableau, a ritual dance.

In Late Classic art, patterns from earlier periods continue. Red remains the most common color of body paint, appearing on both male and female bodies in a range of contexts. Among men there is a noticeable trend for more of the body to be painted red in approximately the seventh and eighth centuries AD, less so by the end of the Classic period (figs. 3.4a and b). The contexts of use vary widely: rulers and nobles wear red paint in scenes of courtly conference, religious ritual, the ball game, and dance; sometimes, too, they are in the process of being painted by attendants in preparation for ritual performances. Paint coverage is often incomplete and appears to have varied regionally and temporally: the hands, inner elbows, and armpits might be left unpainted to avoid smudging (fig. 3.4c), or paint might be applied mainly to the shoulders and upper body to shield them from the sun (fig. 3.4d). Limited body painting frequently emphasizes the face and neck, which are either painted when other parts are not (fig. 3.4e) or left unpainted so as to contrast with the rest of the body (fig. 3.4f). On a small number of Late Classic ceramic vessels, brown to reddish-brown replaces red body paint (fig. 3.5a). This difference may reflect incidental variations in the manufacture of pigments used on bodies or on ceramic vessels, all of which nevertheless fell within a range culturally defined as "red"; alternatively, there may

(a)

(b)

(c)

FIGURE 3.2. *Face and body paint on the Maize God and related deities: (a) detail of the North Wall, Las Pinturas building, San Bartolo (illustration by Heather Hurst © 2004; courtesy of Heather Hurst); (b) detail of an Early Classic plate showing the Maize God with painting around the mouth (photograph © Museum Associates/LACMA, M.2010.115.250); and (c) detail of a Late Classic codex-style vessel with overpainting (K4598) showing a young god with painting around the mouth (photograph © Justin Kerr, used by permission). See plate 2.*

(a)

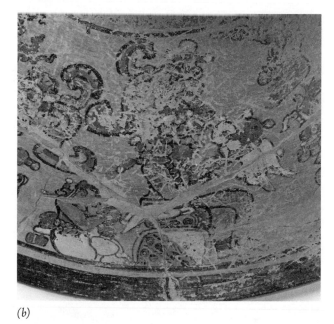

(b)

(d)

FIGURE 3.3. *Early Classic face and body painting: (a) figurine from a burial at Yaxuna (drawing by Nicholas Carter after Fields and Reents-Budet 2005, cat. 116); (b) ruler on a lidded ceramic vessel (photograph © Museum Associates/LACMA, M90_104a-b); (c) two men from the Structure B-XIII mural, Uaxactun; (d) two men and a woman from the Structure B-XIII mural, Uaxactun; and (e) priests and young men from the Structure B-XIII mural, Uaxactun (painting by Antonio Tejeda, © President and Fellows of Harvard College, PM50-1-20/22982). See plate 3.*

(c)

(e)

have been a fleeting or regional trend of using brown paint instead of a saturated red. In other cases, however, there is a clear and intentional distinction between the two colors, as when a king is painted red and several of his attendants brown (fig. 3.5b).

Women at all stages of the Late Classic era tend to appear with only the shoulders, neck, and optionally the face marked with paint. Free application of pigment could stain clothing, of which Classic Maya women often wore more than men; the limited application may also have drawn attention to the paler skin of women who might, if of elite status, avoid much outdoor work. Red or brown paint could be applied to the face in large blocks of color around the mouth, cheeks, nose, or eyes (fig. 3.6a), or exceptionally to the entire body (fig. 3.6b). Lines painted on the face, in the Late Classic period, appear most often on women in the form of an "IL" design on the cheeks (fig. 3.6b), although other designs—a crescent or curl around the eyes (fig. 3.6c), or other forms that also emphasize the eyes (fig. 3.6d)—are also attested, sometimes being drawn on over a base of white paint (fig. 3.6e).

At Chamá, in Alta Verapaz, Late Classic ceramics reveal the same emphasis on red and black body paint seen on lowland painted vessels, with the visual contrast between them sometimes marking social or narrative roles. The two main actors in one scene—a warrior and a man holding a smoking cigar—are both painted black, while their attendants are partly or completely painted red (fig. 3.7a). Early Postclassic mural art at Chichen Itza indicates another, distinct, culture of body painting or its absence. Murals at the Temple of the Jaguars reveal the brightly colored costumes of elite men but contrast their vivid ornaments with unpainted skins. One mural in the Temple of the Warriors does depict body paint, which the artists used to distinguish victors and vanquished in a scene depicting an assault on a village. Naked prisoners' bodies are painted with thin horizontal red stripes, while their captors are painted dark gray except for their faces (fig. 3.7b).

Other Postclassic mural paintings and codices from the northern lowlands offer further images of colored bodies, but since those bodies typically belong to supernatural beings, their relationship to social practices among living humans is not entirely clear. Stephen D. Houston and colleagues (2009, 94–97) identify a shift in the use of color in mural paintings, from an Early Postclassic scheme using the five basic colors of the Maya palette to a division in the Late Postclassic period between a highly polychromatic style and a restrained set of blues and blacks on white backgrounds. Mural 1 in Structure 12 at Tancah, rendered in Early Postclassic style, shows deities covered from head to foot in solid blue paint, except for their hands and the faces of the Maize God and a sacrificial victim (fig. 3.8a). Gods in the Late Postclassic murals of Structure 5 at Tulum are by contrast trichromatic: outlined in black, with dots and short streaks of blue on their white plaster skin (fig. 3.8b). The bodies of supernatural beings in the roughly contemporaneous murals at Santa Rita Corozal are red, gray, yellow, or black, frequently with repeating motifs in a contrasting color that appear as if stamped. Those colors and

(a)

(b)

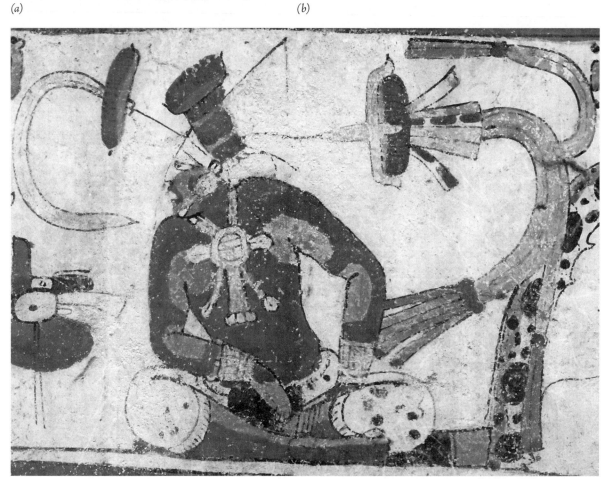

(c)

(d)

(e)

(f)

FIGURE 3.4. *Late and Terminal Classic body painting: (a) detail of an Ik'-style ceramic vessel (K5370) showing abundant red paint; (b) detail of a ceramic vessel in the Señor del Petén style (K9144) showing a courtly scene without body paint; (c) detail of a Late Classic ceramic vessel (K2711) showing body paint avoiding the hands and joints; (d) detail of a Late Classic Fenton-style ceramic vessel (K1392) showing paint on the shoulders and chest; (e) detail of a Late Classic ceramic vessel (K1599) showing paint that avoids the face; and (f) detail of a Late Classic ceramic vessel (K3412) showing a courtier with only his face and neck painted. Photographs © Justin Kerr, used by permission. See plate 4.*

(a)

(b)

FIGURE 3.5. (this page) *Brown body paint: (a) covering the body on a Late Classic ceramic vessel (K1453); and (b) in contrast with red body paint on a Late Classic ceramic vessel (K7021). Photographs © Justin Kerr, used by permission. See plate 5.*

FIGURE 3.6. (right page) *Body and face painting on women: (a) detail of a Late Classic ceramic vessel (K2707) showing two women with red-painted faces; (b) detail of a Late Classic ceramic vessel (K0764) showing brown body and face paint on one woman and red linear details on another; (c) detail of a Late Classic ceramic vessel from the area of Motul de San José (K2573) showing a woman with red body paint and a crescent design around her eye; (d) detail of a Late Classic ceramic vessel (K2695) showing two women with red body paint and painted designs over their eyes; and (e) detail of a Late Classic ceramic vessel from the area of Motul de San José (K4996) showing a woman with a crescent design around her eye over a base coat of white paint. Photographs © Justin Kerr, used by permission. See plate 6.*

(a)

(c)

(e)

(b)

(d)

(a)

(b)

FIGURE 3.7. (a) Late Classic ceramic vessel from Chama (K0593) showing principal interlocutors distinguished from their attendants by black body paint (photograph © Justin Kerr, used by permission); and (b) detail of an Early Postclassic mural from the Temple of the Warriors, Chichen Itza, showing victorious warriors painted dark gray and prisoners painted with red stripes (Morris, Charlot, and Morris 1931, pl. 139). See plate 7.

(a)

(b)

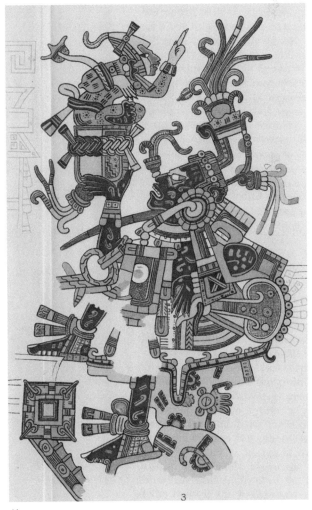

FIGURE 3.8. *Postclassic deities with painted bodies: (a) detail from Mural 1, Structure 12, Tancah, showing blue-painted deities (painting © Felipe Dávalos G.); (b) detail from a mural painting at Structure 5, Tulum, showing deities with blue marks on their bodies (drawing by Nicholas Carter after a painting by Felipe Dávalos G.); and (c) detail of a mural painting from the north wall of Mound 1, Santa Rita Corozal, showing a deity with repeating yellow designs on red-painted skin (Gann 1900, pl. 30). See plate 8.*

(c)

patterns sometimes continue onto the face, but more often the faces are painted with still other colors and designs (fig. 3.8c).

MEANINGS AND SOCIAL ROLES

A strong connection between body or face painting and high or low social rank is difficult to establish from available evidence. For men, using body paint at all may have been more connected with specific ranks or statuses. In scenes of courtly life in the murals at Bonampak, for instance, very few people are painted, and then only in specific settings. The ladies of the royal household wear some red face paint when they receive emissaries, but not when they offer blood; the king Yajaw Chan Muwaan and his sons show contrasts in skin tone between the hands and forearms and the rest of the body in the context of a ritual performance, but not in battle. This differs from an account of contact-period Yukateko warriors, whose whole bodies were "daubed with earth of many colors" (Tozzer 1966 [1941], 49).

Black face and body paint have some associations with pain and violence, being favored in Late Classic representations by hunters (fig. 3.9a) and warriors (fig. 3.9b). A mural at the site of Xultun displays members of an order of ritual specialists whose title of *taaj*, "obsidian," associates them with bloodletting, wearing black cloth headdresses and painted black from head to toe (fig. 3.9c; see Rossi 2015; Saturno et al. 2017). Sacrificers who wear the kind of broad hats and decorated cloaks linked to the underworld deity known as God L sometimes show fields of black paint over their eyes (fig. 3.9d) or spots of it on their cheeks (fig. 3.9e). Yet other kinds of performers also appear with black-painted bodies, including ritual clowns (fig. 3.9f), musicians (fig. 3.9g), and ballplayers (fig. 3.9h). As the Structure B-XIII mural at Uaxactun demonstrates, women also wore some black face paint in other contexts, at least in the Early Classic period. Yet, overall, black paint is more strongly male-gendered than red, especially in the Late Classic.

A link between black paint and sacrifice or deprivation continued into the Late Postclassic period in northern Yucatán, where unmarried young men, and men undergoing a fast, painted themselves black. Blue paint—probably the famous "Maya blue" compounded from indigo and palygorskite (Leona et al. 2004)—was

the preferred body coloring of priests (Tozzer 1966 [1941], 89). Blue body paint is nearly absent from Classic art, although the true Maya blue pigment was in use at least as early as the middle sixth century AD (García Moreno, Strivay, and Gilbert 2008, 1052). In the murals from the Chiik Nahb complex at Calakmul, which appear to depict everyday events in a marketplace, most women—including one low-ranking woman, perhaps a slave (see chapter 1)—have red face paint (Carrasco Vargas and Cordeiro Baqueiro 2012; S. Martin 2012). In light of those murals and the prevalence of face painting among women in the Late Classic ceramic corpus, painting the skin, especially the face, may have been a standard practice among ancient Maya women of all social classes.

Tattooing was practiced by both sexes in Late Postclassic Yucatán, but especially by women, whose upper bodies except the breasts could be covered with delicate designs; unmarried men received only minimal tattoos or scarifications (Tozzer 1966 [1941], 91). Unlike body painting, which frequently extended to the trunk and limbs, tattooing and ornamental scarification among the Classic Maya seem to have targeted the face. Evidence for such practices is abundant in the Classic artistic corpora, but primarily limited to the Maya West, the Gulf Coast, and the Yucatán Peninsula in the Late Classic period and thereafter. At Palenque and along the Usumacinta River, elite men and women both appear with day signs tattooed above their eyes (fig. 3.10a), or with tattooed or scarified "breath scrolls" around their mouths (fig. 3.10b; Houston, Stuart, and Taube 2006, 19–21; Yadeun 1993, 98). Lines of dots along the chin or jawline, depicted in some carvings, may indicate scars or tattoos; three of the noblemen depicted on the carved bench panels from Temple XIX at Palenque, for instance, have such lines (see Stuart 2005). Jaina-style figurines attest to similar practices. In that corpus, elite men, warriors and lords, sport raised scrollwork around their eyes, extending well up onto the brow and down the cheeks to the mouth (figs. 3.10c and d), or else straight scars extending sideways from the corners of their mouths (fig. 3.10e). Women sometimes display the same kind of linear mouth scars (fig. 3.10f), but not the tattooed or incised scrollwork on their upper faces. Unlike ear piercings or the scars left by genital bloodletting, marks of this kind were probably made on

(a)

(b)

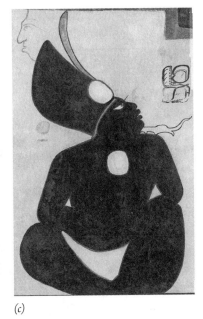

(c)

(d)

FIGURE 3.9. (a) Detail of a polychrome vase (K4151) showing a hunter with black "jaguar spots"; (b) detail of a Late Classic polychrome vase (K5451) showing two victorious warriors with black body paint; (c) detail of a Late Classic mural painting showing a taaj priest with black body paint (Structure 10K2, Xultun, illustration by Heather Hurst © 2012. Courtesy of Heather Hurst); (d) detail of a Late Classic codex-style vessel (K1200) showing a sorcerer with black paint around his eyes (drawing by Nicholas Carter after a photograph by Justin Kerr); (e) detail of a Late Classic codex-style ceramic vessel (K4384) showing a sorcerer with spots of black paint on his face; (f) detail of a Late Classic polychrome vase (K2780) showing performers with black body paint; (g) detail of a Late Classic polychrome vase (K1563) showing musicians with black body paint; and (h) detail of a Late Classic polychrome vase (K2803) showing a ballplayer with black body paint. Photographs except (c) and (d) © Justin Kerr, used by permission. See plate 9.

(e)

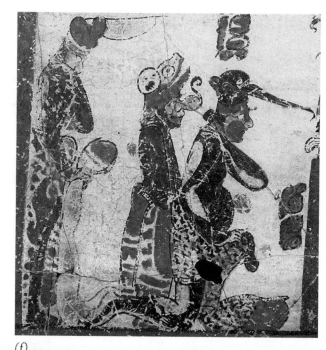

(f)

(g)

(h)

FIGURE 3.9. (continued)

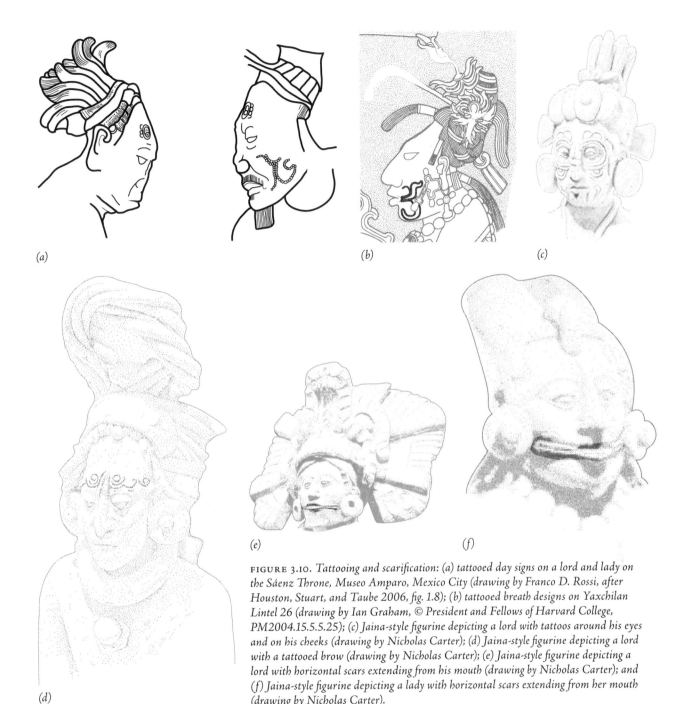

FIGURE 3.10. *Tattooing and scarification: (a) tattooed day signs on a lord and lady on the Sáenz Throne, Museo Amparo, Mexico City (drawing by Franco D. Rossi, after Houston, Stuart, and Taube 2006, fig. 1.8); (b) tattooed breath designs on Yaxchilan Lintel 26 (drawing by Ian Graham, © President and Fellows of Harvard College, PM2004.15.5.5.25); (c) Jaina-style figurine depicting a lord with tattoos around his eyes and on his cheeks (drawing by Nicholas Carter); (d) Jaina-style figurine depicting a lord with a tattooed brow (drawing by Nicholas Carter); (e) Jaina-style figurine depicting a lord with horizontal scars extending from his mouth (drawing by Nicholas Carter); and (f) Jaina-style figurine depicting a lady with horizontal scars extending from her mouth (drawing by Nicholas Carter).*

adolescent or adult bodies to avoid distortions caused by growth (Houston, Stuart, and Taube 2006, 18). As in other preindustrial cultures, ancient Maya tattoos could have been applied using sharp chisel-like implements tapped with wooden mallets against skin prepared with appropriate colorants, potentially soot or vegetable pigments like indigo. Alternatively, sharp blades of obsidian or flint could have been used to cut designs into

flesh, which could then be packed with pigment or simply left to heal into a cicatrix.

CONCLUSION

Body paint had some utilitarian purposes: covering up unpleasant odors, repelling insects, and protecting the skin from the sun's damaging rays. This latter function may go far toward explaining the prevalence of paint on faces and shoulders in Late Classic art. But skin is also the physical boundary between the individual and the rest of the social and material world (Turner 2012 [1980]). As such, it is a major site for socially meaningful modification—either permanent, as with tattooing or scarification, or temporary, through the application of paint, dyes, or makeup. Indeed, the active signaling of identity through skin painting could be more prevalent in imagery than it was in the everyday lives of the ancient Maya. Also, individuals' social relationships and bodily presentations might shift in tandem over time, a change in one reflected by a change in the other (Sault 1994). Because of the paucity of evidence for either children or elders with body paint, it may well be that this kind of decoration was reserved for youthful adults or those in their physical prime in order to reflect their beauty, strength, and reproductive fitness.

Mary Douglas (1970, 141–143) has argued that ritualized bodily practices express concerns about the security and order of the social group. It is clear that strict bodily comportment in both posture and dress was of high importance to the ancient Maya (e.g., Houston 2001; Houston, Stuart, and Taube 2006, 198–201). The impermanence of body and face painting, coupled with the need to remove and reapply decorations appropriate to different social situations, re-created and reinforced Maya ideas of decorous bodies and correct comportment. Not only did situational or long-term social roles need to be inscribed on the skin through the application of paint, but, once applied, keeping it unsmudged meant emphasizing some bodily postures and movements and avoiding others. Body paint must have inhibited actions like leaning against things, scratching the body or limbs, and touching the face, while encouraging an erect posture, careful movements, and spatial awareness. As such, it helped to represent roles and identities and disciplined Maya bodies into the proper enactment of those categories.

CHAPTER 4

The Capped Body

NICHOLAS CARTER AND ALYCE DE CARTERET

In the Maya lowlands, where towns and cleared fields are even hotter than the sweltering forests and scrublands, head coverings were and are a necessity. Ancient Maya headgear shaded the face and protected the crown of the head from direct sun. Hats, headwraps, and other headdresses also concealed or constrained hair, a body part bound up with cultural ideas about sexuality and decorum. Headgear could further signal individual identity, group membership, and social status.

The most basic ancient Maya headdress was a strip of cloth tied about the head: a *pixjol* or *pixol*, "wraphead," in many Mayan languages (Hopkins, Josserand, and Cruz Guzmán 2011, 185; Kaufman 2003, 999). Yukateko vocabulary points to conceptual connections between wrapping or covering (*pix*) and ideas of the animating soul (*pixan*; Barrera Vásquez et al. 1980, 658–659). A related concept, *met*, refers to flexible objects twisted into a circle, including birds' nests but also potentially crowns and cloth head rings (Zender 2017, 18–19). A *pixjol* might be a simple headband or kerchief, keeping the wearer's hair out of his face but otherwise providing little coverage. By themselves, such headbands are rare in Classic Maya portraits, although they would have been worn underneath more complicated headdresses and are the origin of the royal *amate* headband (see below and chapter 5 in this volume). One style of headscarf, historically favored in highland Guatemala, consists of a large square of cloth folded into a triangle and laid over the brow and the crown, with its corners tied behind and the ends left

hanging down at the back of the neck. This fashion is almost unrepresented in the Classic southern lowlands: when it does occur, as on Ceibal Stela 3 (fig. 4.1a), it appears to index the foreign connections of its wearers. Instead, southern lowland Classic Maya headscarves were typically two-piece constructions: a long, broad strip of plainweave cotton cloth wrapped several times around the head and held in place with a thinner, shorter band.

Variations on this assemblage are numerous in Classic art. In one common version, ends of the broader headwrap project in folded peaks from the crown of the head, leaning forward or folded back, their apparent stiffness suggesting a process of starching and pressing. Courtiers in the Early Classic mural painting from Structure B-XIII at Uaxactun wear this style of headwrap, and a logogram mentioned in chapter 2 of this volume for an elite rank, which probably read **EBEET** ("messenger"), depicts a predatory bird doing the same (Houston 2018a, 105; Stuart 2005, 133–136; fig. 4.1b). Another variation, well attested on Late Classic polychrome ceramic vessels from the central lowlands, uses a length of cloth wrapped around the upper forehead, the crown, and some or all of the hair without being folded. The material might be of plainweave, dyed or not, but is frequently netted or gauzy with a brocaded or embroidered hem (fig. 4.1c). Another strip of cloth, bound above the brow, holds the cylinder of cloth in place. Still a third form, favored by elites at Copan and other southeastern lowland sites, used a narrow, extravagantly long band

51

FIGURE 4.1. (a) Detail of Ceibal Stela 3 showing a man wearing a highland-style headwrap; (b) detail of an Early Classic mural painting from Uaxactun Structure B-XIII showing a courtier wearing a peaked headscarf; (c) detail of an unprovenienced Late Classic painted vessel (K5453) showing a courtier wearing a gauzy headscarf with a hem; (d) detail of Copan Altar Q showing a ruler wearing a wide turban; and (e) detail of a Late Classic Fenton-style vase (K558) showing a ruler wearing a headwrap of cloth set with shells. Drawings by Nicholas Carter, (a) after a photograph by Ian Graham, (b) after a painting by Antonio Tejeda, and (c–d) after photographs by Justin Kerr.

of cloth wound around the head to form a wide turban (fig. 4.1d). Yet the most exalted headwrap was structurally the simplest: the "white paper" (*sak hu'n*) headband, made from pounded fig (*Ficus*) or mulberry (*Morus* spp.) bark paper rather than cloth. Adorned with diadems of jade or shell, emblematic of royal authority, such headbands were "raised up to the forehead" (*k'ahlaj tu baah*) of new kings during their accession ceremonies (Stuart 2012a; Zender 2016; see chapter 5 in this volume).

The bands tied around headwraps could be of the same cloth as the wrap, but contrasting colors and textures are common. Headgear also called for materials compositionally distinct from those worn elsewhere on the body. Tiny white shells sewn onto a fabric backing formed a visually striking material that could be wrapped tightly around the hair or formed into voluminous headbands to be worn over headwraps (fig. 4.1e). The elaborate headdresses used in royal ritual performances (see below) called for an abundance of quetzal tailfeathers, but single quetzal plumes or small bundles of such plumes, their bases protected with cloth or paper, could be tucked into headbands. So too could brightly colored flowers, quills, brushes, and accordion-folded bunches of paper. Animal hides are infrequently shown as components of wrapped headgear, but royal men might substitute the skins of spotted cats for cloth in their headwraps or headbands.

Cloth was far from the only material used in ancient Maya headgear. Painted vessels show hunters and travelers of both sexes wearing tall hats, their rounded crowns sometimes topped with ornaments, with broad or short brims (fig. 4.2a). As fine detail on one codex-style vessel makes clear, such hats were plaited from some fibrous material: grass, reeds, or palm fronds (fig. 4.2b). Wider-brimmed sombreros could be adorned with feathers or whole birds, as with the distinctive owl hat worn by God L, an underworld deity and patron of traveling merchants (fig. 4.2c). Well-to-do ladies might wear broad-brimmed hats to protect their complexions even when not on a journey, as suggested by some ceramic figurines from Jaina. During the Late Classic period, sacrificers and the ritual actors in mortuary ceremonies wore a distinctive variation on travelers' hats: cloth, sometimes painted with crossed bones, was affixed to the brim, stretched over the hat, and bound at the peak with strips of cloth or paper (fig. 4.2d).

Other headpieces were designed to protect their wearers from more direct threats than sunstroke. Diego de Landa (1966 [1941], 122) records that Yukatek Maya war captains sometimes wore wooden helmets at the time of Spanish contact. Helmets that can clearly be distinguished from less protective headdresses are rare in Classic art, perhaps best attested in the corpus of Jaina figurines (fig. 4.3a). Warriors' helmets tended to expose the face, but those worn by ritual boxers, who fought each other with conch-shell manoplas, typically covered the whole head except for a T-shaped slit at the front (fig. 4.3b). Bunches of feathers and other ornaments would have helped identify individuals in martial or ritual combat, while a protective headwrap would have stabilized the helmet and cushioned the wearer's head against blows.

Animal heads, real and simulated, feature largely in depictions of headgear during all periods of ancient Maya civilization. Hunters, warriors, and ballplayers are all shown wearing the heads of deer and big cats (fig. 4.3c). Captives, too, were sometimes made to wear deer heads in ceremonies that culminated in their torture and sacrifice as the prey of their captors (Taube 1988). Other animal-head headdresses can only have been artificial constructions, although they could have incorporated actual pelts. These include outsize deer and jaguar headdresses and masks, as well as the heads of fantastic aquatic creatures worn by warriors, courtiers, and dancers in painted scenes from the Ik' polity and Bonampak (see Just 2012; M. Miller and Brittenham 2013). Oversize masks might have been made of papier-mâché, or, as with one remarkably preserved example excavated at Aguateca, molded from cloth impregnated with fine clay and allowed to dry in the sun (Beaubien 2004; Inomata et al. 2001). Genuine or faux, such headdresses relied on the same time-tested technologies for keeping an object on a human head: placed over the crown of the head, they were bound on with headbands or fitted snugly over a wrap in the manner of a hat.

DEITY-IMPERSONATION HEADDRESSES: DEFINING TYPES AND ELEMENTS

While various kinds of wraps were the everyday head covering of choice for ancient Maya courtiers and commoners alike, special occasions called for special headgear.

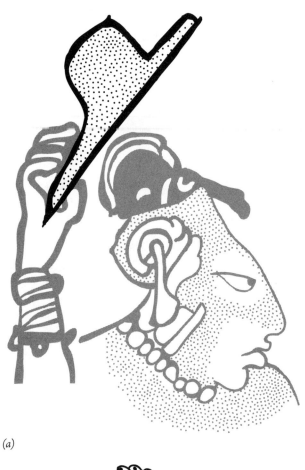

(a)

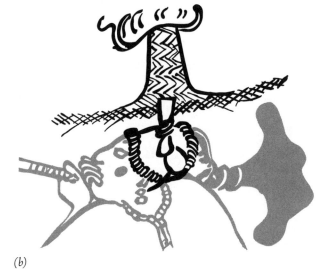

(b)

(c)

(d)

FIGURE 4.2. (a) Detail of an unprovenienced Late Classic painted vessel (K5847) showing a lady with a traveler's hat; (b) detail of a Late Classic ceramic vessel from the area of Calakmul (K1226) showing the Maize God wearing a hat of woven plant fibers; (c) detail of a Late Classic ceramic vessel from the area of Naranjo (K2796) showing God L wearing an animate traveler's hat; and (d) detail of a Late Classic ceramic vessel from the area of Calakmul (K1200) showing a sorcerer wearing a wide-brimmed hat. Drawings by Nicholas Carter after photographs by Justin Kerr.

FIGURE 4.3. (a) Ceramic figurine from the area of Jaina showing a warrior wearing a plumed helmet; (b) detail of an unprovenienced Late Classic ceramic vessel (K500) showing a boxer wearing a wooden helmet; and (c) detail of a Nebaj-style polychrome vase in the Museum für Völkerkunde, Berlin (K2206) showing a warrior wearing a headdress with an animal's head. Drawings by Nicholas Carter, (b) and (c) after photographs by Justin Kerr.

(a)

(b)

3

4

(c)

FIGURE 4.4. (a) Detail of Tikal Stela 2 showing the mask of
the Principal Bird Deity in a ruler's ritual headdress (drawing
by Nicholas Carter); (b) detail of Jimbal Stela 1 showing a ritual
headdress with the Principal Bird Deity conflated with K'awiil
(drawing by Nicholas Carter); and (c) detail of Dos Pilas Stela 11
showing a ritual headdress with the Principal Bird Deity conflated
with Yopaat (drawing © Stephen D. Houston).

For festivals, royal dances, period-ending ceremonies, and other spectacular occasions, elites donned complicated headdresses evidently designed with certain considerations in mind. They had to be large enough to appear clearly from a distance, yet light enough to allow movement and even dance, and they had to communicate information about the wearer—his identity, status, wealth, and role in the proceedings. Drawing on long-distance trade networks, Maya artisans had at their disposal the resources of lowland and montane rain forests, marine coasts, and more distant parts of Mesoamerica. Unsurprisingly, ritual headdresses present a bewildering variety of forms and components, not all of which can really have existed in the way they are portrayed in Classic art. Still, most of them were built up by the addition of optional elements to more foundational ones, and as such they exhibit some broad similarities over time and space.

The basis of most such headdresses was a mask fitted on the head over a cushioning headwrap and perhaps a jeweled headband. In the highlands and southern lowlands, from the Late Preclassic through the Late Classic period, those masks most frequently depict God D in his avian form as the Principal Bird Deity (fig. 4.4a). Masks of the rain god Chahk, his poorly understood aspect Yopaat, and the lightning spirit K'awiil (fig. 4.4b) are the next most common. Also represented are royal ancestors, the "Waterlily Serpent" who embodied floods and waterfalls (witz'); the solar deity "GI" and his nocturnal counterpart, the "Jaguar God of the Underworld"; foreign gods (see below); and other beings. Such masks are nearly always agnathous (jawless), giving the visual impression that the wearer's face is contained in the mouth of the supernatural being, so that he could animate it with his movements and speak for it with his voice.

Feathers are nearly ubiquitous in ritual headdresses. Bundles of quetzal plumes or other figures could be inserted into bejeweled holders or the mouths of animal heads, or else affixed to towering frameworks of cane and matting. Yet when masks of the Principal Bird Deity or other gods are depicted, some feathers are often shown in panaches behind the god's head, emerging from a serpent's mouth, presumably of shell or wood. These serpent-headed wings are a diagnostic characteristic of the Principal Bird Deity dating back to Late Preclassic Kaminaljuyu. For this reason, representations of

rain gods or other beings should be seen as conflations of those entities with God D when accompanied by this kind of artificial wing.

Building upward from the mask, gods and deified ancestors were identified by headgear of their own. On the Late Preclassic Monument 1 at Chalchuapa, a solar deity wears an avian headdress with a hooked beak, potentially presaging Classic lowland hieroglyphic references to the Sun God as an eagle. Yopaat is distinguished in most Classic lowland depictions by two or three dotted curls at the top of his head, K'awiil by the torch or celt protruding from his forehead, and the Waterlily Serpent by a lily-pad headwrap bound about his forehead with the stem of a water-lily blossom from which a fish feeds. An elderly male deity or set of deities responsible for holding up the sky is marked by a netted headscarf that is the origin of the logogram **ITZAM**, "venerable" (S. Martin 2015; Stuart 2007). Kings' headgear instantiated those divine models during ritual impersonations, but whether all the ornaments involved really existed as they are portrayed is questionable: a flaming torch, for instance, would have been a hazardous addition to any costume. The most realistic portrayal of Yopaat's head-curls, on Dos Pilas Stela 11 (fig. 4.4c), leaves some doubt about their composition: "Kaban curls," which can indicate strong smells in Maya iconography (Houston 2010), suggest that they could have been molded from clay or some aromatic gum or resin. Yet in Classic art, some such diagnostic traits might have been meant not to represent visible objects but to denote the deity or indicate the presence of his name in the name of the wearer.

Ritual headdresses could incorporate a wide range of other expensive and significant items. Smaller greenstone masquettes may have indicated that the gods or ancestors they portrayed were with the king who wore them, but their small size and placement in headdresses—above the main component or at the back of the assemblage—suggest that their meanings were subtly different from those of the foundational deity masks. Jester God or other royal diadems often looked out from below the primary headdress element (see chapter 5 in this volume). Other greenstone jewels, including pectoral ornaments and earspools, could be added to the confection to indicate the wearer's lordly wealth. Rulers at some sites, especially Copan, favored a kind

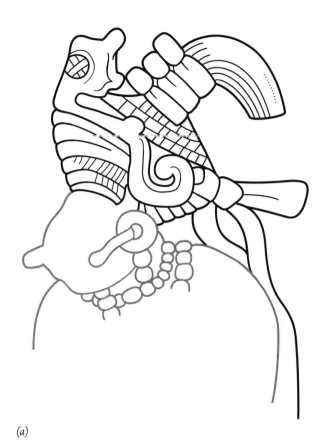

(a)

(b)

(c)

(d)

of tiara, probably of wood, which was associated with the rain god Chahk and whose peak is rendered with crossed bands or circular elements (fig. 4.5a). Woven mat-work, basketry, and canes could increase the height of a headdress at a low cost in weight, serving at the same time to anchor other elements. Likely further signs of wealth, the bodies and body parts of animals are well represented in Late Classic southern lowland headdresses, with western rulers particularly favoring spotted cats' tails and whole birds (fig. 4.5b). Other ornaments alluded to their wearers' prowess as killers and captors. Small bones, perhaps phalanges or the sawn ends of long bones, decorate several Early Classic headdresses at Tikal, but also appear in later headdress assemblages from Naranjo and other sites (fig. 4.5c). Some seventh- and eighth-century royal headdresses include owls or serpent effigies, wrapped in long bundles with feathers or stone blades protruding from their mouths, which could have been perceived to augment or embody kings' power to make sacred war (fig. 4.5d).

SPATIAL AND TEMPORAL VARIATION

Headdresses are present in the earliest Maya depictions of human beings, suggesting that associations between the head and individual identity or essence extend deep into the Preclassic period. On Kaminaljuyu Monument 65, three enthroned rulers and their kneeling captives each wear unique headdresses likely including nominal elements specific to the individual (fig. 4.6). Headdresses incorporating the Principal Bird Deity as their primary element make their first appearance in Late Preclassic art, in some of the earliest representations of Maya kingship. For instance, Kaminaljuyu

Sculpture 11 depicts a ruler wearing a mask of that god surmounted by an early outsize form of the Jester God ornament (fig. 4.7a). In a scene of coronation from the Late Preclassic murals of San Bartolo, a Principal Bird Deity headdress is worn by the priest who offers the diadem of rulership to the new king (fig. 4.7b).

Headdresses emerge as salient markers of cultural identity during the period of intense interaction between Teotihuacan and the Maya region in the Early Classic period. At a swath of sites across the southern lowlands, depictions of Central Mexican warriors and the Maya lords who imitated them emphasize their distinctive headgear, discussed in detail below. Whatever their form, Teotihuacan-style headdresses seem to have been marked by feathers—likely also indicating rank or status, as in a mural at La Sufricaya painted in the style of a Mexican codex (Estrada-Belli et al. 2009). The Central Mexican warrior in the Uaxactun mural wears a headdress with abundant feathers, while the Maya courtiers have few or no feathers in their cloth head-

FIGURE 4.6. Kaminaljuyu Monument 65. Drawing © Lucia Henderson, used by permission.

(a)

(b)

FIGURE 4.7. (a) Detail of Kaminaljuyu Sculpture 11 showing a Jester God ornament on a mask of the Principal Bird Deity (drawing © Lucia Henderson, used by permission); and (b) detail of a mural from the west wall of the Las Pinturas building at San Bartolo showing a priest wearing a Principal Bird Deity headdress (San Bartolo Mural, illustration by Heather Hurst, © 2005. Courtesy of Heather Hurst).

wraps. The same mural provides an early example of a historical woman wearing a shawl as a head covering.

Within a few generations after the introduction of Teotihuacan-style headdresses, Maya headdresses with no obvious Teotihuacan connections likewise began to be represented in monumental art as richly bedecked with feathers. Whether the newfound emphasis on feathers represents a direct aesthetic influence from Teotihuacano artistic and sartorial conventions, or whether it instead reflects some change in the economics of lowland Maya luxury goods, is open to question. Jade ornaments continued to be part of ritual headdresses during the Late Classic period, but not in such abundant quantities as depicted on earlier monuments. A tremendous variety of cloth constructions appear in the profusion of painted ceramic vessels depicting scenes of courtly life that were produced in northern Guatemala and southern Campeche during the seventh and eighth centuries AD. The late-eighth-century mural paintings of Bonampak provide another corpus of Late

Classic headgear (M. Miller and Brittenham 2013). The same bodies of work illustrate a range of headdresses for public and semipublic dances that substitute the artificial or taxidermized heads or bodies of animals for deity masks, a style particularly favored in the Ik' polity (fig. 4.8).

During the Terminal Classic period, conservatism in the styles of headdress depicted in monumental art in some kingdoms coexisted with a growing diversity in others. Beginning with Jasaw Chan K'awiil I, who reigned from AD 682 to 734, rulers from Tikal's Mut dynasty had themselves portrayed wearing a mosaic headdress depicting a supernatural entity important to that royal line (fig. 4.9a). That consistency contrasts with the evident instability of the Mut court itself, which seems to have relocated to Ixlu and Zacpeten between about 830 and 869 (Carter 2014, 181). Figures on most Terminal Classic stelae at Calakmul observe eighth-century conventions of dress, including Principal Bird Deity headdresses. There, conservatism in what costume elements appear on late monuments is at odds with stylistic changes in how those elements are rendered. The content of the figural carving on Stela 84, for instance, adheres to Late Classic traditions, while its proportions are reminiscent of Terminal Classic portraits at Chichen Itza, and the style and format of the accompanying text differ sharply from late Classic practice (fig. 4.9b).

By contrast, the stelae and altars commissioned by Caracol's final generations of kings show them wearing not elaborate headdresses but the same kinds of cloth wraps favored by courtiers and kings on earlier polychrome ceramics. The same simple headgear is shown on Caracol portrayals of kings from allied sites, suggesting a regional turn toward an aesthetic of simplicity and restraint (see fig. 2.4c). At Ceibal, representations of headgear changed even more radically. Whereas early Terminal Classic stelae depict rulers wearing fairly traditional plumed headdresses in the context of ball games and period-ending rituals, later monuments show dramatically different forms. Human and divine characters wear a highland-style *pixjol* (see fig. 4.1a), warrior helmets linked to Chichen Itza (fig. 4.9c), and, on Stela 13, a skeletal mask worn on the back of the head of what may be a personified *k'atun* (fig. 4.9d). Headgear on some Terminal Classic portable objects, including shell pectoral ornaments and vessels decorated by painting or

FIGURE 4.8. *Detail of a ceramic vessel from the area of Motul de San José, now in the Boston Museum of Fine Art (MUS2003.777), showing a lord wearing a bird's head mask incorporating a spotted feline pelt (drawing by Mallory E. Matsumoto).*

incising, shows other forms: simple headwraps and tufts or rows of feathers (fig. 4.9e).

Postclassic examples of headdresses come mainly from figurines, mural art, and a few monuments, plus the four known Maya codices. Mural paintings at Santa Rita and Tulum participate in an "international style" or "coastal Maya mural style" (M. Smith 2003, 182) emphasizing floral imagery, certain deities, and the souls of the noble dead in the form of butterflies and birds (Taube 2010a). Figures in the Santa Rita murals, for instance, wear diadems embodying stylized butterflies or rear-facing masks of the Feathered Serpent (Taube 2010a, fig. 3). The old Maya conventions of ritual headdresses as supernatural descending birds are also present, indeed made more explicit than in most Classic representations (fig. 4.10).

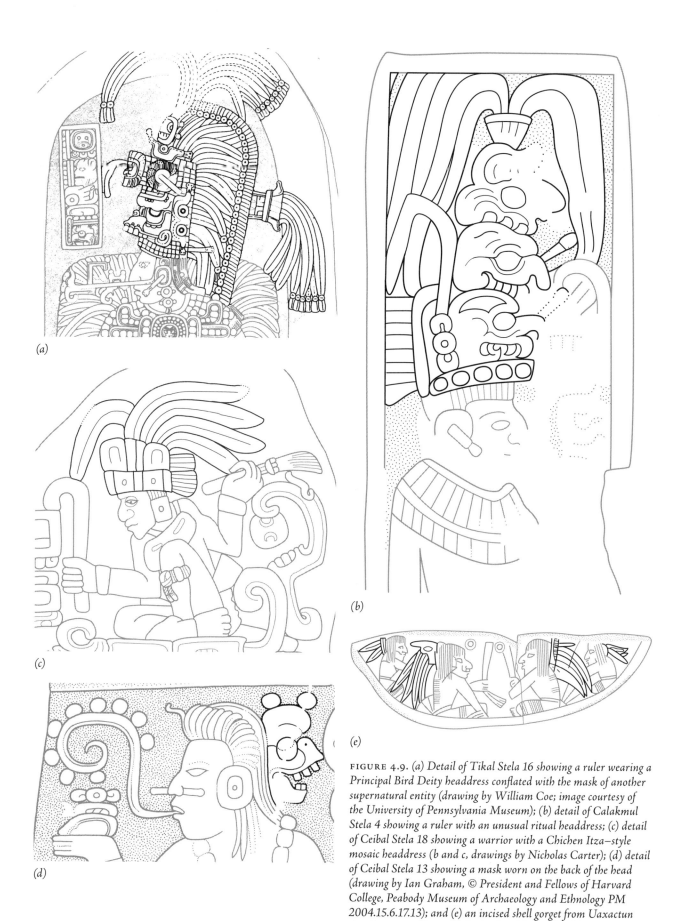

FIGURE 4.9. (a) Detail of Tikal Stela 16 showing a ruler wearing a Principal Bird Deity headdress conflated with the mask of another supernatural entity (drawing by William Coe; image courtesy of the University of Pennsylvania Museum); (b) detail of Calakmul Stela 4 showing a ruler with an unusual ritual headdress; (c) detail of Ceibal Stela 18 showing a warrior with a Chichen Itza–style mosaic headdress (b and c, drawings by Nicholas Carter); (d) detail of Ceibal Stela 13 showing a mask worn on the back of the head (drawing by Ian Graham, © President and Fellows of Harvard College, Peabody Museum of Archaeology and Ethnology PM 2004.15.6.17.13); and (e) an incised shell gorget from Uaxactun showing men with simple feather headdresses (Kidder 1947, fig. 51a).

FIGURE 4.10. *Detail of a mural from the north wall of Mound 1, Santa Rita Corozal, showing God D with a descending quetzal in his headdress (drawing by Nicholas Carter after Gann 1900, pl. 30).*

The headdresses worn by supernatural beings in the Dresden, Grolier, Madrid, and Paris Codices include elements realistic and fantastic, animal and vegetal, which index the identity of the wearer and—for instance, in the case of the Maize God—can even be part of his body. The headwrap worn by the aged goddess Chak Chel, midwife and destroyer, incorporates living serpents but is otherwise a realistic depiction of female headgear made of cloth wrapped around the hair and head.

MEANINGS AND SOCIAL FUNCTIONS

As with many other articles of dress, ancient Maya headgear was strongly tied to social roles and individual identities. Surprisingly, given the close connection between headgear and individual identity, specific gender is not as consistently marked with headwraps and headdresses as it is by other garments, at least in stone and mural art. When gender is thus highlighted in such compositions, it is the female that appears as the marked category: at times, and especially in painted media, women appear in sex-specific shawls or headwraps. Specifically, feminine styles of headwrap are best represented in the cor-

pus of ceramic figurines and ocarinas from the eighth and ninth centuries AD (fig. 4.11a). Stone monuments, on the other hand, tend to show elite ladies in the same kinds of ritual headdresses as their male counterparts, and even on painted ceramics men and women might wear the same types of *pixjol* or travelers' hats. In general, women wear less and simpler headgear. The disparity between the sexes might have to do with the role of headdresses in marking distinctions of rank; in male-dominated courtly societies, both a higher number of distinctions existed for men and a greater importance was placed on such distinctions. Nuances of feminine identity could thus have been expressed by means other than headwear, including by body painting, hairstyling, hair ornaments, and headbands.

Certain headdresses, simpler than those worn for deity impersonation, may have signified courtly ranks or political offices. Potential connections, though, are far from straightforward. Bearers of one aristocratic title, *aj k'uhu'n*, frequently appear on eighth-century polychrome and incised vessels from the southern lowlands wearing a *pixjol* with an ornament of white folded paper, sometimes partially stained red, in their headbands (fig. 4.11b) (M. Coe and Kerr 1997; Lacadena Garcia-Gallo 1996). Yet many individuals with the same headdress are *not* identified as *aj k'uhu'n* in accompanying captions, while a few people with that title (especially on later vessels painted in a style associated with the site of Señor del Petén) wear headwraps without the distinctive ornament. Other headdresses may not have identified specific ranks as such, but could instead have been worn for specific kinds of events. For instance, from the Late Preclassic period to the late eighth century AD, a ritual headdress bearing distinctive tassels and a mask of the Principal Bird Deity appears on the heads of older men overseeing rites of passage by youths, including but not limited to royal accession (fig. 4.11c).

As markers of individual and group identity, headdresses played an especially important role in ancient Maya battles and ball games. Their function as heraldic identifiers is perhaps most dramatically displayed in the battle scenes from the murals at Bonampak, in which dozens of warriors wear unique confections of animal heads, *pixjol*, and small-brimmed hats on their heads (M. Miller and Brittenham 2013, 94, fig. 172). In the context of Classic Maya warfare, with its emphasis

(a)

(b)

(c)

(d)

FIGURE 4.11. (a) Figurine from the area of Jaina depicting a woman wearing a headwrap (drawing by Nicholas Carter); (b) detail of a Late Classic ceramic vessel (K5445) showing a headwrap with a folded paper ornament (drawing by Mallory E. Matsumoto); (c) detail of an unprovenienced Late Classic ceramic vessel (K1440) showing two priests wearing Principal Bird Deity headdresses (drawing by Mallory E. Matsumoto); and (d) detail of La Corona Panel 1 showing a sak wahyas lord whose headdress includes elements typical of people with that title (drawing by David Stuart).

on the personal identities of captives and captors, such diversity could have helped participants in the melee to identify one another as individuals, ensuring that acts of heroism and cowardice would be recognized. At the same time, a confusion of headdresses could well have made it harder to quickly identify group affiliation as opposed to personal identity, especially in a battle as chaotic as the one depicted at Bonampak. There, too, only warriors on the victorious side are shown wearing massive headgear and other finery, while their captives are portrayed already nearly naked. One possibility, then, is that this variety of martial headgear might be partly fictive—meant to signal the identities or names of key players, not to one another in the heat of battle but to the audience of the mural. While headdresses of the type depicted in the Bonampak scenes likely had physical counterparts, we may question whether they were normally used in actual battles.

Just as questionable in their factuality, yet equally central to the role of headgear in painted and lapidary art, are representations of names in headdresses. From their beginnings, highland and lowland Maya artistic traditions identified supernatural and historical individuals by nominal glyphs or glyph-like elements on their heads. The practice makes sense in light of both Mayan languages and cultural concepts of the body—Classic Mayan *baah* is both "head" and "person, self" (Hous-

ton, Stuart, and Taube 2006, 59–81)—and the universal function of the human face as the primary identifier of the whole person. The strong links between Maya iconography and hieroglyphic, almost animate writing would also have facilitated the nominal or heraldic use of masks and other objects in composite headdresses, especially for kings whose names referred to easily recognizable animals or gods. In some cases, the nominal headdresses portrayed on Classic monuments could very well have been real objects, especially if hieroglyphic elements were molded out of lightweight, perishable materials. In other cases, the elements shown on monuments, like the swirling flames of the torch in K'awiil's forehead, were probably not physical parts of the headdresses. At times the Maya may have substituted other materials in the actual costume: dyed paper streamers, perhaps, in place of flame. At other times, the questionable elements may have been conceptually "known" to be present without being seen, like the jeweled breath of living deity masks. In still other instances, hieroglyphic or iconic elements that were neither part of the original headdress nor perceived to be so might have been included in figural representations in order to clarify a person's identity for viewers who knew how to read the visual message. In one sense, the blurry distinction between the world as represented in ancient Maya art and the world as the Maya experienced it complicates any attempt to understand the various indigenous categories of headdress and how they functioned in practice. In another sense, that same fluidity allows scholars to approach the depths of meaning assigned to various kinds of ornament that could not be communicated through more literal representations.

Some headdresses and headdress elements stand in Maya art for regional or cultural identity or for authority derived from a source outside the southern lowlands. Some such elements may correlate with a regionally specific elite title, *sak wayas* (white/resplendent *way*). This title is best attested on codex-style vessels from the Mirador Basin, but was also used by elites at La Corona, El Perú-Waka', El Zotz, and, in a royal name attested on Tikal Altar 5, at Topoxte. The headdress elements proposed to correspond to the title—a jaguar's or ocelot's head, its mouth stuffed with a bundle of quetzal feathers—appear on El Zotz Lintel 1, in the headdress of a king whose mother was a *sak wayas*. On a panel from La Corona, the cat's head is juxtaposed with the logogram **SAK** (white) and a tobacco leaf (fig. 4.11d). Another panel from the same site depicts another *sak wayas* wearing a variant of the same element, with tobacco leaves and a feline head, but with the quetzal plumes missing and the cat's lower jaw defleshed. The head-and-plumes element also appears on the head of a mytho-historical character on a seventh-century vase excavated at Uaxactun who is said to be from Calakmul (Carter 2015).

By far the most widely distributed kinds of headdresses marking cultural affiliation are those connected to the Central Mexican metropolis of Teotihuacan. In southern lowland art, such headdresses appear first in the fourth century AD—around the time that a warlord named Sihyaj K'ahk', a mysterious figure with Teotihuacan connections, intervened in the dynastic succession of Tikal (Stuart 2000). Thereafter, Teotihuacan-style headdresses became integral parts of Classic Maya military imagery, usually forming part of costumes with other Teotihuacan elements: Tlaloc goggles (see below), nose ornaments (see chapter 6 in this volume), spears with tassels below their heads, coyotes' tails affixed to the back of the wearer's belt, and shields, incense bags, pectorals, or other objects with Teotihuacan hieroglyphs or icons.

Teotihuacan-style headdresses can be divided into several categories, to each of which clusters of specific meanings no doubt adhered. One was a kind of hat with a broad, tall brim perimetrically adorned with flat rings of shell like the goggles worn around the eyes of the Central Mexican storm god known to the Aztecs as Tlaloc. Shell or stone bangles could be hung from the brim, while the crown of the headdress might bear, in addition to the ubiquitous feathers, elements including tassels, darts, and feline or ophidian masks. This type of headdress, vividly illustrated in mural paintings at Teotihuacan's Atetelco Palace, seems to have been associated with military orders whose patron predators were eagles and coyotes, analogous to the later Eagle and Jaguar orders of the Aztec Empire. Atetelco-style headdresses are worn by individuals in several apparent portraits carved at sites in Peten during the lifetime of Sihyaj K'ahk' (fig. 4.12a), by seated warriors in a mural at La Sufricaya, as well as by the deceased warriors depicted in modeled ceramic theater censers from Teotihuacan and the Pacific Coast of Guatemala (Estrada-Belli et al. 2009; Taube 2000, 308–309).

In the generations after the *entrada* of Sihyaj K'ahk', Atetelco-style tasseled headdresses became rare in southern lowland art, but other Teotihuacan-related headgear continued to be used and memorialized at sites throughout the southern lowlands—even long after Teotihuacan itself had been sacked and abandoned. Prominent here are shell mosaic helmets (*ko'haw*), sometimes depicting the face of the Feathered Serpent. Stela 31 at Tikal portrays two such helmets, one figural; Panel 2 from Piedras Negras depicts *ko'haw* used by Maya rulers as indicators of rank, with a proud overlord sporting a more elaborate helmet than the vassals who kneel before him. At Palenque, *ko'haw* not only were part of kingly regalia but are also listed among the clothes and ornaments offered to the city's patron gods (see chapter 1 in this volume). Another type of mosaic headdress with connections to Teotihuacan portrays the face of a butterfly, the transmogrified soul of a deceased warrior (Berlo 1983; Taube 2000). In some examples, the butterfly's goggle eyes and curling proboscis are mounted on a headdress that does not obscure the wearer's face (fig. 4.12b); in other depictions, the wearer himself peers through the goggles, which may form part of a mask. Butterfly warrior headdresses are well attested at Yaxchilan, including examples in which the goggle eyes are missing and

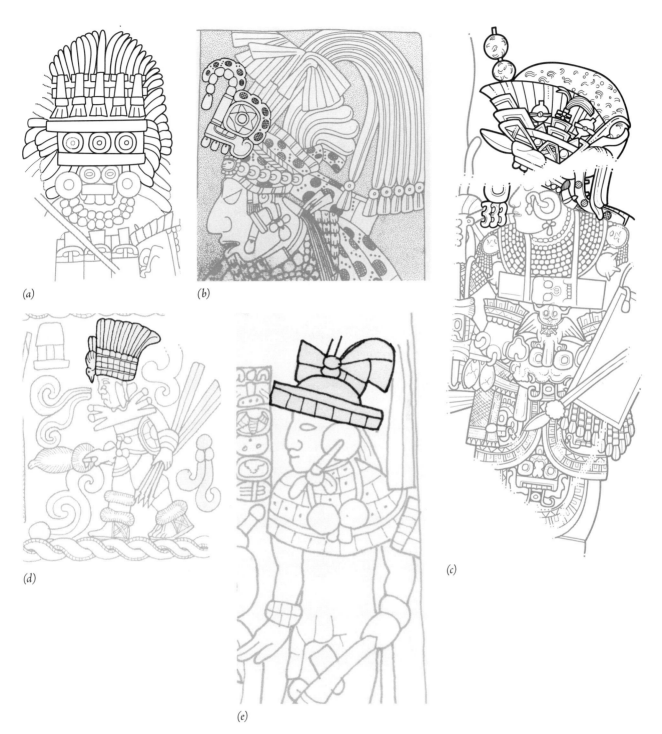

FIGURE 4.12. (a) Detail of Yaxha Stela 11 showing a warrior with an Atetelco-style headdress (drawing by Nicholas Carter); (b) detail of Yaxchilan Lintel 41 showing a ruler with a Teotihuacan-style butterfly mask in his headdress (drawing by Ian Graham, © President and Fellows of Harvard College, PM2004.15.6.6.12); (c) detail from Dos Pilas Stela 16 showing a ruler wearing a Tlaloc mask and a balloon headdress (drawing by Nicholas Carter); (d) detail of a carved register from the interior wall of the Lower Temple of the Jaguars, Chichen Itza (drawing by Linda Schele © David Schele, courtesy of Ancient Americas at LACMA [ancientamericas.org]); and (e) detail of the South Column from Temple 6E1, Chichen Itza (drawing by Linda Schele © David Schele, courtesy of Ancient Americas at LACMA [ancientamericas.org]).

the core of the headdress consists of the platelet-covered proboscis. A related form depicts Tlaloc, whose goggled visage—itself iconically derived from a butterfly—could be worn as a mask or as an ornament at the brow (fig. 4.12c).

During the Terminal Classic period, another category of headdress alluding to the lowland Maya's Central Mexican contemporaries appeared in monuments and mural paintings in the northern Yucatán Peninsula and at a few sites in the southern lowlands. These headdresses, widely represented in monumental art at Chichen Itza and the Central Mexican site of Tula, consist of one or more bands of shell plates on a backing encircling the head, the whole crowned by long feathers stretching vertically upward. Like Teotihuacan-style headdresses before them, these Toltec-style headdresses form parts of larger outfits that frequently include distinctive weaponry—spear-throwers and darts—and a broad, flanged plaque hung from the neck. More typically, Maya-style headgear in the art of Chichen Itza includes broad-brimmed hats adorned with plates and tassels, sometimes worn with a necklace of two large beads or shells, a style with its origins in Late Classic Maya costume (figs. 4.12d and e; see chapter 7 in this volume).

CONCLUSION

The meaning of headdresses is evident from the earliest examples of Maya portraiture, underscoring the fundamental quality of this association. Indeed, while other types of adornment had simple forms in Preclassic art or were de-emphasized, fully fledged nominal headdresses appear in some of the earliest Maya monuments and continued to be rendered in careful detail throughout the whole history of Maya art. Nominal headdresses may have begun as representational conventions rather than the "photographic" representation of physical reality. Yet over time, even imaginary nominal elements may have come to be incorporated into physical dress. In other words, representations and physical manifestations of headgear, like other garments, may have mutually influenced one another over time. Monumental sculpture, figurines, and murals reflected bodily practices to a great extent but did not do so passively; they also played a role in shaping individuals' relationships with their environments.

Close associations in Mesoamerican cultures and Mayan languages between the head or face and the human person meant that the head could serve not only as a *pars pro toto* sign for the whole individual but also as a site for other signs indicating his or her social roles and relationships of affiliation or contrast with other persons. For the ancient Maya, "the face or head establishe[d] individual difference and serve[d] logically as the recipient of reflexive action" (Houston, Stuart, and Taube 2006, 60). This communication could take place on a number of levels (Pancake 1991): names, official titles, political loyalties, ethnicity, and family ties could all have been communicated by this highly malleable and visible article of dress. The close physical connection between the head and the headdress, which at times even incorporated elements of the wearer's hair, does much to explain why the adornment of the head played such an important role in defining and communicating Maya identities and social selves.

CHAPTER 5

The Diademed Body

FRANCO D. ROSSI, KATHARINE LUKACH, AND JEFFREY DOBEREINER

The word *diadem* derives from a Greek term meaning "to bind round" (διαδεῖν). Through time, it has come to signify a "wreath of leaves or flowers worn round the head"; a "band or fillet of cloth, plain or adorned with jewels, worn round the head . . . as a badge of royalty"; and "a crown" denoting honor and royal dignity (*OED* 2013). This term's origin in the presentational act of binding is key to how we think about diadems and headbands more broadly in the Maya area and beyond. For the Classic Maya, headbands and diadems were "raised up" (*k'al*) in presentation, and "wrapped, bound" (*joy*) or "tied" (*kach*) around the foreheads of royal figures (Stuart 2012a; Zender 2016)—powerful actions that were as significant as the adornments themselves (fig. 5.1). There is often an emphasis by Maya artists on the diadem's bejeweled nature, on the inclusion of flowers and plants in its structure, and on its capacity to mark royal and personal identity. These objects of adornment, along with simple headbands and headwraps, were among the oldest and most widespread forms of ancient Maya clothing. Pragmatically, they served many purposes, including holding back hair, wiping away sweat on hot days, and cushioning the forehead when worn underneath heavy headdresses or helmets (see also chapter 4 in this volume). Symbolically, they operated as markers of personal distinction and identity affixed to a visually prominent part of the body.

The head is an exceptional place for display of meaningful and identifying ornaments. In various Maya languages as well as pre-Columbian Maya images and texts, *baah* and related terms acted as pronouns for self-reference—referring reflexively to an individual "body" (Bricker 1986, 112–113; MacLeod 1987, 105; Kaufman 2003, 277). Notions of the "forehead" or "head" were closely linked with this term and its associated concepts of selfhood and individual identity (Houston, Stuart, and Taube 2006, 60–62). *Baah* is bound with one's essence or life force, as seen in the term's incorporation into royal portraiture descriptions and its use in phrases of deity impersonation or invocation (*ubaahil ahn* or *a'n*; Houston and Stuart 1996; Proskouriakoff 1968, 247). A violent end to one's *baah* carried a powerful finality beyond simply death or dishonorable defeat. It is the term employed in contexts of execution and the effectual loss of power (*ch'ak baah*, often glossed as "head axing"), as well as royal accession and the acquisition of power, *k'ahlaj sak hu'n tu baah*, or "the white headband was raised to his (fore)head" (Stuart 1996; Bricker 1986, 113; Houston et al. 2017).

Such associations persisted into the Colonial period and survive in modern Maya expressions in which words derived from Classic-period *baah* function, in reflexive-verb constructions, as terms signifying an individual's own self, spirit, essence, or image and feature (Houston, Stuart, and Taube 2006, 55–58). Headbands and diadems adorned the *baah*, and thus composed an important component of dress that, though related to headdresses, nonetheless constituted a category of adornment

FIGURE 5.1. *Diadem being raised up (Bonampak Panel 1, drawing by Linda Schele © David Schele, courtesy of Ancient Americas at LACMA [ancientamericas.org]).*

all their own. Considering the meanings and identities bound up in marking the head, we discuss headbands and diadems as a category, separate from more complicated headdresses and head- and hair-wrap assemblages (see chapter 4 in this volume).

MATERIALS AND TYPOLOGY

Hu'n refers to headbands, but also to the bark paper from which headbands, books, and other practical and ritual adornments were made. As headbands, *hu'n* were typically worn low on the forehead, occasionally with a larger cloth headwrap. The bark paper constituting these headbands predominantly came from the cortex of amate trees (*kopo'* in several Mayan languages) of the *Ficus* genus, which grow throughout the Maya lowlands. The manner in which such paper was made and used in the Maya area was not all too different from its production and use throughout other parts of Mesoamerica (see von Hagen [1944] for a full survey of Mesoamerican bark papermaking). Cloth-like in texture, bark paper constituted various objects in the Maya area, such as tumplines, ground mats, codex books, and clothing, including the ponchos that were commonly worn by Lacandon Maya of Chiapas, Mexico (Thompson 1930, 62, 97; Tozzer 1907, 29, pl. V, fig. 1). Bark paper's many ritual uses appear in the ethnographic, historical, and iconographic record, and its use as a headband, as depicted in the artistic record, often occurs in contexts of male ritual or public ceremony related to adolescent rites of "first bloodletting" (*yax ch'ahb ak'abil*)—where the headband paper is spotted red with autosacrificially offered blood (Houston 2018, 96–114).

During the Classic period, a specific type of headband, known as *sak hu'n* ("white paper"), usually includes a small "Jester God" diadem jewel. These jewels are explicitly related to kingship, and as such they factor into a multitude of hieroglyphic statements and images involving accession throughout the Classic period (Stuart 2012a, 119; Schele and Matthews 1999, 115, 412). However, while abundant in the ethnographic and iconographic record, paper is notably absent in the archaeology of ancient Maya sites. More enduring evidence turns up in the form of stone bark beaters, tools used to beat out tree cortex into cloth strips and one of which is succinctly described by Francisco Hernández as a "flat stone which has a surface furrowed with grooves" (1959, 83). Bark beaters occur in roughly the same form and appearance not only across Mesoamerica but throughout much of the world where paper cloth was similarly made from the cortex of trees (Bellwood 2011; Chang and Goodenough 1996, 39; Kennedy 1934, 237–238, fig. 2; Skinner 1966).

Though indirect as evidence, bark beaters are perhaps the best archaeological indicators for papermaking. The earliest examples of this instrument in the Maya area date back well into the Middle Preclassic period (900 BC–300 BC) (Hammond 1991, 191; McAnany and Ebersole 2004, 318–319; Willey 1978, 80). As artifacts, bark beaters most commonly turn up in Classic- and Postclassic-period residential contexts and shed light on just how long lived and widespread the manufacture of paper cloth was within Maya society (Aoyama 2006; Aoyama 2009, 48–54; W. Coe 1965a, 599; Kidder 1947, fig. 78h; D. Lee and Piehl 2014, fig. 5.2; Rovner and Lewenstein 1997, 60–62; Rice 1987, 236–238; Woodbury 1965, 165).

In addition to bark beaters, more direct evidence of *hu'n* and *sak hu'n* comes in the form of Jester God diadem jewels that survive (Eberl and Inomata 2001). Though typically made of materials like jade, alabaster, or shell, these diadems were called *sak hu'nal uuh*, or "white papery jewel," by the Classic Maya, because they

were usually attached to the bark-paper headbands of rulers (Stuart 2012a, 119; Pillsbury, Potts, and Richter 2017, pl. 134 and 154) (figs. 5.2a and b). But discoveries of such "jewels" are rare, restricted to contexts associated with the highest socioeconomic classes of society and only one category within the full scope of diadem and headband making throughout the Maya area.

Besides the *sak hu'n*, a wide range of other headband types feature a variety of compositional and decorative elements, including feathers, flowers, shell, and stone— at times tucked in or sewn onto the basic tied assemblage (figs. 5.3a–g). In addition to amate paper, the basic structures of headbands were manufactured from water lilies, leather, coarse fibers of henequen and other plants, as well as the occasionally depicted animal pelt (figs. 5.3f–h) (M. Coe 1973, 49; Houston 2012a). As with many elements of Maya dress, the richest variety of diadems and headbands visible in one place is on the murals of Bonampak Room 1 (M. Miller and Brittenham 2013, 184–185, 189–191).

Most headbands were tied behind the head, often with a substantial surplus of material extending beyond the knot. One Chama-style polychrome vessel figuratively wears a headband around its upper rim, seemingly composed of vertically arranged owl feathers sewn onto a cloth base (fig. 5.4a). The place at which this headband fastens is overlaid with an iconographic flower, and excess feathers and cloth dangle from this point. In some Preclassic representations and several Late Classic polychromes, such knots are placed on the forehead.

The realism or fidelity to actual artifacts must be evaluated in such examples. For corporeal beings, headbands of extreme length and elaborate design (bordering on the fantastic) are often depicted (figs. 5.4b and c). Many such headbands as depicted could not have been manufactured using known Maya materials: they would have been too lengthy to make a viable piece of adornment. Others, especially earspool diadems, appear simply to stay in front of the forehead with no clear mode of attachment in highly stylized portrayals. At times, headbands can even appear as smoking or on fire (figs. 5.4e and f; see also 5.3g). Other examples seem to be more realistic representations of such headbands (fig. 5.4d).

Among images of deities, identifying diadems were commonly included on their foreheads. In these cases, the forehead was used to demonstrate known properties

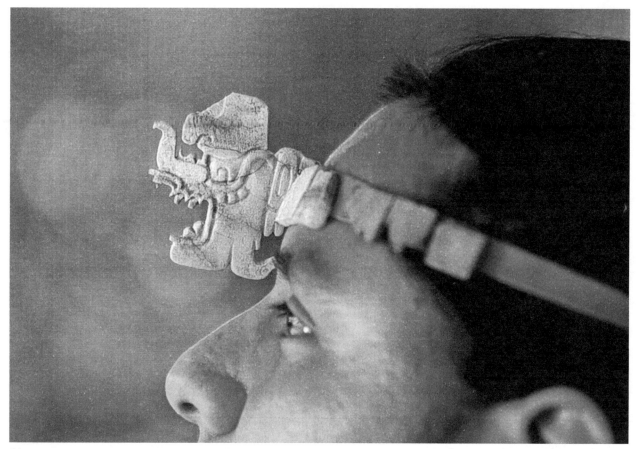

(a)

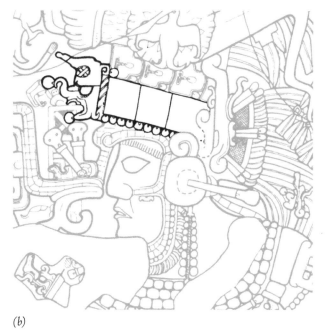

(b)

FIGURE 5.2. (a) Jester God diadem from Aguateca (courtesy of Ceibal-Petexbatun Archaeological Project); and (b) Jester God diadem on Aguateca Stela 7 (after Graham 1961, fig. 17).

of a represented deity: for example, a smoking cigar on (or through) the head of the deity cues *K'awiil*, or an extruded eyeball marks death gods (figs. 5.4e and g). Such diadems, were they ever actually made, would certainly not have been regularly worn. The widespread practice of evoking deities through impersonation would suggest that any such diadems would have been restricted to highly particular contexts. Whether literal burning elements or bona fide human eyeballs were ever actually used remains debatable.

SPATIAL AND TEMPORAL VARIATION

David Stuart (2015) has recently traced the iconography of royal paper headbands across Mesoamerica, making a compelling argument and visual case for their consistent use across Maya, Teotihuacan, Isthmian, Zapotec, and Mexica-Aztec representational systems. Ultimately, he follows Virginia Fields (1991) in tracking such royal headbands back to Olmec iconography, showing deep roots for headbands and their use in ritual

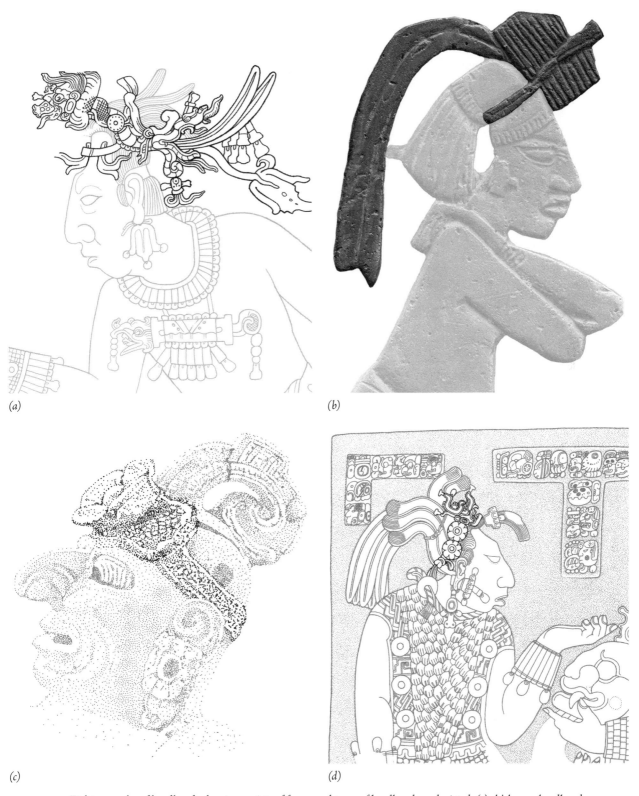

(a)

(b)

(c)

(d)

FIGURE 5.3. *Eight examples of headbands showing variety of forms and types of headbands as depicted: (a) ch'ahoom headband, Temple XIX, Palenque (drawing courtesy of David Stuart); (b) folded paper diadem (Denver Art Museum No. 1969.283, image courtesy of Denver Art Museum); (c) effigy vessel, Kaminaljuyu (Museo Nacional de Guatemala No. 2484, drawing by Franco D. Rossi); (d) flower-motif "Jester God" headband, Lintel 26, Yaxchilan (drawing by Ian Graham, © President and Fellows of Harvard College, PM2004.15.5.5.25); (e) Jaina-style warrior (National Museum of the American Indian Object 23/8366, K2834, drawing by Nicholas Carter); (f) Jaguar pelt headband (University Museum, University of Pennsylvania Object 38-14-1, drawing by Franco D. Rossi); (g) woman with "earspool diadem" (K4358, drawing by Franco D. Rossi after a photograph by Justin Kerr); and (h) tied woven headband (K4113, drawing by Mallory E. Matsumoto after a photograph by Justin Kerr).*

(e)

(f)

(g)

(h)

FIGURE 5.3. (continued)

(a)

(b)

(c)

(d)

(e)

(f)

(g)

FIGURE 5.4. (a) Chama-style vessel wearing owl feather headband, Museo Nacional de Guatemala (photo by Franco D. Rossi); (b) embellished diadem with feathers (K8461); (c) embellished headband with diadem (K2780); (d) realistically portrayed headband (K4996); (e) K'awiil with mirror and cigar on forehead (K5164); (f) flame diadem (K1391); and (g) eyeball diadem (K3924). Drawings (b–g) by Mallory E. Matsumoto after photographs by Justin Kerr.

and as insignia for leadership. In the Maya area, the earliest representations of headbands and diadems occur during the Preclassic period.

Several Late Preclassic monuments at Kaminaljuyu display simple knotted-cloth headwraps, as on Monument 62, or flower headbands as on Sculpture 23 (figs. 5.5a and b). Another monument (Kaminaljuyu Monument 18) similarly shows a headband, only it is adorned with a square diadem of uncertain material (see L. A. Parsons 1986; Henderson 2013, 588–660, for updated catalog of Kaminaljuyu sculpture). At this time, a stronger connection between headbands and kingship appears throughout the Maya world, perhaps nowhere more clearly than in Tikal Burial 85, where a greenstone mask featuring a headband and trefoil diadem marked the grave of an early ruler (fig. 5.5c) (W. Coe 1965b, 1414 and fig. 16). More recently, archaeologists claim to have found the "earliest Jester God" at the late Preclassic site of K'o, where a modeled censer discovered within an early royal tomb depicts a figure wearing the trefoil diadem (Skidmore 2011). Several jades from the Structure 6B cache in Cerros have also been thought to represent Late Preclassic Jester God diadems (Freidel and Schele 1988, 552). Whether they were worn on the forehead or not, these jades—among other artifacts of the period like the K'o ceramic censer or the Dumbarton Oaks Pectoral (fig. 5.5d)—offer compelling iconographic evidence of an emerging centrality of "Jester God" symbolism within representations of Maya kingship.

The San Bartolo murals offer perhaps the most vivid and varied glimpse into diadems and headbands during the Maya Late Preclassic period (Saturno, Taube, and Stuart 2005; Taube et al. 2010). Even though these are worn by mythical actors, their depiction presages some of the symbolic and identifying roles headbands and diadems play in later Maya imagery, as well as some of the materials and techniques used to make them. To take the San Bartolo Sub 1A north wall as one example (see fig. 3.2a for one of these two scenes), we observe two scenes with fourteen figures, eight of whom wear headbands (figs. 5.6a–g). Three of these headbands support diadems (on Individuals 6, 7, and 12; figs. 5.6b, d, and e) (see Saturno, Taube, and Stuart 2005, 8–9, fig. 5 for painted individuals' numerical designation). Additional diadems adorn the Maize God (Individual 9; fig. 5.6a) and the two decorative heads that ornament the offer-

ing baskets carried by Individuals 13 and 14 (fig. 5.6f). Each decorative head wears a trefoil-flower diadem like the mask found in Tikal Burial 85 (fig. 5.5c). The Maize God wears a diadem of a stylized quetzal bird (fig. 5.6a), the bird's iridescent green feathers were closely linked to maize imagery since at least the Middle Formative period (Taube 2005). Individual 12 (fig. 5.6b), argued to be the Maize God's primary consort (Saturno, Taube, and Stuart 2005, 34), exhibits a stiff, multicolored headband with a diadem featuring a mirrorlike pendent topped with ritual items and out of which emerges the head of a waterbird. Individual 11 (fig. 5.6c), another of the Maize God's consorts, wears a woven headband decorated with yellow flowers. Seated in the cave, holding a vessel full of tamales out toward the Maize God, Individual 7 wears a white and yellow headband (fig. 5.6d), seemingly made of platelets and possibly depicting a centipede with a schematic circular head and outcurving fangs, which are present in other Formative representations of centipedes (Chinchilla Mazariegos 2015, personal communication; see illustrations in Taube 2003, fig. 1). Individual 6 (fig. 5.6e), "the diviner," has a feathered headband with a mirror diadem as he watches over the birth of five babies from a bottle gourd. The diadem shows a red and black rim around a central mirror with thorns at its four corners, and a bird's feet and tailfeathers reach upward from its top side, giving the impression that a bird is diving into the mirror. A serpent comes out of the mirror center with a gourd flower in its mouth. The gourd flower would become a Classic-period symbol of kingship and mainstay of the headbands of later *ajaw*-head variant logographs, as well as royal depictions. Nondiademed, papery cloth headbands adorn four figures. Individuals 13 and 14 wear cloth headbands knotted at the front over the top (or part) of ballplayer headgear (fig. 5.6f for Individual 13). Individual 8 wears a red-stained cloth headwrap, with thick bands interwoven around the brow. Individual 1, interpreted as the mythohistorical founding king of the site (fig. 5.6g; Saturno 2009), uses a pure white headband over a ballplayer head assemblage—an early *sak hu'n* headband perhaps. Ball game–related headgear has been associated with leadership at least as far back as the San Lorenzo Olmec. These distinctive headbands all identify the roles and characteristics of each of these figures in some way. By the Late Preclassic, clearly, headbands were conforming to the kinds

(a)

(b)

(c)

(d)

FIGURE 5.5. *Late Preclassic diadems;* (a) *Simple knotted-cloth headwrap (Kaminaljuyu Monument 62, drawing by Franco D. Rossi after Parsons 1986);* (b) *flowery headband, Sculpture 23, Kaminaljuyu (drawing © Lucia Henderson, used by permission);* (c) *greenstone masquette with trefoil diadem, Burial 85, Tikal (drawing by Franco D. Rossi); and* (d) *Dumbarton Oaks pectoral with figure wearing trefoil diadem (drawing © Alexandre Tokovinine, used with permission).*

FIGURE 5.6. *Diadems and headbands on north wall, Sub 1a, San Bartolo (San Bartolo Mural, all illustrations by Heather Hurst, © 2003, courtesy of Heather Hurst): (a) quetzal diadem (Individual 9, the Maize God); (b) mirror-waterbird diadem (Individual 12); (c) yellow flower headband (Individual 11); (d) "centipede" headband (Individual 7); (e) mirror-serpent diadem (Individual 6, "diviner"); (f) red and white headband worn by person, trefoil diadem headband worn by cargo (Individual 13); and (g) white headband (Individual 1).*

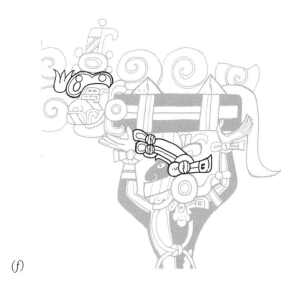

(f)

(g)

of standardized systems of representation that we see during the Classic period, with specific semiotic significance for identity, status, and ritual roles already present in their diagnostic features.

Headbands and diadems remain important during the Early Classic period, with increasing depictions of trefoil and Jester God symbolism that show the heightened importance of kingship in the Maya region. Turning to murals once again, we see glimpses into changing styles of headband and diadem adornment. On the murals of Uaxactun, headbands are shown being worn over the top of large white cloth hats, rather than directly against the forehead. One individual, however, labeled as a *ch'ok*, or "youth," carries a headband against the forehead, and this headband is fronted with a standard Jester God diadem (fig. 5.7a). On the Hauberg Stela, the central figure wears a paper headband beneath his more complex headdress, as an ancestor looks down on him (fig. 5.7b). Crosshatching signals darkened patches on the headband as stained red, a convention used during the Late Classic period as well. The deity peering down emerges from the mouth of a serpent whose body is held by the central figure; that god wears a headband with three leaves tucked beneath the band, pointing downward. The leaves cover the eyes and perhaps signify the deceased status of this ancestor. Three small figures, perhaps deified ancestors as well, are positioned on different parts of the serpent's body and also wear white headbands with crosshatching beneath their more elaborate and distinct headdresses.

At Early Classic La Sufricaya, white headbands show up as central to kingly legitimation. The mural discovered there portrays an elite figure who travels to a distant place (possibly Teotihuacan) in order to receive the right to rule. He is shown standing on the stairs of a temple wearing a white paper headband, while an aged individual confirms his authority with a red-speckled, white paper aspergillum (fig. 5.7c; see chapter 4 for discussion of such elders) (Estrada-Belli 2011, 135–136). The scene recalls another painted on a late Classic Maya vase in the Boston Museum of Fine Arts where an individual wearing the headband and cape of a *ch'ajoom* (see below) is confirmed in similar fashion by a similarly attired elder (K1440; fig. 4.11c). Several ceramic vessels depict nonroyal individuals in headbands, and such figures appear on monuments as well. For example, on the sides of Uaxactun Stela 20, captives wear headbands without Jester God diadems. Many other nonkingly representations of headbands exist from this time, revealing a continued widespread use and consistent meaning for these items.

As with most items of dress, the Late Classic period witnesses a sharp increase in depictions of headbands and diadems. It is during this time that the full array of contexts and materials for headbands and diadems becomes visible—occurring most abundantly on polychrome ceramic vessels, but also featured across other media, including carved and incised objects, monumental and miniature sculpture, murals, and stucco facade work. Headbands and diadems adorn the heads of

(a)

(c)

(b)

FIGURE 5.7. *Early Classic diadems: (a) figure wearing trefoil diadem and red headband on Structure B-XIII mural, Uaxactun (detail of painting by Antonio Tejeda, © President and Fellows of Harvard College, PM50-1-20/22982); (b) headbands on Hauberg Stela (drawing by Franco D. Rossi); and (c) headband worn by traveler on La Sufricaya Mural 6N (illustration by Heather Hurst, courtesy of Heather Hurst).*

mythical beings and historic figures: gods, kings, and *way*, as well as various figures of the court. In many scenes, individuals wear headbands in addition to more elaborate headdresses.

Also, by the time of the Late Classic period, headbands and diadems had come to serve as key diagnostics in logographic glyph signs. The head variant of the number three features the Wind God, *Ik' K'uh*, wearing a textured, woven headband fronted with a flower, a common characteristic of this deity (Taube 2005, 32). At Copan, an as of yet undeciphered glyph signifying sacrifice depicts what looks to be a lacerated face wearing a headband adorned with the kind of curved obsidian blade that would feature in sacrificial events (fig. 5.8a). A logogram **JOY** ("to wrap"), Proskouriakoff's "toothache" accession glyph (Proskouriakoff 1960), features a knotted white headband wrapped vertically around a rodent's head. The *ajaw* title bestowed in such accession events is widely written with either a human or a vulture head wearing a darkened crosshatched headband with the "gourd" flower at its front, or sometimes wearing the Jester God headband (figs. 5.8b and c).

As previously mentioned, headbands similarly serve as diagnostic features on gods and mythical figures, cueing certain deities or aspects of particular deities. God D commonly wears a diadem infixed with the glyph for darkness, or *ak'ab*, in both his aged human and avian forms (fig. 5.8d; Bardawil 1976)—an identifying characteristic visible even in the Late Preclassic San Bartolo murals. Other "Old God" or *itzam* figures, as well as wind and water deities, are often shown with headbands fronted by a darkened, red-trimmed "pad" out of which a water-lily flower emerges (see K1485). Another "Old God," God N, is often depicted wearing a textured, frond-like headband stiffly knotted at his forehead, perhaps made of woven henequen (fig. 5.3h; see S. Martin 2015). A version of this aged deity occurs on a well-known set of polychrome vessels in which he emerges from the mouth of a serpent that has coiled itself around a young woman. This woman is routinely depicted wearing a simple headband with an earflare diadem or sometimes just the earflare diadem, out of which a wisp of hair emerges (fig. 5.9a). The Maize God sometimes wears a similar earflare headpiece, but more often flourishes a diadem with long, elaborate water-lily flowers or maize vegetation extending outward from the forehead.

On one of several codex style vessels (K6979), both such earflare diadems are visible, worn by the Maize God and a woman walking in file behind him (fig. 5.9b, Individuals 1 and 3). Iconographic maize extends outward from the Maize God's earflare diadem, while the wisp of hair emerges from the young woman's earflare diadem. She holds aloft a Jester God diadem and headband, reverently transporting this symbolically charged item.

A variety of other important diadems characteristic of certain Late Classic characters, roles, and deities can be seen in this procession as well; the scene is vaguely reminiscent of the previously discussed north wall of San Bartolo. Individual 2 wears an eyeball diadem, matching a costume with associations of death and God A' (see chapter 2 in this volume). Her hands are extended flat in front of her as though carrying the hieroglyphic text nearby. Fitting with her macabre attire, this text describes the Maize God's death, using a well-known metaphor: "on 7 Ajaw, 7 Sak, he enters the water" (**OCH[I]-ha-HA'**). The Hero Twins are commonly shown wearing diagnostic headbands as well, both in their glyphic numeric head variants and in their artistic depictions. "Xbalanque" (Individual 5), one of the Hero Twins, typically wears a logographic **YAX** diadem, while "Juun Ajaw" (Individual 4) typically wears a white headband of acceding rulers, usually complete with a diadem (see fig. 5.9b). This white headband usually contains red spots or one large red spot at its center—artifacts likely sourced in royal bloodletting events.

In court scenes, rulers often wear diadem headbands that recall those worn by certain deities. The Maize God's flowery water-lily diadem is common in this regard and is usually depicted with the same kind of exaggerations present in mythical scenes. One unprovenienced polychrome vessel from the area of Motul de San José (fig. 5.4d), however, provides a rare glimpse into the appearance of such a diadem. It shows a seated lord with a simple headband into which an erect flower is tucked, awkwardly pointing upward instead of gracefully extending forward out of the forehead.

In many scenes, nonroyal figures and courtly officials are shown with headband diadems as well. On Piedras Negras Stela 12 (fig. 11.5), a captive wearing a headband looks up at his captors, one of whom—a *sajal*, or subsidiary lord—wears a *sak hu'n*, even as the overlord to whom he presents his prisoners does not.

(a)

(b)

(c)

(d)

FIGURE 5.8. *Headbands in texts: (a) glyph with profile head wearing eccentric lithic blade as diadem (drawing by Franco D. Rossi); (b)* **AJAW** *logogram, Palenque Panel of the 96 Glyphs (drawing by Franco D. Rossi); (c)* **AJAW** *in day-sign cartouche wearing headband and diadem, Quirigua Stela D (drawing by Franco D. Rossi); and (d) full-figure* **ITZAM MUUT,** *Tonina (drawing © Simon Martin, used with permission).*

(a)

(b)

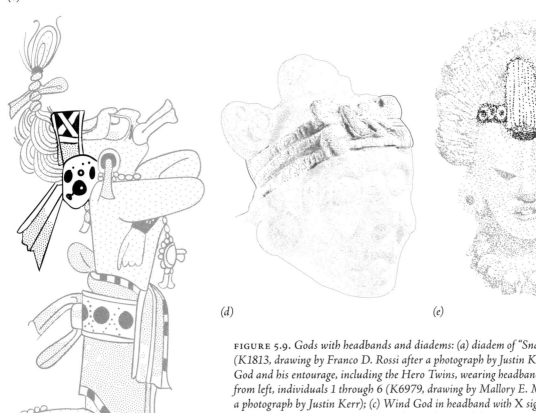

(c)

(d)

(e)

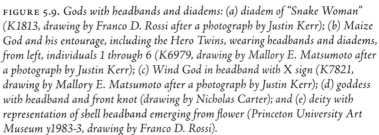

FIGURE 5.9. *Gods with headbands and diadems: (a) diadem of "Snake Woman" (K1813, drawing by Franco D. Rossi after a photograph by Justin Kerr); (b) Maize God and his entourage, including the Hero Twins, wearing headbands and diadems, from left, individuals 1 through 6 (K6979, drawing by Mallory E. Matsumoto after a photograph by Justin Kerr); (c) Wind God in headband with X sign (K7821, drawing by Mallory E. Matsumoto after a photograph by Justin Kerr); (d) goddess with headband and front knot (drawing by Nicholas Carter); and (e) deity with representation of shell headband emerging from flower (Princeton University Art Museum y1983-3, drawing by Franco D. Rossi).*

Such headbands could mark accession to courtly offices, as in the case of Chak Suutz, who is said to have acceded to the post of *yajaw k'ahk* ("fire lord") with the "fire headband" in the text of Palenque's Tablet of the Slaves (Zender 2004c, 298–301). At Bonampak, an individual wearing a white headband, spotted red, pulls the fingernails from a captive's hand as droplets of blood scatter on the temple stair (M. Miller and Brittenham 2013, 110, fig. 209). Headbands could mark accession to certain offices. Figures carrying the title *ch'ajoom*, or "incense scatterer," wear headbands made of water-lily vegetation, which feature two downward-hooking leaf elements symmetrically positioned more or less above the eyes (fig. 5.3a, see headband that crosses forehead). These *ch'ajoom* headbands are sometimes spotted with red, indicating the role of "scatterers" in sacrificial rites.

Straddling the line between headband and headdress, Room 1 at Bonampak depicts a series of lords standing before their new heir, each wearing a different headband diadem that may indicate a personal name or title (see M. Miller and Brittenham 2013, 154, fig. 292). On another unprovenienced polychrome vessel, two women stand near Yajawte' K'inich, a Late Classic king of Motul de San José (K3054). They wear diademed headbands plaited with stone or shell. Shell-beaded headbands often feature in portrayals of important women. Musicians shown on another Late Classic polychrome vessel accompany a performer on stilts, each adorned with slightly different woven and feathered headbands. The foremost musician and the stilted performer wear unique diadems on their similarly constructed headbands, revealing their elevated (literally in the stilted man's case) role in the troupe (K8947; Houston 2018a, 65; see also fig. 9.8e).

The white headband, or *sak hu'n*, is ubiquitous in both mythological and historical scenes. Most prominently at Palenque, but also at other sites, hieroglyphic texts recount a particularly important event in a ruler's life involving the raising of the white headband, which marked accession to rulership. At Palenque there is a specific structure designated as the *k'alhu'n naah*: the "headband-raising house"[1] or "accession house," located in the site core (Stuart 2012a, 122; Zender 2004c, 302).

Sak hu'n in such contexts seems to serve as a gloss for both white headbands as well as Jester God diademed headbands, which by the Late Classic had taken on several different forms. In analyzing these diadems, David Stuart (2012a) as well as Karl Taube and Reiko Ishihara (2012) isolate three forms of the Late Classic Jester God. Each of the authors uses slightly different terminology in describing these forms: the foliated avian or standard Jester God form; the piscine, or *xok*, form; and the trefoil Maize God or trident-blossom form. The last of these has recently been argued by David Stuart (2012a, 122, fig. 8; 2015) to possess its own name, *ux yop hu'n*, or "three amate leaf paper."

While historic, nonglyphic images of the trefoil maize-form diadem are hard to come by during the Classic period, both the standard jester and the *xok* forms occur abundantly in historic scenes. However, Stuart (2012a) sees the standard Jester God as more representative of the paper-like character of the *sak hu'n*, and he argues, along with Taube and Ishihara, that the rarity of actual Jester God jewels in the archaeological record as well as the iconography of this form in other artistic contexts belie the possibility of its actual existence in historical scenes. It is the opposite for *xok*-form diadems, several of which have been documented archaeologically, testifying to their historical actuality (fig. 5.2; Inomata et al. 2002, 314–315). In some representations at Aguateca and Ceibal, a *xok* diadem is visible over the forehead as well as above the ear, suggesting the symmetry of a third diadem on the opposite, invisible, side of the head. This triadic orientation, though of a standard Jester God, is visible in the imagery of Palenque's Temple 19 (Stuart 2005, 10). Although the three Jester God forms should be viewed as distinct, their associations with the number three and paper-cloth headbands, as well as their similar contexts in portrayed and inscribed scenes, suggest their roles overlapped considerably.

The Jester God motif largely disappears from Maya art during the Postclassic period. Styles and iconographies of power change considerably, though with a few intriguing exceptions. One dramatic representation from this time period seems to emphasize that

---

1. Though we adopt the recent translation of "to raise up" for the verb *k'al*, a longtime reading of the term as "to bind" is common in epigraphic

literature. David Stuart used this meaning in his 2012 translation of *k'alhu'n naah* as the "headband-binding house." We acknowledge his reading here, but include this note should any confusion arise over our earlier translation of *k'al* as "to raise up."

point: a single scene from the Chichen Itza ball-court friezes displays an armed Central Mexican–style warrior holding the decapitated head of an individual wearing a jewel strikingly reminiscent of the Jester God diadem (fig. 5.10a). The warrior displays a sun-disk diadem, complete with rays.

During the Postclassic, feathered headbands and beaded headbands continue to be used with stylistic innovations and new diadem forms that play on much older iconographies. Many full animals and animal heads appear in place of diadems, usually in the form of birds with their heads pointed downward, as if diving from the sky (fig. 5.10b). Postclassic ceramic censers reveal another headband motif, often adorning a figure glossed as "the diving Maize God" (fig. 5.10c). Its salient feature is a central triangle diadem spiking upward with its base tucked behind the headband. Moving south from Yucatán across the Maya area, Postclassic artistic representations are perhaps less abundant; however, it seems diadems were nonetheless common elements of dress (fig. 5.10d).

In Postclassic codices, headbands and diadems are worn by many figures, though more so by females than by males. In the Dresden Codex, for example, most of the represented females wear headbands, with motifs that imply production using the same set of materials as mentioned above, as well as apparent representations of complete snakes and other forms (fig. 5.10). While older women at times are depicted without a headband crossing the hair, young women are nearly always shown with them.

The organization of hair is considered a key part of proper comportment for a young Maya woman, and woven sashes are among the most appropriate means by which to control unwieldy hair (Ventura 2003). The proper placement and organization of such hair sashes are necessary to be considered a fully clothed adult. While this contrasts markedly from the traditionally construed "wrapping" nature of the headband—most notably in the use of complex textile motifs—it is worth considering the possible connections between these elements of dress (see chapter 4 in this volume as well).

Forehead elements continue to proliferate among deities in the codices, among which nonrealistic fantastical elements and bird diadems are widespread. These forehead ornaments are also present on structural facades at Uxmal and Chichen Itza, which feature *witz* masks with flowers centered over their foreheads, or even full floral headbands, to make clear the associations these structures have with "Flower Mountain" (Taube 2004, 85). This is further reinforced by the flower headdress–wearing warrior figures present in the carvings surrounding some such facades (Taube 2004, 8). These trends during the Postclassic collectively demonstrate that while the forehead continued to be a locus for displaying personal identity, the operational symbols and social meanings had shifted since the Classic period.

MEANINGS AND SOCIAL FUNCTIONS

The perceived potency of the forehead underscores the significance of headbands in Maya imagery and practice. As mentioned above, the *baah* was widely understood to be the primary locus of one's spirit and identity. In imagery, the forehead commonly served as the place in which key semantic signs were infixed into otherwise indistinguishable heads and faces (Houston, Stuart, and Taube 2006, 60–62). This is perhaps most clearly demonstrated in the headband differences between hieroglyphic godhead logographs, but it also factors prominently in imagery. To return to the example of San Bartolo: the headband helps distinguish the Maize God (Individual 9; fig. 5.6a), who wears a quetzal diadem, overlapping the imagery's verdant green maize stalks and iridescent green quetzal bird plumage; the woman in the cave (Individual 7; fig. 5.6d), adorned with a headband and diadem (perhaps evoking a centipede), indicative of her role in the Maize God's premature death (see Chinchilla Mazariegos forthcoming; 2011, 59–67); the "Diviner" (Individual 6; fig. 5.6e), who wears a mirror as his diadem; and, of course, the born ruler, who wears the *sak hu'n* over the top of his ballplayer headgear (fig. 5.6g; Saturno, Taube, and Stuart 2005; Taube et al. 2010). As mentioned, *sak hu'n* would become synonymous with kingship over the next centuries. By the sixth century AD, the term even came to factor into other courtly titles, such as *ti'sakh'un*, or "speaker for the white headband," an important courtly office (Zender 2004c, 210–221n79).

In headband-related accession statements, *raising up* and *tying* are operative verbs, perhaps presaging the similar rituals that came to surround initiation in the modern

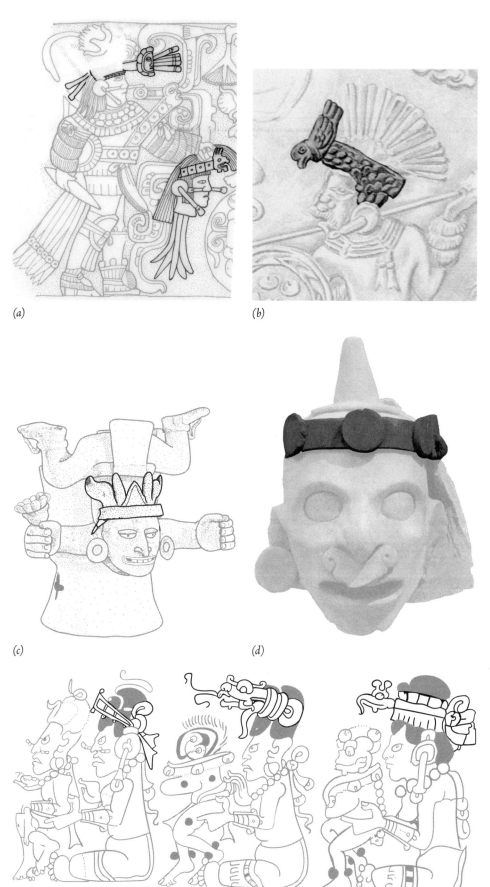

FIGURE 5.10. *Postclassic headbands: (a) headbands on decapitator and decapitated, East Central Panel, Great Ballcourt, Chichen Itza (drawing by Linda Schele © David Schele, courtesy of Ancient Americas at LACMA [ancientamericas .org]); (b) warrior wearing diving-bird diadem on Disk F from the Cenote of Sacrifice at Chichen Itza (reprinted by permission from Lothrop 1952, fig. 34); (c) Diving Maize God with Central Mexican–style headband (Dzibanche Structure 6, drawing by Franco D. Rossi); (d) incense burner with distinctive headband, Iximche' (Museo Nacional de Guatemala, photo by Franco D. Rossi); and (e) goddesses wear assorted headbands (Dresden Codex p. 20a, drawing by Mallory E. Matsumoto).*

(a)

(b)

(c)

(d)

(e)

day (Stuart 1996, 2012a; Schele and J. Miller 1983). Jon McGee (1990) provides a detailed ethnographic account of paper's ritual use among the Lacandon as *chak huun*, or "red paper." *Chak huun* were headbands stained red with the dye of annatto-tree fruit, applied by Lacandon Maya and visually evocative of blood. These headbands formed key ritual objects in a number of offertory ceremonies, some of which featured the symbolic act of presenting and tying *chak huun* around god pots and the heads of men. In what McGee (1990, 99–120) explains as an imitation of blood sacrifice, the red-stained headbands figure prominently in the initiations of male adolescents transitioning into adulthood (the *mek'chul* ceremony; see also Tozzer 1907, 138–145).

Of accession statements during the Classic period, the most discussed are Jester God diadems, at times actually shown as being given to rulers in rites of accession in accompanying scenes (see fig. 5.1), other times held aloft by deities (or perhaps deity impersonators) in procession scenes (fig. 5.9b). The practice of using red-stained paper headbands in initiatory rites can be clearly matched with carved and painted scenes on Classic-period Maya monuments and polychrome vessels in which headbands marked with crosshatching or red coloring to indicate blood are worn by youths (*ch'ok*) during public ceremonies (Houston 2018, 96–118). Similarly, in the art of the Classic period, there are many tableaux in which blood (typically let from the tongue or the penis) falls into bowls, where paper absorbs it (Schele and M. Miller 1986, 174–186). The paper, spotted red with blood, is shown either worn or in bowls ready to be burned in offertory rites—perhaps related to coming-of-age ceremonies like that referenced on the Hauberg Stela (see fig. 5.7b, glyphically referred to as the protagonist's "first bloodletting" or "*yax ch'ahb ak'abil*") or other types of initiation (Houston 2018, 89–117; Schele 1985; Stuart 2008).

Another type of headband called *say hu'n* was recently identified on the Princeton vase and at Aguateca, with the term *say* likely referring to its manufacture from sedge or possibly wild mulberry (Houston 2012a). Artistically rendered with dark crosshatching, the textual reference to the *say hu'n* at Aguateca refers to a preaccession *kach*, or "tying" event. This took place some twenty-two days before the ruler's actual accession to the throne, suggesting a preparatory function for such headbands. Such subtle variation in material, paired with meaningful symbolic differences (preaccession versus postaccession), suggests that, in future studies, close attention must be paid to the differences in materials constituting objects themselves as well as the forms these worked objects take (see Houston 2015 for one such treatment of Maya materiality).

CONCLUSION

Headbands and diadems were key pieces of adornment in Maya society across time. Worn prominently across the forehead, headbands and diadems were important semantic devices for signifying identity, social status, and political position, among other things. Temporary roles within particular ceremonies or events could also be marked by these versatile objects. Constructed from a wide array of materials, both perishable and permanent, headbands and diadems factored into royal ritual, coming-of-age ceremonies, and gender decorum. In understanding their layered and shifting meanings through time, we gain an additional window into the subtleties of how individual, community, and regional identities were constructed, displayed, and contested in Maya social worlds by means of the adorned body.

CHAPTER 6

The Bejeweled Body

NICHOLAS CARTER

Modification of the face through ornament—painting, tattooing, scarification, and especially piercing of fleshy parts like the nose and ears—was part of integration into Maya society, whether for children or, in colonial times, for outsiders such as the shipwrecked Spaniard Gonzalo Guerrero, so heavily marked as to be forever separated from his own people. In all cases, body modification was incremental, permanent, and indicative of status. More than baubles, Maya ear and nose ornaments too were polyvalent signs of social roles, embodiments of vital forces, and foci of aesthetic pleasure.

The Classic Maya applied the word *tuup* and its unpossessed form *tuupaj* (figs. 6.1a and b) to ornaments worn in pierced ears (see chapter 1 in this volume); if separate terms existed for nose or lip ornaments, they have yet to be recognized in the hieroglyphic corpus. A second term, written in Classic times with a logogram depicting an ear ornament or circular bead (figs. 6.1c and d), might have denoted ear ornaments in particular or jewels and wealth more generally. A reading of *kaaj* was proposed by Dmitri Beliaev (2012) for the logogram, though this reading continues to be debated. Used as a toponym, the term names a mythological location connected to a date in 3114 BC, an important station in the Maya Long Count. The same name pertained to multiple real-world sites near Naranjo, Yaxchilan, and potentially elsewhere (Houston, Garrison, and Román 2018, 23). A codex-style vessel (Robicsek 1981,

201), whose dedicatory text names a lord of the Ik' polity but was probably produced in southern Campeche, connects the mythological "Jewel" site to the death and resurrection of the Maize God. In one part of the vase's painted scene, a woman seated in the mouth of a cave, represented as the jaw of a supernatural centipede, offers a *Spondylus* shell ornament to the dancing Maize God. In another part of the scene, the Maize God's sons heft a bundle and a massive bowl full of jewels. The accompanying text tells us that the events were "overseen" (*u kabjiiy*) by a "holy 'Jewel' lord" (*k'uhul ʔkaaj ajaw*). A royal title used by the dynasties of El Zotz and Yaxchilan (Houston 2008b), which uses the same "Jewel" logogram, may thus derive from the mythic lord of a place connected to the death and resurrection of this important deity.

MATERIALS AND TYPOLOGY

Most ancient Maya ear ornaments we see were earflares—that is, the main body of the ornament rested in a pierced, stretched earlobe instead of hanging from a thin string passing through an unstretched perforation. A typological division can be established between simple earflares and composite earflares. The most basic earflares were cylinders of bone, wood, or fired clay. A variation on that form consisted of a solid cylindrical plug with a thinner tail projecting downward behind it. The forward end of the cylinder could be inset with

FIGURE 6.1. *Terms for ornaments in Maya hieroglyphic writing: (a)* **u-tu-pa**, *u tuup, "his ear ornament" (Palenque, Temple of the Inscriptions, middle panel, glyph block M3); (b)* **tu-pa-ja**, *tuupaj, "an ear ornament" (Palenque, Temple of the Inscriptions, middle panel, glyph block A9); (c)* **ʔKAAJ**, *kaaj(?), "ear ornament" or "jewel" (El Zotz Lintel 1); and (d)* **ʔKAAJ**, *kaaj(?), "ear ornament" or "jewel" (Tikal, Structure 5C-4-1st, Lintel 2, glyph block B8) (drawings by Nicholas Carter).*

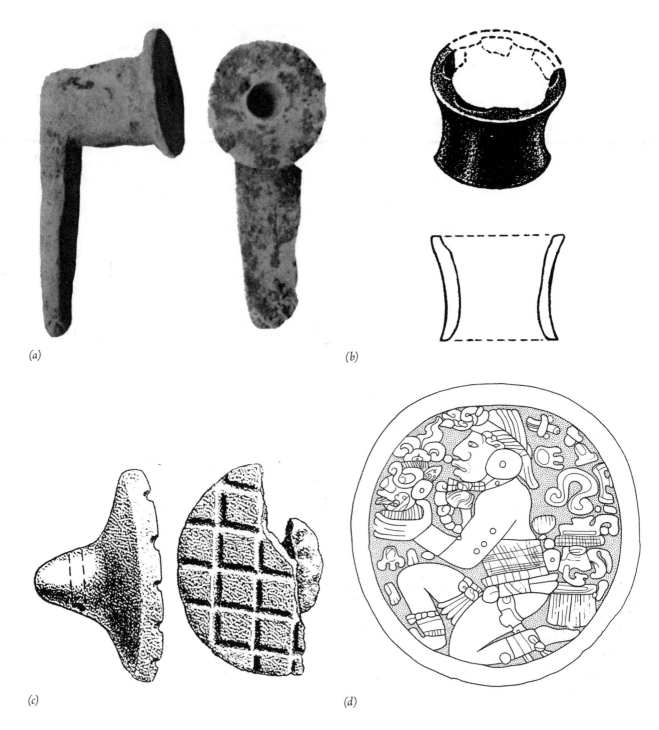

(a)

(b)

(c)

(d)

FIGURE 6.2. (a) L-shaped earflare, from Altar de Sacrificios
(reprinted by permission from Willey 1972, fig. 198); (b) "napkin-
ring" flare, from Altar de Sacrificios (reprinted by permission from
Willey 1972, fig. 74b); (c) plug designed to be held in place with a
thin rod, from Altar de Sacrificios (reprinted by permission from
Willey 1972, fig. 75); (d) carved earflare plaque in the De Young
Museum, San Francisco (drawing by Nicholas Carter after a
photograph by Justin Kerr); and (e) Early Classic earflare plaques
with incising and mosaic inlay, from El Zotz (drawing by Nicholas
Carter).

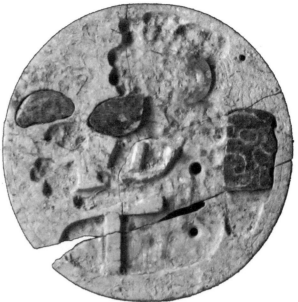

(e)

stones or carved shell or decorated by carving or incising (fig. 6.2a). Small, inexpensive, and easy to make, these L-shaped plugs were in general use among well-off commoners (Moholy-Nagy 2003, 43–45).

Earlobes stretched over time could accommodate larger earflares made of the same materials or of hard stone, especially jadeite, which was rarely used for L-shaped ornaments. These larger earflares might be cylindrical, flared only at the front, or spool-shaped "napkin rings" flared at the front and the back (fig. 6.2b). Most archaeological examples would have been held in place by the earlobe alone, but some were designed to be secured with a thin stick passing through a hole in the plug behind the ear (Willey 1972, 91; fig. 6.2c). The front faces of solid spools could be inlaid with disks of shell bearing carved designs or themselves inlaid with mosaics of shell, obsidian, jade, pyrite, mica, and other materials (figs. 6.2d and e; Carter et al. 2012; Fields and Reents-Budet 2005, 184). Hollow spools were sometimes decorated around their circumference with texts or designs that would have been largely concealed when they were worn.

Composite ear ornaments combined earflares with other elements—counterweights hung behind the earlobe and, more rarely, ornaments projecting forward from the centers of earspools—likely held together with string or adhesive. Widely variable in form and construction, composite ear ornaments are most common in Late Classic archaeological contexts, but are also well attested for earlier periods. The typological diversity discussed below applies mainly, though not exclusively, to composite ornaments.

SPATIAL AND TEMPORAL VARIATION

Late Preclassic representations of ear ornaments in the Maya highlands and lowlands alike tend to show large circular earspools. Many of these presumably depict "napkin-ring" earflares or front-flaring plugs: shown in frontal view, the ornaments appear as plain or concentric circles worn in the earlobes, without obvious additional components. Composite ornaments are more frequent, however, and show temporally specific differences from later forms. Particularly common are four small circles arranged symmetrically around the central holes of earflares. Shown as raised beads in three-dimensional representations, these correspond to sets of four holes drilled in Late Preclassic and Early Classic archaeological examples of composite earflares from Kaminaljuyu and other sites, which probably anchored small ornaments like pearls or beads (Kidder, Jennings, and Shook 1946, fig. 145). At Tikal L-shaped ear ornaments of pottery or

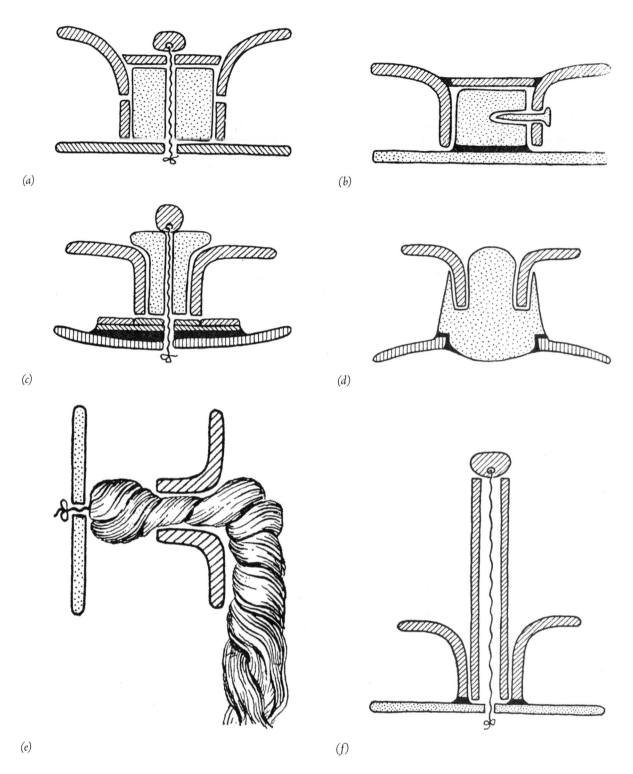

(a)

(b)

(c)

(d)

(e)

(f)

FIGURE 6.3. *Schematic diagrams of Early Classic composite ear ornaments from Kaminaljuyu:*
(a) hollow spool with a throat plate and a core of perishable material, held together with a bead and
string; (b) hollow spool with a throat plate and perishable core, held together with adhesive and a peg;
(c) hollow spool with a perishable core, held together with a bead, string, and adhesive; (d) hollow spool
mounted in wood or another perishable material; (e) hollow spool held to its wooden backing using a
tassel; and (f) hollow spool with a protruding jade tube, held together with a bead and string. Reprinted
by permission from Kidder 1946, fig. 45.

perishable substances were probably in use by the end of the Preclassic period, an inference based on the survival of shell rosettes interpreted as inlays (Moholy-Nagy 2003, 45). Hollow napkin-ring flares at Uaxactun were dated to the Late Preclassic period (350 BC–AD 250) (Ricketson and Ricketson 1937, pl. 696), but Late Classic examples are also attested at Piedras Negras and Altar de Sacrificios (Willey 1972, 93).

Early Classic composite ear ornaments from Kaminaljuyu (figs. 6.3a–f; see Kidder, Jennings, and Shook 1946, 106–108, for a fuller description) consisted of a hollow cylindrical stem, worn in the ear, with a flare in front and a disk-shaped backing closing off the ornament at the other end of the stem. Flares might be continuous with the stem or a separate piece; the backings were always separate, attached to the stem with resinous adhesives. Flares at Kaminaljuyu were typically solid pieces of jade, but they could also be jade mosaic work or made from shell, pyrite, or even fragrant resins; indeed, across the Maya world, ceramic flares are not uncommon (e.g., Willey 1972, 89–91). Kidder and colleagues distinguished between two types of flaring ear ornament: one with a narrow, curving face and a wide central opening that might be closed off by a jade disk in the mouth of the flare and the other with a flatter, wider face and no interior disk. At Kaminaljuyu and Early Classic Tikal, paired earflares tended to be cut from a single piece of jade (Moholy-Nagy 2003, 43–45). Backings and separate stems were usually of perishable materials, probably wood, but stems were sometimes made from jade or shell and backings from shell or slate. With little archaeological evidence for counterweights, these Early Classic ornaments may have been assembled and kept in place using string, wood, or some other perishable material.

Other elements of ear ornaments, present already in the Late Preclassic but especially prominent in Early Classic representations, are strips of cloth or paper knotted above or below circular plaques so large that they cover the entire ear. By the Early Classic period, knots of this kind were depicted with the heads of agnathous (jawless) serpents attached to them. If such heads were real objects rather than an iconographic convention, they were likely made of perishable materials. Widespread in sixth-century representations, knots adorned with serpents' heads bound outsize plaques to the cheek pieces

FIGURE 6.4. *Detail of Caracol Stela 16. Drawing by Nicholas Carter.*

of Principal Bird Deity headdresses (see chapter 4 in this volume), not to the actual ear of the wearer (fig. 6.4). Bracelets and anklets in Early Classic art exhibit a similar construction technique, with circular plaques and agnathous snake heads bound to wrists and ankles (see chapter 10 in this volume).

Late Classic lowland representational and archaeological data indicate a shift in the construction of high-value earflare assemblages, which now tended to include counterweights hanging behind the ear. Late Classic earflare assemblages can be divided into two types of their own: those that incorporate plaques and those with hollow earflares meant to be worn in the lobe. In the former type, a circular plaque was placed in front of the earlobe. A cord passing through a small hole in the center and the pierced lobe held an earflare made of jade or bone against the plaque in front, with heavy jade counterweights dangling behind. Such ornaments could have been worn by persons whose earlobes had not yet been stretched sufficiently to accommodate larger spools or plugs. In the latter type of assemblage, hollow jade flares were inserted into stretched earlobes. A cord threaded through the flare connected counterweights to a frontal decoration consisting of a long tube and a final bead. Visually similar ceramic assemblages, made of fine-paste ceramic coated with green stucco and stained with cinnabar, might not require counterweights. Instead, the projecting rods were affixed to the necks of the flares, and the whole assemblages held in the lobes, using thin sticks or strings inserted through transverse holes (fig. 6.5a). Details of composite earflare assemblages are especially masterfully rendered in late-eighth-century

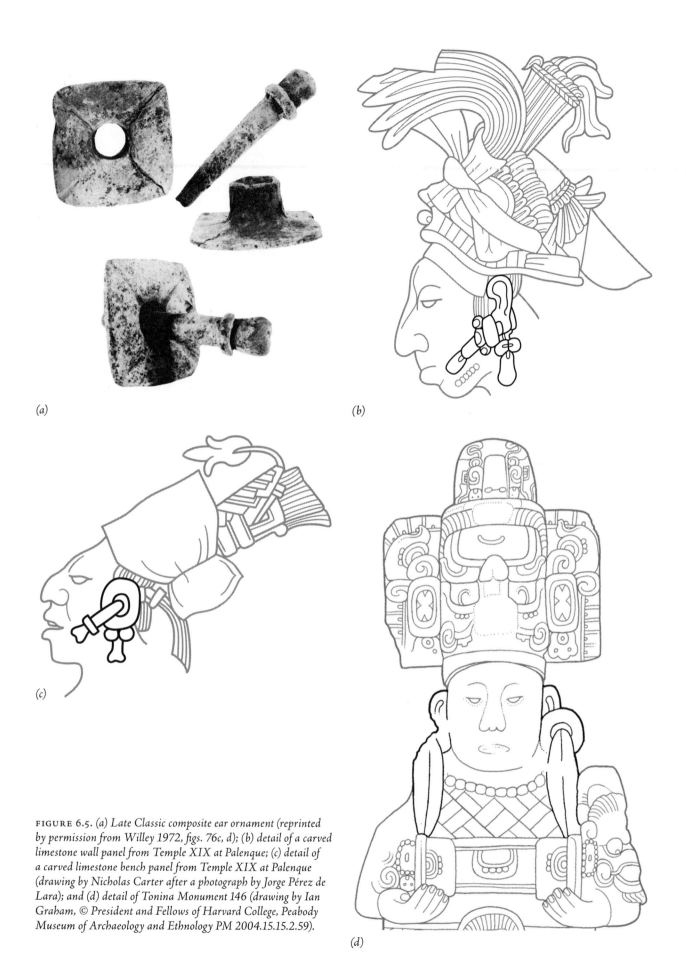

(a)

(b)

(c)

(d)

FIGURE 6.5. (a) Late Classic composite ear ornament (reprinted by permission from Willey 1972, figs. 76c, d); (b) detail of a carved limestone wall panel from Temple XIX at Palenque; (c) detail of a carved limestone bench panel from Temple XIX at Palenque (drawing by Nicholas Carter after a photograph by Jorge Pérez de Lara); and (d) detail of Tonina Monument 146 (drawing by Ian Graham, © President and Fellows of Harvard College, Peabody Museum of Archaeology and Ethnology PM 2004.15.15.2.59).

(a)

(b)

(c)

FIGURE 6.6. (a) Detail of a Late Postclassic ceramic statuette of Itzamná from Mayapan; (b) composite earflare assemblage from the Dresden Codex; and (c) simple earspool from the Grolier Codex. (Drawings by Nicholas Carter.)

stone and stucco sculptures at Palenque (figs. 6.5b and c), among other sites.

At some places and times, trailing feathers or paper or cloth streamers passed through earflares in place of beads and counterweights. Such feathers are common in the art of Tonina, for instance, until the end of the site's royal monumental tradition in the mid-tenth century (fig. 6.5d). Much later, ceramic sculptures from the

Postclassic site of Mayapan depict similar ornaments, which seem to characterize the aged God D or his impersonators (fig. 6.6a). Other Postclassic representations, however, make it clear that more traditional ear ornaments remained in vogue. Plaques or spools with long, protruding beads are well attested in mural and monumental art at Mayapan and Santa Rita Corozal and are virtually the only naturalistically rendered ear ornaments in the Dresden, Madrid, and Paris Codices (fig. 6.6b). The painter of the Grolier Codex, on the other hand, preferred simple plugs or earspools, a choice in keeping with the mixing of Maya and Central Mexican artistic styles in that document (fig. 6.6c; M. Coe et al. 2015, 132).

NOSE AND LIP ORNAMENTS

Representations of nose ornaments in ancient Maya art can be divided into three categories. The first and most numerous consists of conventional representations of jewels as metaphors for breath, which do not necessarily have archaeological correlates and are treated elsewhere (Houston, Stuart, and Taube 2006, 141–142). The second includes ornaments, some of them archaeologically attested, that were worn in holes pierced through the septum, the nostrils, or the skin over the bridge of the nose. The third category encompasses a variety of temporary, noninvasive modifications made to the nose and brow using perishable materials.

In most settings in which they do appear, ornaments for pierced noses seem to function as markers of status and group membership—whether affirming or contrasting with local identities. One of the bound prisoners on the Late Preclassic Kaminaljuyu Monument 65 wears a horizontal bar through his septum, while the other prisoners and victorious lords in the same carving have "beads" of breath in place of material nasal ornamentation (fig. 6.7a). In the Early Classic period, flat, angular nose ornaments—probably made of cut shell—denote Teotihuacan origin or affiliation (fig. 6.7b). Other nasal decorations, with one scalloped edge and internal markings like those of the **CHAK** (red) or **YAX** (green) logograms, lack clear connections to Teotihuacan-style articles of dress. These might represent feathers or shell ornaments worn in the septum.

Nasal jewelry is rare in lowland Maya portraiture

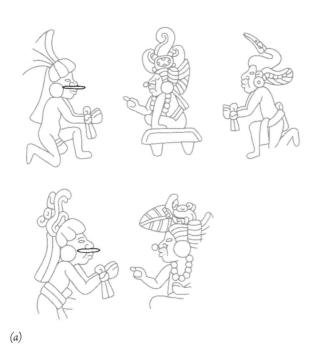

(a)

(b)

FIGURE 6.7. (a) Prisoners with nasal ornaments on Kaminaljuyu Monument 65 (drawing by Lucia Henderson; used with permission); and (b) warrior with a Teotihuacan-style nasal ornament on Yaxha Stela 11 (drawing by Nicholas Carter).

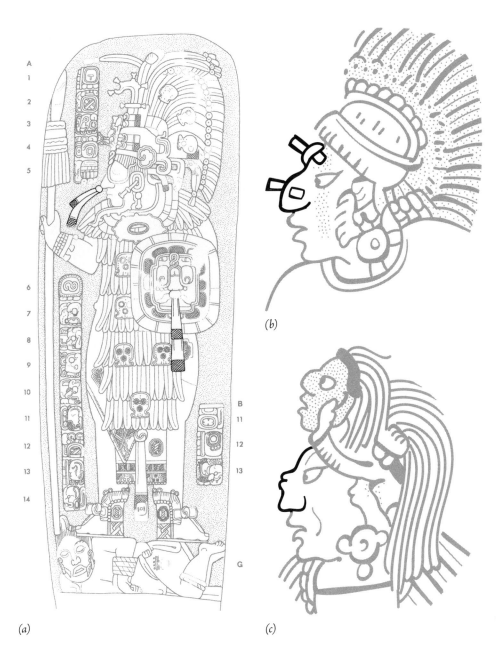

(b)

(a)

(c)

FIGURE 6.8. *Late Classic nasal ornaments: (a) Naranjo Stela 21 (drawing by Ian Graham, © President and Fellows of Harvard College, PM2004.15.6.2.37); (b) warrior with two skewers through the skin of the bridge of his nose on a Nebaj-style polychrome vase in the Museum für Völkerkunde, Berlin (K2206, drawing by Nicholas Carter after a photograph by Justin Kerr); and (c) warrior with a scarred nose on the same vessel (drawing by Nicholas Carter after a photograph by Justin Kerr).*

during the Late Classic period, after the end of Teotihuacan's active involvement in the region. One exception involves a conventional costume attested at sites in eastern Peten, whereby kings impersonated the Jaguar God of the Underworld in martial ceremonies. A stela from Naranjo (fig. 6.8a) depicts a ruler wearing a bead in his nose from which strips of cloth or paper descend; the face of the Jaguar God on his shield has an identical ornament in its nose, suggesting that the monument depicts physical objects rather than metaphors for breath. To the south, in the higher country around Chama and

Nebaj, several polychrome painted vessels depict warriors wearing short sticks or reeds thrust through the skin at the bridges of their noses (e.g., K413, K593, K2206, K2352, and K7107; fig. 6.8b). The simplicity of the ornaments and the difficulty of healing such "surface piercings" raise the possibility that these were temporary, perhaps penitential. Bumps on the bridges of other men's noses, depicted on some of the same vessels, might indicate scarring from the procedure (fig. 6.8c).

Nose piercings began to feature more prominently in lowland art during the Terminal Classic period, as

FIGURE 6.9. (a) Detail of Ceibal Stela 3 (drawing by Nicholas Carter); (b) detail of Ceibal Stela 13 (drawing by Ian Graham, © President and Fellows of Harvard College, PM2004.15.6.17.13); (c) detail of South Column, Temple 6E1, Chichen Itza (drawing by Linda Schele, © David Schele, courtesy Ancient Americas at LACMA [ancientamericas.org]); (d) jade nose bead recovered from the Cenote of Sacrifice, Chichen Itza (drawing by Nicholas Carter after Proskouriakoff 1974, fig. 47a); and (e) detail of a Late Postclassic mural on the north wall of Mound 1, Santa Rita Corozal (drawing by Nicholas Carter after Gann 1900, pl. 29).

part of a new package of aesthetic elements with foreign or innovative valences that were connected to Chichen Itza and the Central Mexican site of Tula. Whereas Teotihuacan-style nose ornaments were broad and flat, hanging down over the mouth, the new Toltec style called for straight beads of jade or topaz (Tozzer 1941, 126; Villela and Koontz 1993, 4) that projected to either side of the septum. Such transverse bar ornaments feature among the adornments of Terminal Classic lords at Ceibal, wearing otherwise fairly conventional "Classic Maya" outfits, but they also appear in much more innovative portraits that may depict foreigners (figs. 6.9a–b). At Chichen Itza, they appear to have been de rigueur for members of the warrior elite (fig. 6.9c), although semi-circular septum ornaments are also attested in the art and archaeology of the site (fig. 6.9d). Nasal bar ornaments continued to be depicted through the Postclassic period, joining earflares and necklaces as essential parts of the Maize God's costume as represented in the codices. Angular plaques worn in the nose, reminiscent yet distinct from the earlier Teotihuacan style, also feature in depictions of deities at Santa Rita Corozal (fig. 6.9e).

Ancient Maya people in some regions, especially along the Gulf Coast and adjacent inland zones, apparently wore nasal prostheses that emphasized their prominent noses and in some cases extended them well up onto the forehead. Such prostheses have left no archaeological remains; they could have been made from any number of perishable materials, including wood, latex, or other tree resins, perhaps painted together with the face, and likely adhered to the nose using some gum or resin. Appliqués of this kind are especially notable at Palenque, where they were favored by elite men. There, fine lines in some relief carvings clarify the distinction between the prosthesis and the wearer's own nose (fig. 6.10a). They also appear on Jaina-style figurines depicting elite male warriors, courtiers, and other actors (fig. 6.10b). Women in the Jaina-figurine corpus often wear related ornaments: either nasal prostheses like the men's or, more frequently, beads adhered to the brow just above the nose (fig. 6.10c). Unlike ear ornaments, a gender-based distinction in nose and brow ornamentation is evident here.

Lip piercings are very rare in Maya art, although an intriguing example comes from a hieroglyphic spelling on Sacul Stela 1 (AD 761). There, the head variant for the logogram **NAAH** (first or great) depicts the face of the Maize God with tattooing or scarification around his mouth and a thick, cylindrical labret (fig. 6.10d)—part of the spoils from his sojourn in the underworld and triumphant resurrection. L-shaped ornaments found in archaeological contexts have sometimes been interpreted as labrets (e.g., A. Smith and Kidder 1943, fig. 54b). The interpretation is plausible when a single ornament with a suitably short tab is found in the vicinity of the lower jaw, but if labrets were in widespread use, then their virtual absence from human portraits in ancient Maya art is hard to explain. Among the Late Postclassic Aztecs, labrets marked masculine achievements on the field of battle (R. Joyce 2000b, 479), yet there is little to indicate that most Maya groups had a similar custom.

MEANINGS AND SOCIAL FUNCTIONS

Incorporated into the face, ear, nose, and lip ornaments were well suited to mark status. They were, for instance, salient markers of class distinctions: at Tikal L-shaped ornaments of pottery or perishable materials like marine shell were found in the burials of well-to-do commoners, while more complicated earflare assemblages incorporating jade appear restricted to royalty and aristocracy (Moholy-Nagy 2003, 43–45). Several Late Preclassic and Early Classic monuments show individuals wearing a superfluity of ear ornaments, sometimes in settings other than the ears, in conspicuous displays of wealth. A string of seven earflares hangs from the headdress of a lord or deity on the Late Preclassic Altar 13 at Tak'alik Ab'aj. Early Classic rulers at Tikal sometimes appear with an even greater profusion of ear ornaments: for instance, on Tikal Stela 31, the king Sihyaj Chan K'awiil wears massive ear plaques attached to his headdress and a necklace made of three strands of earspools, while another strand of seven plaques or spools bound together hangs from a second headdress that he holds aloft. Additional ear ornaments adorn the king's belt as well as the ears and (as tokens of precious breath) the noses of the gods and ancestors whose masks he wears or carries (fig. 6.11). Most prevalent in Early Classic art, strings of earspools had more or less disappeared from depicted royal costumes by the middle of the seventh century AD.

Among the ancient Maya, ear piercing was likely part

(a)

(b)

(c)

(d)

FIGURE 6.10. (a) Detail of Palenque, Temple XXI, south bench panel, showing a nasal prosthesis (drawing by Nicholas Carter after a photograph by Jorge Pérez de Lara); (b) Jaina-style figurine depicting a warrior (drawing by Nicholas Carter); (c) Jaina-style figurine depicting a woman with a brow ornament (drawing by Nicholas Carter); and (d) hieroglyphic spelling on Sacul Stela 1 depicting the head of the Maize God with a labret (drawing by Nicholas Carter after a photograph by Ian Graham).

of a process of socialization beginning in childhood, in which the transition from slimmer to wider, heavier ornaments kept pace with advancing maturity. A link between ear ornamentation and blood sacrifice may also be inferred from the example of the Late Postclassic Aztecs, among whom, when young children offered blood from their ears for the first time, the lobe was pierced through with an awl and a cotton thread inserted in the hole to keep it open (R. Joyce 2000b, 477–478). Replacing normal ear ornaments with strips of paper emphasized penance and the sacrificial dimension of ear piercing. At the same time, it denoted the suspension of the wearer's ordinary social status, whether voluntary or involuntary. Paper is most commonly depicted in the ears of captives—but other prisoners are shown still wearing their jewelry, if little else, and in some cases, such as the mural painting in Room 2 of Structure 1 at Bonampak, successful warriors appear with paper in their earlobes. Far rarer in Classic art, but again attested in the Bonampak murals, are strips of spotted feline hide worn in the ears like bark paper. Such ornaments likely referenced bark paper, with its sacrificial connotations, but they are not attested for captives.

Ear ornaments also announced the kinds of sounds it was appropriate for their wearers to hear: the flowery, beautiful speech of the well bred; the entreaties of captives; the advice and blessings of ancestors. The placement of ear ornaments—in the ears and on either side of the face—created wearable versions of a standard tableau in Maya art, in which a central figure receives offerings from ancestors, deities, or subordinates. Such offerings could include blessings or advice, captives, game animals, riches, or religious objects, many of them explicitly rendered on disks set into solid plugs (Carter et al. 2012). Appropriately, then, the text on a pair of ear ornaments from the tomb of K'ihnich Janab' Pakal at Palenque describes their dedication in terms of "hearing" (*ubjiiy*, "it was heard") (Houston, Stuart, and Taube 2006, 156, fig. 4.18).

The ear ornaments of particular deities are remarkably consistent in Maya art across time and space, indicating that ear ornamentation could point to individual identities in much the same way as headdresses. For instance, through the end of the Classic period, representations of a nocturnal solar deity known as the Jaguar God of the Underworld include earflares with four

FIGURE 6.11. *Tikal Stela 31, front, showing abundant ear ornaments (image courtesy of University of Pennsylvania Museum).*

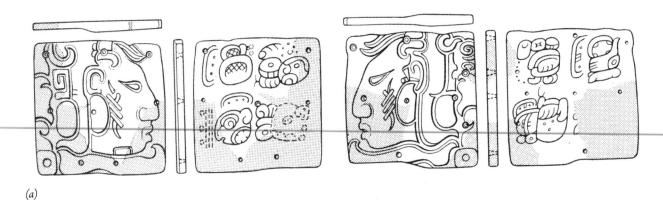

(a)

(b)

FIGURE 6.12. *(a) Two jade plaques from the Cenote of Sacrifice, Chichen Itza (reprinted by permission from Proskouriakoff 1974, pl. 49b); and (b) detail of Lacanha Panel 1 showing a Serpent Bar with earspool-like objects at either end (drawing by David Stuart; used with permission).*

pearls or beads on their faces, a style of great antiquity that is perhaps best archaeologically attested at Early Classic Kaminaljuyu and on the friezes discovered at El Zotz (see Kidder, Jennings, and Shook 1946; Houston et al. 2015). But a few other items that the ancient Maya called *tuupaj* are hard to understand as ear ornaments at all. For example, the obverse sides of two square jade plaques recovered from the Cenote of Sacrifice (fig. 6.12a) depict human faces emerging from the jaws of supernatural serpents or centipedes, in the manner of deceased ancestors, a motif widely attested in Classic Maya depictions of so-called Serpent Bars. An inscription on the reverse of one of the plaques calls the objects the *tuup* of a "heart god" (*u tuup ohlis k'uh*). Pierced by small drill holes, the plaques appear unlikely to have been worn in human ears; instead, they could have been sewn to clothing or to a headdress assemblage. Alternatively, they could have been affixed to either end of a Serpent Bar, which are often shown with large earspool-like objects at their ends (fig. 6.12b).

CONCLUSION

Ear and nose ornaments, like headdresses and diadems, were closely tied to individual and group identities because of their placement near the face. Classic southern lowland Maya conventions of dress allowed for considerable variety in ear ornamentation across space, time, and social rank, presumably signaling fine gradations of status and role. Meanwhile, nasal ornaments as such usually appear to signify non-Maya identities, or at least, as at Chichen Itza, a Maya take on larger Mesoamerican identities and beliefs. At the same time, *tuupaj* exhibit much less formal and compositional variation than headgear, no doubt in part because of technological constraints.

Like *uuhaj*, *tuupaj* were closely connected to Classic Maya concepts of breath and life. The death and resurrection of the Maize God and the defeat of the chthonic God L (see Taube 1992b, 79–88) are represented in Late Classic vase painting in terms of the donning or stripping of jewelry. Associations between vitality and *tuupaj* may not have been limited to ear ornaments: even though physical nasal jewelry usually denotes specific, marked identities in Classic Maya art, nonphysical jewels depicted at the nostrils conventionally represent breath. When they were worn by living human beings, nose ornaments may have had the same connotations. Floral motifs, well attested in Late Classic composite earflare assemblages, point to further associations among hearing, breath, and smell and to connections among visual, olfactory, and aural beauty. While such connections may be most marked in the elaborate jewelry worn by Maya lords and ladies, they also mattered

to the commoners, who wore shell, bone, and wooden plugs set with stones or carved with flowers. Ornaments made from quickly perishing substances—flowers, paper, hide—were semiotically marked, deviating from and referring back to conventionally harder materials and pointing out the special status of their wearers.

Nose and lip ornaments, being less well represented than ear ornaments in ancient Maya art, have received less scholarly attention, but we can speak of certain patterns in time and space. During the Classic period, nasal piercings tend to signal special statuses or identities: affiliation with Teotihuacan, manifestation of certain gods, or, in the Terminal Classic, connections to the economic and cultural world of the Gulf Coast. A similar geographic orientation characterizes nasal prostheses and technologically similar brow ornaments, which are best attested in the Chontal-speaking region of the Maya West and in the art of the Jaina polity on the west coast of the Yucatán Peninsula. The near absence of lip ornaments in Maya art, meanwhile, presents a puzzling contrast with Mesoamerican societies to the west of the Maya world and perhaps also a contrast with evidence from the archaeological record—if, indeed, L-shaped ornaments include labrets as well as earplugs. Clearly, many of these subtle inflections of status, gender, and ethnicity signaled through such ornaments remain to be understood.

CHAPTER 7

The Collared Body

MALLORY E. MATSUMOTO AND CARA GRACE TREMAIN

Their ubiquity in imagery, frequent recovery in excavations, and mention in some texts attest to the central social role that beaded or jeweled neck ornaments fulfilled in Classic Maya culture. Their production engaged a variety of artisans who had mastered the techniques of working a broad range of materials, ranging from archaeologically ephemeral plant fibers to more durable shell and greenstone. Not all materials were accessible to everyone, however, nor were all neck ornament forms equally attested across space, time, or society. Some patterns in the distribution of necklaces, collars, and pectorals correspond to temporal or regional differences across the Maya region. Other trends, however, may reflect differentiation in status, identity, symbolism or other social markers. In this respect, Maya neck ornaments provide a glimpse into the material and cultural realities of their producers and wearers.

The ancient Maya referred to accoutrements worn around the neck as *uuh-*, from Proto-Mayan **uuh-* (Houston, Stuart, and Robertson 1998, 282; Kaufman 2003, 299, 1030; see chapter 6). *Uuhaj* could be written using purely syllabic spellings such as **u-ha** > *uuh*, "neck ornament" (Palenque Temple of the Inscriptions, center tablet, block I7 [M. Robertson 1983, fig. 96]), or one of several variants of the logograph **UUH**, meaning "necklace, jewel, or bead" (Stuart and Houston 1994, 45; Macri and Looper 2003, 159). Neck ornaments were frequently possessed, as demonstrated by occurrences of **yu-ha** > *yuuh*, "his/her/its neck ornament" (Houston 2012c, fig. 261), and **yu-UH** > *yuuh* (Spinden 1913, fig. 196b). Some such forms were also suffixed with the abstractivizing *-il*, to become **yu-UH-li** > *yuuhil*, particularly if the possessor was supernatural (Houston, Robertson, and Stuart 2001, 26–32).

Classic-period texts drastically underrepresent the great variety of neck ornaments attested by material artifacts and iconography, as *uuhaj* are mentioned only sporadically in writing. However, Colonial-period and contemporary linguistic data suggest that the term *uuhaj* itself was semantically general, with distinctions between types of *uuhaj* probably conveyed by modifiers. The *Diccionario de Motul*, for instance, defines Yukateko *v* [*u*] as a "necklace or string or choker that is worn at the neck" (Ciudad Real 2001 [1577], 436), whereas Alfredo Barrera Vásquez and colleagues (1980, 896) describe *ú* more specifically as a "necklace or string of beads."[1] Fray Domingo de Ara (1986, 407) also defines Tzeltal *uhal* as "necklace," generally referring to something placed around the neck "like a string of trinkets." As an example, he mentions *cuhal taquin*, a necklace of "iron, silver [or] all metals" (377, 407).

Charles Wisdom (1950a, 286) similarly registers Ch'orti' *yuh* as "necklace, anything worn or wrapped around in necklace fashion" (cf. Pérez Martínez et al.

---

1. All translations of non-English-language sources are by Mallory E. Matsumoto, unless otherwise noted.

1996, 268), but he also provides a few examples of specific neck ornaments, such as *yuh e sakir* (necklace of white seeds), *yuh e chakar* (necklace of red seeds), and *yuh ta'k'an* (gold necklace). The use of modifiers to specify the type of *uuhaj* is attested in the hieroglyphs by rare allusions to particular types of ornaments, some of which may not have been worn at the neck, like the *sak hu'nal uuh* (white paper diadem jewel) of a deity named on the center tablet of the Temple of Inscriptions at Palenque (M. Robertson 1983, fig. 96; Guenter 2007, 34–36; see chapter 1 in this volume).

MATERIALS AND TYPOLOGY

The materials used to manufacture neck ornamentation varied widely and included both expensive materials, such as jadeite and *Spondylus* shell, and more commonplace components, such as fiber. Archaeological excavations have recovered a range of other resources, including limestone, quartzite, obsidian, pyrite, amazonite, bone or teeth, alabaster, and ceramic (e.g., W. Coe 1959, 53, 62; Ekholm 1985; Inomata and Eberl 2014, figs. 6.17s–z, 6.24k, 6.5h). Although some of these materials, like amazonite, were relatively rare, most would have been more readily available than the luxuries of jadeite or *Spondylus*. Gold, copper, and other precious metals are attested only rarely in the pre-Columbian Maya region, and most known examples of neck ornaments containing these materials, such as the clay beads covered in gold leaf retrieved from the Cenote of Sacrifice at Chichen Itza, are thought to be of non-Maya origin (S. Lothrop 1952, 28–29, 72–74, 83–84, 94).

Nonetheless, some pendants and pectorals were surely formed from wood, ceramic, or less valuable stone covered in plaster and stucco, like the elaborate Teotihuacan-style form worn by the central, seated figure on an unprovenienced ceramic vessel (K1463). This manufacturing technique is attested by finds such as the painted stucco objects recovered from Burial 9 at El Zotz (Newman et al. 2015, 147–156) and a pectoral, likely of alabaster and originally plastered and adorned with iconography and hieroglyphs, from Xultun Burial 15 (Saturno et al. 2014, 277, fig. 3.2.52). Neck ornaments could also incorporate perishable components such as textiles, rope, trophy heads, flowers, feathers, or wood. Although such materials are occasionally found in excavation (e.g., palm

nut beads, Moholy-Nagy and Ladd 1992, 359), they are primarily attested in imagery (e.g., Ishihara-Brito and Taube 2012, 461–462) and ethnohistoric records (e.g., Roys 1931, 309).

To account for the morphological and functional variety of ancient Maya *uuhaj* that confronts us in artifact assemblages and iconography, we make a basic typological distinction between necklaces, collars, and pectorals.

Necklaces

Necklaces are composed of leather or fibers such as cord, twine, fabric, or paper that encircle the neck and, in many cases, suspend large pendants in front of the chest. The range of necklace forms illustrated in artifacts and imagery largely correlates with diversity in materials used. Preservation bias has generally skewed the archaeological sample in favor of necklaces containing nonperishable materials, but iconographic evidence reveals that some were composed entirely of perishable substances, such as cloth and woven textiles (Halperin 2014, fig. 3.26; K. Taube and Houston 2010, fig. 1; von Euw 1977, 17). Many modern reconstructions of necklaces are also based primarily on images, more so than on spatial associations between beads and pendants in excavated contexts (Coggins and Shane 1984, 67).

Although sometimes left unadorned (fig. 7.1a), the basic necklace form of a loop around the neck was frequently strung with elements made from precious stones, shell, or other materials. Many, if not most, Maya necklaces contained beads—some smaller than one centimeter in diameter (Kidder 1947, fig. 80b; Kidder, Jennings, and Shook 1946, 111–112). Although the exterior surfaces of many beads were smooth, others featured detailed carvings (García Moll et al. 1990, cat. 45, 48; W. Coe 1959, fig. 49g). Yet it is difficult to determine the average number of beads per necklace in antiquity because, as William Welsh (1988, 103) notes, many field reports do not enumerate those recovered from burials (but see, e.g., Kidder 1947, 63). Furthermore, decay of the organic material that once held beads together can cause them to fall from their original placement, and therefore it is often unclear as to what ornament (if any) they originally belonged.

The simplest beaded necklace, which is also the most prevalent type in iconography, consisted of a single strand of identical beads (fig. 7.1b). More intricate forms

FIGURE 7.1. *Examples of necklaces: (a) unadorned necklace worn by captive on Yaxchilan Lintel 17; (b) bead necklace on Uaxactun mural; (c) double-stranded bead necklace on Motmot Marker from Copan; (d) San Bartolo murals, north wall; (e) necklace with beads of different sizes and counterweight on El Cayo Altar 4; (f) bead necklace with pendant on Uaxactun mural; (g) necklace with multiple identical pendants on Tikal Stela 31; (h) necklace with more elaborate pendants in geometric shapes on Naranjo Stela 33; (i) necklace with quatrefoil pendant on vessel found at Structure 5C-49, Tikal (K2697); and (j) necklace with trophy head in Bonampak murals, Room 2, north wall. Drawings by Mallory E. Matsumoto.*

(g)

(h)

(i)

(j)

FIGURE 7.2. *Detail from Copan Altar T showing two beaded necklaces with pendants. Drawing (SD-1019) by Linda Schele, © David Schele, courtesy Ancient Americas at LACMA (ancientamericas.org).*

articulated multiple strands or combined beads of different shapes, sizes, or materials (figs. 7.1c–e). The 118 jadeite beads in the necklace with which K'ihnich Janab' Pakal was buried, for instance, represent forms ranging from cylindrical, pyramidal, or oblate to flower, gourd, or even animal shaped (Ruz Lhuillier 1992, 197–199, figs. 222–224).

Some beaded or plain necklaces suspended a pendant in the center of the wearer's chest. Unlike beads, pendants were asymmetrical with respect to the hole by which they were strung. In some instances, a combination of pendants and pectorals were worn together (Culbert 1993, fig. 68a). Many luxurious pendants were richly carved with iconographic motifs, glyphic texts, or both (W. Coe 1959, fig. 49a; Fields 2012; Houston 2012c). Pendants could be used alone (fig. 7.1f); alternatively, a single necklace could combine multiple, and often identical, pendants (fig. 7.1g). Pendant form could vary widely, from simple circles, square plaques, or other geometric shapes to more complex forms embellished with beads (fig. 7.1h; Inomata and Emery 2014, figs. 8.12b, 8.20h; Tate 1992, fig. 130a). More elaborate pendants were shaped as quatrefoils, woven mats, anthropomorphic or zoomorphic figures, or even trophy heads (figs. 7.1i–

j). The latter forms, at least some of which were artificial (Coggins and Shane 1984, catalog entries 53–56; Willey 1972, fig. 83), served as a physical reminder of conquest and subjugation and thus a symbol of military and political power as well (Berryman 2007; Houston, Stuart, and Taube 2006, 70–72). Nonetheless, they are often worn outside of explicit contexts of warfare, and their use was not restricted to warriors (K8008; I. Graham and von Euw 1977, 39). Necklace length varied from tighter, choker-like forms that wrapped along the base of the wearer's neck to longer forms that would have hung down over the chest (figs. 7.1a–j and 7.2; Finamore and Houston 2010, pls. 24, 98). Some choker necklaces were tied in front and likely made of cloth or another perishable material (T. Joyce 1933, pl. V, fig. 8; K. Taube and Houston 2010, fig. 1), and many lacked beads or pendants (fig. 7.1a). A few also featured long ties in the back that were presumably aesthetic embellishments (Bullard and Bullard 1965, fig. 12a; S. Martin 2012, fig. 13). Some are worn by ballplayers, for whom their shorter length would have ensured that they did not hinder rapid movements (Hellmuth 1987). At the other end of the spectrum were longer dangling necklaces, usually strands of beads enhanced with a pendant (fig. 7.2). Those that fall to the wearer's knees illustrate the extremes of this variant (García Moll et al. 1990, fig. 151; Sears 2016, 669), which were particularly common in the northern Yucatán (I. Graham 1992, 87; I. Graham and von Euw 1992, 163).

The weight of the beads and pendants usually required that the necklace include a counterweight, allowing for a more comfortable positioning and lessening the strain on the back of the wearer's neck. This could take the form of an extra strand of beads, a larger nonbead element, or a combination of the two dangling down the wearer's back (figs. 7.1b and e; Foncerrada de Molina and Lombardo de Ruiz 1979, 47; S. Lothrop 1936, pl. 7). It is unclear if their use was motivated by aesthetics (for instance, to keep the necklace from hanging too low on the torso) or comfort (to relieve pressure against the back of the neck). Clearly, however, many counterweights, particularly those that are the most visually complex component of the neck ornament (fig. 7.1e; K1453; Gordon 1925, pl. VIII), were aesthetically salient, suggesting that the necklace was not intended to be viewed from the front only.

Collars

Collars are assemblages of varied objects, usually appearing as thick bands of decorative jewelry, which cover more of the upper chest than necklaces and pectorals. Similar to necklaces, collars wrap around the wearer's neck. But in contrast to necklaces, they spill over onto the shoulders and do not hang as low or loose on the chest. The simplest collars appear to have been lengths of textile, leather, or other perishable materials that wrapped around the base of the neck and covered the chest, secured with a tie behind the neck. This base also served as a surface onto which motifs were woven or other ornaments were sewn (de Vega, Melgar, and Lourdes Gallardo 2010; M. Miller and Martin 2004, pl. 47). As with other neck ornaments, however, perishable material components of collars rarely survive in the moist climate of the Maya region.

Collars are particularly popular among ruling elites and are often seen on monuments, where they are worn by both males and females (El Perú Stela 34 [Cleveland Museum of Art object no. 1967.29], Yaxchilan Stela 24 [Schele and M. Miller 1986, pl. 62]). They appear less frequently in ceramic scenes, particularly those of the royal court, where they are worn only by males (Tremain 2017, 209). They are also uncommon among figurines, though a similarly shaped ornament with an elongated central element does appear around the necks of boxers (T. Joyce 1933, pl. VIII: 2) and warriors (Triadan 2014, fig. 2.3e).

Collars tend to be composed of multiple rows of beads (fig. 7.3a) or of regularly shaped shell or greenstone pieces woven onto a material backing to create a mosaic-style ornament (fig. 7.3b). The garment recovered from Tomb 1 at Oxtankah, which strongly resembles the shape of a collar, consisted of more than fifteen hundred shell pieces that were individually shaped, perforated, and polished (de Vega, Melgar, and Lourdes Gallardo 2010). While many collars would have consisted primarily or even exclusively of nontextile ornaments, others incorporated perishable materials such as twisted fibers (fig. 7.3c). They often, but not necessarily, included distinctive pieces of ornamentation placed within or atop the body of the basic collar. These elements, which contrasted in form or size with the pattern of the underlying collar to which they were affixed, could come in the form of a single pendant (fig. 7.3d) or multiple ornaments of either the same (Trik 1963, 8) or different forms (González Cruz 2011, 49, 212). They could be dispersed evenly along the body of the collar or fringe (Wanyerka 1996, figs. 1, 10) or arranged as a series of tassels spaced around the edges (de Vega, Melgar, and Lourdes Gallardo 2010, fig. 14). Other ornaments, such as pectorals (fig. 7.3e), were frequently layered atop collars.

Pectorals

Like pendants, pectorals are invariably suspended on a simple necklace with or without beads or on a collar. However, they tend to be larger than pendants, covering a much greater surface area of the chest, and are displayed in the center of the wearer's body. Their distinctive shape, in its most basic form, features single or double elements, usually horizontal tubes, bars, or plaques, hanging from the neck in a manner that emphasizes the chest. Nonetheless, the central element was more oval or circular in some pectorals, particularly in the case of polished mirrors (fig. 7.4a). In most cases, they rested at chest height, although some rested higher on the body, across the clavicle. More rarely, pectorals dangled lower, in front of the hips or legs (fig. 7.4b).

Pectorals consistently maintain bilateral symmetry on an invisible vertical axis that bisects the horizontal plaque or tube. Yet like other necklace types, they were highly diverse in both form and relative degree of elaboration. More elaborate pectorals may vary in shape and

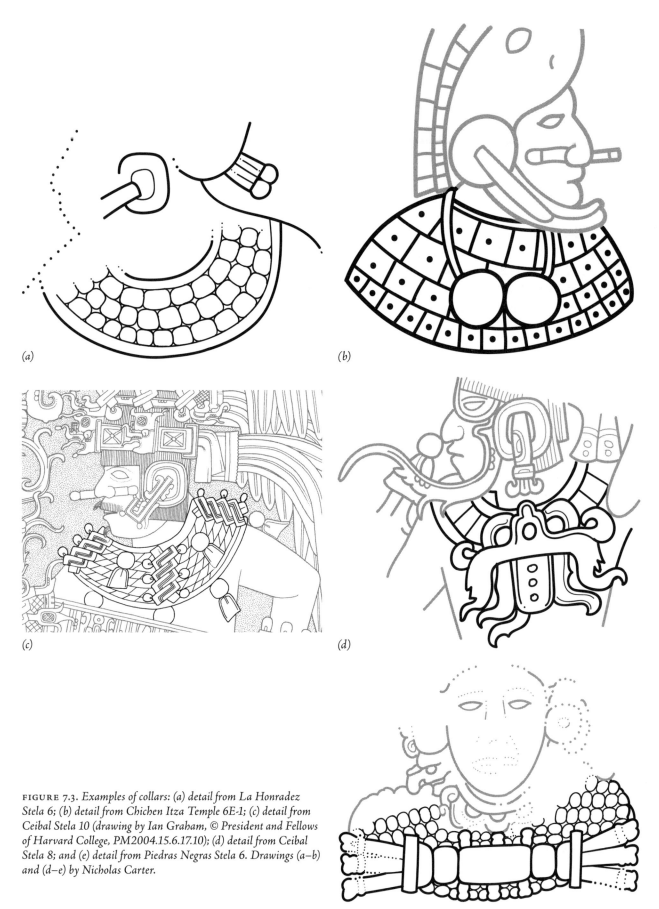

FIGURE 7.3. *Examples of collars: (a) detail from La Honradez Stela 6; (b) detail from Chichen Itza Temple 6E-1; (c) detail from Ceibal Stela 10 (drawing by Ian Graham, © President and Fellows of Harvard College, PM2004.15.6.17.10); (d) detail from Ceibal Stela 8; and (e) detail from Piedras Negras Stela 6. Drawings (a–b) and (d–e) by Nicholas Carter.*

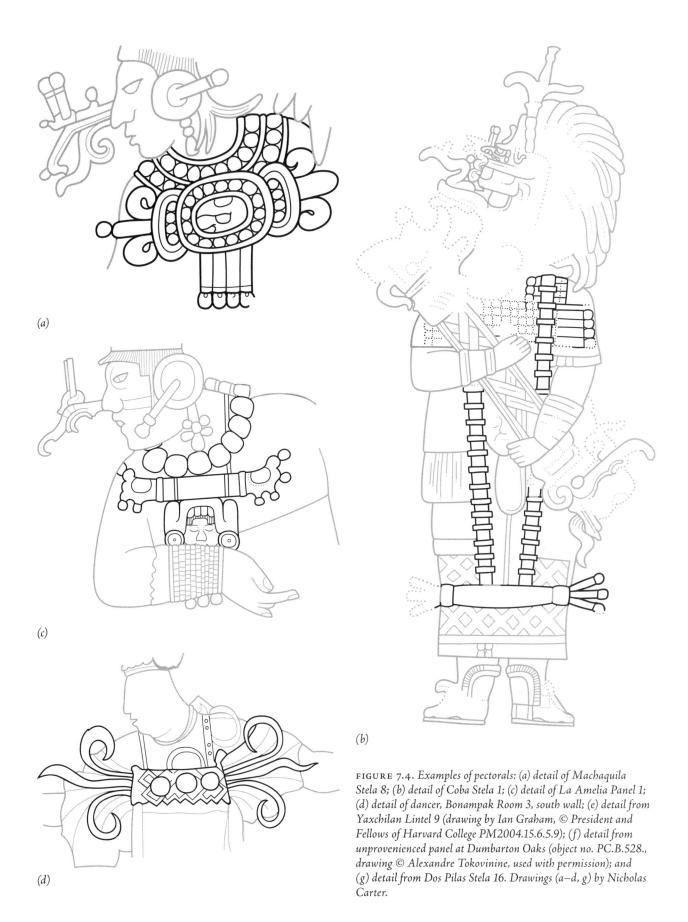

FIGURE 7.4. *Examples of pectorals: (a) detail of Machaquila Stela 8; (b) detail of Coba Stela 1; (c) detail of La Amelia Panel 1; (d) detail of dancer, Bonampak Room 3, south wall; (e) detail from Yaxchilan Lintel 9 (drawing by Ian Graham, © President and Fellows of Harvard College PM2004.15.6.5.9); (f) detail from unprovenienced panel at Dumbarton Oaks (object no. PC.B.528., drawing © Alexandre Tokovinine, used with permission); and (g) detail from Dos Pilas Stela 16. Drawings (a–d, g) by Nicholas Carter.*

(e)

(f)

(g)

FIGURE 7.4. (continued)

include elements below, above, atop, or adjacent to the central bar. Based on iconographic evidence, stiff tubular beads projecting outward from the top, middle, and bottom of both ends of the horizontal bar appear to have been the most common enhancement of the basic pectoral form (fig. 7.4b). In other instances, the elements at the end of pectoral bars were stylized shapes (figs. 7.4c–d) or even perishable material such as feathers (fig. 7.4e). Elements could also dangle down from the middle or the underside of pectorals (fig. 7.4a), or, more rarely, project upward from the top (fig. 7.4f). Although pieces affixed to either end of the horizontal bar were usually arranged in sets of three (fig. 7.5), some pecto-

FIGURE 7.6. *Detail from Palenque Palace Oval Tablet. Drawing (SD-143) by Linda Schele, © David Schele, courtesy Ancient Americas at LACMA (ancientamericas.org).*

rals featured just one or two on each side (Culbert 1993, fig. 68a; M. Miller and Martin 2004, pl. 118). Pectorals could also be strung on necklaces with other plaques—a configuration common in the Pasión region (Browder 1991, 67–68)—or with smaller pendants, such as the face-like ornaments above the horizontal bar worn by Yaxuun Bahlam IV on Yaxchilan Lintel 9 (fig. 7.4e).

The surface of pectorals was often incised or otherwise ornamented. One relatively common motif was the T-shaped **IK'** (wind) symbol (fig. 7.6; Proskouriakoff 1974, pl. 50a, 65b; Pillsbury, Potts, and Richter 2017, pl. 131). One such example recently excavated in Tomb 5 at Nim Li Punit closely matches that carved on that site's Stela 15 (Borrero, Azarova, and Braswell 2016, 202–203, figs. 12–13; Prager and Braswell 2016). The woven mat was another prominent motif, albeit restricted to a handful of sites (Browder 1991, 63). Anthropomorphic faces, some with skull-like features, embellished other pectorals (fig. 7.4g). However, the small size of skull-like pectoral ornaments that have been recovered archaeologically suggests either that they were

FIGURE 7.5. *Detail from Copan Altar T showing a pectoral with two pendants, worn with a long, beaded necklace. Drawing (SD-1019) by Linda Schele, © David Schele, courtesy Ancient Americas at LACMA (ancientamericas.org).*

enlarged for emphasis in imagery or that those recovered as artifacts are small-scale copies of those worn by the elites depicted on monuments. Still other pectorals manifest glyphic texts, some of which explicitly record the ancestral connotations attached to those ornaments (Houston, Stuart, and Taube 2006, 50–51, fig. 1.54).

A minority of pectorals were elaborately ornamented mosaics composed of multiple worked pieces, likely beads, which would either have been affixed to an underlying slab of material or woven together to create the basic structure of the pectoral (Looper 2003, fig. 3.31). Other pectorals featured multiple horizontal bars arranged vertically in a tier (S. Lothrop 1952, fig. 20d), and some combinations of horizontal bars even featured rounded, "medallion"-like central elements (Houston 1993, fig. 3.27). Many ornaments associated with pectorals were engraved with iconographic motifs or glyphic texts, which often identified the owner (Borrero, Azarova, and Braswell 2016, fig. 12; M. Coe and Thacher 1966). Among all classes of Maya neck ornaments, pectorals have probably received the most scholarly attention to date, with particular emphasis on their value as indices of social status (e.g., Browder 1991, 60–86; González Cruz 2011, 178; Rossi 2015, 106–133; Viel 1999).

SPATIAL AND TEMPORAL VARIATION

Owing to the difficulty of recovering perishable components of neck ornamentation from archaeological excavations, and of accurately reconstructing the artifacts that they held together, understanding of the temporal and regional distributions of neck ornamentation is largely aided by iconography. Erin Browder's (1991, 87–88) image-based study, for example, reveals that collars remained relatively narrow and loose around the wearer's neck through much of the Early Classic, until they acquired a larger surface area and were wrapped more tightly around the base of the neck beginning in the early sixth century. This change in morphology appears to accompany a general elaboration of collars over the course of the Classic period. Dicey Taylor (1983, 75–76) makes a similar observation about necklaces, suggesting that while long, loose beaded necklaces were common in Early Classic images like the Uaxactun Structure B-XIII murals (Sharer 2006, fig. 7.13), they gave way to tighter-fitting chokers in the Late Classic.

Clearly, however, regionally and more locally situated preferences also influenced necklace choice. At Yaxchilan, for example, kings often wear uniformly small and round beads at the base, onto which more elaborate pendants were affixed, and longer beaded strands persisted well into the Late Classic (I. Graham and von Euw 1977, 13, 17, 53–54). In contrast, the collars of rulers at nearby Piedras Negras more commonly integrate beads of differing shapes and sizes (M. Miller and Brittenham 2013, fig. 299). Yaxchilan rulers and their affiliates are also much more likely to feature anthropomorphic pendants on their collars than are their antagonists to the north (La Pasadita Lintel 2 [Tate 1992, fig. 38b]; but see Piedras Negras Stela 1 [Stuart and Graham 2003, 18]).

Other clear regional trends can be seen in the style of collars at Chichen Itza, where large planar gorgets with spiked ends are affixed to the collars of some Terminal Classic figures (fig. 7.7; Tozzer 1957, figs. 546–552). Such styles seem to be unique to that region and era, and images of warriors wearing these distinctive neck ornaments have been cited as evidence of Chichen Itza's close cultural ties with the non-Maya settlement of Tula in Central Mexico (Kowalski 2007, 273–275; S. Lothrop 1952, 39; Tozzer 1957, 157–158). The lords of Peten sites under the tutelage of the Kaan dynasty, in turn, seem to have preferred attaching to their collars a large elliptical pendant with a central perforation and a series of rounded nodules evenly distributed around its outer edge—likely *Spondylus* or other marine shells, perhaps imitations (Stuart, Canuto, and Barrientos 2015, fig. 5; Grube et al. 2012, fig. 8). However, it is possible that these pendants may be attached to a necklace rather than to the collar, similar to those worn by the two central standing figures on K2695 (Browder 1991, 78). In contrast, the beaded chokers with suspended shells depicted on Tikal Stela 31 (fig. 7.1g; Jones and Satterthwaite 1982, figs. 51–52), like their shell-less counterparts on Yaxha Stela 11 (Morley 1937, pl. 161b), evince clear stylistic influences from Teotihuacan (cf. Copan Stela 1 [Proskouriakoff 1950, fig. 50a]).

The beads with which necklaces were strung transmuted over time as well. In the assemblage of shell beads from Tikal, for example, Hattula Moholy-Nagy (1989, 155) observed that long-barrel and irregularly shaped *Spondylus* beads appeared in the Early Classic, whereas

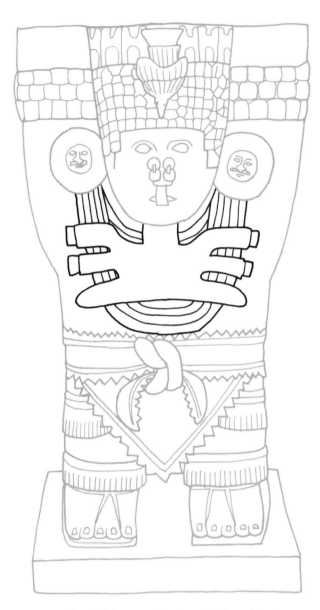

FIGURE 7.7. *Leg of Atlantean Altar from the Upper Temple of the Jaguar at Chichen Itza. Drawing (SD-5077) by Linda Schele, © David Schele, courtesy Ancient Americas at LACMA (ancientamericas.org).*

commonly appear as a horizontal bar flanked on either end by three tubular projections (Barrientos, Escobedo, and Houston 1997, 9). In addition to differing in suspension height, as illustrated by the lower-hanging pectorals at Coba, the forms of pectorals differed by site; neighboring Quirigua and Copan, for example, evince differing affinities toward medallion versus bar pectorals, respectively (Browder 1991, 62, 66).

The great variety of necklaces and other neck ornaments is not attested equally among all segments of Maya society, nor were all pendant forms equally likely to be donned by a given wearer. Those with increasingly complex iconography and geometrically irregular shapes, including pectorals, are much more characteristic of royal attire. Forms like trophy heads, for instance, appear to have been restricted to rulers or eminent military elites (M. Miller and Brittenham 2013, fig. 125; I. Graham and von Euw 1977, 29–30). Nonetheless, high-ranking nobles, rulers, and even deities sometimes donned simple bead necklaces, albeit often as one of multiple neck ornaments (I. Graham 1996, 17; K2698). Conversely, lower-ranking nobles could in certain contexts wear images of deities, *Spondylus* pendants, and other luxurious ornaments on their necklaces (Culbert 1993, fig. 68a; M. Robertson 1985b, figs. 274–275).

Based on representations from across the Maya region during the Classic period, it is likely that social standing influenced the general distribution of necklaces and collars more strongly than gender. Browder (1991, 87) suggested that collars are characteristic of females, no doubt influenced by the fact that they do appear on a higher percentage of women than men in monumental imagery. Yet collars often appear on men as well (M. Miller and Brittenham 2013, fig. 301; I. Graham 1967, figs. 54–55; I. Graham and von Euw 1977, 23). More consistent is the trend that those depicted with collars were usually the more elite subjects in a given image. A similar pattern of elite association is apparent with pectorals as well, but with a more clearly gendered dimension: men are more likely than women to be illustrated wearing pectorals, perhaps reflecting their association with rulership (Browder 1991, 60; Viel 1999), although women did don them as well (I. Graham and von Euw 1977, 35). These observations may additionally explain why collars and pectorals in particular are frequent in monumental iconography, which

"ring-like and collared" forms were added to the repertoire later during the Classic period. As for pectorals, Browder (1991, 62) suggested they were relatively consistent components of elite neck ornament assemblages across the Maya region during the Late Classic. She also noticed that they were clearly a favored neck ornament of ruling males, and occasionally of prominent females, in the Usumacinta River kingdoms of Piedras Negras and Yaxchilan (1991, 74). At these sites, pectorals most is generally dominated by figures of elevated status. For instance, females depicted on painted ceramics and murals often lack ornamentation around the neck or wear strands of beads rather than larger pectorals or collars (K2695; K2707; M. Miller and Brittenham 2013, fig. 160). Nonetheless, women on carved sculpture tend to wear more elaborate neck ornamentation than in other representational contexts, indicating that these patterns may reflect distinctions in iconographic content by medium or genre, rather than a strictly gendered social phenomenon.

MEANINGS AND SOCIAL FUNCTION

Choice of material for neck ornamentation was likely influenced by varying access to resources and the morphological features of different ornaments—feathers were more easily integrated into collars than necklaces, for instance, and clay could be worked much more expediently than jadeite. Undeniably, however, personal preference and local tradition played a role in material selection as well. Consequently, the materials used in a neck ornament, in addition to its visual content and quality of production, surely had their own impact on the artifact's meaning and social function.

The most valuable raw materials included jadeite and *Spondylus* shell, which for most Maya communities were only obtainable via long-distance trade networks. The Motagua River Valley region in Guatemala constitutes the only documented source of jadeite in Mesoamerica (Bishop, Sayre, and Mishara 1993; Seitz et al. 2001). In addition to its geographically restricted availability, jadeite required extensive processing to produce refined ornaments, a laborious task even for trained specialists, whose work further elevated jadeite's value (Kovacevich 2011, 152–159). The collar of the Red Queen of Palenque, for example, comprised more than 170 circular and quadrangular jadeite beads (González Cruz 2011, 49, 177–187), while Burial 116 at Tikal yielded a spectacular collar consisting of 114 spherical jadeite beads that collectively weighed in at nearly four kilograms (Trik 1963, 8; see W. Coe 1990, 606). Jadeite was also used by nonroyals, however, among whom the precious good appears to have been a significant marker of status, depending on the quality and quantity of material to which one had access (Andrieu, Rodas, and Luin

2014, 153–161; Kovacevich 2007, 82; Scherer 2015, 65). Other greenstones were used in addition to or in place of jadeite, but they were probably considered less valuable, perhaps in part because they were more widely and locally available, as well as less arduous to work (Dunham 1996, 327–328; Tremain 2014, 140–141).

Spondylus americanus was a popular material for beads, pendants, and pectorals since at least the Late Preclassic (Aizpurúa and McAnany 1999, 123; González Cruz 2011, 178; Moholy-Nagy 1989, 152). This shell with an orange-red hue is locally obtainable only along the coast of what is now Belize and southern Guatemala, where extracting the specimens with the most vibrant colors required experienced divers to retrieve them (E. Graham 2002, 410; Pillsbury, Potts, and Richter 2017, xiv; Velázquez Castro 2017, 92–93). The material's value is apparent, for instance, in the *Spondylus* beads recovered from Burial 9 at El Zotz that show evidence of careful reworking or repair (Newman et al. 2015, 166–168). Pearl was another prized marine resource used to produce neck ornaments primarily for elite consumption, often in combination with *Spondylus* and jade (Moholy-Nagy 1989, 147–150).

Other shells considered less precious than *Spondylus* or pearl, like *Olivella* (fig. 7.8), were also used for beads and pendants, particularly among lesser elites and nonelites (Aizpurúa and McAnany 1999; Masson and Freidel 2012, 471–475; Moholy-Nagy 1989, 142–150). Some larger shell ornaments were adorned with intricate carvings (Finamore and Houston 2010, pl. 45)—modifications that presumably would have increased the pieces' value, in addition to preserving information about their contexts of creation and use. Of these materials, conch shell was the most prevalent material for beads in the Maya lowlands during the Middle Preclassic (Stanchly 2014). Unlike *Spondylus* beaded ornaments, those composed of less precious shell were more frequent in construction fill or residential contexts rather than in burials, indicating differential patterns of consumption and eventual retirement or discard (Moholy-Nagy 1989, 142–150). Although *Spondylus* had been the elite shell of choice since the Late Preclassic, it declined sharply as a material for bead manufacture at Tikal in the Late Classic and was replaced by other, less valuable, options (Moholy-Nagy 1989:153). However, Moholy-Nagy (1989, 155) does not identify a parallel shift in bead

FIGURE 7.8. Olivella *shell beads from Campeche, Mexico.*
National Museum of the American Indian, Smithsonian
Institution (23/6371). Photograph: NMAI Photo.

morphology, indicating that changing economic and political conditions more likely influenced this transition
than did changes in bead style.

For those unable or unwilling to procure such costly
resources for neck ornaments, imitations could be fabri-
cated to mimic more prestigious raw materials. The contents of Burial 128 at Altar de Sacrificios, for instance,
included clay beads covered in stucco and painted to im-
itate the blue-green hue of jadeite (A. Smith 1972, 267).
Similarly, Rulers 3 and 4 at Piedras Negras were both
buried wearing strands of clay beads painted a similar
color, presumably to mimic the high-status resource that
was in particularly short supply in that region (Escobedo and Houston 1997, 221; Scherer 2015, 63–65; see
W. Coe 1959, figs. 58a, 64). Ruler 3's tomb also yielded
four clay pendants shaped like bivalve shells (W. Coe
1959, 71, figs. 58b–c). In contrast to other ornaments
that manifested their wearer's access to the resources
from which they were made, these necklaces were explicitly manipulated to obscure their true nature.

In addition to materials, the identity of the wearer
also factored into a neck ornament's meaning and social
function. It is clear from visual studies that necklaces
and their associated forms were not a mode of dress reserved exclusively for humans. Deities often wear neck
ornamentation, as illustrated by the small K'awiil figure
in the lap of the Palenque ruler's mother on an unprovenienced panel at Dumbarton Oaks (M. Miller and Martin 2004, pl. 117). Some animals, both supernatural and
earthly, also display adorned necks (see figs. 7.2 and 7.5.;
Doyle 2010; Tozzer and Allen 1910). It is possible that
by wearing such objects, animals become "humans" and
enter a world in which they are co-sentients, interlocutors with humans (Stephen D. Houston, personal communication 2016; see chapter 1 in this volume).

The decision to cover areas of the body with ornamentation like necklaces or collars may have been motivated by a socially infused desire to beautify the body
(Reischer and Koo 2004). Scholarship exploring concepts of beauty among the ancient Maya has acknowledged aesthetically motivated practices such as crossing
the eyes, filing teeth, and shaping the head (M. Miller
2009; Landa 1941, 88), but Rosemary Joyce (2002, 88–
89) hints that strands of beads were in some way also
associated with beauty in ancient Mesoamerica as well.

Much scholarship on necklaces in non-Maya contexts relates beauty with the female gender (Leurquin 2003; Mascetti and Triossi 1997); however, male beauty was also esteemed among the Maya (Houston 2009). Neck ornaments may thus have been considered genderless, or gender-inclusive, forms of beautification in Classic Maya society.

Polished iron-ore mirrors, like those seen in painted scenes of court life (K2695), were also strongly associated with aesthetics. Examples recovered from burials in the Maya region have been found near the head, chest, groin, back, and feet of interred individuals (Healy and Blainey 2011, 232; Kidder, Jennings, and Shook 1946, 126–133; Willey 1972, 141–143). Their recovery from the chest areas of interred individuals in particular suggests that they may have been worn as pectorals like they were at Teotihuacan (Taube 1992a), a use that perhaps reflects a concern with beautification and aesthetics. Nonetheless, their significance extended beyond mere enhancement of physical beauty, given mirrors' symbolic associations with ritual and supernatural beings (Blainey 2016; Healy and Blainey 2011; Saunders 1988).

The most basic evidence supporting the role of neck ornamentation in enhancing personal beauty is the fact that the primary function of objects hung around the neck seems to have been to draw attention to this area of the body. Even those components that would appear to serve a more pragmatic role, such as counterweights, were often embellished beyond the basic form necessary for them to fulfill this purpose (fig. 7.1e). More innovative or morphologically unusual necklaces would have been particularly effective in attracting the viewer's gaze. Attempts to repair necklace beads, like those found in Tombs A-1/1 and B-4/6 at Altun Ha (Pendergast 1979, 61; 1982, 88), suggest that the wholeness of ornamentation was important as well. Missing beads in a necklace or broken attachments to pectorals may have lowered the quality of the ornament, thus diminishing the beauty or standing of the wearer. Ironically, the desire to impress with quality and expense is attested most vividly by mimicry of exotic or rare materials, as in the case of the aforementioned clay beads at Piedras Negras that were painted to resemble greenstone and *Spondylus*.

Although no strand of beads can defend the body from harm in the same way as a shield or the padded cotton armor that a Maya warrior bore into battle, certain neck ornaments may have been ascribed protective powers, similar to protective necklaces and amulets worn in some contemporary Maya communities (Kunow 2003, 54, 68). Other neck ornaments may themselves have been curative or featured pendants containing medicine or other substances. In pre-Columbian Nahua communities, for example, necklaces made from *tlacopatli* and *iyacualli* plants were worn by children to relieve illness and prevent the *tonalli* from escaping the body (Austin 1988, 219–220). Similarly, nursing mothers in some contemporary Maya communities wear the medicinal plant wild poinsettia (*Euphorbia pulcherrima*) around their necks to increase milk supply (Arvigo 1994, 190). Other natural necklace elements are used among Ch'orti' speakers, for whom a *yuh e tz'i'* represents a "necklace of lemons placed around a dog's neck (to cure it of a cold)" and a *yuh e chakar* constitutes a "necklace of red seeds (worn as a protection against evil eye)" (Wisdom 1950a, 286).

The form of the object worn around the neck also bore symbolic relevance in many cases. Neck elements assuming the shape of the ik' sign, for instance, evoked the "breath" or "life" emanating from the wearer's chest, and thus the soul and the afterlife, in addition to comparing the encircled head with a fragrant flower (Houston, Stuart, and Taube 2006, 141–149; e.g., M. Miller and Martin 2004, pl. 25). Yet the symbolic value of ornaments and their features was not contingent on their visibility or ease of perception. Some feature intricate incisions or carvings that would have been imperceptible to others at a distance (Pendergast 1979, figs. 18b, 20b; Willey 1972, fig. 64h). For example, pendants with intricately carved images of seated rulers may have represented ancestral or dynastic ties (fig. 7.9). Their association with kingship would have been reinforced if worn by a living ruler who embodied the carved motif in the flesh.

The symbolic potential of neck accoutrements on the body also extended to contexts in which they were absent. Although present in most scenes, neck ornaments are not worn in every image, even those that illustrate fine details of dress and ornamentation (compare Corson 1973, 32; S. Martin 2012, figs. 4, 6, 10, 31). Stripping finery from captives, for one, was a method of shaming or denigrating them (Houston, Stuart, and

Taube 2006, 202–207). But there are also instances in the service of those donning elaborate ornaments in which elites are represented with a bare neck out-side of contexts of warfare (K8006; K2707; Pendergast 1982, fig. 119K). Although some neck ornaments may be temporarily missing from an as yet incompletely attired body, their absence in other contexts suggests that wearing ornaments around the neck was, at least for some segments of society, a discretionary, rather than mandated, custom, in contrast to other conventions of dress in Mesoamerica (Anawalt 1980). In particular, the apparent preference for neck ornaments to be depicted on high-status individuals in sculptural representations, versus their more frequent absence on figures in painted scenes and figurines, may reflect differences in expected viewership and the context in which an artwork was visible (S. Martin 2012, fig. 4; Halperin 2014, fig. 3.25c; K8002). Perhaps neck ornamentation was an expected component of the elite's public outfit, necessary to construct a complete social person. Its absence, in contrast, may have signaled a lesser degree of personhood or increased subordination, an association particularly evident in the case of captives who have been stripped of their adornment and individuals with bare necks shown

in the service of those donning elaborate ornaments (K6298).

Finally, neck ornaments were not only intended to be worn. Although necklaces, collars, and pectorals are almost exclusively shown on the body in iconography, archaeological excavation and occasional images attest to their circulation and use as portable objects as well. An especially important context for handling neck ornaments would have been in their exchange as political gifts and tribute (Houston, Stuart, and Taube 2006, 247; Stuart 2006; e.g., K1452, K8872; Halperin 2014, figs. 3.26a–c; see fig. 5.1 in this volume). As possessions, they could also be passed between generations as heirlooms, as attested by the Olmec pectoral excavated at Nakum (Źrałka et al. 2012) or the ik'-shaped pendant from Nim Li Punit (Borrero, Azarova, and Braswell 2016, 203; Prager and Braswell 2016; see also Carter 2010). Some ultimately transitioned from an ornament intended for wear to an inherited object given as an ancestral offering, a change that may have been signaled by physical modification. J. E. S. Thompson (1939, 194), for example, reports that the jade pendant recovered from Burial A2 at San Jose had a plug inserted into the suspension hole. This feature may have been added to change the pendant's function, perhaps ensuring that it remained with the interred individual and would no longer be deployed in a living context by successive generations (R. Joyce 2000c).

FIGURE 7.9. *Jadeite pendant illustrating seated man with headdress. Courtesy of the University of Pennsylvania Museum, object #NA5896.*

CONCLUSION

Of the wide range of neck ornaments crafted and worn by ancient Maya individuals, this chapter provides only a glimpse. Clearly, such objects were fundamental components of bodily adornment for much of ancient Maya society. However, they also demonstrate great diversity with respect to form, function, and context of use. Ranging from the precious to the remarkable to the mundane, the resources from which adornment for the neck was fashioned reflect the broad diversity of raw materials that were accessible to their Classic Maya producers and users. The near ubiquity of neck ornaments in iconography and the frequency with which their traces, particularly beads, are encountered in excavations suggest that they were present in a wide range of contexts across Maya society. Yet their distribution within society was unequal. Particularly lavish ornaments, like the luxury goods from which they were often fashioned, were the purview of the ruling class and other elites; the absence of any ornamentation around the neck frequently correlated with lesser status or, in the case of captives, a loss of status following defeat. In short, neck ornamentation was socially inflected by such factors as access to material resources, sociopolitical standing, activity, and the social context in which their very human wearers were embedded.

(a)

(b)

PLATE 1. *Application of body paint on Late Classic polychrome painted vessels: (a) paint applied with a cloth (K0764); (b) an old god applying paint to his mouth with a brush as a young goddess with painted designs on her face holds up a mirror (K0530); (c) handprints in black paint (K2345); (d) a painted couple dancing together (K0554); and (e) one hunter applying paint to another (K1373). Photographs © Justin Kerr, used by permission.*

(c)

PLATE I. *(continued)*

(d)

(e)

(a)

PLATE 2. *Face and body paint on the Maize God and related deities: (a) detail of the North Wall, Las Pinturas building, San Bartolo (illustration by Heather Hurst © 2004; courtesy of Heather Hurst); (b) detail of an Early Classic plate showing the Maize God with painting around the mouth (photograph © Museum Associates/LACMA, M.2010.115.250); and (c) detail of a Late Classic codex-style vessel with overpainting (K4598) showing a young god with painting around the mouth (photograph © Justin Kerr, used by permission).*

(c)

PLATE 2. *(continued)*

(a)   (b)

PLATE 3. *Early Classic face and body painting: (a) figurine from a burial at Yaxuna (drawing by
Nicholas Carter after Fields and Reents-Budet 2005, cat. 116); (b) ruler on a lidded ceramic vessel
(photograph © Museum Associates/LACMA, M90_104a-b); (c) two men from the Structure B-XIII
mural, Uaxactun; (d) two men and a woman from the Structure B-XIII mural, Uaxactun; and
(e) priests and young men from the Structure B-XIII mural, Uaxactun (painting by Antonio Tejeda,
© President and Fellows of Harvard College, PM50-1-20/22982).*

(c)

(d)

PLATE 3. (continued)

(e)

(a)

(b)

PLATE 4. *Late and Terminal Classic body painting: (a) detail of an Ik'-style ceramic vessel (K5370) showing abundant red paint; (b) detail of a ceramic vessel in the Señor del Peten style (K9144) showing a courtly scene without body paint; (c) detail of a Late Classic ceramic vessel (K2711) showing body paint avoiding the hands and joints; (d) detail of a Late Classic Fenton-style ceramic vessel (K1392) showing paint on the shoulders and chest; (e) detail of a Late Classic ceramic vessel (K1599) showing paint that avoids the face; and (f) detail of a Late Classic ceramic vessel (K3412) showing a courtier with only his face and neck painted. Photographs © Justin Kerr, used by permission.*

(d)

(e)

PLATE 4. (continued)

(f)

(a)

(b)

PLATE 5. *Brown body paint: (a) covering the body on a Late Classic ceramic vessel (K1453); and (b) in contrast with red body paint on a Late Classic ceramic vessel (K7021). Photographs © Justin Kerr, used by permission.*

(a)

(b)

(c)

PLATE 6. Body and face painting on women: (a) detail of a Late Classic ceramic vessel (K2707) showing two women with red-painted faces; (b) detail of a Late Classic ceramic vessel (K0764) showing brown body and face paint on one woman and red linear details on another; (c) detail of a Late Classic ceramic vessel from the area of Motul de San José (K2573) showing a woman with red body paint and a crescent design around her eye; (d) detail of a Late Classic ceramic vessel (K2695) showing two women with red body paint and painted designs over their eyes; and (e) detail of a Late Classic ceramic vessel from the area of Motul de San José (K4996) showing a woman with a crescent design around her eye over a base coat of white paint. Photographs © Justin Kerr, used by permission.

(d)

(e)

PLATE 6. (continued)

(a)

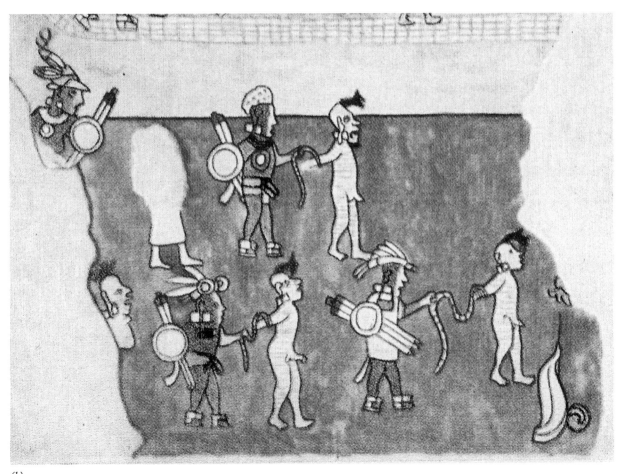

(b)

PLATE 7. (a) Late Classic ceramic vessel from Chama (K0593) showing principal interlocutors distinguished from their attendants by black body paint (photograph © Justin Kerr, used by permission); and (b) detail of an Early Postclassic mural from the Temple of the Warriors, Chichen Itza, showing victorious warriors painted dark gray and prisoners painted with red stripes (Morris, Charlot, and Morris 1931, pl. 139).

(a)

PLATE 8. *Postclassic deities with painted bodies: (a) detail from Mural 1, Structure 12, Tancah, showing blue-painted deities (painting © Felipe Dávalos G.); (b) detail from a mural painting at Structure 5, Tulum, showing deities with blue marks on their bodies (drawing by Nicholas Carter after a painting by Felipe Dávalos G.); and (c) detail of a mural painting from the north wall of Mound 1, Santa Rita Corozal, showing a deity with repeating yellow designs on red-painted skin (Gann 1900, pl. 30).*

(b)

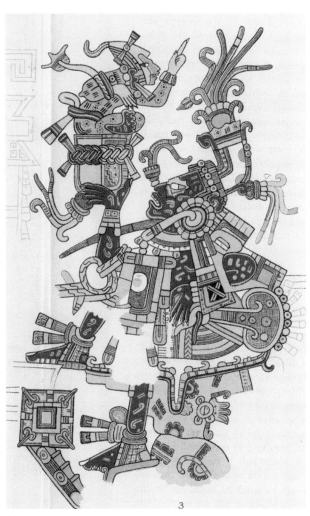

(c)

3

(a)

(b)

PLATE 9. (a) Detail of a polychrome vase (K4151) showing a hunter with black "jaguar spots"; (b) detail of a Late Classic polychrome vase (K5451) showing two victorious warriors with black body paint; (c) detail of a Late Classic mural painting showing a taaj priest with black body paint (Structure 10K2, Xultun, illustration by Heather Hurst © 2012. Courtesy of Heather Hurst); (d) detail of a Late Classic codex-style vessel (K1200) showing a sorcerer with black paint around his eyes (drawing by Nicholas Carter after a photograph by Justin Kerr); (e) detail of a Late Classic codex-style ceramic vessel (K4384) showing a sorcerer with spots of black paint on his face; (f) detail of a Late Classic polychrome vase (K2780) showing performers with black body paint; (g) detail of a Late Classic polychrome vase (K1563) showing musicians with black body paint; and (h) detail of a Late Classic polychrome vase (K2803) showing a ballplayer with black body paint. Photographs except (c) and (d) © Justin Kerr, used by permission.

(c)

(d)

(e)

PLATE 9. *(continued)*

(f)

(g)

(h)

PLATE 9. (continued)

CHAPTER 8

The Girded Body

ALYCE DE CARTERET AND JEFFREY DOBEREINER

In even the earliest instances of ancient Maya art, belts and bands of various kinds gird Maya bodies. Belts and sashes cinch waists and hips. Armbands wrap around forearms; bracelets and cuffs hang around wrists. Legbands wrap around thighs and shins, while anklets and other lashings bind ankles. Essential to Maya costume, belts and bands represent some of the most ubiquitous elements of Maya dress as seen in iconography.

For the purposes of this chapter, armbands and legbands are defined as elements of dress wrapped around the limbs, which are distinct and clearly delimited from gloves and footwear. The term *belt* is used to denote any item of clothing that is fastened around the waist or hips and does not further cover the legs. This definition includes belts, sashes, and loincloths, while excluding kilts and skirts. Although belts and kilts often appear together, belts are evaluated separately here.

Specific words for "belt" and "sash" appear in a number of Mayan languages. Terrence Kaufman reconstructs **paas* as the root for "belt" or "sash" in Eastern Mayan languages, including K'iche', Kaqchikel, Poqom, Mam, and others (Kaufman 2003, 1018). In Ch'ol, which is more closely related to the language of the hieroglyphic inscriptions, "belt" is glossed as *kajchil näk*, which can be further broken down into *kajch*, "scarf," or "bandana," and *näk*, "belly" (Hopkins, Josserand, and Cruz Guzmán 2011, 93). *Kajch* may be related to Yu-

kateko Mayan's *k'ax*, which denotes something that is tied, knotted, or bound (Pfeiler 2003, 385).

The concept and visual conceit that links all of these items of dress together is the knotting, tying, wrapping, or bundling of materials around the body, either the limbs or the waist. Through these conceptual similarities, belts and bands may have been associated with the sacred practice of bundling, a practice whereby the soul becomes fixed to the body. But before these deeper meanings are considered, this chapter reviews the materials that compose belts and bands and how they adorned ancient Maya bodies over time.

MATERIALS AND TYPOLOGY

Evidence for the vast array of materials used to gird the ancient Maya body comes primarily in the form of visual culture, although a smaller subset of materials does preserve in archaeological contexts. Excavations of royal burials in the Maya area often recover beads of hardy materials like shell, jade, and other kinds of stone (see Fitzsimmons 2009, appendix 3). These objects, commonly recovered from elite interments, may have adorned royal bodies in death or may have been accoutrements in the wrappings of the bundled corpse (Fitzsimmons 2009, 78). In imagery, beads like these are common (figs. 8.1a–c). Simple strings of beads, represented in most cases by a linear set of three circles,

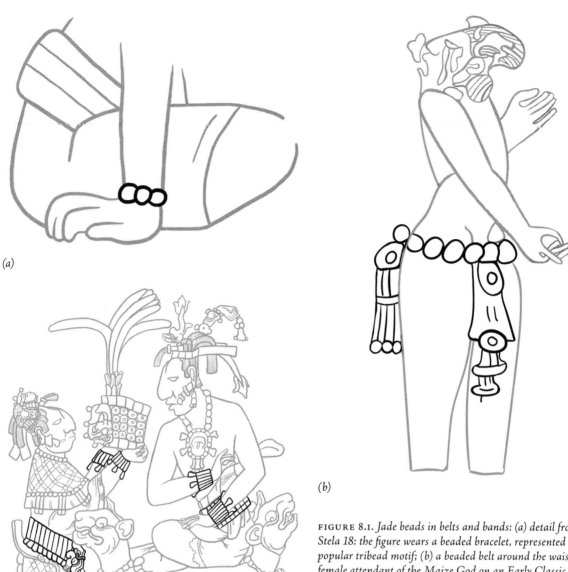

(a)

(b)

(c)

FIGURE 8.1. *Jade beads in belts and bands: (a) detail from Izapa Stela 18: the figure wears a beaded bracelet, represented by the popular tribead motif; (b) a beaded belt around the waist of a female attendant of the Maize God on an Early Classic blackware vessel (K6547); and (c) altar from Palenque House E: in an accession scene, the queen mother passes her son, the king, the crown; she wears a royal plaque belt and cuffs, and he wears a beaded belt and jade plaque cuffs (after Stuart and Stuart 2008, fig. 49a). Drawings by Alyce de Carteret.*

adorn wrists and ankles (and in rare instances waists). Similar iconography is employed for beaded necklaces; however, while beaded bracelets and anklets have only a handful of standardized forms, necklaces can feature more complex and ornate designs.

Cloth is the most commonly depicted material for belts and bands, although items of cloth rarely survive archaeologically. Visual evidence (figs. 8.2a–b) demonstrates that cloth bands appear in myriad contexts and

can signal vastly different stations high and low, from divinity to captivity. Beginning in the Preclassic period, strips of knotted cloth are shown tied around the wrists of deities as well as those of elites performing ritual ceremonies. Cloth can appear on its own, or it may affix other materials to the arm or the leg, such as jade celts and strips of paper (figs. 8.3a–d). In these cases, cloth bands reflect exalted status, but cloth can denigrate, too. Scenes of captivity show prisoners with arms and legs bound to one another with strips of cloth or rope. These bonds, at times the only material on an otherwise nude body, humiliate and incapacitate. In contrast to limb bands, belts of cloth do not correlate with social status and appear on rulers and captives alike. The simplest and most common belts consist of long strips of cloth tied around the waist, often with a long flap extending down between the legs to form a loincloth (see chapter 2 in this volume). Cloth belts and sashes can have a plain appearance, or they can be decorated with rich geometric designs (a feature seen in some Late Classic depictions; for example, see figs. 8.6a–b).

Cloth girdles also appear on the bodies of warriors, ballplayers, and other athletes. Helmeted boxers, for instance, feature cloth-wrapped wrists and heavy padding affixed to the hips with cloth straps (see Taube and Zender 2009). An unprovenienced Late Classic polychrome vase depicts three such boxers that don conch shells attached to their hands with cloth wrappings (K500). Players of the Classic Maya ball game made ex-

tensive use of cloth in their attire as well. In one scene on another unprovenienced polychrome (K1209), two bedecked ballplayers engage in gameplay with simple strips of cloth knotted around their wrists; in another, incised on the surface of a Chocholá-style vessel (K4684), more elaborate textile wrappings fan out from the forearms. The loose-ended bands like these, flowing behind the athlete's wrists, would have drawn attention to his limbs as he moved about the ball court, allowing the observer's eye to follow the game.

When it comes to materials, belts exhibit more variety in their composition than do limb bands. Belt assemblages range from simple to more complex arrangements. As noted above, simple cloth belts, sashes, and

---

FIGURE 8.2. *Cloth belts and bands: (a) detail from Kaminaljuyu Monument 65 showing a captive with wrists bound in cloth; and (b) figure on San Bartolo's west wall shown with extensive leg wrappings (after painting by Heather Hurst). Drawings by Alyce de Carteret.*

(a)

(b)

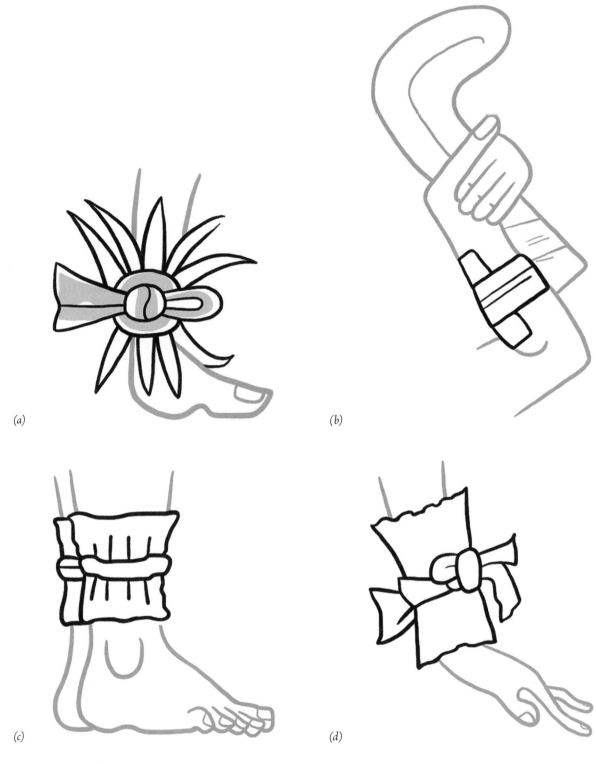

FIGURE 8.3. *Cloth bands as affixers: (a) detail from the west mural, San Bartolo, Las Pinturas building (after painting by Heather Hurst); (b) detail from Izapa Stela 3; (c) detail from the Tablet of the Cross, Palenque (after Stuart and Stuart 2008, 63); and (d) detail from a Late Classic Ik'-style polychrome vase (Museum of Fine Arts, Boston; 1988.1168). Drawings by Alyce de Carteret.*

(a)

(b)

(c)

(d)

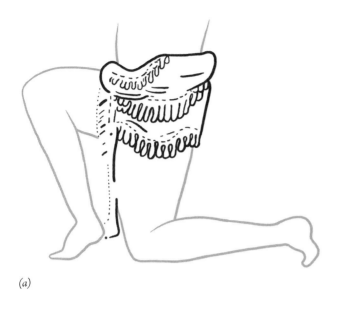

(a)

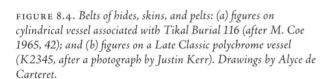

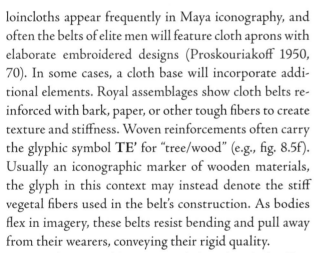

FIGURE 8.4. Belts of hides, skins, and pelts: (a) figures on cylindrical vessel associated with Tikal Burial 116 (after M. Coe 1965, 42); and (b) figures on a Late Classic polychrome vessel (K2345, after a photograph by Justin Kerr). Drawings by Alyce de Carteret.

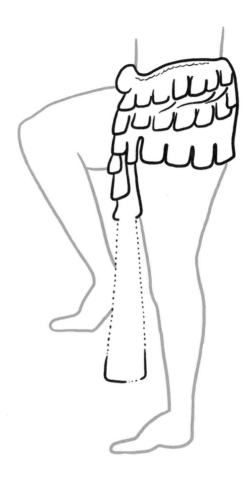

(b)

loincloths appear frequently in Maya iconography, and often the belts of elite men will feature cloth aprons with elaborate embroidered designs (Proskouriakoff 1950, 70). In some cases, a cloth base will incorporate additional elements. Royal assemblages show cloth belts reinforced with bark, paper, or other tough fibers to create texture and stiffness. Woven reinforcements often carry the glyphic symbol **TE'** for "tree/wood" (e.g., fig. 8.5f). Usually an iconographic marker of wooden materials, the glyph in this context may instead denote the stiff vegetal fibers used in the belt's construction. As bodies flex in imagery, these belts resist bending and pull away from their wearers, conveying their rigid quality.

For other assemblages, animals lent their hides (figs. 8.4a–b). On Late Classic polychrome vessels, long strips of deerskin, represented in iconography with a distinctive frilled pattern but otherwise undecorated, wrap around the waist two or three times before being secured under the navel. Belts of jaguar pelts could appear on men of high status. Lords and elite ballplayers

are sometimes shown wearing jaguar-pelt girdles, featuring the large feline's characteristic rosettes. Other kinds of sumptuous materials could be used for simple belts as well. Jade plaques, strung together with twine made from henequen or other fibers, hang on the hips of rulers and other elites in Classic-period imagery (e.g., fig. 8.6e). The likely tomb of Yuknoom Yich'aak K'ahk', ruler of Calakmul in the late seventh century AD, contained a belt of jade plaques among other precious items of adornment (Martin and Grube 2008, 111). Women may have worn similar belts of large jade beads, like those shown on wrists and ankles. Preclassic and Early Classic iconography depicts female attendants of the Maize God wearing jade-bead belts and little else (e.g., fig. 8.1b); however, this imagery is rare and seems to be limited to mythic scenes.

On cloth, leather, and bark-fiber bases, belts could be layered and adorned with additional materials. Late Classic depictions show men of elite status wearing bark-reinforced belts wrapped around more pliable

(a)

(b)

(c)

(d)

(e)

(f)

cloth sashes. As will be discussed in greater detail below, the accompanying sashes are often brightly colored with geometric designs. Strings of whole sea-snail shells dangle from more ornate belts and sashes, particularly on the royal belt assemblages carved into monumental stelae. As many of these images depict lords leaping in dance, one can imagine the sonorous jingling that would have been produced by the suspended shells as the body moved. Additionally, complex belts worn in ritual contexts could include heads, likely made of perishable materials like papier-mâché or perhaps precious stone, meant to represent ancestors or deities (Proskouriakoff 1950, 65). The heads, in most cases, have jade or shell pendants suspended from them and can appear isolated or in triplets. Accessories like these appear in many permutations; some belts have shell pendants, others have bark reinforcements and heads, and many have all of these features.

By the Late Classic period, a handful of distinctive belt assemblages appear in iconography (figs. 8.5c–f and 8.6a–e). The most distinctive of these, which is termed here the royal composite belt, had three integral components: a cloth base stiffened with bark or other rigid fibers, a row of complete shell pendants hanging from this base, and a series of heads from each of which a handful of polished celts are suspended (figs. 8.5d–f). Oftentimes a jaguar kilt will be paired with this belt, although it is not a necessary component. A similar assemblage, the royal plaque belt, substitutes a string of jade or shell plaques and beads for the bark-reinforced cloth and sags around the hips of its wearer (indicating the greater flexibility of this particular item when compared with the rigid royal composite belt) (figs. 8.6d and e). Finally, warriors and athletes don a combat belt assemblage, which includes a deerskin or jaguar-pelt base and a row of shell pendants (as with the royal composite belt) (fig. 8.6c). A loincloth apron may also be apparent.

Rings worn around fingers are vanishingly rare in ancient Maya art, yet archaeological specimens attest that they were worn in the Late and Terminal Classic periods, perhaps especially by elites in the eastern part of the Maya world. Finger rings were carved from shell or bone and could be incised with designs or texts, carved to show figural or abstract motifs, or set with pearls or precious stones. Incised inscriptions on two bone rings from Cahal Pech name the ornaments' owner and apparently provide the Classic Maya word for "ring," potentially *osib*, from a verb meaning "to insert" (Santasilia 2013, 120–122).

SPATIAL AND TEMPORAL VARIATION

The visual depictions of belts and bands undergo marked changes through time, from the earliest Preclassic images to Postclassic renderings millennia later. Abundant Late Classic iconography shows the most complex assemblages, which incorporate a wide variety of materials in, at times, idiosyncratic ways. The earliest and latest pre-Columbian images, on the contrary, depict a smaller repertoire of adornment in a smaller set of genres. This section will describe the apparent trends in belts and bands throughout time, focused primarily on the images produced in these different periods.

Belts and limb bands in the Preclassic period (with most evidence coming from Late Preclassic iconography) are simple, consisting in most cases of either a string of beads or knotted cloth. These patterns extend across media, from carved stelae to murals. Simple beaded bracelets and anklets are frequently depicted. Common is the three-bead motif, consisting of three adjacent circles spanning the width of the wrist or ankle (see fig. 8.1a). Cloth bands are particularly numerous as well and often appear as strips of cloth wrapped once around the wrist or ankle (or both) and tied in place. Visually, there is consistency in how this ornamentation is represented: the knot is circular with a closed loop on one side and two loose ends on the other. More elaborate wrappings utilize this same convention. A figure, who crowns the seated *ajaw* in the accession scene on San Bartolo's west wall, has his forearms and calves fully wrapped in cloth (see fig. 8.2b). In this example, the wrappings are still secured by a single knot at the wrist and ankle, as seen in other images. The social status of the wearer does not affect the way in which cloth is affixed to the body: deities,

FIGURE 8.5. *The royal composite belt: (a) detail from Izapa Stela 4; (b) detail from Kaminaljuyu Stela 11 (after drawing by John Montgomery); (c) detail from Tikal Stela 40; (d) detail from Copan Stela B (after drawing by A. Dowd in Baudez 1994, fig. 5); (e) detail from Tikal Stela 5 (after Jones and Satterthwaite 1982, fig. 7); and (f) detail from Ceibal Stela 10 (after drawing by Ian Graham). Drawings by Alyce de Carteret.*

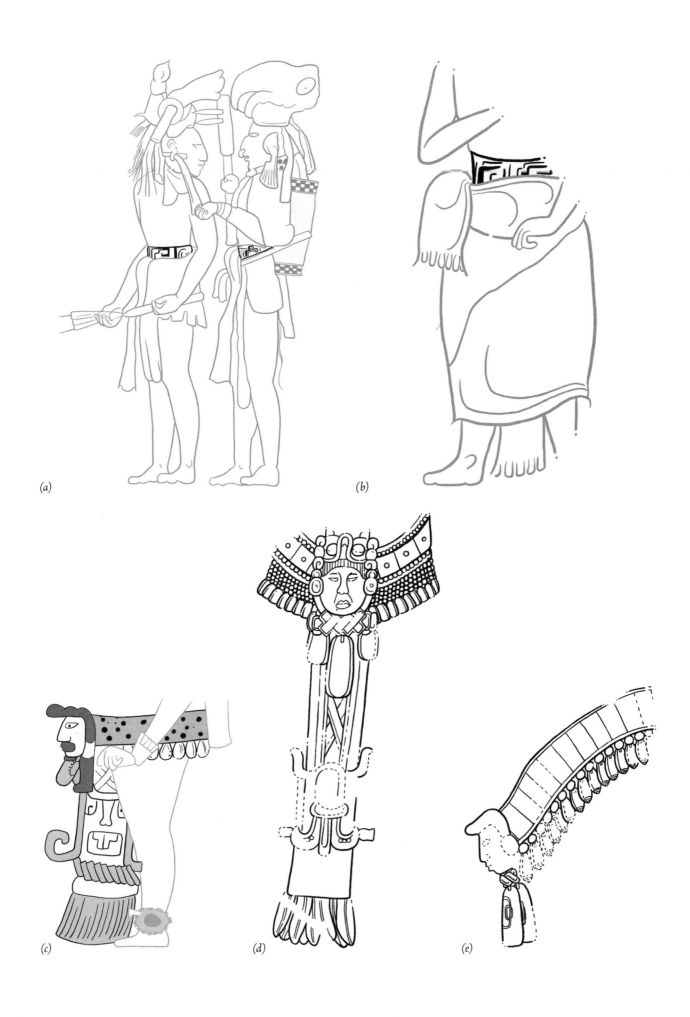

(a)

(b)

(c)

(d)

(e)

elites, and captives alike are bound with the same knots. In some Preclassic depictions, cloth wrist- and legbands are accompanied by a simple cloth necklace, shown with the aforementioned artistic conventions.

In early iconography, cloth binds precious materials to divine and elite bodies (fig. 8.3a). Among the most notable examples are jade celts tied to the upper arms or thighs of deities (fig. 8.3b). Jade celts as objects are common inclusions in Formative-period caches at both Olmec and Maya sites and have intimate associations with divinity, sustenance, and the sacred breath of life (see Taube 2005). Affixing celts to the body linked the individual (divine or regal) with the symbolic potency of the items. In these scenes, the cloth appears functional but superfluous to the larger visual message. The convention was discarded in later periods, and celts and other glyphic markers began to be inscribed directly into divine arms and legs, forgoing the cloth binding (see central seated figure on K504 or central standing figure on K595 for examples). In this way, cloth-bound celts are antecedents to these elemental "god signs" that appear on the skin of divinities during the Classic period. Cloth could bind other kinds of materials to arms and legs as well. Figures on San Bartolo's west wall engage in acts of self-sacrifice at the four corners of the world, represented by four world trees. Here, leaves and grass are tied to the figures' wrists and ankles—and, in one case, the knees—with strips of red cloth (e.g., fig. 8.3a). Later Classic-period examples similarly show deities and lords performing sacred rites with strips of paper and other materials bound to their arms and legs with cloth (figs. 8.3c–d), indicating the importance of this adornment for the ritual acts being undertaken.

Preclassic belt assemblages tend to be more complex than arm- and legbands, as tends to be the case in ensuing time periods. Ornaments in the form of heads—both anthropomorphic and zoomorphic—secure cloth belts

and loincloths around the waists of deities and kings. On Izapa Stela 4 and Kaminaljuyu Stela 11 (figs. 8.5a and 8.5b, respectively), divine figures wear belts with stylized heads affixed at the navel and long embroidered aprons that hang almost to the ankles. Also note the strips of knotted cloth bound to the wrist and ankles of the figures (and around the knees of the figure on Izapa Stela 4). The similarities this belt assemblage shares with the royal composite belt, which does not appear in its fully realized form until Late Classic iconography, suggest it may be its predecessor.

The evocative San Bartolo murals provide a glimpse into the potential variety of Preclassic belts and bands, with the caveat that these scenes depict mythologized events and not necessarily everyday dress. Male attendants of the Maize God, who provide the deity with a variety of offerings on the mural's north wall, have multiple strips of cloth knotted around their waist (see fig. 3.2a, Individuals 8, 13, and 14; Saturno, Taube, and Stuart 2005, 8–9). Their wrists and ankles are also wrapped in cloth, secured with a single knot. Another figure (Individual 7) in the scene kneels before the Maize God; she wears a skirt with a cloth belt cinched at the back, as well as simple beaded bracelets and anklets. Two other kneeling women (Individuals 10 and 11) also wear beaded jewelry, one with an accompanying beaded belt and another with a more enigmatic girdle. On the latter (Individual 10), skeletalized crania, perhaps belonging to crocodiles or caimans, appear interspersed with the standard circular beads. The details of this mural are singular—either they are representative depictions of Preclassic dress and ideas about dress, or they are the idiosyncratic images of a particular place at a particular time. Regardless, despite some evidence for complexity in belt and band assemblages in this formative era, truly complex arrangements do not begin to concretize until the following centuries.

Iconography in the Classic Period exhibits the greatest complexity in belts and a striking degree of variety in arm and leg apparel, especially on the bodies of rulers and other people of high status (although keep in mind that imagery is biased in representing primarily elite individuals). Among these varied forms, some common motifs emerge. Wrist and ankle cuffs, constructed of jade plaques or beads of shell or bone, are popular accoutrements at this time (see Proskouriakoff 1950, 71,

FIGURE 8.6. *Standardized belt assemblages. The courtier belt: (a) detail from the murals of Bonampak (after painting by Heather Hurst and Leonard Ashby); (b) polychrome sherd from Caracol. Combat belt: (c) figure on a Late Classic polychrome vessel (K787). Royal plaque belt: (d) detail from Piedras Negras Stela 13 (after drawing by John Montgomery); and (e) detail from Tikal Temple 3, Lintel 2 (after Jones and Satterthwaite 1982, fig. 72). Drawings by Alyce de Carteret.*

80). Plaque cuffs consist of a row of oblong plaques or tubular beads that cover the lower forearm or ankle. In some examples, the cuff includes an additional row of rounded, semicircular beads along its proximal side, creating an ornamental border (fig. 8.1c). Beaded cuffs will have four or more rows of circular beads, either strung together or sewn onto a cloth or leather backing. These may also have an ornamental border of rounded beads or beaded tassels. Additionally, some examples show the cuff's ornate clasp in profile. Both men and women wear these cuffs, and they appear in scenes of accession, sacrificial rites, and warfare, among others.

As in Preclassic iconography, cloth bands affix paper or other fibers to Classic-period wrists and ankles in supernatural and ritual contexts. Historical figures appear on Tikal Altar 5 (a scene of tomb reentry and reburial, fig. 2.13b) as well as Palenque's Temple of the Cross (an accession scene, fig. 8.3c) wearing strips of paper visibly tied to their wrists. This motif, however, more commonly appears on the bodies of deities in various media (fig. 8.3d; K688). In the examples described above, these specialized forms of wrist and ankle adornment denote the wearer as a participant in a certain ritual act and visually communicate the person's role in the ceremony.

The most common form of belt in Early Classic imagery is the cloth belt or sash. These may appear in isolation as part of a loincloth or as a fastener in a more complex kilt assemblage. During this time, cloth belts gird the waists of men alone, and women's waists are only rarely defined by belts of any kind. In the few scenes where women do wear belts, all of which are supernatural or mythic in nature, simple beaded belts hang loosely around their hips. An Early Classic blackware vessel (K6547) shows female attendants of the Maize God mourning his bundled corpse; other than their simple beaded belts, with beaded aprons hanging down the front (fig. 8.1b), they are shown completely nude. Beaded belts do not appear in other circumstances.

The royal composite belt continues to develop in Early Classic representations. Three early examples appear on the Hauberg Stela and Tikal Stelae 2 and 40 (fig. 8.5c) (see Schele 1985; Jones and Satterthwaite 1982, fig. 2; Valdés, Fahsen, and Muñoz Cosme 1997). These Early Classic depictions show a cloth base with bark reinforcements in a crisscross pattern and a knotted apron connected to the base from which a supernatural head

is suspended. The belt form and suspended supernatural head in these examples clearly build on late Preclassic iconographic conventions (see Izapa Stela 4, fig. 8.5a; and Kaminaljuyu Stela 11, fig. 8.5b). Staying with these representative examples, Tikal Stelae 2 and 40 also depict two anthropomorphic or zoomorphic heads affixed directly to the belt, each with three celts hanging below.

Another common motif on Early Classic royal composite belts consists of circles interspersed with the woven knot or *pohp* designs, perhaps part of belts' vegetal reinforcement (see fig. 8.5c). This combination of circle and mat does not readily appear in Late Classic examples. As Proskouriakoff (1950, 65) notes, "These circular elements are a fairly reliable indication of the Early Period." The two lords shown on Copan's Motmot Marker also wear such belts, although the assemblage is slightly obscured by their seated positions (W. Fash, B. Fash, and Davis-Salazar 2004, fig. 4.4). On the Motmot Marker, each figure has a bark-reinforced base, depicted with the repeating crisscross-circle motif, and a belt-dangle assemblage attached at the back, consisting of an anthropomorphic head with three pendants.

Late Classic depictions of the royal composite belt are ubiquitous in carved imagery, particularly on stelae. While there is some degree of variability in the woven base—some examples exhibiting the classic crisscross pattern of the fibrous reinforcements, others with more complex configurations—the belt has a fully developed, standardized form at this time (see figs. 8.5d–f): a bark-reinforced cloth base, a row of sea-snail shell pendants, and deity with three pendant celts apiece. A single head may be affixed at the navel, or multiple heads may appear, with one at the navel, one at the back, and one on either side of the hips (a maximum of three are usually shown, depending on the position of the figure in the image) (fig. 8.5d). A long, embroidered apron will often hang between the legs from the center of the belt, often incorporating a more stylized, two-dimensional take on the supernatural heads evident in Preclassic and Early Classic examples. At the height of Classic Maya political complexity, the belt appears on innumerable stelae, adorning the bodies of mostly royal men who participate in period-ending and scattering ceremonies, thus constituting a fundamental element of the regal wardrobe and public displays of authority. As some major political centers began to dissolve during the Terminal Classic period, appearances of the belt became less frequent and less standardized. On Ceibal Stela 10, for instance, the woven bark-reinforced cloth base is visually conflated with a skyband (although the glyphic **TE'** markers remain, see fig. 8.5f).

Other standardized forms develop in the Late Classic period. Simple cloth belts and sashes remain common, but they bear more distinctive designs and bright colors. Sashes continue to be used as fasteners for kilt assemblages, as well as backing for more complex ornamental belts. On the murals of Room 2 at Bonampak, male figures wear cloth or leather kilts wrapped around fitted girdles (fig. 8.6a; see also M. Miller and Brittenham 2013). Each girdle is made of light blue cloth and features a black geometric design. While there is some variation in the designs, the appearance of the girdles is remarkably consistent from one figure to the next. A polychrome sherd excavated from Caracol depicts the same assemblage (fig. 8.6b): the male figure sports a kilt of rosy-hued cloth fastened around a light-blue girdle, which is fitted snugly around the waist. Considering the uniformity of the girdle in its representation, particularly across a variety of media and a wide geographic range, the assemblage may have signified the specific rank or role of its wearer. As these figures appear to be members of the royal court, it is reasonable to suggest that the girdle identifies its wearer as a courtier or other high-ranking figure.

Belts of strung jade plaques appear with some frequency on royal bodies in Late Classic imagery (see figs. 8.6d–e). Unlike the royal composite belt, this assemblage can adorn both men and women who participate in royal ceremonies. Palenque's Oval Palace depicts the accession of K'ihnich Janab' Pakal in AD 615 (Martin and Grube 2008, 161). His mother, Lady Sak K'uk', presents him the crown wearing this plaque belt (fig. 8.1c). In terms of composition, the plaque belt shares its standardized features with the royal composite belt. Often, a centrally located head with three pendants will be affixed to the belt in the front, perhaps securing it in place, and in nearly every example a row of shell pendants hangs from the jade plaques. Unlike the rigid royal composite belt, however, the royal plaque belt hangs loosely around the hips, sagging with the weight of the affixed head and pendants. An image carved into Lintel 2 of Tikal Temple 3 depicts this belt assem-

blage hanging below its elite wearer's protruding belly (fig. 8.6e; see also Jones and Satterthwaite 1982, fig. 72).

Among the specific assemblages of belts and bands that arise during the Late Classic period, the combat assemblage—worn by both warriors and athletes—is also worthy of mention (fig. 8.6c; see also figs. 11.3 and 11.7). Albeit distinctive in the contexts of its use, the belt in this assemblage shares similarities in form and composition with the royal belts discussed above. A firm, inflexible band of leather, cloth, or jaguar pelt will gird the waist. In many examples, a row of shell pendants will hang from the leather band. Ornamental loincloth aprons may also hang from the front, back, or both. On ballplayers, the combat belt may appear alongside a single kneepad or a pair of kneepads. The kneepad consists of a circular element, perhaps a cushion made of leather or cloth, tied to the knee with a cloth band and decorated with tassels. When only one kneepad is shown, it is worn on the player's dominant side, which would have received the force of his dives (Schele and M. Miller 1986, pl. 100–104). One can imagine the spectacle of an athlete wearing this assemblage during gameplay, the aprons and tassels flowing, the shells clamoring.

The standardization apparent in Classic-period depictions of belts and bands does not persist into the Postclassic period, where surviving iconography reveals greater idiosyncrasy in bodily adornment. On murals, monumental carvings, and etchings on portable objects, variety abounds. While symmetry was common in earlier periods, for instance, Postclassic imagery shows no concern for matching the bands worn on the right and left sides of the body. Other aspects of dress are changing as well. Taking the golden disks dredged from the cenote at Chichen Itza as just one example, every figure depicted has a unique assemblage of items of adornment (see Lothrop 1952; Pillsbury, Potts, and Richter 2017, pl. 170–172). The balkanization of dress at this time indicates a comfort with individual assertive style, at least at an artistic level (Wiessner 1985).

Postclassic iconography (figs. 8.7a–c) shows beaded bracelets, leather wristbands, and arm wrappings made of overlapping courses of grass or perhaps some kind of animal fur. Examples from this period also highlight a variety of knee bands, which are relatively rare in earlier representations. These include cloth strips with beaded pendants, leather cuffs, leather pads affixed with cloth

(a)

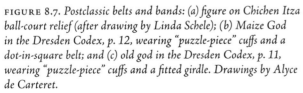

(b)

(c)

FIGURE 8.7. *Postclassic belts and bands: (a) figure on Chichen Itza ball-court relief (after drawing by Linda Schele); (b) Maize God in the Dresden Codex, p. 12, wearing "puzzle-piece" cuffs and a dot-in-square belt; and (c) old god in the Dresden Codex, p. 11, wearing "puzzle-piece" cuffs and a fitted girdle. Drawings by Alyce de Carteret.*

strips, and cloth wraps that extend from the knee down to the ankle (see fig. 9.10c). Imagery from Chichen Itza, including the aforementioned disks as well as murals, depicts martial scenes and reveals great variety in the adornment of warriors (Ringle 2009; see also Lothrop 1952; Morris, Charlot, and Morris 1931; Tozzer 1957). Knee bands, armbands, and belts appear integral to wartime costume, in addition to helmets, neckwear, and sandals. Belts are relatively simple, consisting in many examples of a long strip of cloth wrapped around the waist, sometimes three or four times. A loincloth or leather codpiece may hang from the front. Fuzzy wrist- and armbands adorn arms; grass, furs, or fringed cloth may give these items their fuzzy appearance. Some examples involve multiple layers of wrappings tied around the upper arms, and others consist of simple cuffs at the individual's wrist. While more common in Postclassic imagery, the motif has its beginnings in the Classic period: an unprovenienced polychrome vessel (K5763) depicts a row of hunters, each with three fuzzy cuffs around their forearms.

Dress in the Postclassic codices exhibits more internal uniformity compared with other media (see figs. 8.7b–c). Individuals shown in the Dresden, Paris, and Madrid Codices wear a nearly invariable assemblage of wrist and ankle cuffs. In the Paris and Madrid Codices, these are represented by a pair of overlapping or interlocking "puzzle-piece" elements, angular in shape, each with a central perforation. The puzzle pieces are flanked by two longer rectangular elements, perhaps beads or bones, that run along the length of the arm. A similar motif can be seen on the ankles of some figures. In the Dresden Codex, the same cuffs have rounded, nearly circular puzzle pieces and flanking elements that curl proximally. Additionally, some figures in the Dresden Codex wear other kinds of wristbands, including jade plaque bracelets and eyeball baubles. Belts are generally simple, and loincloths featuring dot-in-square motifs are particularly numerous. Some individuals wear bulkier cloth belts that bear a crisscross pattern similar to Classic-period royal composite belts.

Postclassic depictions of belts and bands, while varied, are relatively simple. Yet it is worth mentioning the context of this pattern: a shift in the thematic content of Maya art during a politically volatile time. The complexity of belts during the Late Classic period reflects in large part the proliferation of royal images, as the most complex belt assemblages adorn royal bodies. For the ensuing Postclassic period, the artistic focus on warriors and battle provides a window into the dress of a distinct class of people, and adornment would be expected to vary accordingly. The patterns discussed above have as much to say about changing sociopolitical structures in Maya society and the shifting genres of Maya art as they do about changes in dress more specifically.

MEANINGS AND SOCIAL FUNCTIONS

In Classic Maya culture, the use of belts and limb bands was linked conceptually, and oftentimes visually, with the symbolic practice of bundling. Precious items and tribute were offered in tightly wrapped bundles of cloth. Royal corpses were wrapped in textiles and knotted cords before interment, a pattern documented iconographically as well as archaeologically (Scherer 2015, 51–104). Excavations in a number of Early and Late Classic royal tombs, at sites like Tikal, Copan, and Calakmul, recovered pieces of textiles that had once wrapped the body (Fitzsimmons 2009, 76–78). Ethnographic analogy suggests that the practice protects the inner essences of the thing being bundled. For the modern Tzeltal Maya community of Zinacantan, located in the highlands of Chiapas, Mexico, binding and bundling rituals are used to secure souls in their place. Mothers of newborns must refrain from many activities in order to protect the vulnerable infant: they cannot leave the house, do chores, or eat certain foods. Above all, she must "keep the baby wrapped up and hidden from view," and as part of this practice she "binds its wrists and ankles to keep in the soul" (Vogt 1969, 182). Arm- and legbands may have served a similar symbolic function, binding body to soul. Soundly bound and safely ensouled, the wearer could be considered a complete person, which helps shed light on the ubiquity of these items in all periods of Maya iconography.

Beyond the general symbolic association with bundling, the use of belts and bands seems to be linked to or emblematic of particular roles and duties. The combat belt assemblage is especially illustrative of this quality, as it only appears in the contexts of warfare or athletic competition and does not appear to distinguish different participants from one another. Similarly, the royal composite belt, appearing primarily on monumental architecture in public spaces, is associated exclusively with rulers conducting important ceremonies. Lords wearing the belt commemorate period endings and engage in scattering rites. The royal plaque belt appears in similar contexts, although it can adorn individuals of varying royal status, both men and women. Those wearing the belt can be primary or secondary figures in the scene and can be involved in a variety of acts, including deity impersonation, dance, and accession.

Royal belt assemblages also appear unadorned, separate from the body. On Piedras Negras Stela 10, for example, the primary components of these belts—a head with three pendants, a woven band, and a string of sea-snail shells—encircle the jaguar-skin throne of the ruler. The jaguar skin covering the throne could be considered an analog to the jaguar kilt often worn in conjunction with these belts. The visual connection between the belt and the throne further emphasizes the royal nature of the assemblage. When a ruler wears the royal composite belt, he effectively wears the throne and performs acts as a "living embodiment" of rulership itself (Taube 2005, 30).

As a final observation, the marked imbalance of adornment along gendered lines is noteworthy. While women are often shown wearing necklaces, armbands, and wristbands, women rarely wear belts. Examples to the contrary are limited and confined to supernatural scenes (e.g., the attendants of the Maize God who wear beaded belts) or royal ceremonies (e.g., the queen mother inaugurating her son). These examples further emphasize that belts are more closely linked with particular activities and roles than they are with an individual's identity. However, these exceptions also make clear that the identity of belt wearers is only rarely female. More commonly, elite women wear loose-fitting garments that obscure the waist, masking the shape of the body (e.g., huipils). The ancient Maya appeared to avoid defining a woman's waist through adornment, perhaps suggesting that the female abdomen was especially taboo in its exposure and representation, or that a defined waist signaled masculine roles and modes of dress.

CONCLUSION

In the diverse world of Maya dress, belts and bands have adorned Maya bodies in consistent fashion. Even relatively unadorned bodies in Preclassic iconography wear loincloths, bracelets, and anklets. Cloth straps and strings of beads, materials common in all periods, could bear additional decorations. Cloth, leather, stiff fibers, jade beads and celts, shell—these materials could be interwoven, suspended, and strung together to create complex assemblages that girded the body. Whether simple or complex, these items appear to be some of the most essential elements of ancient Maya dress through time, at least for male bodies.

In the Classic period, and especially the Late Classic period, specific belt assemblages denote the assumption of particular roles, duties, and responsibilities. The royal composite belt adorns royal men performing royal rites. Flexible plaque belts hang loosely over the hips of royal men and women engaging in important ceremonies. Athletes and warriors don combat belt assemblages. Along with headdresses, belts appear to be particularly important in signifying the ephemeral identity of the role the wearer is performing in the moment of its adornment. Specific tasks required specific costumes, and belts and bands were potent adornments, serving not only to decorate but to protect as well. A body girded with belts and bands was a bundled one, a soul protected.

CHAPTER 9

The Shod Body

FRANCO D. ROSSI AND ALYCE DE CARTERET

Footwear is a neglected item of ancient dress, commonly worn but rarely constituting a primary topic for study. Yet footwear was as vital in antiquity as today—toes and soles need protection from hard, rocky, or muddy surfaces and ankles need some support against sprains. In this, the Classic Maya were no exception. Despite thin material evidence (few shoes or sandals survive), imagery reveals a rich variety of footwear among the pre-Columbian Maya, with examples from the most mundane (traveling footwear) to the most extravagant (quetzal-headed sandals for public ceremonies). This chapter explores Maya footwear by probing the archaeological and artistic corpus, surveying available materials and methods of manufacture, and touching on various fashions from the Preclassic through Postclassic periods.

Footwear relies on certain resources and expertise in working leather, cordage, feathers, cloth, beads, and even metals. Looking to historical documents from Central Mexico, Justyna Olko (2005, 294) has identified no fewer than twenty-one Nahuatl terms for different types of sandals (*cactli*) in Nahua and Early Colonial Mexican society. These include basic terms for a sandal's appearance, such as "thin sandals" (*canhuac cactli*) or "embroidered sandals" (*tlamachcactli*), or they might embrace cultural or social meanings, as in "lordly sandals" (*tecpilcactli*). There were many material-specific terms too, from "rubber sandals" (*olcactli*) to "wolf skin sandals" (*cuetlachcactli*) and "obsidian sandals" (*itzcactli*).

Although Bernardino de Sahagún focuses on Nahua peoples of early colonial Central Mexico, his writings are helpful in thinking about sandal making and decoration throughout pre-Columbian Mesoamerica and among the Maya in particular.

In book 10 of the *Florentine Codex*, Sahagún's informants describe "the sandal-maker/seller" in sixteenth-century Nahua society, detailing an array of relevant production methods and types:

> He [the sandal-maker] adorns the sandals with flowers. [He who] sells sandals, sells sandals of cured leather, of maguey fiber—of tight stitching, of thin stitching, of thick stitching, of tangled stitching, basted, of loose stitching; loose, straight and long, straight, shiny, no dragging—in no way dragging, with gathered tabs—tabs which are gathered, with short tabs; white, black, tawny, green, blue; with designs, with feathers, with dyed fur, with the ocelot claw design, with the eagle claw design, with streamers, with the shield jewel, with the wind jewel, narrow, wide, long; large sandals, small sandals, children's sandals; tangled ones; enlarged ones; creaking, noisy, noise-making ones; distended ones. (1961, 74)

Although this lexical and descriptive spread of terms does not appear in colonial documents from the Maya area, Classic-period images point to many categories,

constituent materials, decorative methods, and even meanings that recall Nahuatl examples.

FIGURE 9.1. *Huarache sandal—foot vessel. Yale University Art Gallery (courtesy of Yale University Art Gallery, Leonard C. Hannah Jr., Class of 1913, Fund).*

MATERIALS

Sandals abound in the Classic-period images, which show a standard method of binding sandals to the feet with two straps or ropes passed between the first and second and then the third and fourth toes (or sometimes the fourth and fifth toes; fig. 9.1). This form is consistent with modern *huarache* sandals, called *xana'* by Yukateko speakers, commonly manufactured and sold today in the markets of Mexico. Early-twentieth-century accounts by Alfred Tozzer note another manner of binding, "by a strap or rope passing between the first and second toes" (1907, 32), a method more in line with beach "flip-flops" today. This binding sandal may have been in use during the Classic period, although it has yet to be documented in imagery.

Among K'iche' speakers, leather sandals are typically called *lej xajab*, or "tortilla sandals," referring perhaps to the flat, tortilla-like nature of a leather sole (Edmonson 1965, 66, 145). Alfonso Villa Rojas (1985, 401) also describes Tzeltal Maya men's use of leather sandals during the early twentieth century. Modern *huarache* sandals are made of leather, though this is usually cowhide, which would not have been available to pre-Columbian populations (Hirth 2009, 91). However, other types of leather were evidently in use.

The most commonly cited leather used was manufactured from deer hide, both tanned and untanned (Landa [in Tozzer 1941], 9; Roys 1972, 23, 154; Tozzer 1907, 29, 32; Herrera [in Tozzer 1941], 17; one could also see, in limited cases, reptile or even fish hide; see Grey et al. 2006; Reed 2005). The tanning of hides probably consisted of sun drying the animal skins (Roys 1972, 23) or possibly mirrored tanning methods employed by pre-Columbian Nahua peoples, in which leached ash was used to derive the lye required for the tanning process (Sahagún, book 10, 1961, 73–74). In Yukateko Mayan, one term for sandals, *yahaw sasak tzimin*, is defined in the *Cordemex* dictionary as "henequen-fiber sandals" (Barrera Vásquez 1980, 962). The inclusion of the word *tzimin* in the name of these particular sandals also suggests the pre-Columbian use of tapir (*tzimin*) hides for leather soles. The term *tzimin*, present-day Yukateko for "horse," originated as a word for "tapir," an animal that, though once widespread, is now rare in regions that speak Yukateko (Kaufman and Norman 1984, 163).

Henequen (*Agave sisalana* and *A. fourcroydes*) grows in abundance in the northern Maya lowlands, and its fibers make cordage and cloth that are usually whitish in color (fig. 9.2a). Henequen fibers (*sak ki* or *tsots ki* in Yukateko) appear to have been used historically for various types of sandals (Roys 1972, 154; Barrera Vásquez 1980, 313). *Sisal* and other *Agave* fibers are easily spun into cordage for sandal making, as we see in surviving pre-Columbian examples in other parts of the Americas; Friar Diego de Landa, too, records the use of henequen fibers in the construction of footwear in the sixteenth century (Tozzer 1941, 89). Cloth sandals, ostensibly woven from agave fibers, are abundantly represented in pre-Columbian imagery as well, first appearing in the Maya area during the Early Classic and remaining "in style" through the Postclassic. This footwear resembles the "white sandals" (*iztac cactli*) of the Aztec ubiquitously depicted in the codices of Central Mexico. It seems also to be the primary type of footwear depicted on the Postclassic-period murals of Chichen Itza and other Postclassic imagery of the Northern Maya Lowlands.

Woven henequen or combination henequen/leather sandals would have been used by the Classic-period Maya (figs. 9.2a and b), possibly along with rubber sandal soles like those documented in pre-Columbian Central Mexico (Tarkanian and Hosler 2011, 470–480). Evon Vogt (1969, 96) notes a traditional everyday sandal worn by Tzotzil Maya men called the *varachil*, made with leather straps fitted to thick rubber soles cut from automobile tires. Accounts at the time of Spanish contact reveal that rubber was already a widely traded material in pre-Columbian Mesoamerica. Several archaeological discoveries of rubber objects preserved in anaerobic conditions support these accounts, indicating that rubber processing and use extend as far back as the Early Preclassic/Early Formative periods (Hosler, Burkett, and Tarkanian 1999). These discoveries include twelve rubber balls found at the Olmec site of El Manatí (1600 to 1200 BC), a variety of rubber artifacts dredged from the Cenote of Sacrifice at Chichen Itza and dated between AD 850 and 1550 and, most recently, rubber balls found at Teotihuacan in Central Mexico (Ortíz and Carmen Rodríguez 1999; Coggins and Ladd 1992, 353–357; Lakhani 2017). Another material most likely existed as well: in Yukateko a type of boot or "high shoe" is referred to as *bolon yokte' xanab* (Barrera Vásquez 1980, 64), or, literally, the "nine" or "many footsteps wood shoe." This shoe is discussed further below, but its name probably refers to a wooden sole or heel, making it "high" or elevated.

Perishable materials like leather, cloth, wood, and rubber do not easily survive in the hot, tropical climate of the Maya area, yet nonperishable materials, like metal, do endure in select contexts. In fact, several metal sandal bases constitute the only known, material evidence of pre-Columbian footwear from the Maya area (fig. 9.2c). These objects are part of a larger corpus of gold-copper sheet-metal objects, excavated from the Sacred Cenote at Chichen Itza (Cockrell 2014). However, the Cenote sandals lack formal equivalents from other regions of the Americas and could hardly be regarded as the norm in pre-Columbian Maya societies. In fact, in a recent restudy, Bryan Cockrell (2014) contends that these objects may not be of Maya manufacture at all. In Cockrell's research, the only historical analogues to such sandals that he found were in the sixteenth-century account of Bernal Díaz del Castillo. In that account, Díaz del Castillo mentions such sandals twice: first noting that provincial indigenous leaders from around Río Grijalva (in modern Tabasco) brought "two golden soles like the ones on their own sandals" (2012, 48) as tribute for the Spanish and, second, that the Mexica leader Motecuhzoma II wore "soles of gold and, on the upper part, clusters of very precious stones" (2012, 192). Cockrell argues that such objects likely "reached the Cenote directly or indirectly by means of the Mexican tributary system" (2014, 32).

That being said, although metal was rarely (if ever)

(a)

(b)

(c)

used in the Maya area to make sandals, Classic Maya footwear nonetheless incorporated many other decorative and valued materials, as well as various designs and manufacturing techniques akin to those described by Sahagún for Nahua peoples. Jaguar skins were commonly used in elite sandal design (figs. 9.3a and c). In certain instances of impersonation or ritual dance, figures are seen wearing complete jaguar paws or avian claws, either authentic or replicated, on their feet. Bird heads are a common component, as are woven *pohp* designs and flowery ornamentation, perhaps real in some contexts (fig. 9.3b). A variety of colors were available for dyeing or painting sandals, as were various jewels, feathers, and streamers (fig 9.3c). Sandals also featured tightly fitted featherwork in their construction, as well as beads and shell plaques woven or glued onto a cloth backing (figs. 9.3d, e). Sandal noisemakers were probably made from rattles incorporating natural materials such as turtle carapaces in their construction. A supernatural character on a stucco frieze at Tonina is identified in relation to such footwear; in fact, his name, *Ahk Ook Chamiiy,* "turtle foot death," seems to specifically refer to the use of turtle carapaces in this capacity (fig. 9.3f). Sizing would have always been a concern in sandal making, alluded to above in Sahagún's mention of "large sandals, small sandals and children's sandals" among Nahuatl speakers.

In describing "the Nahuatl Sandalmaker," Sahagún repeatedly mentions various "stitchings" and "tabs." Key components to any sandal, these sandal elements are nonetheless difficult to discern in Maya images. The most informative evidence comes largely from the Postclassic period and takes the form of ceramic foot vessels. These objects are made in the shape of a foot with upper ankle/lower calf, disembodied and depicted within a highly realistic sandal. One example in the Yale Art Gallery reveals surprising detail about distinct san-

dal components, knots, fasteners, and overall sandal structure, granting a reasonably accurate view into how Maya sandals were assembled (fig. 9.1). The sole was one component, stitched to the heel wrap beneath the heel or along the base, although this latter base stitching is not visible in the depiction. The heel wrap connected the sandal sole to the ankle strap, with the stitch line between the heel wrap and ankle strap clearly visible—this is as close as we will likely get to stitch size and variation from such artifacts. The ankle strap wraps the back of the ankle and ends over the foot in two loose tabs, each with small notches for fixing and fastening the two sandal thongs. Such details emphasize a customizable component to the sandals, allowing wearers to tighten or loosen to some degree. The thongs then extend down over the center of the foot's bridge, where they meet and are knotted tightly. From this knot, the thongs then reach even farther down the foot to the toes, where they run between the first and second toes and fourth and fifth toes before attaching to the sandal sole underneath. In this example, the toes hang off the front of the sandal sole, a practice mirrored in other contemporary Postclassic examples as well. The Tancah, Tulum, and Santa Rita Corozal murals depict sandals in this way, a curious detail to include were it not at least somewhat accurate (figs. 2.5c and 3.8a-c). Other examples of foot vessels show varied methods of sandal manufacture, constituent materials, and forms that sandals could take, all based on the sandal structure just described.

TYPOLOGY

There is too much variety in the imagery of ancient Maya footwear to discuss every specific variant or nuanced type of sandal. However, continuing to build on groundbreaking work by Tatiana Proskouriakoff (1950) and soon after, by Samuel Lothrop (1952), we seek to create general categories of depicted Maya footwear, grouping them into specific types according to their basic structure and the forms devised from that structure. At the broadest level of categorization, these are simple sandals, woven sandals, and unconventional footwear (figs. 9.4a–c).

Most sandals in ancient Maya iconography are elaborations on what we call the "simple sandal," typified by the ceramic Yale "foot vessel" explained above. The simple

FIGURE 9.2. *(a) Henequen fiber being used in sandal construction, 2009 (photograph by Franco D. Rossi); (b) Late Classic period depiction of woven sandals (drawing © Simon Martin, used with permission); and (c) gilded copper sandals (image courtesy of Metropolitan Museum of Art, from Pillsbury et al. 2017, no. 178, p. 250; Peabody Museum Expedition, 1907-1910. @President and Fellows of Harvard College, Peabody Museum of Archaeology and Ethnology, Harvard University, PM 10-71-20/C7419).*

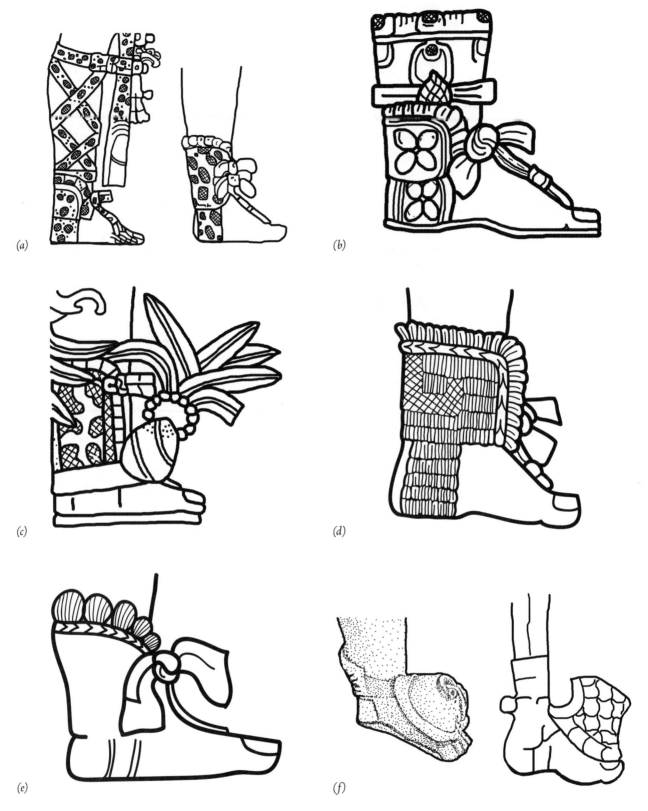

FIGURE 9.3. (a) Jaguar pelt sandals, from Palenque Temple of the Cross (left) and Bonampak Mural, Room 2 (right); (b) flower-design sandals (from Naranjo Stela 2); (c) sandals featuring feathers and jaguar pelt (from Ceibal Stela 10); (d) tightly knit feather work sandals (from Bonampak Stela 2); (e) sandals with seashells (Aguateca Stela 18); and (f) turtle carapace sandals, from "Standing Lord" Figurine, Kimbell Art Museum AP 1984.03 (left), and Tonina "Dreamlords" Frieze (right). Drawings by Franco D. Rossi.

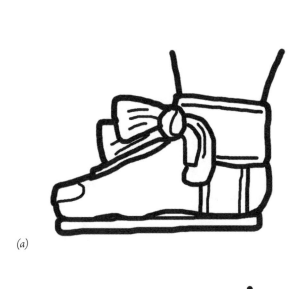

(a)

(b)

(c)

FIGURE 9.4. *Sandal categories: (a) simple sandal (Aguateca Stela 19); (b) cordage sandal (Caracol Stela 3); and (c) unconventional sandal (Izapa Stela 1). Drawings by Franco D. Rossi.*

sandal consists of a sole, a heel wrap or band, an ankle strap, and thongs connecting the ankle strap and the sole, which pass between the first and second and then third and fourth toes (or sometimes fourth and fifth toes).

The most common elaboration on the simple sandal is the fan-backed sandal, which includes an extended heel wrap bringing the sandal up past the ankle and farther up the base of the calf. Fan-backed sandals featured additional spaces for sandal adornment and decoration and also would have probably provided more ankle support.

On monumental architecture and polychrome vessels, these sandals usually appear to have been made from thick bands of leather or white, likely henequen,

cloth. In color depictions, the leather seems at times to have been painted or dyed, and other components could be brightly colored. Sandals could take on the form of small effigy depictions (figs. 9.4c and 9.5d) and would often feature decorative flowers, streamers, or puff balls in their design (figs. 9.2b and 9.3c). Thongs were typically knotted or bound over the bridge of the foot (figs. 9.3e, 9.4a, and 9.5a–b). Should one wish to hide these visible knots, loose thong tabs could also be pulled into or completely through different types of bridge ornaments that would serve the same function (figs. 9.3c, 9.5c, and 9.5e).

The most common designs on fan-backed sandals are the mat or *pohp* motif, commonly situated within a quatrefoil on the fan (fig. 9.6b). Often featuring feathered

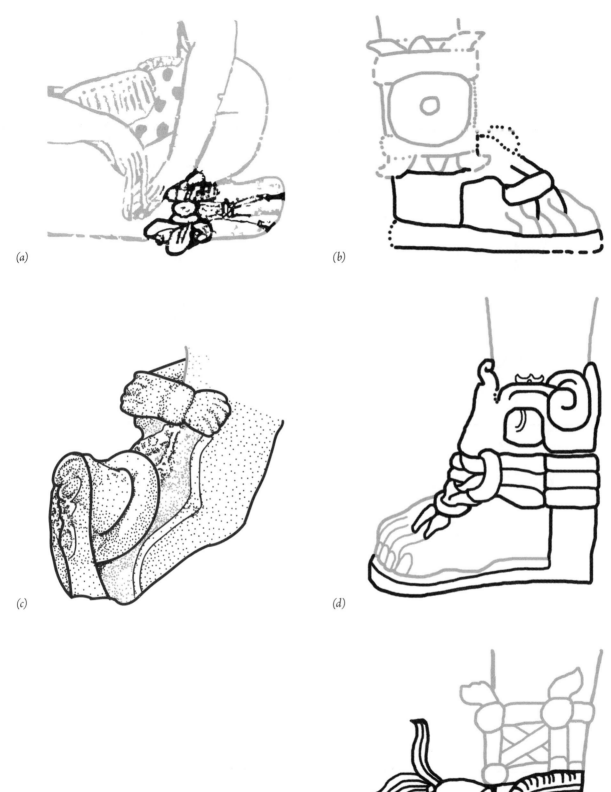

FIGURE 9.5. *Simple sandal variations: (a) unprovenienced Late Classic polychrome vessel, New Orleans Museum of Art; (b) Tikal Stela 27; (c) figurine of a seated lord (after Schele and Miller 1986, pl. 3); (d) Copan Stela B; and (e) Dos Pilas Stela 17. Drawings by Franco D. Rossi.*

(a)

(b)

(c)

(d)

(e)

rims, fan-backed sandals could also be decorated in a number of other ways, with masks attached to the heel wrap or bundled threads, bunches of feathers, and even rattles attached to the thong (fig. 9.6; see also figs. 9.3, 9.5d, and 9.5e). In certain instances, especially in contexts of ritual or ball play, fan-backed sandals had a tiled or mosaicked appearance, perhaps representing the attachment of individual plaques of shell or stone onto a cloth backing (fig. 9.6h). On simple cloth sandals, the fan can appear with or without added designs (fig. 9.6a). As a side note, Evon Vogt observed that very similar high-backed sandals, called *chak xonobil*, were used in ceremonial dances and other ritual contexts by Tzotzil Maya people in Zinacantan, Mexico (Vogt 1969, 98). This led him to draw parallels with Classic-period monumental depictions and their portrayed scenes and even to suggest the *chak xonobil* were survivals from the remote past.

Woven sandals frequently appear in early imagery and sculpture, especially during the Late Preclassic and Early Classic periods (Proskouriakoff 1950, 86–88). Although nearly all these portrayals of sandals fitted neatly into our "woven sandal" category, there is a surprising variability in types across the monuments on which they occur (figs. 9.7a–h). These sandals are similar in construction to the simple sandal, yet rather than employing a heel wrap to connect the sole with the ankle strap, a length of rope, leather, or cloth loops up and around the ankle strap from the sole (figs. 9.7a–b, d–e, and h); at times, this is also represented by a length of twisted cordage (fig. 9.7c). In some cases, these sandals appear with additional rope bindings wrapped up around the length of the calf (fig. 9.7e). Simple cloth sandals with similar cloth wrappings for the calf appear in the Early Classic and in Postclassic examples from the Yucatán. An interesting detail on the woven sandals depicted on the Leiden Plaque (fig. 9.7h) is the difference in appearance between the sandal inseam (undecorated) and out-seam (decorated). Such examples reveal that particular sandals were made with public viewership in mind, as out-seam designs were intended to be seen in profile.

The "unconventional" Maya footwear category contains examples that fall outside the more frequent forms of sandal construction discussed above. These include examples of footwear made specifically to evoke jaguar

paws and raptorial bird talons during royal ceremonies (figs. 9.8a–d). In these depictions, the claws or paws often look as though a human had simply taken on the morphological traits of these revered animals: i.e., the performing agent's feet and hands had become talons or paws. However, a few instances reveal some of the mechanics behind such costumes and how they were made. An instructive example on Dos Pilas Stela 2 reveals such footwear to be more like long socks or booties made of jaguar skin (fig. 9.8b). In this example, three claws of unequal length poke visibly out from the jaguar sock in a line perpendicular to how they would be positioned on actual jaguar paws. A representation on Aguateca Stela 2 displays the feet of a jaguar-avian composite costume in which the same kind of jaguar skin booties are used, yet only thick, artificial-looking bird claws poke out—two from the toes and one from the heel (fig. 9.8d).

Another notable example of unconventional footwear occurs on a Classic-period polychrome vessel (fig. 9.8e). On it, we see a stilted performer at the head of a musical troupe welcomed by an enthroned figure, who is referred to glyphically as *ik'il ook*, or "musical [windy] feet" (Houston 2018a, 65). Although such footwear appears largely during the Late Classic and Early Postclassic periods, a few examples also occur during the Late Preclassic. On Izapa Stela 1, a figure impersonating a rain god wears unconventional sandals that take the form of bat heads (fig. 9.4c). Interpreted as a depiction of ritualized and costumed performance (Guernsey 2006), this portrayal highlights unconventional footwear as a longstanding component of ritual dress, a usage continuing into later times and consistent with broader Mesoamerican practice.

SPATIAL AND TEMPORAL VARIATION

Sandals are common features of pre-Columbian art from as early as the Late Preclassic, when they begin to appear regularly on public monuments throughout the Guatemalan highlands and along the Pacific Coast, as at El Baul, Takalik Abaj, Izapa, and Kaminaljuyu. In Late Preclassic art, the inclusion or exclusion of sandals seems to be associated with the nature of the scene and individual.

Although nearly all Late Preclassic portrayals of sandals fit neatly into our "woven sandal" category, there

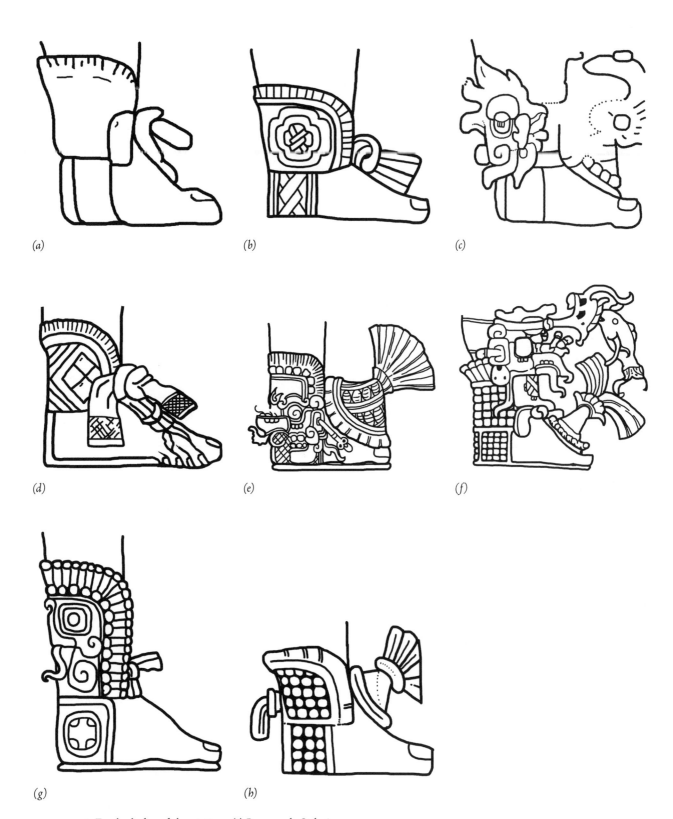

FIGURE 9.6. *Fan-backed sandal variations: (a) Bonampak, Stela 1,*
Room 1, mural painting; (b) Naranjo Stela 6; (c) Xultun Stela 4;
(d) Dos Caobas Stela 1; (e) Quirigua Stela K; (f) Aguateca Stela 7;
(g) Cancuen Stela 2; and (h) Yaxchilan Lintel 32. Drawings by
Franco D. Rossi.

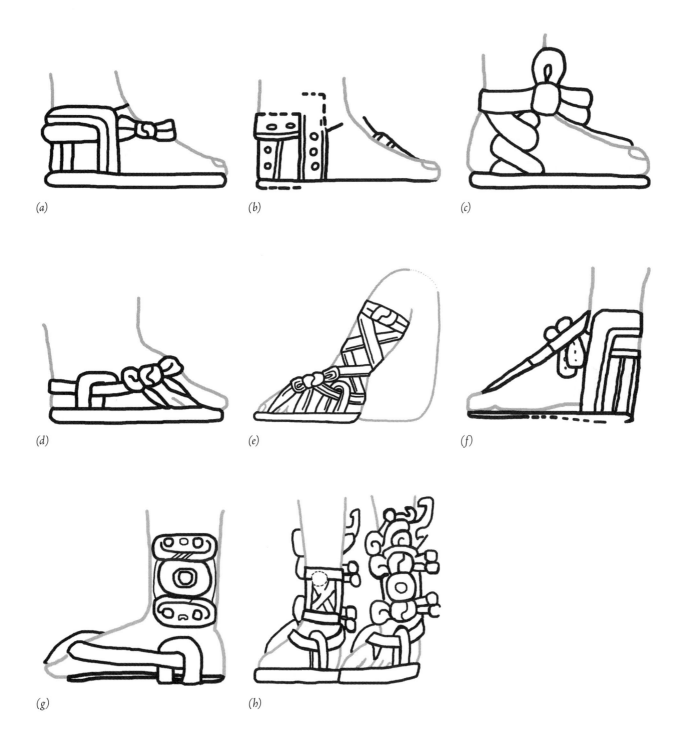

FIGURE 9.7. *Woven sandal variations: (a) Yaxha Stela 6;*
(b) Copan Stela 2; (c) Temple of the Jaguars, Chichen Itza;
(d) Tikal Stela 1; (e) Dzibanche Monument 20; (f) Caracol
Stela 5; (g) Hauberg Stela, Princeton University Art Museum;
and (h) Leiden Plaque, National Museum of Ethnology,
Netherlands. Drawings by Franco D. Rossi.

FIGURE 9.8. *Unconventional sandal variations: (a) Seibal Stela 8;*
(b) Dos Pilas Stela 2; (c) Tohcok Stela 1; (d) Aguateca Stela 2; and
(e) from Late Classic Polychrome, Kerr No. 8947. Drawings by
Franco D. Rossi.

is great variability in woven sandal types visible across early monuments. On Kaminaljuyu Sculpture 15, for example, sandal straps crisscross up the legs of the figure, being tied in a knot just below the knee (fig. 9.9a; Henderson 2013, 603). Takalik Abaj Stela 12 shows a similar crisscrossing of straps up the leg (Graham and Porter 1976–78). The soles of the sandals on both of these portrayals are quite thick, but those shown at Kaminaljuyu are flat-bottomed, while at Takalik Abaj the sandal bottoms occur with two divots. Kaminaljuyu Sculptures 24 and 88 also depict thickly soled, flat-bottomed, and woven sandals, yet without the crisscrossing straps; the woven, mat-like nature of the sole is just visible (fig. 9.9b; Henderson 2013, 612). Kaminaljuyu Sculpture 67 displays two different, thinly soled, woven sandals on a figure standing before a captive, the right sandal strap tied just above the ankle, while the left sandal strap is wound as a single strand around the leg and bound just below the knee (fig. 9.9c; Henderson 2013, 621). An early portrayal of a fan-backed sandal may be on Kaminaljuyu Sculpture 89, a rarity in costume during the Late Preclassic period (fig. 9.9d; Henderson 2013, 633). On Stela 1 at El Baul, the portrayed individual, dressed as if traveling, is shown with footwear whose soles are barely visible beneath his feet; cloth or leather wraps around the point at which the ankle meets the leg, akin to slippers (fig. 9.9e; Schele and Miller 1986, fig. 8). Intriguingly, the variety of footwear at Kaminaljuyu and other nearby Preclassic sites of southern Guatemala (highlands and Pacific Coast) is not attested in the imagery of contemporaneous sites in central Maya lowlands to the north. Despite many parallels in the art of these regions at this time, figures in Preclassic art of the central lowlands often appear without footwear (see fig. 3.2a).

Many Early Classic sandal styles are simply continuations from earlier Preclassic styles we see in southern Guatemala. An updated version of the sandals worn on Takalik Abaj Stela 5 appears on a figure from an unprovenienced celt fragment at Dumbarton Oaks (figs. 9.9f and g). This figure wears sandals fastened by two vertical straps around the ankles to an elaborate decorative extension running up the leg. The straps ultimately fasten below the knee, marked by the tied knot as well as a crocodilian head out of whose mouth issues the excess strap. During the Early Classic, the woven sandal (figs. 9.7e, g, and h), though still popular, nonetheless

began to lose ground to the white cloth simple sandal, which appeared with increased frequency in imagery (figs. 9.4a and 9.9h). These cloth sandals feature a thick, vertical strap attaching a thin horizontal ankle strap to the white sole, leaving the very back of the heel exposed. The appearance of cloth sandals may signal increased contact between Central Mexico and the Maya area at the time of entanglements with Teotihuacan, where this type of sandal seems relatively common. During the Early Classic, such sandals suggestively occur most often in the Maya area on Teotihuacan-associated art and artifacts (Estrada-Belli et al. 2009; Graham 1986, 143; Kidder, Jennings, and Shook 1946, figs. 173f, 204a). Cloth sandals continued to be depicted across the Maya area even after the decline of Teotihuacan, through the Late Classic period and into the Postclassic period, when trade with Central Mexico increased once again.

Fan-backed sandals also gain popularity during the Early Classic period, soon becoming frequent in monumental depictions of rulers and nobility. The backs of these early fan-backed sandals are already quite elaborate, with intricate decoration and even semantically meaningful symbols (Jones and Satterthwaite 1982, figs. 1, 83). On Tikal Stela 31, the monument protagonist's father, and previous Tikal ruler Yax Nuun Ayiin, stands with decorated, fan-backed sandals—part of an ensemble that proclaims his connection to the distant metropolis of Teotihuacan in Central Mexico (fig. 9.9i; Stuart 2000; Jones and Satterthwaite 1982, fig. 31a).

During the Late Classic period, there is a variety in footwear more consistent with Sahagún's description of contact-period Nahua footwear, that is, more elaborate fan-backed sandal depictions increase in number (figs. 9.6a–h). Such footwear mostly occurs on stelae monuments showing rulers in scenes of public ritual and ceremonial dance. Dyed leather, jaguar hide, and feather rims all became commonplace in artistic depictions (figs. 9.3a–e, 9.5a–e, and 9.6a–h), and increasingly complex designs build on Early Classic trends and peak during this time.

During the Postclassic, sandal design remains largely the same, though variations emerge in the styles and adornments of Maya footwear, a feature most visible in the art at sites like Chichen Itza (figs. 9.10a–e). Depictions of cloth sandals increase once again in frequency at this time. On murals from the Upper Temple of the

FIGURE 9.9. *Preclassic to Early Classic: (a) Kaminaljuyu
Sculpture 15; (b) Kaminaljuyu Sculpture 24; (c) Kaminaljuyu
Sculpture 67; (d) Kaminaljuyu Sculpture 89; (e) El Baul Stela 1.
Early Classic: (f) Takalik Abaj Stela 5; (g) Dumbarton Oaks
celt; (h) Uaxactun Stela B-XIII mural; and (i) Tikal Stela 31.
Drawings (a–d) by Lucia Henderson; drawings (e–i) by Franco D.
Rossi.*

Jaguars at Chichen Itza, cloth sandals are worn by nearly every warrior (see E. Morris, Charlot, and Morris 1931). This is in stark contrast to earlier depictions of the Late Classic period, where sandals were rarely displayed outside scenes of courtly events or public ceremonies. At Chichen Itza, all three types of sandals (simple, woven, and unconventional) are represented (figs. 9.10a–d). Many occur with a variety of topknot adornments and heel decoration, and are sometimes paired with wraps wound tightly up the shins from the sandals (fig. 9.10c; see chapter 8). In the codices, sandals are relatively rare, but those that occur are often simple sandals, either of cloth, leather, or a combination. The soles are usually not visible in these depictions, and several depicted in the Maya codices recall previously mentioned footwear in the Tancah, Tulum, and Santa Rita Corozal murals in which toes hang off the front end of the sandals (fig. 9.10c; see also figs. 2.5c and 3.8a–c). Stilts also occur in the Maya screenfold books. On page 36 of the Madrid Codex, a figure is shown wearing stilted footwear (fig. 9.10g). He stands next to two disembodied blue feet wearing what appear to be sandal topknots (though no sandals are discernible on the feet). This is one of several pairs of disembodied feet hinting at the presence of sandals, although the overall significance remains unclear.

MEANINGS AND SOCIAL FUNCTIONS

Many items of dress are highly gendered, and there is some limited evidence that this pattern extended into Maya footwear, at least according to historical documents. Writing about colonial Yucatán, Ralph Roys noted that "women usually went barefoot, but wore sandals when on the road" (Roys 1972, 23). Alfred Tozzer (1907, 29–30) attests to the same trend among the Lacandon, stating that although men and women were more often than not barefoot, men would sometimes don simple sandals when working in fields. In Zinacantan, Vogt found that "Zinancanteco women always went [go] barefooted" (Vogt 1969, 96), while men routinely wore the heavy, rubber-soled varachil sandals mentioned earlier. During earlier periods, such distinctions were less clear. Although depictions of women wearing footwear occur less frequently than depictions of shod men, this may be a matter of sampling, an issue acknowledged in earlier chapters: far more men are rep-

resented in the corpus of Maya art than women. When footwear is worn by women, it does not seem distinct from male footwear. Most of the various styles of sandals described above probably could have been donned by either gender. The degree to which sandals might have reflected certain social standing or class is equally difficult to say. In the scant portrayals of nonelite individuals, as on the Chiik Nahb murals of Calakmul, individuals are shown both wearing shoes and going barefoot (figs. 2.2a, 2.8c, and 2.11f; see also Carrasco Vargas and Cordeiro Baquiero 2012; Martin 2012). Indeed, many Maya elites are depicted without footwear.

Throughout Maya history, travel and journeys were important moments when footwear was deemed necessary. Travelers, emissaries, merchants, and sometimes soldiers were shown in sandals, even when other figures in shared scenes were not. Yet it is difficult to track down any clear linguistic reference to "walking" sandals or travel footwear of any kind. The closest example is the previously mentioned boot or "high shoe," called *bolon yokte' xanab* (literally, the "nine" or "many footsteps wood shoe") (Barrera Vásquez 1980, 64)—likely referring to shoes featuring a wooden sole or heel. The epithet *Bolon Yokte'* or "the nine or many footsteps, wood" was also used to label "a group of related deities that perform foundation rituals through the act of walking a ritual circuit" (Vail and Hernandez 2013, 436). The importance of such circuits and similar procession is well known ethnographically, ethnohistorically, and even epigraphically for the Classic Maya. The "many footsteps wood shoe" could thus also reflect its use within such circuits in which "many footsteps" were part and parcel of ritual performance (see also Gillespie and Joyce 1998, 288–289).

In battle it seems Late Classic Maya warriors elected not to wear shoes, as can be seen in the melee depicted in Bonampak's Room 2 (M. Miller and Brittenham 2013, 94, fig. 172). Polychrome vessels often show hunters and soldiers similarly unshod. Warfare during the Late Classic period likely required quick and nimble movement that would have been hindered by wearing sandals with thick ankle wraps and soles, particularly in the forested lowlands. Yet there are counterexamples to this trend. Piedras Negras Lintel 2 exhibits various young warriors, dressed for battle and wearing sandals. When warriors of the Late Classic period do sport footwear,

FIGURE 9.10. *Terminal Classic: (a) woven sandal with heel knot, inner column, Upper Temple of the Jaguars, Chichen Itza; (b) simple sandal with heel decoration, south bench, Temple of the Chacmool, Chichen Itza; (c) simple sandal with heel decoration and calf wrap, outer pier, Lower Temple of the Jaguars, Chichen Itza; (d) simple sandal with feathery ankle strap, Pier 5, South Temple, Chichen Itza; (e) bird-talon unconventional footwear, Column 17, Temple of the Warriors Colonnade, Chichen Itza; (f) cloth simple sandal, Dresden Codex, p. 26c; and (g) stilts as unconventional footwear next to disembodied feet, Madrid Codex, p. 36a. Drawings by Franco D. Rossi.*

it usually takes the form of simple cloth sandals in military preparations or processions (see K8933). Such footwear might have been useful for marches, but more of a nuisance or hindrance in fast-paced jungle warfare or the hunt. In contrast, representations of battles in the murals of Postclassic Yucatán show each figure adorned with a pair of sandals. This distinct shift in martial costume suggests a difference in the way the Maya conducted battle in these two regions and time periods. Perhaps it related not only to changing battle strategies but also to the different environmental settings in which battles took place.

Oddly, captives are sometimes shown in sandals, prompting reflection and discussion on footwear and its social meanings for the defeated and dishonored. Captives usually appear without shoes, aligning well with the conspicuous absence or simplicity of clothing that marks this social category more generally. However, captives sometimes are shown wearing woven sandals, often with cloth wrap extending up the calf (fig. 9.7e). Their dress is not like that of captors, however, with the possibility that clothing was stripped and other costume added in preparation for sacrifice or related ceremonies. Captives may, in fact, have been replicating roles in mythic events, with all the clothing suitable to such impersonation (Houston, Stuart, and Taube 2006, 202–226).

There is also the ball game to consider. Ballplayers are often shown wearing tiled, fan-backed sandals, but simpler cloth and leather sandals also appear with some frequency. As with other items, symmetry or consistency was unnecessary when it came to shoes. In some instances, shoes adorn both feet; in others, the participant appears without shoes. Usually, ballplayers wear a single shoe on the same side of the body adorned by a single kneepad and arm wrap (see chapter 8 in this volume). The solitary shoe in these examples consists of an anklet or ankle wrap and a rope extending from this wrap along the top of the foot and terminating at the toes. A sole is usually not visible in these depictions. Such a configuration provided protection for the foot when its wearer dived to the ball-court floor. At the same time, the sandal would have been light enough to allow free movement in a game that prized agility and sure footing.

Meaning is always difficult to infer from past images

and materials. But there are nonetheless several examples in which footwear, at least as it occurs in the artistic record, conveys meaning, especially in Classic-period imagery. As a general example, jaguar skins can be seen only on the sandals of high-ranking individuals, usually rulers, deities, or military commanders. Sandal adornment was usually tied to larger costume ensembles. In this sense, it resembles similar cases among the Aztec, including the "obsidian sandals" (*itzcactli*) of Tezcatlipoca, or "blue-painted sandals" (*tlaxihuihcuilolli cactli*) as a means for showing an individual's "Toltec-ness" (Olko 2005, 295–297). For the Maya, such footwear was normally reserved for elite men in acts of royal ritual on monumental sculpture.

Animate masks built into fan-backed footwear helped rulers embody various deities and were often worn in concert with other accoutrements as part of impersonations (Houston and Stuart 1996). Animating sandals in this way was especially popular in Waxaklajuun Ubaah K'awiil's eighth-century program of stelae at the site of Copan (fig. 9.5d), but it was also commonplace elsewhere in the Maya lowlands during the Late Classic. As mentioned, there are many scenes, both on monuments and on polychrome vessels, in which sandals were explicitly linked to their wearers' costumes. These referents are perhaps most noticeable on depictions in which individuals adopt jaguar or avian costumes, since the unconventional footwear in such scenes is made to resemble an actual jaguar paw or bird claws (figs. 9.8a–d and 9.10e).

Regional and site-specific trends emerge when footwear depictions are analyzed closely. For example, at Naranjo, the *pohp* symbol (mat) or the four-petal flower is commonly infixed into rulers' fan-backed sandals (figs. 9.3b and 9.6b). The *pohp* symbol was emblematic of rulership throughout the Maya area from as far back as the Preclassic period, yet, for unknown reasons, it is favored for Naranjo sandals more than anywhere else. At the site of Xultun, nearly every Late Classic monument portrays a ruler with fan-backed sandals equipped with different avian heads: a quetzal, a goggled quetzal, a vulture, and so on (fig. 9.6c for quetzal sandal example). The reasons for wearing certain avian sandals over others at Xultun remain obscure, though we do see similar (if not the same) pairs of avian sandals worn by different rulers. For example, on two different sets of stelae (Xultun Stelae 4 and 5 and Xultun Stelae 23, 24, and 25), the protagonist wears similar quetzal sandals, yet each set of stelae was erected decades apart by different rulers. It is thus unclear whether these sandals referred to a local deity, served as family heirlooms, were coming back into style again, or discharged yet other functions. However, there is a recurring female name at Xultun that features *k'uk'* ("quetzal") as its main component; such sandals' prominence in imagery may be related to this name.

At Late Classic Caracol, artists portrayed their rulers with sandals styled after the footwear traditions of the Late Preclassic and Early Classic periods, with clear depictions of woven cords as straps (see fig. 9.7f). Similar anachronistic references appear at other Late Classic sites, sometimes reviving older Teotihuacan-style accoutrements of war and sacrifice (B. Fash 2011, 111, fig. 134). In these settings, sandal decoration is more often tied to the larger costume ensemble being represented. At Yaxchilan the tiled fan-backed sandals in scenes of dancing, ball playing, and bloodletting mirror the scale-like helmets of the Teotihuacano "war serpent" style (fig. 9.6h). Such examples of Teotihuacan-inspired footwear may invoke the memory of a time when there were strong connections between the local dynasty and the powerful yet distant Teotihuacan. Such loose historical references through costume are rarely anchored in specific years and seem more to signal a nostalgic rhetoric, indeed, long after the collapse of the Mexican city. In these and many other examples, a wide variety of historical, regional, mythical, and exotic referents underscore the political overtones evoked by certain footwear.

CONCLUSION

Footwear expressed connections to foreign powers, linked lords (and sometimes captives) to revered ancestors or gods, and showcased an individual's place of origin. Sandals could be important markers of rank or social status and were also key accoutrements in ceremonial costumes. Yet unlike other items of dress, such as headgear and loincloths, footwear also appears to have been relatively unnecessary in routine adornment. Up into the Postclassic period, sandals occur in imagery, but this is most common in ceremonial contexts, and even elite individuals are regularly shown barefooted. In the scant portrayals of non-elite individuals, as on the murals of the Chiik Nahb complex at Calakmul, individuals are often unshod (Carrasco Vargas, Vázquez López, and Martin 2009). This implies that sandals had little utility in the day-to-day lives of non-elite and elite individuals alike. By and large, the wearing of footwear for the ancient Maya was reserved for ceremonial events, ball play, and travel; use in battle became commonplace by the Postclassic period.

Footwear that was decorative, rather than utilitarian, marked elite status by its very presence. Along with belts and limb bands, such shod feet constituted an important part of an elite dress code required of royal individuals in the practice of dynastic rites. By understanding how these items of dress were created, used, and represented, we can not only explore technologies of Maya footwear production and consumption, but interpret the evolving styles, subtle messages, and deep cultural histories painted, woven, and embroidered on their surfaces.

CHAPTER 10

The Varied Body

CARA GRACE TREMAIN

Identity is a cross-cultural experience that involves appreciating who we are and the similarities and differences between ourselves and others. Although it is often thought of as an extremely personal (and thus internal) experience, identity is also exterior to us and can be expressed in various ways. While dress (which is used here as an inclusive term that does not refer to any particular form of attire) can communicate information about the identities of its wearers, it is not simply a passive reflection of identity—it has a powerful relationship to how individuals understand themselves and interact with others.

Many aspects of Maya dress beautified or eroticized bodies (Houston, Stuart, and Taube 2006, 23), while also helping to create and advertise identities (R. Joyce 2000a, 13). Much evidence for Maya dress comes from pictorial imagery, where the most visible identities are perhaps those of status, gender, and age. Such evidence can be supplemented with items of dress recovered from archaeological excavations, to create a sizable data set to help understand how Maya dress related to identity. This chapter specifically examines the way in which textiles, ornamentation, hair, and body modification were related to the status, gender, and age of the ancient Maya.

STATUS

The Maya visually communicated wealth and power through the way in which they constructed outfits, the items they wore on their bodies, and the types of body modifications they performed. The quantity and quality of dress items is one of the most popular means of interpreting status from dress. For example, Triadan (2007, 286) suggested that the elaborateness of dress on figurines from Aguateca may represent different social ranks or sociopolitical contexts. Conversely, in instances where royalty and elites have been stripped of their most visible finery (e.g., Monument 122 from Tonina), the absence of dress indicates lack of status.

The effect of dress on bodily movement can be another avenue to identifying status. Houston, Stuart, and Taube (2006, 26) proposed that heavy dress elements graphically embodied the duties of high rank. Since large amounts of finery "must have been heavy and awkward, necessitating cautious, measured movement to maintain balance and dignity" (Schele and Miller 1986, 67), it is likely that high-status dress required slow, purposeful movements.

It is important to consider how body form and positioning also inform these questions of dress and identity. For example, perhaps one of the most conspicuous instances in which body form guides our understanding of status lies in the painted figure of Yajawte' K'inich of Motul de San José (the "Fat Cacique"). His corpulence is often taken as a direct indicator of wealth, prosperity, and royal status (Gillespie 2008, 129; Kerr 1989, 32). This, in turn, guides how we read the accoutrements of dress that he dons. Similarly, Miller and Martin (2004,

25) have argued that depictions of powerful females often exaggerated their girth to indicate wealth.

As well as being larger in size, rulers are positioned higher in pictorial scenes or shown frontally (Houston 1998, 343). Subsidiary figures are usually shown in profile (Looper 2009, 56) or are positioned on the viewer's left (Houston 1998). Females are also relegated to subordinate positions (Bruhns 1988, 111; Guernsey 1992, 59; Proskouriakoff 1961, 84), and ceramic scenes such as K4996 show a female seated behind male rulers. In this scene, the seated woman's face is painted white with designs rendered in red, and she wears an earflare diadem, a necklace of greenstone beads, bracelets, a shoulderless dress, and flowers in her hair. Her position, although subordinate to the ruler, is high ranking, and the adjacent text confirms her status. Conceivably, her dress could be read as expected raiment for an individual who seems to have been both the ruler's bride and a prominent noblewoman in her own right attending court.

Hand gestures can also be a means of inferring the status of individuals. Both Benson (1974) and Miller (1981) have demonstrated that certain hand gestures can indicate submission, and thus relative hierarchy. Other small details, such as the representation of long fingernails and toenails, may have signaled the absence of hard manual labor and therefore betokened elite status (Houston, Stuart, and Taube 2006, 25).

Finally, the status of individuals can be inferred from their proximity to the dominant figure of a scene—which Houston and Stuart (2001, 63) have referred to as "hierarchical space." Elsewhere, Houston, Stuart, and Taube (2006, 37) suggested that social distance was close among courtiers but expanded greatly with rulers and high-ranking lords, who often sit apart. Furthermore, they proposed that parasols in Maya imagery not only offered protection from the sun but also framed the sanctified space around rulers (2006, 38).

Textiles
Although no complete examples survive (see Fasquelle and Fash 1991 and Morehart et al. 2004 for examples of partial remains), textiles were undoubtedly an important communicator of status among the Maya (see chapter 2 in this volume). They may have even acted as currency (Baron 2018), with the more elaborate or intricate

examples being of higher value. McAnany (2013, 233) asserted that the brocaded huipiles (see below) worn by Lady K'abal Xook of Yaxchilan were bequeathed to her daughter(s) and would have been valuable possessions if the royal family fell into difficult circumstances. Similarly, she proposed that lesser textiles were given away to cement alliances, settle disputes, or meet tribute obligations (2013, 234).

Although the production of textiles was by no means limited to elites (Chase et al. 2008), it was often larger in scale and intensity in elite contexts (Halperin 2016, 436). The most elaborate textiles were commissioned, worn, and perhaps even created by elites. Clark and Houston (1998, 41) argued that some elite women may have hired other women to do their spinning and weaving and proposed that if the maker was of high status, it may have affected the value of their products. Detailed representations of textiles in art, such as Yaxchilan Lintel 24 or the Lagartero figurines (Eckholm 1979), are examples of the high level of skill and intricacy of clothing worn by the elite. Elaborately brocaded and embroidered designs may have been reserved for upper classes, as may the incorporation of materials such as feathers. Though such clothes were not necessarily everyday items, and palace scenes often show elite figures in less elaborate and relatively undecorated textiles as well (e.g., K8006 [Tremain 2017]).

Status probably also played a key part in who wore textiles of certain materials; it is often suggested that cotton was reserved for elites, while maguey or other coarse fibers were used for lower-status garments. This is based on Fray Diego Durán's observation of Aztec sumptuary laws: "Only the king is allowed to wear the fine mantles of cotton. . . . [T]he common people will not be allowed to wear cotton clothing . . . but only garments of maguey fibre" (Heyden and Horcasitas 1964, 131).

This is not to say that cotton was the only fiber worn by the upper classes. Archaeological analysis revealed that three of the four textiles found in Tomb 19 at Río Azul were manufactured from a plant fiber that was not cotton (Carlsen 1986, 147), and 58 percent of the fibers sampled from Cueva del Lazo in Chiapas (associated with high-status child burials) were a combination of cotton and agave (Domenici and Valenzuela 2016). As we have seen, coarse fibers are useful in belts, hair ribbons, headbands, footwear, and many other types of clothing; they simply require the correct kind of spindle whorl (McCafferty and McCafferty 2000; Parsons 2001).

The way in which textiles covered the body may also have had a relationship to status. Guernsey (1992, 59) proposed that the female huipil—a long garment that covered the shoulders, chest, and hips—was a modest textile that covered the body and was thus appropriate for a woman's (subordinate) position as caregiver to men. Stone (2011, 169) has also correlated body surface coverage to status, proposing that female garments that revealed the breasts were more commonplace among lower-class women. An alternative method of interpreting textiles is not in the amount of body surface they cover but the time, resources, and labor required to produce them. A huipil, because of its size, required more fibers to weave than a male loincloth, and therefore increased time was spent in its manufacture. The increased energy and resources dedicated to producing such garments may have heightened the status of women who wore them.

Ornamentation
Ornamenting the body included adorning it with jewelry, coloring it with pigments, and wearing specific items such as headdresses or footwear (see chapters 5–8 in this volume). The material from which a piece of ornamentation was produced has often been correlated to status. "Exotic" materials that can be accessed only through specific trade routes and materials that took many hours to manufacture are both associated with wealth and high social status. One of the most important materials in the production of jewelry was jadeite, not only because of its symbolic value (Taube 2005), but also because it was geographically restricted to the Motagua Valley in Guatemala (Foshag and Leslie 1955; Seitz et al. 2001) and difficult to procure and shape (Tremain 2014, 140). The appropriation of powerful animals is another indicator of high status, and the incorporation of jaguar skin into outfits was a mark of high status. Likewise, quetzal feathers are regarded as a marker of status because of the symbolic importance of the bird and the difficulty in procuring its feathers (Houston 1984; Taube 2005; Tremain 2016).

The presence of ornamentation in burials has often been used to interpret the status of interred individuals (Welsh 1988, 103). Healy, Awe, and Helmuth (2004) identified items such as jade jewelry, marine shells, and slate-backed pyrite mosaic mirrors among the attributes of regal burials. Unfortunately, as recognized by Fitzsimmons (2009, 87), there is tremendous variation in the number and form of these items within royal interments. A clearer association between such items and status is their size and weight. Large and cumbersome jewelry likely signified high status—much like the eight-and-a-half-pound necklace worn by Tikal ruler Jasaw Chan K'awiil in his tomb at Temple 1 (Trik 1963, 8).

Certain items of ornamentation have been recognized as "badges of social status" (R. Joyce 2001, 113). A well-known example is the *hu'n* or *sakhu'n* headband, long recognized to be an indicator of rulership (Fields 1991; see chapter 5 in this volume) and donned by rulers to signal their coronation (Looper 2003, 2). Houston, Stuart, and Taube (2006, 83) suggested that the metaphor of "bundling" a ruler at his accession may have given rise to the use of the headband to "wrap" the divine king in office. Another symbol of status appears to be the practice of piercing the septum, identified as a marker of royalty as well (figs. 10.1a–b; see chapter 6 in this volume; see also Houston, Stuart, and Taube 2006, 19).

Finally, there may have been a relationship between status and body paint (see chapter 3 in this volume). Certain colors likely had specific meanings attached to them, which possibly dictated when they were used. Although Landa (in Tozzer 1966 [1941], 89) did not necessarily emphasize the meanings attached to body paint—making only the generalized statement that the Maya "had the custom of painting their faces and bodies red. . . . [T]hey thought it very pleasing"—he did touch on some of the relationships between this practice and social and religious customs. For example, he points out the relationship between blue body paint and sacrifice (Tozzer 1966 [1941], 118). He also discusses in depth the practice of painting the body black with soot among young unmarried men up until their time of marriage and during periods of fasting (Tozzer 1966 [1941], 124–125, 152, 161). Black paint was washed away at the end of such fasts, followed by the application of a red ointment for celebrations related to the new year (1966 [1941], 152–153)—a practice seemingly mirrored on an eighth-century Maya mural at the site of Xultun (Rossi 2015, 61–65). In line with these observations, Mat-

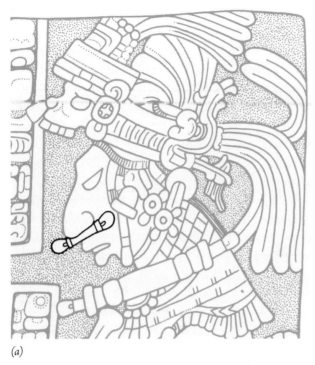

(a)

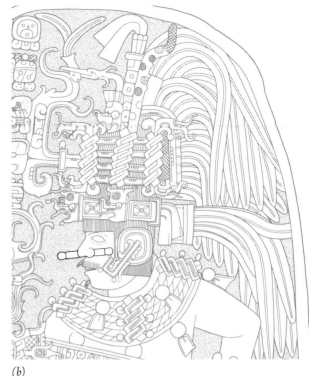

(b)

FIGURE 10.1. *Pierced septa: (a) detail of Yaxchilan Lintel 17 (drawing by Ian Graham, © President and Fellows of Harvard College, PM2004.15.6.5.16); and (b) detail of Ceibal Stela 10 (drawing by Ian Graham, © President and Fellows of Harvard College, PM2004.15.6.17.10).*

thew Looper (2010, 35) proposed that red body paint may have symbolized the east, warmth, and the powers of life and birth and was thus an appropriate color for such public ceremonies. Similarly, Knub's (2014) study of body paint within the royal court concluded that red was the most prevalent color, which she suggested could be used to emulate deities. However, this type of body modification does not appear to be exclusive to particular individuals. The Calakmul murals confirm that body paint was not restricted to elites (Vargas and Baqueiro 2012).

The use of cinnabar (a toxic sulfide of mercury) for coloring the bodies of interred individuals has long been recognized among the ancient Maya and is epitomized by the burial of Palenque's "Red Queen" (González Cruz 2000, 2011). Archaeometric studies of red pigments preserved inside of ceramics in funerary contexts

have revealed that the Maya created "recipes" consisting of cinnabar mixed with hematite—likely to mitigate risks associated with applying toxic mercury sulfide to the skin (Vázquez de Ágredos Pascual and Vidal Lorenzo 2017, 163). Thus, as well as color being an important factor in ornamenting the body, choice of mineral or material was undoubtedly associated with status.

Hair

Generally, high-status individuals are represented with tidy, bound hair. At sites such as Palenque, it appears that a common practice was to shave the sides of the head in horizontal cuts, giving a "stepped" appearance (fig. 10.2). Hair is rarely shown as completely shaved off, but baldness is a distinguishing feature of certain deities, such as God L and God M (Coe 1978, 16, 64; Martin 2015) and an individual that Hellmuth (1996) refers to as "the old patron of deer hunting" (see Pendergast 1966 for an example). Unkempt and unbound (or loosely bound) hair, often seen on depictions of prisoners (fig. 10.3a), is considered to be a marker of lost status (M. Robertson 1985a, 33). Houston (2001) has argued that carefully controlled appearances reflected morally appropriate behavior among the Maya and were in con-

FIGURE 10.2. *Detail of the Oval Palace Tablet at Palenque showing K'inich Janab Pakal's stepped hairstyle. Drawing by Cara Grace Tremain.*

trast to individuals with disheveled hair and contorted limbs. Messy hair likely signaled loss of self-control.

The decoration of hair with beads, ribbons, and other adornment may have been a marker of status as well. Beaded and decorated hair appears on portraits of rulers at Bonampak (Miller and Brittenham 2013, fig. 283) and Lacanha (e.g., panel 1), in addition to warriors on unprovenienced vases (e.g., K1403). Virginia Miller (2018) has recognized that beaded hair is a style associated with prisoners and sacrificial victims at Chichen Itza—similar to the image of a prisoner on a bone from Tikal (fig. 10.3a). Many of the examples of beaded hair at Chichen Itza are from murals, where individuals have yellow-colored hair. Miller (2018) suggests that light-colored hair was used to express otherness and perhaps even divinity. Elsewhere in Mesoamerica (e.g., the Cacaxtla murals [Brittenham 2015]), pictorial evidence also shows individuals with colored hair, demonstrating that altering its color was likely a common practice. Changing hair color may have been achieved naturally,

(a)

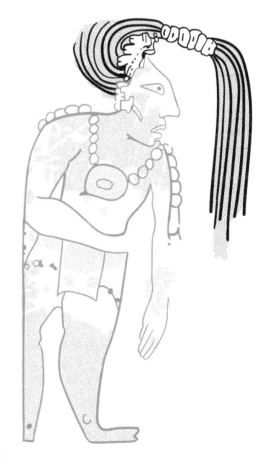

(b)

FIGURE 10.3. *Classic Maya men with long hair: (a) detail from a carved bone in Burial 116 at Tikal showing a prisoner with long, disheveled, beaded hair (drawing by Franco D. Rossi); and (b) detail of a polychrome painted vase from Burial 116 at Tikal showing a courtier with long, bound hair (drawing by Cara Grace Tremain, after Culbert 1993, fig. 75b).*

from too much sun exposure, or dyes might have been used as in some modern communities (see Cordry and Cordry 1968, pl. 5). Perhaps, as with body paint, specific colors marked status, but at present little is known about the meanings of ancient Maya hair color.

Body Modification

Cranial modification was perhaps the most discernible permanent body alteration, achieved by constricting and shaping the skulls of infants (Tiesler 2011). Tozzer reported that the Yukateko Maya believed "this custom . . . gives us a noble air, and our heads are thus better adapted to carry loads" (1966 [1941], 88). Consequently, cranial modification has long been assumed to be an indicator of high status. However, recent studies by Tiesler (2011, 124–125; 2014, 210) have demonstrated that there was no clear association between cranial modification and status, just as there was no clear favored artificial head shape among the Maya. She found more than 80 percent of pre-Columbian skulls are modified in some way, arguing that head shape may have communicated ethnic statements rather than status (Tiesler 2011, 118, 127).

Another body modification that left visibly lasting results was the alteration and decoration of teeth (Romero 1970). The Maya modified teeth by filing them into different shapes or drilling cavities into their surface and decorating them with inlays of jadeite, iron pyrite (hematite), or turquoise. The inlays were either set with a cement or fitted perfectly to the cavities drilled into the teeth. Alternatively, cavities were filled with a paste of powdered pyrite. Since teeth recovered from both high- and low-status burials exhibit evidence of modification (Romero 1970, 56–58; Williams and White 2006), there is little evidence to link tooth modification to status. Furthermore, Landa (in Tozzer 1966 [1941], 125) recorded that the Yukateko Maya considered tooth shaping to be "elegant," and it may thus have been associated with aesthetics rather than status.

Other body modifications included tattooing and scarification (Mayer 1981; see chapter 3 in this volume). The difference between the two practices cannot be easily discerned from iconography. The Maya may not have considered a strict division between the two, and they perhaps overlapped in meaning and symbolism. Landa

(in Tozzer 1966 [1941], 91, 124) described tattooing as both a punishment and a method of celebrating bravery, while Thompson (1946) proposed that tattooing and scarification were a privilege of persons of noble blood. Those with scars or tattoos were perhaps considered to have undergone death and rebirth (through practices of cutting/piercing and healing of the skin), even resembling a divine power that was limited to elites or nobles.

GENDER

Outside the discipline of archaeology, dress is one of the most heavily explored areas of gender identity (Barnes and Eicher 1992). It is no surprise then that dress has been one of the principal methods by which genders have been outlined in Maya studies—particularly because overt sexual characteristics tend to be de-emphasized pictorially (R. Joyce 1992, 1996, 2002). In rare cases, such as Protoclassic burial S.D.C117B-5 at Caracol, organic and inorganic dress items have also been used to study the relationship between dress and gender (Brown 2003).

Although there are plentiful representations of male gender in Maya imagery, the same cannot be said for females. As Proskouriakoff (1961) and Reese-Taylor et al. (2009) note, females only appear in the art and inscriptions of specific sites, and overall females occur in a very small percentage of royal court scenes (Tremain 2017, 181). Women are more frequently represented in figurine form, but heads are often separate from bodies when recovered archaeologically, so a full understanding of their attire is not possible (Looper 2014).

Some scholars have also explored "other" genders through dress. R. Joyce (1996) suggested that the muting of biological and sexual differences between males and females created a unified elite identity that created "other" genders. Looper (2002) has furthered this, proposing that rulers could claim an identity as a third gender through the use of the beaded-net costume. Houston, Stuart, and Taube (2006, 51–52) contend that claims for a third gender have no support because the costume of the Maize God has been misinterpreted; they argue that the costume related to a particular category of deity, not a blurring of genders.

Textiles

The textile garments worn by the Maya were strongly gender specific. Traditionally, those worn by females covered more of the body compared to the clothing worn by males. Huipils were worn exclusively by females, as were long garments tied under the arms that resemble modern sarongs. In contrast, male garments consisted of a loincloth, a long or short skirt, and (less frequently) a cape. The manufacture of textiles is also strongly linked to gender identity in Mesoamerica—particularly female gender (Brumfiel 1991, 2006; Chase et al. 2008; Hendon 2006; McCafferty and McCafferty 1991). Pictorial sources often demonstrate the close association between females and weaving (fig. 10.4), and ethnohistoric documents also link females to weaving and spinning (Tozzer 1966 [1941], 127). Indeed, even among modern Maya communities, one of the essential qualities for a wife is to be able to weave good clothes for herself and her husband (Vogt 1969, 192).

Archaeological evidence of textile manufacture is often found in the form of tools such as spindle whorls, needles, brocade picks, and awls (Hendon 1997). Recent evidence suggests that another tool used in the process of textile manufacture may have included "donut stones" (Tomasic 2012). Some tools, such as spindle whorls, are often recovered exclusively from female burials, as is the case at Uaxactun and Tikal (Chase et al. 2008). Other strong links to female gender include the bone needles reportedly recovered from the burial of a royal female at Naranjo (Dacus 2005). The needles were inscribed with *u puutz'* and *u puutz' baak* ("the needle of" and "the needle bone of"), along with the name of a female owner. Houston and Stuart (2001, 7) have cautioned that the inscriptions fail to tell us whether the female owner actually used the tools, yet they appear to be symbolic of female gender.

Despite strong correlates between certain tools and females, Halperin (2008, 112) complicates this seemingly straightforward association by pointing out that items associated with textile production have also been found in male burials. Bone awls were recovered from the Hunal Tomb at Copan, which is thought to contain the remains of male ruler K'inich Yax K'uk' Mo (Bell, Canuto, and Sharer 2004, 133), and bone pins occur in male and female burials at Caracol (Chase et al. 2008,

FIGURE 10.4. *Female weaver in the Madrid Codex. Drawing by Cara Grace Tremain after Villacorta and Villacorta 1993, folio 79c.*

134–135). Additionally, needles have been recovered from male burials at Altun Ha (e.g., Tombs A-1/1, B-4/7, and B-4/2 [Pendergast 1969, 1979, 1982]) and Copan (e.g., Burial 37-1 [Bell, Canuto, and Sharer 2004]).

The apparent association between males and textile tools reminds us that while females were usually associated with weaving, males were involved in other stages of textile manufacture (Halperin 2016, 435–436). For example, Fray Bernardino de Sahagún (Dibble and Anderson 1961, 35) observed male tailors in Aztec Mexico who designed, stitched, and embellished clothing. Additionally, although they have suggested there were seamstresses rather than tailors in the Maya region, Clark and Houston (1998) recognize that males were involved in the process of planting and growing cotton as well as creating dyes and colorants.

Ornamentation

Despite specific textile garments aligning with certain genders, it is unclear if this was the case for body ornamentation. R. Joyce (2000a, 74) has observed that "women wear ornaments indistinguishable from those of men on their head, hands, and feet" on monumental media, and Bruhns (1988, 113) noticed that jewelry or other dress such as footwear does not seem to differ much between males and females. However, the author found that royal court scenes reveal a more noticeable nuance; females do not tend to wear the same range of headdresses or ear ornamentation as males, nor do they don certain types of jewelry such as pectorals, collars (see chapter 7 in this volume), or nose ornamentation (Tremain 2017).

Burial data are also ambiguous in terms of revealing gendered distinctions in ornamentation. Welsh (1988, 146) determined that male and female burials were comparably furnished at many sites in the Maya lowlands, and Haviland (1997) reported that most grave goods at Tikal were placed in both male and female graves. Similarly, burial data from Lamanai and Altun Ha demonstrate that female elite burials are almost as frequent as elite male burials and occur with similar grave goods of jade and shell ornaments, copper bells, and sometimes gold (Graham 1991, 473–474). C. Robertson verified these patterns in her study of burials from Pacbitun, suggesting that "gender as expressed in burial treatment . . . may represent a fluid ideology of gender" (2010, ii).

A stronger association with gender might be seen with *Spondylus* shells, which have been considered to be symbolic of female gender (Ardren 2002, 76). Landa's (in Tozzer 1966 [1941], 106) description of young girls wearing shells around their loins has often been taken as evidence that the placement of shells on the waist of an individual signifies female gender (e.g., Trachman and Valdez 2006; see also chapter 3 in this volume). Individual 12 from the north wall of the San Bartolo murals has been identified as a female based in part on "a spondylus shell belt piece" (Saturno, Taube, and Stuart 2005, 34), for example, despite wearing a garment in the shape of a loincloth (see fig. 3.2a). Burial 61 at El Perú-Waka' also contained the remains of an adult with a *Spondylus* shell on the lower torso. Based on the shell and an alabaster vase (see below), the remains have been interpreted as Lady K'abel (El Perú-Waka' Archaeological Project 2012).

Spondylus shells have also been found in the pelvic region of interred males, such as in Tomb 4 at Calakmul (Vargas et al. 1999, 53) and Tomb B-4/2 at Altun Ha (Pendergast 1982, fig. 57 and pl. 35). Rather than being solely representative of gender, *Spondylus* shells in burials may have been representative of the necessary funerary paraphernalia for the transition to the watery un-

derworld (Fitzsimmons 2009, 90). Alternatively, since "gender relations were surely dynamic and probably varied from place to place" (Haviland 1997, 10), perhaps *Spondylus* shells were associated with a specific gender during a certain time period or life stage.

Hair

Hair is another aspect of dress that may be associated with gender identity. Locks of long hair are often considered to be feminine attributes among the ancient Maya (Bruhns 1988, 112; Saturno, Taube, and Stuart 2005, 38)—a relationship that is strengthened by the glyph for lady or woman (*ix-* or *ixik*), which often has a long strand of hair (Proskouriakoff 1961, fig. 1). Indeed, the association between hair and female gender seems in some instances to be stronger than other dress items—as is the case with Goddess I in the Dresden Codex (Tremain 2013, 10). The alabaster vase found inside Burial 61 at El Perú-Waka', which has a brief glyphic text that names its owner as Lady K'abel, depicts a mature individual with a "strand of hair in front of her ear" (El Perú-Waka' Archaeological Project 2012) and is another instance that associates female gender with long hair.

Long hair has also been used as a way to identify the individuals in Drawing 18 at Naj Tunich cave; Drawing 18 depicts two individuals embracing one another. Both are considered to be biologically male, but one is considered socially female because "the queue of hair trailing down her back is a conventional sign of female gender" (Stone 1995, 145). The strand of hair may be related to a satirical performance (Taube 1989; Taube and Taube 2009) or may be related to Landa's observation that the Yukateko Maya "wore their hair long like women" (Tozzer 1966 [1941], 88).

Despite the seemingly strong correlation between hair length and female gender, long hairstyles were not reserved exclusively for women. As previously discussed, male prisoners are often shown with long unbound hair—such as the captive on an incised bone from Tikal (fig. 10.3a). Noncaptive males are also shown with long hair, as demonstrated on a vase from Tikal (fig. 10.3b) and a vase from Actun Balam cave (Pendergast 1966). Although not as long in length, the hair on several male figures on a vase from Ratinlixul seems notably similar (Mason 1943, pl. LII). Thus, the assumption that "women wore their hair longer than did men" (Schele and Miller 1986, 67) is unsupported, and in fact it seems that males and females could share the same hairstyles (as demonstrated by M. Robertson 1985a).

Facial hair is a more secure identifier of gender than length of head hair, and various pictorial sources show males with facial hair (fig. 10.1b). Schele and Mathews (1999, 145), however, claimed that beards were a rare feature among Maya men and proposed that the long beard worn by Waxaklahun Ubaah K'awiil on Copan Stela C was false. This may be because Landa (in Tozzer 1966 [1941], 88) observed that the Maya of Yucatán "did not grow beards . . . [;] their mothers burned their faces in their childhood with hot cloths, so as to keep the beard from growing." Tozzer also noted that men were "accustomed to pull out the beard with tweezers" (1966 [1941], 88).

Body Modification

Tiesler (2011, 2014) has determined that cranial modification was not a gender-distinguishing type of dress because both male and female skulls were shaped using the same techniques, and no one shape was used exclusively by either sex. However, both R. Joyce (2001, 125–128) and Tiesler (2014, 4) have explained that most practitioners of cranial modification were female, and the practice of altering skull shape may have inadvertently indicated female gender. As for tooth modification, although more men than women appear to have had their front teeth inlaid, there is no clear correlation to gender (Tiesler 2014, 21–22; Williams and White 2006). Dental filing appears to have begun in the Early Preclassic, whereas dental inlay was introduced in the Middle Preclassic (Williams and White 2006, 139). Therefore, differences in tooth modification may have been associated with certain time periods rather than gender. In terms of the relationship between gender and impermanent forms of body modification, Landa (in Tozzer 1966 [1941], 89, 91) observed that both men and women were tattooed, and it does not appear that body modifications were necessarily restricted to specific genders.

AGE

Age is perhaps the least common identity to have been explored through the study of dress, even in modern

studies (Twigg 2007). Unfortunately, representations of individuals at different stages of life in Maya art are uncommon. The ability to identify age categories other than adults is hindered by the available evidence, which show an extremely limited variation in age (R. Joyce 2000a, 122). Scholars seem to have applied categories of young, old, and everyone else in between to their studies of the ancient Maya, despite modern Maya communities recognizing many differences between life stages (Vogt 1969).

Age has often been interpreted from the size of individuals in Maya art, or bodily form and appearance, rather than dress. Studies of elderly individuals throughout Mesoamerica have relied on artistic conventions of sagging and wrinkled skin, sunken eyes, toothless mouths, and prominent cheekbones, jaw, or stomach (Houston, Stuart, and Taube 2006, 16, 49; Joralemon 1981). For example, the face on the alabaster vase discovered inside Burial 61 at El Perú-Waka' is thought to resemble an aged Lady K'abel because of the "lined face" (El Perú-Waka' Archaeological Project 2012). In contrast to the details used to identify individuals of advanced age, the identification of children has usually relied on their small size. The difference in size between adults and children can often be seen in Maya sculpture (e.g., Piedras Negras Stela 3 [Graham and von Euw 1975, 17]), and figurines (e.g., Halperin 2014, fig. 3.37; Triadan 2014, 286–287)—though figurines of children themselves appear to have been uncommon.

Whereas studies of aged deities have long been incorporated into scholarly studies of the Maya, studies of childhood in Mesoamerica are somewhat recent (Ardren and Hutson 2006; R. Joyce 2000b). This is surprising, considering it has long been recognized that children held important roles in ancient Maya society. For example, Pakal took the throne at Palenque at the age of twelve (Stuart and Stuart 2008, 149), and a woman dubbed the Lady of Tikal appears to have coruled the site at the age of six (Martin 1999; Martin and Grube 2008, 38). Additionally, young nobles, dubbed *ch'ok* ("sprout"—relating them to the maize plant), were involved in various roles within the social, political, and economic arenas at Maya sites (Houston 2009, 2018; Miller and Martin 2004, 26).

In addition to their political importance, children also had symbolic importance. Throughout Mesoamerica there is archaeological evidence for child sacrificial rites (Berrelleza and Balderas 2006; Fitzsimmons 2009, 93; Follensbee 2006, 266), and ethnohistoric sources describe the killing of children (Chamberlain 1948, 241; Roys 1943, 27, 81; Tozzer 1966 [1941], 116). Iconographic sources present evidence for infant sacrifice and child bloodletting rites in the Maya region as well (Miller and Martin 2004, fig. 11; Houston 2018, 96–114; Taube 1994, 669).

Textiles

An observable pattern between textiles and age appears to be their absence on the bodies of infants and young children. Indeed, Landa (in Tozzer 1966 [1941], 125) observed that children were not clothed until the age of four or five. Two figurines from Altar de Sacrificios show a female holding a small child; one appears to be completely naked, while the other has ornamentation and appears to be clothed (Willey 1972, figs. 34b, 34g)—suggesting that the child without dress is younger. Similarly, R. Joyce (2014) has observed that aged figurines from Playa de los Muertos, Honduras, wear more cloth than youthful figurines.

The process of textile manufacture may also have been associated with different age categories. R. Joyce (2008, 94) recognized that for young girls in Aztec Mexico, learning to weave embodied the transition to adulthood. Moreover, Sahagún (in Dibble and Anderson 1969, 201) reported that infant males in Aztec Mexico were provided with tools such as a bow and arrow and clothes in the form of a breechclout and cape, while infant girls were provided with tools for spinning fibers and clothes in the form of a skirt and shift.

Ornamentation

Some of the richest deposits of jewelry in the Formative period are from infant and child burials—though it is impossible to be sure whether young individuals from lavish burials were so attired when alive (Looper 2014, 419). However, in general, burial data does not show a consistent relationship between ornamentation and young individuals. At K'axob, offerings of shell and jade beads, shell pendants, and shell tinklers were found among burials of all ages, but those who died under the age of five generally lacked offerings (Storey and McAnany 2006). In contrast, juveniles at Pacbitun re-

ceived adornments only if they were interred alongside adults (C. Robertson 2010).

The inconsistency in the dress associated with young individuals in burials is upheld in Maya art. Evidence of children and adults wearing similar dress can be seen in Yaxchilan Lintel 2, where Bird Jaguar IV and his young son, Shield Jaguar IV (labeled with his childhood name, "Chelew Chan K'inich," in the lintel's text), wear similar headdresses (fig. 10.5a; Martin and Grube 2008, 133). Similarly, R. Joyce (2000a, 122) has recognized that figurines often (though not always) represent children costumed identically to adults. In contrast, on Yaxchilan Lintel 52 Bird Jaguar IV and his son wear different headdresses (fig. 10.5b).

The size of jewelry and other ornamentation may be an indication of age. For example, R. Joyce (2001, 115) has argued that earspools are one of the major markers of adult status in Postclassic Mesoamerican societies (see also chapter 6 in this volume). The diameter of earspools may directly relate to age, with small-shaft diameters likely used early in the process of widening the pierced hole during childhood (Follensbee 2006, 267). Respectively, it is likely that as the size of earspools increased, so too did the age of the wearer. Correspondingly, very large beads for necklaces or very heavy headdresses were probably worn by adults rather than children.

Finally, the Maya may have associated heirlooms with particular age categories (R. Joyce 2000c). Examples of heirlooms include an Olmec pectoral excavated from a Late Classic period burial at Nakum (Źrałka et al. 2011), a pair of earplugs in Early Classic Tomb 4 at Calakmul that feature incised glyphs in an earlier calligraphic style (Vargas et al. 1999, 53), and helmet bib pendants, which date stylistically to the Preclassic (see Proskouriakoff 1974, 11), in Early Classic caches at Blue Creek (Guderjan 2007, 33). Body ornamentation like this, kept for generations, may have been related to particular stages of life among the Maya.

Hair

Differences in hairstyles by age may have existed among the Maya, especially since Landa (in Tozzer 1966 [1941], 125–126) observed that adult hairstyles were different from those of children (with the latter including "horns" worn by young girls until they reached a certain age). R. Joyce (2001, 122) has observed images of children

(a)

(b)

FIGURE 10.5. (a) Yaxchilan Lintel 2 showing Bird Jaguar IV and his son wearing similar headdresses (drawing by Ian Graham, © President and Fellows of Harvard College, PM2004.15.6.5.2); and (b) Yaxchilan Lintel 52 showing Bird Jaguar IV and his son wearing different headdresses (drawing by Ian Graham, © President and Fellows of Harvard College, PM2004.15.6.6.26).

in Mesoamerica with uncut and unbound hair. Allowing the hair to grow freely may be associated in some way to the belief held by highland Guatemalan communities: that cutting the hair of young boys affects their knowledge, reason, and speech (Duncan and Hofling 2011, 203).

Facial hair was likely a strong indicator of age for the ancient Maya, undoubtedly indicating puberty and the growing body—thus distinguishing young men from children. Indeed, elsewhere in Mesoamerica there was a relationship between facial hair and age as the Nahuatl terms *ye tentzonixhua telpuchtli* and *ye tentzonquiza telpuchtli* (young man whose beard is sprouting) help to demonstrate (Austin 1988, 286). However, as previously discussed, Landa observed that boys in Yucatán had their faces burned to prevent beards from growing. Perhaps then, beard growth was a regional custom or custom of a particular time period.

Body Modification

There seems to be little evidence linking tooth modification to status or gender, yet there is an association with age. Romero (1970, 55) observed that while it is not a practice exclusive to adults, it is rarer for children to have modified teeth. He cautioned that it is difficult to estimate age from human remains, so the osteological data may be unable to reveal trends in relation to children of different ages. As an example of this, the teeth recovered from Burial 2 at Piedras Negras had dental inlays, but excavators could not be sure if the individual was a child or young adult (W. Coe 1959, 122–123). Even in instances where modification to deciduous teeth has been found (e.g., Braswell and Pitcavage 2009), it has been considered a postmortem practice.

In contrast, cranial modification was exclusively limited to infants, because after the age of two or three years, the skull loses flexibility and malleability (Tiesler 2011, 118). Another practice that was enacted on individuals at a very young age was crossing the eyes (Tozzer 1966 [1941], 88). Although such modifications were limited to infants, they do not seem to have been used principally to communicate age or youth. Both were permanent body modifications that remained with individuals at all stages of life and would not have visually signified one particular age category over another.

Finally, tattooing, like tooth modification, appears to be related to adulthood rather than childhood. Landa (in Tozzer 1966 [1941], 91) explained that young men do not tattoo much until they are married, and R. Joyce (2001, 122) has observed that images of children in Mesoamerica are represented without tattoos. Houston, Stuart, and Taube (2006, 18–19) have suggested that, in order to avoid distortion of design that might result from physical growth, tattooing was probably carried out on fairly mature bodies—perhaps beginning at puberty in preparation for marriage. If the relationship to marriage is accurate, perhaps tattooing signified not age itself but sexual and social maturity. In contrast, Austin (1988, 288) explains that among the ancient Nahuas, girls were marked with small cuts on their breasts and hips in ceremonies to the deities. This may relate scarification to the protection of children, rather than identity.

CONCLUSION

Of the dress items discussed here, those that appear to be most strongly associated with identity were textiles. Garments clearly communicated male and female gender, and spinning and weaving were strongly associated with females of all ages. Elaborately decorated textiles marked high status, and lack of clothing appears to have marked both low status and young age. The materials used to manufacture garments were also likely associated with status, with cotton marking high status and coarse fibers marking low status (although the latter were incorporated into high-status clothing as well). However, textile tools have been found in both male and female burials, so alone they cannot be used as markers of identity.

Body ornamentation was associated with identity as well, but in a less clear manner. Items such as the Jester God headband, exotic materials, large size, and substantial weight all appear to be markers of high status, but they do not indicate other aspects of identity. While the size and weight of ornamentation may have been smaller and lighter for children, this was likely the result of practicality rather than an intentional index of young age. However, the absence of body painting for children may have been a marker of youth.

The appearance and style of hair was another dress form associated with aspects of identity. High-status individuals appear to have worn their hair in a tidy, bound manner, while lower-status individuals often had unkempt hair. Decorated hair may also have been related to identity, perhaps in the form of marking "otherness." Facial hair appears to have been associated with male gender and maturity, but it is not clear if it was grown to intentionally communicate these aspects of identity. What is clear is that length of hair was not a marker of gender, since both males and females could wear their hair long.

Finally, body modifications have long been considered strong markers of identity. Recent research has demonstrated that cranial modification was shared by individuals of all statuses, genders, and ages and was unlikely to have been an intentional marker of these kinds of identity. Similarly, while perhaps less common among youth, tooth shaping and decoration do not have any strong association with identity. Tattooing and scarification also appear to have been less common among young age groups and may have marked other identities via design or color.

Dress had a myriad of meanings and was used in a variety of ways—some to mark important aspects of identity such as status, gender, and age, and others not. Certain dress items were likely more strongly associated with aesthetics and in this sense should be considered as markers of beauty. Continued study of dress is an important means of learning about the people who made, wore, traded, and cherished items of clothing and adornment in the ancient Maya world.

CHAPTER 11

The Moving Body

MALLORY E. MATSUMOTO

The living body is a moving body, constantly transitioning between varying stages of activity and rest. The dress in which we adorn our bodies and the objects that we carry with them are necessarily involved in that movement as well. To express such movements, Classic Mayan speakers would have mobilized what linguists refer to as positional verbs, a class of verbal roots characteristic of Mayan languages that canonically denote a physical position, quality, or state of being (see, e.g., Kaufman 1990, 45). Compared to the hundreds of positional roots attested in many modern Mayan languages (e.g., England 1983, 78–83), precious few are preserved in the hieroglyphic record (Bricker 1986, 160–165), of which the most relevant to the movements described in this chapter are *chum*, "sit," and *wa'*, "stand upright." The full range of standardized Classic Maya movements cannot be covered here, and even the few typical cases discussed below are treated only in brief. But by highlighting select motions of special social and ritual significance, this chapter draws attention to the need to consider the context in which all of the accessories addressed in this volume—objects borne by a living body—would have been worn or used and how ensembles of objects may have acquired additional, collective significance when used in a particular activity.

HUNTING

As a pursuit that largely occurred in the wild territory that was spatially and conceptually distant from the safe, socially ordered settlement, hunting implicated both ritually established and situationally improvised movements (e.g., Taube 2003; Wisdom 1940, 72–73, 426). Scenes of ancient Maya hunting are known primarily from portable, painted objects, most of which are unprovenienced; the activity was apparently not of the nature to be regularly recorded on public monuments, apart from a few exceptions from the northern lowlands (Colas 2006; Proskouriakoff 1950, 165; Stone 1995, 238; e.g., Voss and Kremer 1998, fig. 1). Known glyphic expressions related to hunting, too, are scarce, representing a handful of attestations of *aj chij* (hunter; lit., "deer person") and of spearing (*jul*) prey (Justeson 1984, 349). Archaeological evidence of the hunt has been largely limited to projectile points (Wiseman 1983, 159), the occasional conch trumpet (M. Coe 1982, 120–123, fig. 163), and faunal remains of hunters' quarry.

The constellation of participants likely differed by activity. Pre-Columbian iconography and ethnographic comparison suggest that hunting of deer in particular was a collective undertaking (Wisdom 1940, 71–73). Thus, in addition to the standard motions implicated in tracking and taking prey, it would have required some form of communication among the participants, perhaps through hand gestures (Houston, cited in Doyle 2012, 133). Individual hunters are recognizable by their distinctive headgear, often a wide-brimmed, sombrero-like hat or an animal-shaped headdress (table 11.1), and their accessories, most commonly conch-shell trumpets

TABLE II.I. *Elements of bodily adornment commonly depicted on Classic Maya hunters*

FEATURE		EXAMPLE	CITATION
Body paint		K1373	
Clothing	loincloth	El Perú-Waka' figurine	Pérez Robles 2010, fig. 2.16
	skirt	K4546	
Footgear	bare feet	K1226	
	sandals	K1116	
Headgear	wide-brimmed hat	K4151	
	animal-shaped headdress	K5534	
Jewelry	neck and ear ornaments	Tabi stela	Voss and Kremer 1998, fig. 1

FIGURE II.I. *Hunter butchering deer on page 40b of the Madrid Codex. Drawing by Cara Grace Tremain after Brasseur de Bourbourg (1869, pl. XVII).*

FIGURE II.2. *Hunter carrying deer on page 41a of the Madrid Codex. Drawing by Cara Grace Tremain after Brasseur de Bourbourg (1869, pl. XVI).*

and spears or other weapons (fig. 11.1; K0771; K4805; K4922; Pérez Robles 2010, fig. 2.16). Some successful hunters are shown bearing bundled animals, usually deer, on their backs (fig. 11.2; K0808; see also Pérez Robles 2010, fig. 2.14). Others wear distinctive body paint, which is thought to represent camouflage or scent applied to deceive their prey (Houston 2010; Taube 2003, 473). Otherwise, hunters tend to be sparsely dressed in loincloths or longer skirts (*pih*) (table 11.1). With few exceptions, their upper bodies are noticeably bare of

TABLE 11.2. *Examples of Mayan-language verbs denoting hunting activities*

ACTIVITY	EXAMPLE (LANGUAGE)	CITATION
hunting (general)	*korm* (Ch'orti')	Hull 2005, 63; Wisdom 1950, 103
hunting with a spear or other thrown weapon	*huri* (Ch'orti')	Wisdom 1950, 80; compare Maxwell and Hill 2006, 101; Tozzer 1966 [1941], 121
hunting with a trap	*caje'* (Chontal)	Keller and Luciano 1997, 328
	nup' (Yukateko)	Barrera Vásquez 1980, 590; compare Vail 1997; Wisdom 1940, 74–77
hunting as a physical act of grabbing or capturing	*chuki* (Ch'orti')	Hull 2005, 24; Pérez Martínez et al. 1996, 49; Wisdom 1950, 50
	chuk (Yukateko)	Barrera Vásquez 1980, 111
	*chuq (Proto-Mayan)	Kaufman 2003, 904

jewelry or clothing, allowing them to move easily and discreetly through the landscape.

Hunters are generally represented either in the act of chasing and capturing an animal, butchering their quarry, or, more frequently, in a standing or walking pose that suggests that they are in transit to or from the hunt (K0771; K1373; Pohl 1983, fig. 3.2). The range of potential activities implicated in hunting is more aptly expressed in the variety of terms in modern Mayan languages for hunting activities (table 11.2). Each of these verbs implicates a difference not only in equipment employed but also in physical proximity and engagement, according contextual factors such as type of game pursued. For instance, most, though not all (compare K1991), uses of the verb *chuk* "capture," refer to human victims, alluding to a conceptual divergence between hunting animals and intrahuman violence. Nonetheless, the hunt served as metaphor for warfare, as well as for courtship and sexual pursuit (Braakhuis 2001; Looper 2009, 56; Taube 1988). In addition, it symbolized elite power and authority in pre-Columbian Maya society, as illustrated by depictions of rulers dressed in hunting attire, particularly when presiding over capture and sacrifice events (Staller and Carrasco 2010, 17; Taube 1988; e.g., Kerr 1992, 112, fig. 7.7; Taube 2003, 473–474; see also Pohl 1981, 524–525).

WARFARE

Of all forms of aggressive violence and indeed of purposeful movement generally, warfare is one of the most prevalent in Classic Maya hieroglyphic and iconographic representation. Warriors' generally sparse clothing reflects their need to execute rapid, coordinated motions (table 11.3). Various images from monumental and portable art depict the fierce thrusting and throwing of spears (*jub*, "fall; take down"), hand-to-hand combat, wrestling, and decapitation (*ch'ak*, "ax; cut; decapitate") that accompanied many military campaigns (Grube, cited in Stuart 1995, 311; Orejel 1990; e.g., Bonampak Room 2, Miller and Brittenham 2013, fig. 172; Itzimte Stela 12, von Euw 1977, 29; Lothrop 1952, figs. 32, 34; K1082). Simple loincloths leave many soldiers' torsos and legs free, with their feet sandaled or bare. Nonetheless, some wear more elaborate skirts or tunics, which may have served a protective function in some cases (Ethnologisches Museum Ident. Nr. IV Ca 48207 and IV Ca 4938).

Bodily adornment is often limited to a headband, a headdress (fig. 11.3)—including animal-shaped ones like those worn by hunters (see Taube 1988)—or the rare Teotihuacan-style mosaic helmet (*ko'haw*); body paint; and a modest quantity of neck and ear ornaments. In war scenes, even those taking place on open waters (Houston 2019, figs. 2–3; Lothrop 1952, fig. 35), the fighters are turning and twisting, arms raised, elbows and knees bent to indicate a bodies in motion (K2206; Yaxchilan Lintel 8, I. Graham and von Euw 1977, 27). The chaos of the battlefield embodied in the combatants' frenetic movements would have been augmented in some cases by musical instruments, particularly drums and trumpets, sounding during combat or marches (Miller 1988; e.g., K5027; Bonampak Room 2, Miller and Brittenham 2013, fig. 172).

Such dynamism is particularly common in images on portable media and murals (K2036; Chichen Itza, Upper Temple of the Jaguars, Coggins 1984, figs. 18–19). Carved monumental representations, in turn, tend to be more static, often focusing on images of the victors or of captives taken in battle (Piedras Negras Panel 15, Clancy 2009, fig. 5.1; Coba Stela 1, I. Graham and von Euw 1997, 21–22; though cf. Bonampak Lintels 1–3, Miller and Brittenham 2013, figs. 45–47; Kabah jambs, Proskouriakoff 1950, figs. 103a–b). They also contrast in this respect with illustrations of hunters pursuing animal prey, in which even those actively engaged in killing or butchering tend to hold a more erect posture or bend stiffly at the waist, with less visual emphasis on the mobility of the knees compared to combatants (K1373; K5857; though cf. Pohl 1983, fig. 3.9).

Yet warriors also appear in less frenetic, more restrained poses, as when performing a dance (K1229; Itzimte Stela 3, von Euw 1977, 11), marching in procession (K1206; K1403), or calmly standing or sitting at attention while observing a sacrifice or other ritual (K2781; K3469; Bonampak Room 2, North Wall, Miller and Brittenham 2013, fig. 190). In these latter contexts, they are particularly likely to be elaborately dressed in heavy jewelry, backracks (*paat pih*) (see chapter 1; Tokovinine 2008, 281), capes, or larger headdresses that would have been unwieldy in active combat (table 11.3).

No war costume was functionally complete without weapon and shield in hand (K2036; Itzimte Stela 12, von Euw 1977, 29). The value placed on these implements is even documented in titles used to honor outstanding warriors, such as *baah took'*, "head flint," or *baah pakal*, "head shield," which linked their prowess to specific instruments that they wielded (Houston 2008). The weapons wielded included clubs, axes, slingstones, spears, lances, and Central Mexican–inspired atlatls (spear-throwers), which, with the exception of the latter, were mostly designed for close combat (Hassig 1992, 96–97; e.g., K0971; Díaz del Castillo 2008, 5; Tozzer 1966 [1941], 121–122). Shields, which are only rarely illustrated before the Late Classic, were largely either small, round, and rigid or large, rectangular, and flexible (Hassig 1992, 95–96; e.g., fig. 11.3; K2503; Miller

TABLE 11.3. *Elements of bodily adornment commonly depicted on Classic Maya warriors*

FEATURE		EXAMPLE	CITATION
Body paint		K5124	
Clothing	loincloth	Naranjo figurine	Halperin 2014, fig. 4.6a
	skirt	Yaxchilan Lintel 8	Graham and von Euw 1977, 27
	tunic	K2352	
	cape	Naranjo Stela 30	Graham 1978, 79
Footgear	bare feet	K0503	
	sandals	Chichen Itza Gold Disk F	Lothrop 1952, fig. 34
Headgear	headband	K1116	
	headdress	K9063	
	headdress (large)	Uaxactun Stela 5	Graham 1986, 143
	mosaic helmet (*ko'haw*)	Piedras Negras Panel 2	Miller and Martin 2004, pl. 109
Jewelry	neck and ear ornaments (sparse)	Unprovenienced figurine	Miller and Martin 2004, pl. 112
	neck and ear ornaments (abundant)	Yaxchilan Lintel 16	Graham and von Euw 1977, 41
Backrack		La Corona Panel 1	Stuart, Canuto, and Barrientos 2015, fig. 5

it, too, in lieu of the burdensome, stifling casques and cuirasses they had brought from home (Díaz del Castillo 2012, 8, 21, 41–42).

It should be noted, however, that the precise composition of a warrior's outfit varied across time and space. For example, Linda Schele and David Freidel (1990, 146–148) note that the Teotihuacan-inspired war costume, with its distinctive balloon headdress adorned with bird feathers, first appears in Tikal and its environs in the late fourth century AD before spreading to other Maya sites (fig. 11.4; Estrada-Belli et al. 2009, figs. 6, 12). Monumental depictions of combat in Chichen Itza also indicate that synchronic differences in costume could be salient identifiers between opponents on the battlefield, in this case presumably between local Mayas and individuals designated as foreign or nonlocal (Ringle 2009; Hassig 1992, 125; Lothrop 1952, 37–44). In contrast, artisans at some sites, such as Palenque and Tonina in the western Maya region, only rarely thema-

FIGURE 11.3. *Jaina-style figurine of standing warrior. Photograph courtesy of the Art Institute of Chicago (inventory no. 1963.272), CC0 Public Domain Designation.*

and Martin 2004, pls. 110–112). Warriors could maximize their combative potential by selectively employing a given form: big, flexible shields appear to have been particularly popular among spear users, whereas those wielding clubs and axes tended to carry more modest circular shields (Hassig 1992, 96). The padded cotton armor that Maya warriors were wearing at the time of European contact was so effective at resisting penetration by razor-sharp obsidian and chert points—and simultaneously light enough to bear in the hot and humid tropics—that the Spaniards themselves eventually adopted

FIGURE 11.4. *Teotihuacan-style war costume with balloon headdress on the upper portion of Piedras Negras Stela 35. Drawing by Nicholas Carter.*

tized warfare and warriors in their monumental iconography (Benson 1985, 158).

Nonetheless, one aspect of this thematic complex that was especially prolific in monumental representations was a key human outcome of war: captives. Scenes of *chuk* (capture) acts, which are particularly common on monuments from sites in the western Maya area, including Tonina (see I. Graham and Mathews 1996), usually show the captor looming over the fallen, categorically male *baak* (bone; captive). The latter's physical position reveals his subordination: he is typically on or in the act of falling to the ground, a fistful of his hair held tightly in the conqueror's hand, his limbs fastened in skeins of rope (K6414; La Mar Stela 3, Golden and Scherer 2015, fig. 1; Bonampak Room 2, North Wall, Miller and Brittenham 2013, fig. 125). Later episodes may represent the victorious warrior presenting bound captives to his overlord (fig. 11.5; K6650), often as a prelude to their eventual sacrifice (K0593; K0680; K3059). Clothing, or rather lack thereof, is a salient index of captive status, as hostages are usually shown having been partially or fully stripped of their jewelry and dress, some also bound around their necks (see Houston, Stuart, and Taube 2006, 202–226; e.g., fig. 11.5; Coba Stela 20, I. Graham and von Euw 1997, 60; Ixkun Stela 1, I. Graham 1980, 138–139). Many captives on monuments are named by glyphic captions on their bodies, which, unlike those of noble persons, were open surfaces for scribal inscription (Houston, Stuart, and Taube 2006, 204–205; e.g., fig. 11.5; Tonina Monument 83, I. Graham and Mathews 1996, 113). Images of captive domination also provide the few illustrations of women in contexts of warfare, lavishly dressed and standing atop (male) captives on a dozen early-seventh- to early-eighth-century stelae from Calakmul in southern Campeche, Naachtun and Naranjo in the Peten, and Coba in northern Yucatán (Fritzler 2005; Reese-Taylor et al. 2009).

BALL PLAYING

A more strictly ritualized and spatially confined form of violence was the ball game. The sanctioned combat implicated in playing ball (*pitz*) in designated ball courts provided popular entertainment and facilitated sociopolitical negotiations (Fox 1996; Gillespie 1991, 342–344; Taube and Zender 2009, 175–178; Zender

2004b). The Classic Maya ballplayer is known to us today primarily from iconographic sources, particularly depictions on carved monuments and painted ceramics (see, e.g., Cohodas 1991, 255ff). Although the precise rules likely varied by region, era, and even type of ball court, the game's fundamental aspects have been reconstructed (Cohodas 1991, 251–255; Taladoire 2001, 98). Two individuals or teams endeavored to keep a bouncing rubber ball in motion by deflecting it toward the opposition, an action that, at least in the game's most common form among the Maya, required using only certain body parts other than the head, hands, or feet (Ekholm 1991, 243; Taladoire 2001, 100). The pose in which players are typically depicted reflects this feature of the game: facing and kneeling to one side as if crouching to engage with a ball that, if shown, appears in front of them (Proskouriakoff 1950, 109; e.g., K2731; K3842; La Corona Element 13, K2882). That the direction in which they face indicates their preferred side of the body for play is suggested by the typical position of their single kneepad, a bundle of what appears to have been cloth or another malleable material bound to the knee of the kneeling leg for protection during play (Ekholm 1991, 244; Proskouriakoff 1950, 84, 145, fig. 129). Points could be earned by deflecting the ball into a designated end zone or by maneuvering it through a small ring installed in one of the court's side walls (Miller and Houston 1987, 47).

Hieroglyphic and iconographic references to the ball game indicate that participants were usually young or mature adults, a reasonable bias when considering the dangers that the heavy ball and violent moves inherent to the game would present to children or the elderly (e.g., Coe 2003, 197–198). Most of their outfit, like the kneepads, was designed to allow nimble movement while concurrently protecting vulnerable body parts from injury (table 11.4). Ballplayers' characteristic yokes or girdles of leather, wood, and cloth are tied around the waist to protect their midsection (Ekholm 1991, 243–244; Jones 1985, 44; Shook and Marquis 1996, 19). These, too, are frequently oriented with the bulk of the padding on the kneeling side (K7694; Chinkultik Ballcourt Marker, Miller and Martin 2004, pl. 43). To the front of the girdle was sometimes attached an *hacha*, a relatively thin, flat object whose function remains unknown (Shook and Marquis 1996, 63, 235). Some images also show them donning leather forearm protectors—again,

often on the arm corresponding to the direction in which their kneepad and yoke are oriented—or shielding their upper legs and midsection with aprons or kilt of leather (Grube 2014, 174). Such clear alignment of multiple components of protective gear may indicate the side of the player's dominant hand (Stephen D. Houston, personal communication, 2015).

Yet for the ancient Maya, ball playing (*pitz*) was more than a mere physical sport; it was also a ceremonial activity that mediated between residents of this world and those of the underworld (Grube 2014, 175; Houston 2014a; Schele and Freidel 1991, 290–293). Texts recording symbolic impersonation of ballplayers by both human elites and supernatural figures indicate that personal identity was subsumed by the ballplayer's participatory identity in the ritualized game (Cohodas 1991, 266–267; e.g., "the image of" the Ceibal king dressed as a ballplayer on Ceibal Stela 7, I. Graham 1996, 25). The sport was a spiritually charged event conducted under the auspices of the gods, ancestors, and human elites (e.g., Cohodas 1991, 259–261; Miller and Houston 1987, 60–63; Tokovinine 2002), although more informal "pickup" games surely also occurred in less controlled, nonritual settings (Day 2001, 73; compare Leyenaar 2001; Miller and Houston 1987, 47; Schele and Freidel 1991, 309–310).

Correspondingly, some ballplayer accoutrements seem to have been less protective and functional, and many are donned by participants in other elite rituals. Many ballplayers wear wristlets or anklets (Proskouriakoff 1950, 80–81); some even have sandals on their feet (table 11.4; see chapter 9 in this volume). Other accessories may include earspools, earflares, or neck ornaments (see chapters 6 and 7 in this volume). One of the most prominent components is the headdress. Some are relatively modest, taking the form of lower-lying headdresses or hats (see chapter 4 in this volume). However, like those also found in scenes of other elite activities, headdresses on ballplayers vary widely in form and may include, for instance, images of deities, bird or jaguar heads, quetzal plumes, or a combination of these attributes. Particularly common were those depicting animal heads, especially those of deer that are often found on hunters' headdresses, indicating the conceptual link that the Maya drew between hunting and the ball game (Cohodas 1991, 267; Grube 2014, 174–175; e.g., K1871; Miller and Martin 2004, pl. 45).

FEATURE		EXAMPLE	CITATION
Clothing and protective gear	loincloth	Tonina Monument 171	I. Graham et al. 2006, 116
	apron or kilt	K6660	
	girdle	Tikal figurine	Halperin 2014, fig. 3.15h
	forearm protector	K4040	
	kneepad	La Amelia Stela 1	Proskouriakoff 1950, fig. 129
Footgear	bare feet	K1921	
	sandals	Great Ballcourt frieze, Chichen Itza	Miller and Houston 1987, fig. 6
Headgear	low hat	El Perú-Waka' figurine	Pérez Robles 2010, fig. 2.2
	headdress	La Corona Element 13 (Ballplayer Panel 1)	Art Institute of Chicago, object no. 1965.407
Jewelry	wristlet	Jaina figurine	Whittington and Bradley 2001, fig. 106
	neck and ear ornaments	La Corona Element 17 (Ballplayer Panel 5)	Whittington and Bradley 2001, fig. 113
	anklet	La Corona Element 18 (Ballplayer Panel 6)	Schele and Miller 1986, pl. 104

Although they often appear to be awkwardly large, particularly for an athlete required to move with agility and speed, these headdresses, perhaps in a less cumbersome dimension, may have in fact been worn during play for aesthetic reasons (Grube 2014, 174; e.g., K2022).

As a final note, the ball game, or at least its representation, was strongly gendered: only a handful of depictions of female ballplayers are known from ancient Mesoamerica, many of which are from non-Maya regions (Bradley 2001; Day 2001, 74; Whittington 2001, 135). Similarly, no hieroglyphic reference to a ballplayer has been identified that clearly denotes the individual as female. Such partiality indicates that the Maya ball game was a male-dominated enterprise, at least at the elite level of the formal, sanctioned ritual recorded by painters, carvers, and scribes (though see McKillop 2004, 215–216).

BOXING

Another form of ritualized violence was boxing, a practice only recently identified in the Maya region (Taube and Zender 2009). Across Mesoamerica, this traditional form of sanctioned combat was conceptually and ritually related to rainmaking and agricultural fertility (Taube and Zender 2009, 170–173; Zender 2004a, 7–8). Although no hieroglyphic reference to boxing itself is attested, Zender (2004a) has tentatively identified a logogram for *jatz'*, "strike, hit," a verbal root that has been reconstructed for Yukateko, Tzeltalan, Ch'olan, and Q'anjob'alan languages (Kaufman 2003, 920; Kaufman and Norman 1984, 121). In light of iconographic evidence for boxers wielding stone weapons, it is noteworthy that the hieroglyph used to spell this verb form illustrates a left hand grasping another element that, when functioning as a stand-alone logogram, carries the value **TUUN**, "stone" (Zender 2004a, 5–8).

Most evidence of boxing comes from portable media, with few monumental representations of boxing having been identified (though cf. Taube and Zender 2009, figs. 7.6d, 7.7). Indeed, the diversity of poses and movements in which boxers are depicted, representing the stages before, during, and after combat, may be a function of their appearance on smaller, less controlled, and

TABLE II.5. *Elements of bodily adornment commonly depicted on Classic Maya boxers*

FEATURE		EXAMPLE	CITATION
Clothing and protective gear	loincloth	Jaina-style figurine	Taube and Zender 2009, figs. 7.23a–b
	girdle	Unprovenienced figurine	Schele and Miller 1986, pl. 99
	forearm protector	K0500	
	kneepad	Piedras Negras Miscellaneous Sculpted Stone 10	Houston, in Taube and Zender 2009, fig. 7.7
Footgear	bare feet	El Perú-Waka' figurine	Pérez Robles 2010, fig. 2.19
Headgear	headdress	K8545	
	helmet	Lubaantun figurines	T. Joyce 1933, pl. VII.1–22
Jewelry	wristlet	Late Classic vessel	Taube and Zender 2009, figs. 7.11a–b
	neck and ear ornaments	El Perú-Waka' figurine	Pérez Robles 2010, fig. 2.18
	anklet	Late Classic vessel	Taube and Zender 2009, fig. 7.3a

more privately viewable media than public monuments. More static representations simply portray boxers from the front, standing upright, dressed in their gear but not yet engaged (T. Joyce 1933, pl. 7). Two figurines recovered from Burial 39 at El Perú-Waka' model dwarf boxers poised for a match, left arm fully extended out in front of the chest, wrist flexed, and palm facing away from the body, perhaps reaching out to an unknown opponent (Pérez Robles 2010, figs. 2.18–2.19). A panel from the Structure K-6 ball court at Piedras Negras shows two opponents initiating confrontation, squaring off at a distance, knees bent and torsos leaning backward, presumably before exchanging blows (Taube and Zender 2009, fig. 7.7).

Fighters depicted in the act of boxing have their knees bent and arms raised, with their upper bodies inclined forward to engage with the opponent (Taube and Zender 2009, fig. 7.3a). In some cases, their limbs are entangled, evidence that wrestling was also inherent in such combat (fig. 11.6; Barrera Rubio and Taube 1987, foto 10; Taube and Zender 2009, fig. 7.22b). The image of a completed match's outcome on El Baúl Monument 27 depicts the victor upright and with his padded hands on his hips, still clutching his stone weapons, as he looms over his noticeably smaller vanquished foe,

who is falling backward onto the ground (Taube and Zender 2009, fig. 7.6d; compare K3264). In other rare scenes, individuals dressed in boxing attire are engaged in dance, lending additional weight to the significance of boxing outside of direct, physical confrontations (Taube and Zender 2009, 167–168).

Boxers are generally identifiable by their wrapped torsos, relatively exposed lower bodies, headgear, and handheld weapons, although not all of these elements are consistently depicted (table 11.5; compare fig. 11.6; K0500; Taube and Zender 2009, fig. 7.7). Unlike participants in the ritualized violence of the ball game, boxers are more explicitly outfitted to draw blood. Much of their equipment appears to be functional, including perhaps their most distinctive piece of gear: sturdy helmets that obscure their faces, except for small openings for the eyes and sometimes also the mouth (fig. 11.6). Many boxers are also prepared with kneepads, forearm protectors, or even a padded girdle similar to those worn by ballplayers (Taube and Zender 2009, 164). Yet other clothing and accessories donned by some—including bracelets, loincloths, and elaborate headdresses—are not unique to boxers. In their hands, the fighters usually wield a weapon, most commonly manoplas, stone weapons to cover and reinforce the knuckles; rounded

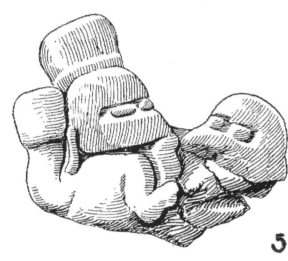

FIGURE 11.6. *Figurines from Lubaantun depicting boxers in action. Reprinted with permission from T. Joyce (1933, pl. 8, nos. 1 and 5).*

stones; clubs; or sharpened conch shells (Taube and Zender 2009, 180–194, 197–209; e.g., K0500; Taube and Zender 2009, figs. 7.6d, 7.11, 7.24, 7.29a–b). Some of these weapons are also attested archaeologically, including manoplas, stone spheres (some with a hole to be swung from a rope), and stone clubs (Taube and Zender 2009, 188–197, 207–209).

DANCE

Although widely represented in ancient imagery, pre-Columbian Maya dance has only recently attracted scholarly attention as an activity of ritual and sociopo-

litical import (see Grube 1992; Houston 1984, 2006; Houston, Stuart, and Taube 2006, 252–276; Looper 2009, 2012). Cosmologically, dance was closely associated with the Maize God and particularly with his resurrection, symbolized by the growth of corn (Taube 2009, 49). The importance and diversity of dance across the region is reflected in the four roots for "dance" attested in Mayan languages, of which only one is known from the hieroglyphic record: *ahk'oot* or *ahk'ut* in Yukateko and Greater Tzeltalan languages (Kaufman 2003, 747–748), usually written in hieroglyphic texts with the logogram T516 **AK'** (Grube 1992).

Dancers in Classic Maya iconography tend to demonstrate a relatively restricted repertoire of motions, perhaps reflecting increased social, ritual, and spatial constraints. The characteristic position depicts the protagonist from a frontal view, head turned to the side, knees bent, with one heel raised (Miller 1981, 131–133; e.g., fig. 11.7; K5880; K9143), although this pose does not define all images of dancing Maya elites (Individ-

FIGURE 11.7. *Detail of dancer on an unprovenienced polychrome vase (K5233), Los Angeles County Museum of Art object no. M.2010.115.504. Drawing by Mallory E. Matsumoto.*

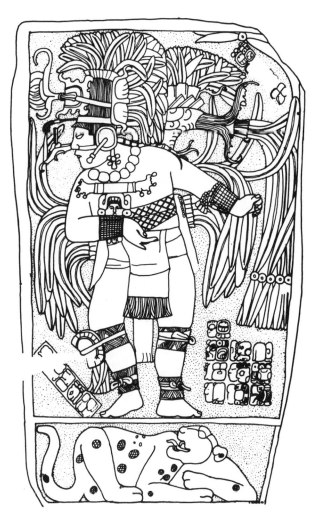

FIGURE 11.8. *La Amelia Stela 1. Drawing (SD-7315) by Linda Schele, © David Schele, courtesy Ancient Americas at LACMA (ancientamericas.org).*

ual 10 in West Wall mural from San Bartolo, K. Taube et al. 2010, fig. 32a; see Looper 2009, 47–49). Other motions may be indicated more subtly by a bend in the knee or the placement of one foot in front of the other (Looper 2009, 88–90; e.g., K0554). That dancers' waists also tend to bow, inclining their torsos to one side, further indicates the dynamism recorded in these images (Miller 1981, 133; e.g., fig. 11.8; K0791).

Many of the objects worn by dancers, like loose loincloths, capes, or feathered headdresses, would have accentuated and visually amplified their movements as they swayed in time with the steps (Miller 1981, 133; e.g., fig. 11.7; K4825; Xcalumkin Jamb 6, Proskouriakoff 1950, fig. 95a). Dancers tend to be elaborately and

colorfully dressed in elements that also appear in other scenes of elite ritual activity, such as wristlets, anklets, pectorals, necklaces, earflares, and other jewelry; kneepads or girdles characteristic of boxers and ballplayers; as well as belts and animal and supernatural headdresses (Looper 2009, 49; 2012, 100–102; e.g., fig. 11.8; Yaxchilan Lintels 2–3, 1. Graham and von Euw 1977, 15, 17; K9085). The backrack is another prominent object worn by dancers on their upper bodies, although some appear to have been too cumbersome to permit any vigorous movement (Looper 2009, 48, 50; e.g., fig. 11.8; K0517; K5976). Other ornaments, like tinklers and celts of shell and jade, were likely positioned on the upper or lower body to reflect light or to generate sound accompanying the dancer's movements (Looper 2009, 50; e.g., Newman et al. 2015, 169).

In general, dancers' gestures and poses largely emphasize movement of the lower body, particularly the legs and feet, whether sandaled or bare (Houston 2006, 144; Miller 1981, 131). Yet while the greatest trajectory of motion appears to come from their feet and legs, dancers' upper bodies clearly did not remain static. They often reach one or both arms out asymmetrically from their bodies, in a stance usually only otherwise found among ballplayers (Looper 2009, 91; Miller 1981, 134; e.g., Bonampak Room 3, Miller and Brittenham 2013, fig. 241). Their wrists and fingers may be extended in variable positions, with one particularly common position showing the wrist flexed back, palm out (Looper 2009, 91; Miller 1981, 134; see fig. 11.9). These poses and gestures clearly belong to the canon of representing dance in Maya art, but many are not unique to dancers and their precise physical correlates and nuanced meanings remain to be explored (Looper 2009, 92–95).

Furthermore, the limited variety of dancing motions preserved in Maya imagery suggests either that the diversity of dances alluded to in the inscriptions has failed to penetrate the visual record or that diagnostic differences between these dances were indicated by other means, such as performance setting or costume (see Houston 2006, 143–144; Looper 2009, 49). Speed of movement, for instance, may have been a salient variable, as suggested by Colonial-period Maya sources such as Fray Tomás de Coto (1983 [1656], 60), who defines the Kaqchikel, *ekal ti xaho, ti liiyax*, as a slower step done "like women dance." Texts on both monumental and

FIGURE 11.9. *Dancer on an unprovenienced polychrome plate. Drawing (JM03200) © 1993 John Montgomery, courtesy Ancient Americas at LACMA (ancientamericas.org).*

portable media only allude to the variety of dances that would have been performed and observed (see Grube 1992), including the *pitzil* (ball playing) (K3296; see Looper 2009, 47–49), **xuʔ-ku-pi** (Yaxchilan Lintel 2, I. Graham and von Euw 1977, 15; see Looper 1991), and **K'AN-ʔ-o-ma** dances (Yaxchilan Lintel 54, I. Graham 1979, 117; see Looper 2009, 236–239).

The most visually striking indices of such variation are probably the ritual objects that dancers often hold, whether a staff, rattle, *K'awiil* scepter, ax, fan, or other item, varying by image and by dance (table 11.6; Grube 1992, 205–206; Looper 2009, 50–52; Looper 2012, 90–92). Some dances were themselves named after the items implicated in them, including the *jasaw chan* (flapstaff) dance commonly depicted at Yaxchilan (Grube 1992, 206–208). Although limited evidence of such variation has survived from the Classic period, colonial sources record a variety of dances implicating different objects, such as Yukateko dances done with canes (*hats'lam che'*) or reeds (*hech*) (Barrera Vásquez 1980, 185, 194), and Kaqchikel *vuqh*, a "dance that they do turning a round stick with their feet," or even *xq'ul*, one that "they often do in twos or threes with their masks . . . and they put some sticks or bones through the mouth and throat,

and through the nose, hitting themselves on the chest" (Coto 1983 [1656], 61, 71). Another instrument that would have dramatically altered dance movements was stilts, attested primarily in the Postclassic Madrid Codex and early colonial Yucatán and Guatemalan highlands, though Classic-period identification (Coto 1983 [1656], 124; Thomas 1882, 79; Houston 2018a, 65; see chapter 9 in this volume, figs. 9.8e and 9.10g).[1]

One of the most salient dance accessories was the mask (*k'oj*), which was intimately associated with the deity impersonation and transformation experiences that were often ritually inherent to dancing (Freidel, Schele, and Parker 1993, 262; Grube 2004, 71; Houston and Stuart 1996, 297–300; Houston, Stuart, and Taube 2006, 256, 270–276; Looper 2009, 47, 50, 2012, 90; Schele and Miller 1986, 69). These accoutrements are depicted most explicitly in profiles that show a cutaway image of the dancer's head just behind the mask (K0533; K4606; K6888). Many such artifacts likely decomposed long ago in the warm, humid climate, as indicated by a rare find at Aguateca of a mask composed of layers of cloth fibers that had been covered with a clay slip, layered and formed around a mold, and subsequently painted (Beaubien 2014). Such displays of material wealth on their bodies and in their hands highlighted elite dancers' access to prestige goods, which, in addition to their participation in this ritual activity, were behavioral indices of their elevated status and authority (Looper 2009, 50). These objects signaled their bearers' roles as dancers and the type of dance under way, as well as more broadly the social ritual nature and function of the activity of dancing itself.

Yet the dances named in monumental inscriptions and texts on portable artifacts likely represent only a sampling of those performed by elites. In contrast to

---

1. The best-known source from the Guatemalan highlands that mentions a dance on stilts is the colonial-era K'iche' *Popol Wuj* (see Houston, Stuart, and Taube 2006, 257; Looper 2009, 211). Transcription of the K'iche' term, which appears as <chitic> in the oldest extant manuscript copied by Fray Francisco Ximénez that is now at the Newberry Library in Chicago (Ayer MS 1515; see fol. 29v, l. 19), has been inconsistent in extant publications; Dennis Tedlock (1996, 132) and Adrián Recinos (1947, 175) translate it as "stilts" (*chitik*) but Allen Christenson (2003, l. 4383) interprets it as "injury" (*ch'itik*). However, a comparison with Coto's (1983 [1656], 124) record of Kaqchikel *qhitic* as "dance" atop "the stilts that they make out of sticks" lends support to *ch'itik* "stilts," an interpretation of Sam Colop (1999, 108; 2008, 116).

TABLE 11.6. *Examples of objects held by Classic Maya dancers*

OBJECT	EXAMPLE	CITATION
axe	Dumbarton Oaks Panel (PC.B.528)	Miller and Martin 2004, pl. 117
conch trumpet	K6508	
fan	Bonampak Room 3	Miller and Brittenham 2013, fig. 241
insect	K2942	
K'awiil scepter	Yaxchilan Lintel 53	Graham 1979, 115–116
loincloth	K6341	
mask	K3296	
rattle	Site R Lintel 5	Looper 2009, fig. 1.18
serpent	Site R Lintel 4	Grube 1992, fig. 15
shield	Copan molded vessel	K4651
staff	Yaxchilan Lintel 2	Graham and von Euw 1977, 15
stone	K2942	
vessel	K6508	

colonial-era Maya and Spanish accounts that record large-scale dances involving dozens, if not hundreds, of participants and spectators (Houston 2006, 143–144; Inomata 2006b, 192–195; see also Looper 2012, 95), most Classic-period sources attest to dances only by isolated individuals (see Looper 2009, 55; e.g., panel at Dumbarton Oaks, Miller and Martin 2004, pl. 117). Furthermore, the ritual nature of the dances recorded in hieroglyphic texts renders it unlikely that all were open to members of every social class in Classic Maya society (see Houston 2006; Inomata 2006a-b; Looper 2009, 56–57; Looper 2012). Few, if any, nonelite dances receive notice. Although participation does not appear to have been categorically restricted by age or gender, evidence suggests that some dances were "age-grade" (Houston 2006, 144). The iconographic association of most dance-specific objects with men suggests a bias toward male performance, at least in surviving records (Looper 2009, 49; Looper 2012, 96–98).

TRAVEL

Longer-distance movement facilitated the circulation of people, goods, and ideas throughout the Maya region. Yet despite the archaeological and epigraphic evidence of such interaction and exchange between pre-

Columbian communities, traveling figures are relatively rare in Maya iconography. Their actions are nonetheless recorded in the hieroglyphic inscriptions (table 11.7), all perhaps aided by a knowledgeable guide (*aj payal*) when traversing a less familiar or more dangerous route (Schele and Grube 1994a, 16). Most travelers recognizable as such—who are, again, consistently male—are engaged specifically in economic or diplomatic undertakings or a combination of both (Tokovinine and Beliaev 2013). Merchants and emissaries (*ebeet*) especially would have been tasked not only with transporting goods and messages between communities, but also with negotiating the economic and political relationships implicated in these exchanges, including tribute offerings (Houston, Stuart, and Taube 2006, 241–249; Tokovinine and Beliaev 2013, 171–194). Other travel would have been ritually motivated, like the processions to or around sacred roadways and enclosures expressed in some hieroglyphic inscriptions with the verb *tek'* (Saturno et al. 2017, 12–13; e.g., Landa 1941 [1566], 109–110, 139–149). Even death was often described metaphorically as a journey (*ochbil*) that brought one to the underworld (Houston, Stuart, and Taube 2006, 194; compare Christenson 2003, l. 2033–2120).

Without beasts of burden, most overland journeys would have been realized by foot on roads (*bih*). Proper footwear would have been vital equipment for such journeys, though not necessarily available for every traveler (see chapter 9 in this volume). The forward movement entailed in overland travel was generally indicated by some combination of staggered legs in profile view, individuals lined up as if following each other one by one, or footprints marking the way along a strip of path, the latter an extended form of the logograph for **BIH** itself (Uayma mirror back, Taube 1992, fig. 40b; La Sufricaya murals, Tokovinine and Beliaev 2013, fig. 7.7; San Bartolo north wall mural, fig. 3.2a in this volume; compare Wisdom 1940, 25–26). Another mode of travel, albeit available only to those with sufficient authority, was to enlist others to carry them by litter (K0594; K5534). In many areas of the Maya region, water was an important transportation option as well, although it is less commonly illustrated than are terrestrial journeys. Travelers in canoes are sometimes shown with the same bundles and headgear worn by those journeying by land (Taube 1992, fig. 43a). More commonly, however, they are bareheaded supernatural figures who seem to trek relatively unburdened, suggesting that their purpose was perhaps more ritual than economic in nature (Tokovinine and Beliaev 2013, 178–179; e.g., Trik 1963, figs. 3, 4, 6, 7).

Those undertaking a journey are generally shown relatively unencumbered in their dress. Loincloths allow unrestricted motion of the legs and keep the lower body cool (fig. 11.10; Robicsek 1978, fig. 159; Tokovinine and Beliaev 2013, figs. 7.7, 7.10). A wide-brimmed hat shields their head from insects and the sun (K5534; Miller and Martin 2004, pl. 10). It is frequently the freight that they carry (*kuch-*), rather than the clothing that they wear, that most saliently distinguishes travelers in iconography. Bulkier or weightier items were suspended down the back with a tumpline anchored across the forehead, the bearer leaning forward to counterbalance the weight (fig. 11.10; Martin 2012, fig. 25; compare Wisdom 1940, 26). Goods could either be carried in bundles (*ikaatz*), as in the processional scene in K8089, or packed into backpacks, as shown with the toad-like traveler on K7727 (fig. 11.10; Tokovinine and Beliaev 2013, 189; see Stuart 1998, 410–416). They may clutch a staff in one hand, which, in addition to serving as a walking aid, could also double as a weapon or to prop up the backpack when at rest (Santana Sandoval, Vergara Verdejo, and Delgadillo Torres 1990, 333, figs. 3–4; Taube 1992, 81, figs. 40b, d).

The archetypal traveler of the Classic era is God L, an aged deity associated with merchants who is frequently depicted with bundles of wares on his back or at his feet (Taube 1992, 79–88). His iconic broad-brimmed hat is trimmed with avian features, including feathers and not infrequently a complete or partial bird (Taube 1992, 79–81). In addition, he may be depicted with jewelry, such as large earspools, necklaces, or anklets, as well as a cape (Taube 1992, fig. 41a; Tokovinine and Beliaev 2013, fig. 7.11a). The primary merchant deity of the Postclassic, God M, can also be identified by the spear or staff in his

TABLE 11.7. *Classic Mayan verbs denoting activities related to traveling*

ACTIVITY	CLASSIC MAYAN TERM	CITATION
run, flee	*ahn-*	Houston, Stuart, and Robertson 1998, 279; Houston and Lacadena, cited in Stuart 2019
go	*bix-n-i*	Stuart 1998, 388–389; Stuart 2012b
arrive	*hul-i*	Grube 1990, 60; MacLeod 1990, 340–341; Schele and Grube 1994a, 16
go down	*koj-*	Houston, Robertson, and Stuart 2000, 333
leave	*lok'-*	Grube and Lacadena, cited in Schele and Grube 1994b, 21–22
enter	*och-/ook-*	Stuart 1998, 388–389; Stuart 2012
return	*pak-x-i*	MacLeod and Stone 1995, 177–178
come, arrive	*tal-*	MacLeod 1990, 339–340
rise, go up	*t'ab-*	Stuart 1998, 417

FIGURE II.10. *Detail of unprovenienced polychrome vase (K7727) showing a standing toad dressed as a traveling merchant, carrying a large pack on his back with a tumpline. Drawing by Mallory E. Matsumoto.*

hand and the backpack that he carries, sustained by a tumpline (Taube 1992, 88–92; Tokovinine and Beliaev 2013, 191). Perhaps unsurprisingly, these two merchant patrons appear to merge in the Postclassic, a phenomenon most visible in the Madrid Codex (Taube 1992, 90–92).

Another class of travelers were those conveying goods between very specific, elite individuals. Couriers deliv-

ering tribute are shown at Bonampak, Yaxchilan, and Tikal dressed in long cloaks, sometimes of white cotton edged with intricate embroidery. They often wore *Spondylus* jewelry around their necks and quetzal or similar feathers in their headdresses (Houston, Stuart, and Taube 2006, 244–246; Miller and Martin 2004, 27, 39). Bundles of tribute (*patan*) resting nearby, some labeled to indicate their contents, index the purpose that brought them to the overlord (Stuart 1998, 410–416; Stuart 2006; e.g., K1728; K2914; Culbert 1993, fig. 68a). Their relatively fine bodily adornment, as reconstructed from tribute presentation scenes, stands in contrast to many other travelers and indicates their elite affiliation. Stephen D. Houston and colleagues (2006, 248) argue that despite this signaled affiliation, they were nonetheless "relatively disposable figures" sent by those in whose name the tribute was being offered. They were representatives whose loss would be less politically fraught were they not to return.

Such disparities in dress raise a broader question concerning the extent to which travelers specifically dressed for the journey versus their purpose upon arrival. In other words, it is possible that the relatively simple presentation of individuals shown on the road was specifically for traveling and they would have, upon arrival, donned other attire more specific to their mission—in the case of tribute bearers, for instance, an audience with an overlord or king—rather than wearing the same clothing or type of clothing throughout. Merchants vending goods in the Chiik Nahb murals at Calakmul, in contrast, are shown in relatively simple attire, with little to no jewelry but often wearing a broad hat very similar to those shown undertaking a journey (Martin 2012, figs. 6, 10, 16, 19, 21).

CONCLUSION

Clothing worn and objects carried are not mere accessories for the static body; they also accompany the body in motion. What one wears and carries is conditioned by the activities in which one is engaged, or at least intends to engage. Merchants cannot conduct their business without the goods they transport upon their backs, and ballplayers don their distinctive protective gear in preparation for a match. Yet the same dress and handheld accoutrements simultaneously condition what the body is able to do (comfortably) at a particular moment in time. When agility and speed are required, as in the pursuit of game or the foray of battle, heavy or excessive clothing can hinder performance. Alternately, moments of more austere movement, such as presenting tribute at courts or participating in certain dances, provide the chance to don a more elaborate costume, perhaps including elements otherwise considered too precious or too unwieldy to wear.

In Classic Maya depictions of the moving body, more elaborate costuming generally correlates with more restricted movements. However, it remains an open question whether this trend indeed reflects a pragmatic adaptation of clothing to functional context or instead differences in status between each activity's participants. Contrasts between images of those engaged in the ball game and rulers impersonating ballplayers, for instance, or between the nobility and their attendants at court, would seem to suggest the latter. As reflected in the preceding discussion, most people illustrated in these scenes of movement are males, in large part because women figure minimally, if at all, in scenes of hunting, warfare, the ritualized combat of the ball game and boxing, dance, or travel. Where women do occur more consistently is in depictions of the royal court, in which they appear either as attendants to the ruler (K6316)—with their elaborate dress often suggesting that they in fact occupied an elevated status within the court—or, on occasion, as elite visitors (K2573). In this sense, the objects worn and carried by the moving body operate as an ensemble to influence and express the individual's momentary activity and social role, reflecting the necessity of understanding them in the contexts in which they were actively employed.

Coda

STEPHEN D. HOUSTON, FRANCO D. ROSSI, AND NICHOLAS CARTER

The adorned body displays, expresses, allures, and, above all, transforms. For the ancient Maya, dress and adornments did not just cover the body but altered its essence by assembling, attaching, daubing, and layering in ways mediated by individual choice, political necessity, intersections of gender and age, relative access to material, and aesthetic or ritual impulse. By consistent and methodical comparison, this book has analyzed such modes of dress through time and space, isolating idiosyncratic adornment and discerning constituent materials in a set of diverse chapters working to shared purpose; where possible, it has extracted the specific histories of particular objects. Surveys of visual and textual documentation through time can be "a valuable primary source for the stuff of dress, cultures, and associated meanings and values, both past and present" (McDowell 2015, 297), with the proviso that such portrayals often reflect only a small, privileged segment of society. Archaeology offers a useful corrective by retrieving and studying tangible objects employed by others of lesser rank.

Yet for all the evidence of coherent patterns, ancient Maya dress responded to dualities and contradictory tendencies.

CONFORMITY VERSUS IDIOSYNCRASY

Regardless of time and place, ancient Maya images reveal clear-cut uniformity in items of dress and orna-ment. Certain forms of dress marked status across various kingdoms. The *sak hu'nal* diadem signaled regal power (see chapter 5 in this volume), and similar dress or accoutrements corresponded to courtly posts (see chapter 2 in this volume and Rossi, Saturno, and Hurst 2015). A remarkable tenacity of costume persisted over time, rooted in Preclassic practices and continuing into the Postclassic period. "Jester god" diadems are one example, a trilobed jewel that also morphed subtly in its referents, if always with the idea that the head and brow formed a key site of personal and social identity. For its part, jewelry worn in the earlobes, on the chest, or more rarely in the nostrils was tied to breath, wind, and fragrance. Jaguar pelts, clinking jade adornment, and resplendent quetzal feathers indicated high status and rank. Nakedness, especially exposure of the privates, denoted defeat and subjugation. Among these steady themes, we find strongly gendered garments of plain composition—loincloths for men and sarongs and huipils for women—as the foundation on which other adornment rests. Supplementing these adornments, body paint not only defended against sun and insects but also transmitted complex meanings. Painted facial markings, particularly on women (chapter 3 in this volume), were remarkably constant through time.

Beyond the regionally shared and chronologically conservative elements of Maya dress were more idiosyncratic trends. Different cities or regions favored particular symbols, costumes, and dances over others. Individual rulers preferred certain modes of dress in their representations. Dynasties emphasized singular objects at different times, such as the "drum major" headdress at Palenque (chapter 4 in this volume), the quetzal sandals at Xultun (chapter 9 this volume) or the *ik'* pendant from Nim Li Punit (chapter 7 in this volume). As with the crowns of Europe or imperial regalia of Japan, these objects likely had their own stories of commission, inheritance, and use, with secure evidence of identifying names or labels; regalia could be visible at a distance or, just as often, recognizable only when held and scrutinized up close. Such objects displayed the shared decorative and symbolic elements of a wide cultural sphere, but they were also unique items in line with Georg Simmel's (1957) celebrated understanding that a basic human tension exists between *imitation of* others and *distinction from* others. In dynastic practice, a grounding in broad institutions, such as kingship and its ritual duties, accompanied a local need to be the ruler of this or that place in particular.

AESTHETICS VERSUS
RITUAL EFFICACY

Public ceremony and performance constitute many of the scenes analyzed in this volume. For the individuals (often rulers) depicted in such scenes, it would have been challenging to navigate movement while wearing such weighty and physically awkward adornments. Fan-backed sandals ornately embellished the feet, and elaborate racks, presumably of light wood or cane, "wrapped the back" (*pohtzaj u paat*) (Stuart, Canuto, and Barrientos Q. 2015; for *potz*, see also Prager 2018). Bracelets or coverings of ankles, knees, or elbows protected areas with a certain notional vulnerability. Other pieces functioned as fetishes with their own identities and ritual emanations. Yet by color, shape, texture, combination, and play of light, that dress conformed to ideas of what would be pleasing to the eye. Adroit, practiced movement was necessary to undergird and affirm such aesthetic appeal: no amount of fancy dress would overcome the negative effects of stumbling, jerky motion, or, in sport, a bad fall. The overriding impression is that Maya rulers were viewed as ferocious and intimidating, their ladies a picture of dignified reserve. But at times, lords were also meant to be beautiful and wealthy be-

yond reckoning, their bodies festooned with warranted, if enviable, wealth.

PERISHABLE VERSUS IMPERISHABLE

In the tropics, objects decay quickly. A key duality in Maya dress is the contrast between the ephemeral and the lasting. In "The Clothed Body" (chapter 2), Carter, de Carteret, and Lukach explore clothing (*buhk*) and the most perishable of Maya adornments, fabrics, and textiles. Maya imagery shows the prevalence of perishable materials in clothing and adornment: hide, cloth, wood, cordage, body paint. Aside from the bare fact of their use, artistic details tell us how such materials were tied, wrapped, cut, or assembled. Property qualifiers, conventional marks used in both Maya art and hieroglyphic writing (Houston 2014b, 10–25; Stone and Zender 2011, 13–15), clarify that some objects incorporated wood, leaves of particular species, feathers of certain colors, and pieces of shaped stone.

Unlike perishable clothes, wraps, and other adornments, ornaments of stone, shell, metal, and the like survive in the archaeological record as pectorals, collars, parts of headdresses and caps, earspools, diadems, bracelets, and other jewelry. Such ornaments offer rich information about production techniques—sawing, drilling, incising, polishing, inlaying—shedding light on production chains and the complex economy of dress. Some finds are matchable to items of dress in ancient Maya art (see chapters 5 and 7 in this volume). Nonperishable items draw attention to the perishable, whether through impressions of woven material on ceramic surfaces, examples of brocade picks and weaving awls dated deep into the Preclassic, or spindle whorls that are found in archaeological deposits, especially in layers that date to the start of the Late Classic period (see chapter 7 in this volume). A noblewoman's container for *uchuub*, perhaps "makeup," from El Peru, Guatemala, attests explicitly to elite use of this popular female accessory (David Stuart, personal communication, 2018); objects like stone bark beaters indicate widespread bark paper and cloth making (see chapter 5 in this volume). Yet the purpose of enduring materials is also, as shown by numerous examples, to "migrate matter," to reflect or materialize perishables of wood, leather, basketry, gourds, hide, and feathers in imperishable form (Houston 2014b, 32–48).

The results could be illusory in intent or derive from a near-magical process that both evoked and transformed an original.

"REALITY" VERSUS THE IDEAL

In a sense, most Maya imagery anticipates present-day concepts of "virtual reality," an immersion in a depicted world (Bergson 1962, 171) and a "technology that convinces the participant that he or she is actually in another place," or, to the knowledgeable viewer, in the same experiential frame as the depicted (Damer and Hinrichs 2014, 17). Indeed, virtuality "vanishes with its own success," when a distinction between a "this world" and a "that one" "fades into the background" (Heim 2014, 111). As noted before, a play of materials hints at an interest, perhaps a delight, in deceiving the eye, or, more seriously, in reproducing or transferring an actual essence. There might be also an optical effect at work, a close view of how cloth wrinkles and folds or the human flesh sags or dimples. Did this come from a novel commitment to preparatory sketching, or did it arise from a more philosophical consideration, of things seen by the eye as opposed to those merely thought or known to be present? (The former privileges human sight, what the eye beholds, the latter a checklist of necessary, identifiable items.) In some moments more than others, portraiture blends conceptual images—name glyphs, "breath beads," flaming torches, and so on—with more literal depictions of material objects. An element of dress might take on an elaborate, largely fictive form in one context and in another seem more within the bounds of actual possibility. To the ancient Maya, a hard divide between the two might have been a boundary of little consequence. In the West, fidelity of depiction as "realism" comes from influences as diverse as attention to observable facts that proved or disproved theories about the world; a claim to artistic sincerity; critiques of social conditions; the anatomical study of dissected bodies that could be condensed, despite their origins in varied bodies, into generic images of skin, skeletons, and muscles; and, after the nineteenth century, a wide array of responses to the development of photography (Rubin 2003). Clearly, as a term, "realism" deserves careful thought and hedged use.

Presumably, for the Maya, each time and place had codes for understanding what was being shown and why,

and it remains unclear what a viewer in the Late Classic period would have made of all details in a Late Preclassic image. Depictive codes might have been disseminated by a variety of means, from inherited clothing and regalia (the Bonampak murals demonstrate that some were stored in special boxes [M. Miller and Brittenham 2013, figs. 133, 135–136]). Other sources for consultation might have been books, figurines, or carved monuments, with the likelihood that few of these remained accessible for more than a few centuries. But echoes existed: at Caracol, woven sandals recalled earlier ones (see chapter 9 in this volume). Moreover, that arc to the distant and even mythic past might have expressed a tenet of belief—that certain dress was always just so, unaltered from antiquity, and in ways established as mythic prototypes by gods and remote ancestors (Houston and Martin 2012).

Consider the sparseness of dress on the north wall of the San Bartolo murals (fig. 3.2a). These ancestral figures are stripped down to the basic elements of dress: loincloths and simple skirts, beaded bracelets or paper wrappings at the wrists and ankles, necklaces of beads or cloth, earflares, and in the case of Individual 9 a pectoral. While it is possible this scene reflects normal dress at the time, contemporary images within the same room and elsewhere in the Maya region suggest otherwise. Individual 6, the elusive deity in the neighboring scene on the same north wall, wears elaborate and ornate dress (Saturno, Taube, and Stuart 2005, 8). Later in a coronation scene on the west wall of the same building, ostensibly further along in time in the overall mural narrative, an ornate headdress is presented to the figure seated on a scaffold by a figure in a beautifully rendered, weftless garment and elaborate headdress (fig. 4.7b). In southern highland and Pacific Coast representations from the same period, rulers don ostentatious and technologically sophisticated costumes (see fig. 4.7a). Taken together, the sparse dress worn by the ancestral figures in the north wall scene seems to reflect a view of how the earliest humans would have dressed in a context where no images from the imagined time existed (for a Late Classic example, see Houston and Inomata 2009, 257, fig. 9.5).

LOCAL VERSUS FOREIGN

Perhaps no single event in Maya history so affected the visual record as the "entrada" of Teotihuacan, a tumultuous intervention in the central part of the Maya region by a powerful and distant city (Stuart 2000; Coggins 1975). Monumental depictions began incorporating styles and accoutrements that evoked that far metropolis. In later centuries, this pivotal event was refracted in many ways, often mediated through dress and adornment, some of which (especially jade and sundry shells) was not found naturally in the urban centers of Maya civilization. For the ancient Maya, dress became a primary means by which individuals displayed ties to the distant center even after it had declined. A variety of figures appear in this role of the foreigner, including many that are not otherwise attested in the key texts relating to Tikal and other sites in what is now northern Guatemala (K9317). Several may be figures dressed in archaic, foreign clothing; others represent individuals from earlier times who served in a much fuller (and largely lost) narrative of contact with Teotihuacan. In ninth-century Maya art, headgear, nose ornaments, and other articles of dress likewise marked connections with distant regions including Veracruz and the central Mexican highlands. The sheer exoticism of these figures might also, on occasion, border on the contemptible and risible: decorous Maya movements contrasted with unusual hunched postures, angular motions of the hands, and heads thrust back in evident, perhaps unintelligible, cries, speech, or song (Houston, Martin, and Taube 2016). Other representations highlighted local identities by emphasizing adornments not used elsewhere, as with the nasal prostheses favored at some sites (see chapter 6 in this volume).

Other dualities could be brought to bear—the everyday and the exalted; the human versus the animal, and how that distinction expressed variable meanings. All inquiries are by nature incomplete, and there is much still to explore about ancient Maya dress. This book represents an expedition of sorts, a project to map Maya dress in time and space. Future studies should push beyond a systematic study of the general, the normative, and the expected. Instead, they should seek the idiosyncratic. Microchronologies of dress and adornment on a site-by-site basis are needed to identify and evaluate the decisions Maya individuals were making about what to produce, wear, bestow, or discard as well as what to layer (as on god impersonators) or strip (as from captives). Which objects were potent essentials to particular ensembles, and which were replaceable? Were the aesthetic oscillations we witness reflective of local tradition, available material, or personal whim? Artifacts and their rigorous comparison are central here, as the means to track fluctuations in economic fortunes, political alliances, and dynastic tastes. There are also texts and dates that can be correlated with particular ensembles (see Rossi 2019, 44–45). In depiction, rulers often embody or impersonate others through specific ensembles. But what did it mean to wear a heavy collar of jade, and why strap bracelets on the wrists? Which items were meant to be heard, clinking and swishing, and not just seen? Of the functions of dress, how are we to stress one over the other? Tensions are always at work in human experience, and dress provides a singular window into many of them. Inequality, unstable status, the conflictive meanings of rulership and empire, what it meant to be a man or a woman, a child or grandparent—all would have troubled and affected the ancient Maya. Through dress, they explored how to be dutiful and boasting, alluring and menacing, conforming and contrastive, how, in short, to project a sense of the self by adorning the body.

References

Aizpurúa, Ilean Isel Isaza, and Patricia A. McAnany. 1999. "Adornment and Identity: Shell Ornaments from Formative K'axob." *Ancient Mesoamerica* 10 (1): 117–127.

Aldana, Gerardo. 2005. "Agency and the 'Star War' Glyph: A Historical Reassessment of Classic Maya Astrology and Warfare." *Ancient Mesoamerica* 16 (2): 305–320.

Anawalt, Patricia R. 1980. "Costume and Control: Aztec Sumptuary Laws." *Archaeology* 33 (1): 33–43.

———. 1981. *Indian Clothing before Cortés: Mesoamerican Costumes from the Codices.* Norman: University of Oklahoma Press.

———. 1990. "The Emperor's Cloak: Aztec Pomp, Toltec Circumstances." *American Antiquity* 55 (2): 291–307.

Ancona-Ha, Patricia, Jorge Pérez de Lara, and Mark van Stone. 2000. "Observaciones sobre los gestos de manos en el arte maya." Translated from "Some Observations on Hand Gestures in Maya Art," by Patricia Ancona–Ha, Jorge Pérez de Lara, and Mark van Stone, in *The Maya Vase Book: A Corpus of Rollout Photographs of Maya Vases*, vol. 6, edited by Justin Kerr, 1072–1089. Mesoweb. Electronic document. www.mesoweb.com/es/articulos/Gestos.pdf.

Andrews, E. Wyllys, V. 1986. "Olmec Jades from Chacsinkin, Yucatan, and Maya Ceramics from La Venta, Tabasco." In *Research and Reflections in Archaeology and History: Essays in Honor of Doris Stone*, edited by E. Wyllys Andrews V, 11–47. Middle American Research Institute Publication 57. New Orleans: Tulane University, Middle American Research Institute.

Andrieu, Chloé, Edna Rodas, and Luis Luin. 2014. "The Values of Classic Maya Jade: A Reanalysis of Cancuen's Jade Workshop." *Ancient Mesoamerica* 25 (1): 141–164.

Aoyama, Kazuo. 2006. "Political and Socioeconomic Implications of Classic Maya Lithic Artifacts from the Main Plaza of Aguateca, Guatemala." *Journal de la Société des Américanistes* 92 (1–2): 7–40.

———. 2009. *Elite Craft Producers, Artists, and Warriors at Aguateca: Lithic Analysis.* Monographs of the Aguateca Archaeological Project First Phase, 2. Salt Lake City: University of Utah Press.

Ara, Domingo de. 1986. *Vocabulario de lengua tzeldal según el orden de Copanabastla.* Fuentes para el estudio de la cultura maya. Mexico, DF: Universidad Nacional Autónoma de México.

Arathoon, Barbara Knoke de. 2007. *Sown Symbols.* Guatemala City: Museo Ixchel del Guatemala, Traje Indígena.

Ardren, Traci. 2002. "Death Became Her: Images of Female Power from Yaxuna Burials." In *Ancient Maya Women*, edited by Tracy Ardren, 68–88. Walnut Creek, CA: Altamira.

Ardren, Traci, and Scott R. Hutson, eds. 2006. *The Social Experience of Childhood in Mesoamerica.* Boulder: University Press of Colorado.

Ardren, Tracy, T. Kam Manahan, Julie Kay Wesp, and Alejandro Alonso. 2010. "Cloth Production and Economic Intensification in the Area Surrounding Chichen Itza." *Latin American Antiquity* 21 (3): 274–289.

Arvigo, Rosita. 1994. *Sastun: My Apprenticeship with a Maya Healer.* New York: Harper.

Aulie, H. Wilbur, and Evelyn W. de Aulie. 1978. *Diccionario ch'ol: Ch'ol-español, español-ch'ol.* Mexico, DF: Instituto Lingüístico de Verano.

Austin, Alfredo López. 1988. *The Human Body and Ideology: Concepts of the Ancient Nahuas.* Translated by Thelma O. de Montellano and Bernard O. de Montellano. Salt Lake City: University of Utah Press.

Bacon, Wendy J. 2007. "The Dwarf Motif in Classic Maya Monumental Iconography: A Spatial Analysis." PhD diss., University of Pennsylvania.

Bardawil, Lawrence. 1976. "The Principal Bird Deity in Maya Art: An Iconographic Study of Form and Meaning." In *The Art, Iconography, and Dynastic History of Palenque*, pt. 3, edited by Merle Greene Robertson, 195–209. Pebble Beach, CA: PARI and Robert Louis Stevenson.

Barnes, Ruth, and Joanne B. Eicher, eds. 1992. *Dress and Gender: Making and Meaning.* Oxford: BERG.

Baron, Joanne P. 2018. "Ancient Monetization: The Case of Classic Maya Textiles." *Journal of Anthropological Archaeology* 49: 100–113.

Barrera Rubio, Alfredo, and Karl A. Taube. 1987. "Los relieves de San Diego: Una nueva perspectiva." *Boletín de la Escuela de Ciencias Antropológicas de la Universidad de Yucatán* 14 (83): 3–18.

Barrera Vásquez, Alfredo, Juan Ramón Bastarrachea Manzano, William Brito Sansores, Refugio Vermont Salas, Davíd Dzul Góngora, and Domingo Dzul Poot. 1980. *Diccionario maya Cordemex: Maya-español, español-maya.* Mérida, Mexico: Ediciones Cordemex.

Barrientos Q., Tomás, Héctor L. Escobedo, and Stephen D. Houston. 1997. "PN 1: Excavaciones en la Estructura O-13." In *Proyecto Arqueo-*

lógico Piedras Negras Informe Preliminar No. 1: Primera Temporada, 1997, edited by Hector L. Escobedo and Stephen Houston, 1–20. Informe preliminar entregado al Instituto de Antropología e Historia. Guatemala City: Brigham Young University/Universidad del Valle de Guatemala.

Bartlett, Djurdja. 2011. "Moscow on the Fashion Map: Between Periphery and Centre." *Studies in East European Thought* 63 (2): 111–121.

Bartman, Elizabeth. 2001. "Hair and the Artifice of Roman Female Adornment." *American Journal of Archaeology* 105 (1): 1–25.

Baudez, Claude F. 1994. *Maya Sculpture at Copan: The Iconography*. Norman: University of Oklahoma Press.

Beaubien, Harriet F. 2004. "Ceramic Laminates: Introduction to the Craft Technology behind Aguateca's Mask." *SAS Bulletin* 27 (4): 11–13.

———. 2014. "Ceramic Laminates." In *Life and Politics at the Royal Court of Aguateca: Artifacts, Analytical Data, and Synthesis*, Aguateca Archaeological Project First Phase Monograph Series, vol. 3, edited by Takeshi Inomata and Daniela Triadan, 118–126. Salt Lake City: University of Utah Press.

Beeton, Isabella. 1861. *Beeton's Book of Household Management*. London: S. O. Beeton.

Beetz, Carl P., and Linton Satterthwaite. 1981. *The Monuments and Inscriptions of Caracol, Belize*. University Museum Monograph. Philadelphia: University Museum and University of Pennsylvania.

Beidelman, Thomas O. 1968. "Some Nuer Notions of Nakedness, Nudity, and Sexuality." *Africa* 38 (1968): 113–131.

Belfanti, Carlo M. 2009. "The Civilization of Fashion: At the Origins of a Western Social Institution." *Journal of Social History* 43 (2): 261–283.

Beliaev, Dmitri. 2012. "Ancient Maya Homers: Classical Rhetorical Devices in Maya Hieroglyphic Texts." Paper presented at Rhetorical Structures and Literary Aspects of Classic Maya Texts, March 10–11, Antigua.

Beliaev, Dmitri, David Stuart, and Camilo Alejandro Luin. 2017. "Late Classic Maya Vase with the Mention of Sihyaj K'ahk' from the Museo VICAL, Casa Santo Domingo, Antigua Guatemala." *Mexicon* 39 (1): 1–4.

Bell, Ellen E., Marcello A. Canuto, and Robert J. Sharer, eds. 2004. *Understanding Early Classic Copan*. Philadelphia: University of Pennsylvania Museum of Archaeology and Anthropology.

Bell, Ellen E., Robert J. Sharer, Loa P. Traxler, David W. Sedat, Christine W. Carrelli, and Lynn A. Grant. 2004. "Tombs and Burials in the Early Classic Acropolis at Copan." In *Understanding Early Classic Copan*, edited by Ellen E. Bell, Marcello A. Canuto, and Robert J. Sharer, 131–157. Philadelphia: University of Pennsylvania Museum of Archaeology and Anthropology.

Bellwood, Peter. 2011. "Holocene Population History in the Pacific Region as a Model for Worldwide Food Producer Dispersals." *Current Anthropology* 52 (S4): S363–S378.

Benson, Elizabeth P. 1974. "Gestures and Offerings." In *Primera Mesa Redonda de Palenque*, pt. 1, edited by Merle Greene Robertson, 109–120. Pebble Beach, CA: PARI and the Robert Louis Stevenson School.

———. 1985. "The Classic Maya Use of Jaguar Accessories." In *Fourth Palenque Round Table, 1980*, edited by Elizabeth P. Benson, 155–158. San Francisco: PARI.

Berdan, Frances F. 1975. "Trade, Tribute, and Market in the Aztec Empire." PhD diss., University of Texas.

———. 1987. "Cotton in Aztec Mexico: Production, Distribution, and Uses." *Mexican Studies/Estudios Mexicanos* 3 (2): 235–262.

Berger, John. 1972. *Ways of Seeing*. London: Penguin.

Bergson, Henri. 1962. *Matter and Memory*. London: George Allen and Unwin.

Berlo, Janet. 1983. "The Warrior and the Butterfly: Central Mexican Ideologies of Sacred Warfare and Teotihuacan Iconography." In *Text and Image in Pre-Columbian Art: Essays on the Interrelationship of the Visual and Verbal Arts*, edited by Janet Berlo, 79–117. BAR International Reports 180. Oxford: British Archaeological Reports.

Berrelleza, Juan Alberto Román, and Ximena Chávez Balderas. 2006. "The Role of Children in the Ritual Practices of the Great Temple of Tenochtitlan and the Great Temple of Tlatelolco." In *The Social Experience of Childhood in Mesoamerica*, edited by Traci Ardren and Scott R. Hutson, 233–248. Boulder: University Press of Colorado.

Berryman, Carrie A. 2007. "Captive Sacrifice and Trophy Taking among the Ancient Maya: An Evaluation of the Bioarchaeological Evidence and the Sociopolitical Implications." In *The Taking and Displaying of Human Body Parts as Trophies by Amerindians*, edited by Richard J. Chacon and David H. Dye, 377–399. New York: Springer.

Bishop, Ronald L., Edward V. Sayre, and Joan Mishara. 1993. "Compositional and Structural Characterization of Maya and Costa Rican Jadeites." In *Precolumbian Jade: New Geological and Cultural Interpretations*, edited by Frederick W. Lange, 30–60. Salt Lake City: University of Utah Press.

Blainey, Marc G. 2016. "Techniques of Luminosity: Iron-Ore Mirrors and Entheogenic Shamanism among the Ancient Maya." In *Manufactured Light: Mirrors in the Mesoamerican Realm*, edited by Emiliano Gallaga Murrieta and Marc G. Blainey, 179–206. Boulder: University Press of Colorado.

Bonfante, Larissa. 1989. "Nudity as a Costume in Classical Art." *American Journal of Archaeology* 93 (4): 543–570.

Boot, Erik. 2004. "Vocabulary in the Ch'olti' Language: A Transcription of the 'Bocabulario Grande' by Fray Francisco Morán (1695)." Foundation for the Advancement of Mesoamerican Studies. Electronic document. www.famsi.org/mayawriting/dictionary/boot/cholti_moran 1695_revised.pdf.

Borrero, Mario, Maya Azarova, and Geoffrey E. Braswell. 2016. "In the Palace of the Wind God: The Discovery of the Nim Li Punit Wind Jewel." *Research Reports in Belizean Archaeology* 13: 193–206.

Bourdieu, Pierre. 1984. *Distinction: A Social Critique of Judgement of Taste*. London: Routledge and Kegan Paul.

Braakhuis, H. E. M. 2001. "The Way of All Flesh: Sexual Implications of the Mayan Hunt." *Anthropos* 96 (2): 391–409.

Bradley, Douglas E. 2001. "Gender, Power, and Fertility in the Olmec Ritual Ballgame." In *The Sport of Life and Death: The Mesoamerican Ballgame*, edited by E. Michael Whittington and Douglas E. Bradley, 33–39. Charlotte, NC: Mint Museum of Art with Thames and Hudson.

Brasseur de Bourbourg, Charles É. 1869. *Manuscrit Troano: Études sur le système graphique et la langue des Mayas*. Paris: Imprimerie Impériale.

Braswell, Geoffrey E., and Megan R. Pitcavage. 2009. "The Cultural Modification of Teeth by the Ancient Maya: A Unique Example from Pusilha, Belize." *Mexicon* 31: 24–27.

Bricker, Victoria R. 1986. *A Grammar of Mayan Hieroglyphs*. New Orleans: Middle American Research Institute, Tulane University.

Brittenham, Claudia. 2015. *The Murals of Cacaxtla: The Power of Painting in Ancient Central Mexico*. Joe R. and Teresa Lozano Long Series in Latin American and Latino Art and Culture. Austin: University of Texas Press.

Browder, Erin C. 1991. "A Study of Elite Costume and Emblem in Classic Maya Art." PhD diss., University of California, Berkeley.

Brown, Linda A. 2005. "Planting the Bones: Hunting Ceremonialism at Contemporary and Nineteenth-Century Shrines in the Guatemalan Highlands." *Latin American Antiquity* 16 (2): 131–146.

Brown, Shayna L. 2003. "An Analysis of a Protoclassic Female Costume from the Site of Caracol, Belize." Master's thesis, University of Central Florida.

Bruhns, Karen O. 1986. "The Role of Commercial Agriculture in Early Postclassic Developments in Central El Salvador: The Rise and Fall of Cihuatan." In *The Southeast Maya Periphery*, edited by Patricia A. Urban and Edward M. Schortman, 247–282. Boston: Springer.

———. 1988. "Yesterday the Queen Wore . . . : An Analysis of Women and Costume in the Public Art of the Late Classic Maya." In *The Role of Gender in Precolumbian Art and Architecture*, edited by Virginia E. Miller, 105–134. Lanham, MD: University Press of America.

Brumfiel, Elizabeth M. 1991. "Weaving and Cooking: Women's Production in Ancient Mexico." In *Engendering Archaeology: Women and Prehistory*, edited by Joan M. Gero and Margaret W. Conkey, 224–251. Oxford: Basil Blackwell.

———. 2006. "Cloth, Gender, Continuity, and Change: Fabricating Unity in Anthropology." *American Anthropologist* 108: 862–877.

Bullard, William R., and Mary R. Bullard. 1965. *Late Classic Finds at Baking Pot, British Honduras*. Occasional Paper: Art and Archaeology. Toronto: Royal Ontario Museum, University of Toronto.

Bushman, Richard. 1993. *The Refinement of America: Persons, Houses, Cities*. New York: Vintage.

Butler, Judith. 1990. *Gender Trouble: Feminism and the Subversion of Identity*. New York: Routledge.

———. 1993. *Bodies That Matter: On the Discursive Limits of "Sex."* New York: Routledge.

Callmer, Johan. 2008. "The Meaning of Women's Ornaments and Ornamentation, Eastern Middle Sweden in the 8th and Early 9th Century." *Acta Archaeologia* 79: 185–207.

Cannadine, David. 2001. *Orientalism: How the British Saw Their Empire*. Oxford: Oxford University Press.

Carlsen, Robert S. 1986. "Analysis of the Early Classic Period Textile Remains: Tomb 19, Rio Azul, Guatemala." In *Río Azul Reports Number 2: The 1984 Season*, edited by Richard E. W. Adams, 122–155. San Antonio: Center for Archaeological Research of the University of Texas at San Antonio.

———. 1987. "Analysis of the Early Classic Period Textile Remains: Tomb 23, Rio Azul, Guatemala." In *Río Azul Reports Number 3: The 1985 Season*, edited by Richard E. W. Adams, 152–160. San Antonio: Center for Archaeological Research of the University of Texas at San Antonio.

Carlsen, Robert S., and David A. Wenger. 1991. "The Dyes Used in Guatemalan Textiles: A Diachronic Approach." In *Textile Traditions of Mesoamerica and the Andes: An Anthology*, edited by Margot Blum Schevill, Janet C. Berlo, and Edward B. Dwyer, 359–380. Austin: University of Texas Press.

Carrasco Vargas, Ramón, and María Cordeiro Baqueiro. 2012. "The Murals of Chiik Nahb Structure Sub 1–4, Calakmul, Mexico." In *Maya Archaeology 2*, edited by Charles Golden, Stephen Houston, and Joel Skidmore, 8–59. San Francisco: Precolumbia Mesoweb Press.

Carrasco Vargas, Ramón, et al. 1999. "A Dynastic Tomb from Campeche, Mexico: New Evidence on Jaguar Paw, a Ruler of Calakmul." *Latin American Antiquity* 10 (1): 47–58.

Carrasco Vargas, Ramón, Verónica A. Vázquez López, and Simon Martin. 2009. "Daily Life of the Ancient Maya Recorded on Murals at Calakmul, Mexico." *PNAS* 106 (46): 19245–19249.

Carter, Nicholas. 2010. "Pectoral Ornament in the Form of a Bivalve Shell, 200–400." In *Fiery Pool: The Maya and the Mythic Sea*, edited by Daniel Finamore and Stephen D. Houston, 132–133. New Haven, CT: Yale University Press.

———. 2014. "Kingship and Collapse: Inequality and Identity in the Terminal Classic Southern Maya Lowlands." PhD diss., Brown University.

———. 2015. "Once and Future Kings: Classic Maya Geopolitics and Mythic History on the Vase of the Initial Series from Uaxactun." *PARI Journal* 15 (4): 1–15.

Carter, Nicholas P., Rony E. Piedrasanta, Stephen D. Houston, and Zachary Hruby. 2012. "Signs of Supplication: Two Mosaic Earflare Plaques from El Zotz, Guatemala." *Antiquity Project Gallery*. antiquity.ac.uk/projgall/carter333.

Carter, Nicholas P., and Lauren M. Santini. N.d. "The Lord of Yellow Tree: A New Reference to a Minor Polity on Sacul Stela 9." Forthcoming in *PARI Journal*.

Caso Barrera, Laura, and Mario Aliphat Fernández. 2006. "Cacao, Vanilla, and Annatto: Three Production and Exchange Systems in the Southern Maya Lowlands, XVI–XVII Centuries." *Journal of Latin American Geography* 5 (2): 29–52.

Chamberlain, Robert S. 1948. *The Conquest and Colonization of Yucatan, 1517–1550*. Washington, DC: Carnegie Institution of Washington.

Chang, Kwang-Chih, and Ward H. Goodenough. 1996. "Archaeology of Southeastern Coastal China and Its Bearing on the Austronesian Homeland." *Transactions of the American Philosophical Society* 86 (5): 36–56.

Charlton, Cynthia L. Otis. 1993. "Obsidian as Jewelry: Lapidary Production in Aztec Otumba, Mexico." *Ancient Mesoamerica* 4: 231–243.

Chase, Arlen F., Diane Z. Chase, Elayne Zorn, and Wendy Teeter. 2008. "Textiles and the Maya Archaeological Record: Gender, Power, and Status in Classic Period Caracol, Belize." *Ancient Mesoamerica* 19: 127–142.

Chase, Arlen F., Nikolai Grube, and Diane Z. Chase. 1991. *Three Terminal Classic Monuments from Caracol, Belize*. Research Reports on Ancient Maya Writing 36. Washington, DC: Center for Maya Research.

Cheetham, David. 2004. "The Role of 'Terminus Groups' in Lowland Maya Site Planning." In *The Ancient Maya of the Belize Valley: Half a Century of Archaeological Research*, edited by James F. Garber, 125–148. Gainesville: University Press of Florida.

Cheong, Kong F., Roger Blench, Paul F. Healy, and Terry G. Powis. 2014. "Ancient Maya Musical Encore: Analysis of Ceramic Musical Instruments from Pacbitun, Belize and the Maya Subarea." *Flower World— Mundo Florido* 3.

Chinchilla Mazariegos, Oswaldo. Forthcoming. "Where Children Are Born: Centipedes and Feminine Sexuality in Ancient Maya Art." Forthcoming in *Witchcraft and Sorcery in Ancient and Contemporary Mesoamerica*, edited by Jeremy Coltman and John Pohl. Boulder: University Press of Colorado.

———. 2011. *Imágenes de la Mitología Maya*. Guatemala: Museo Popol Vuh, Universidad Francisco Marroquín.

———. 2012. "Bead." In *Ancient Maya Art at Dumbarton Oaks*, edited by Joanne Pillsbury, Miriam Doutriaux, Reiko Ishihara-Brito, and Alexandre Tokovinine, 193–195. Pre-Columbian Art at Dumbarton Oaks, no. 4. Washington, DC: Dumbarton Oaks.

Christenson, Allen J. 2003. *Popol Vuh: Literal Poetic Version, Translation and Transcription*. Vol. 2. New York: O Books.

Ciudad Real, Antonio de. 2001 [1577]. *Calepino Maya de Motul*. Vol. 1. Providence, RI: John Carter Brown Library.

Clancy, Flora S. 2009. *The Monuments of Piedras Negras, an Ancient Maya City*. Albuquerque: University of New Mexico Press.

Clark, John E., and Stephen D. Houston. 1998. "Craft Specialization, Gender, and Personhood among the Post-Conquest Maya of Yucatan, Mexico." In *Craft and Social Identity*, edited by Cathy L. Costin and Rita P. Wright, 31–46. Archaeological Papers of the American Anthropological Association 8. Arlington, VA: American Anthropological Association.

Clark, Kenneth. 1956. *The Nude: A Study in Ideal Form*. New York: Pantheon Books.

Clarke, Alison, and Daniel Miller. 2002. "Fashion and Anxiety." *Fashion Theory* 6: 191–214.

Cockrell, Bryan. 2014. "The Metals from the Cenote Sagrado, Chichén Itzá as Windows on Technological and Depositional Communities." PhD diss., University of California, Berkeley.

Coe, Michael D. 1965. "Artifacts of the Maya Lowlands." In *Archaeology of Southern Mesoamerica*, pt. 2, edited by Gordon Willey, 594–602. Handbook of the Middle American Indians, 3. Austin: University of Texas Press.

———. 1973. *The Maya Scribe and His World*. New York: Grolier Club.

———. 1978. *Lords of the Underworld: Masterpieces of Classic Maya Ceramics*. Princeton, NJ: Art Museum, Princeton University.

———. 1982. *Old Gods and Young Heroes: The Pearlman Collection of Maya Ceramics*. Jerusalem: Israel Museum.

———. 2003. "Another Look at the Maya Ballgame." In *Il sacro e il paesaggio nell'America indigena*, edited by Davide Domenici, Carolina Orsini, and Sofia Venturoli, 197–204. Bologna: CLUEB.

———. 2015. "Oyohuallis and Intergender Identity among the Toltec-Maya." Paper presented at the Fifth Annual Maya at the Lago Conference, Davidson, NC, May 1.

Coe, Michael, Stephen Houston, Mary Miller, and Karl Taube. 2015. "The Fourth Maya Codex." In *Maya Archaeology 3*, edited by Charles Golden, Stephen Houston, and Joel Skidmore, 116–167. San Francisco: Precolumbia Mesoweb Press.

Coe, Michael, and Justin Kerr. 1997. *The Art of the Maya Scribe*. New York: Abrams.

Coe, Michael D., and John S. Thacher. 1966. *An Early Stone Pectoral from Southeastern Mexico*. Studies in Pre-Columbian Art and Archaeology. Washington, DC: Dumbarton Oaks.

Coe, William R. 1959. *Piedras Negras Archaeology: Artifacts, Caches, and Burials*. Philadelphia: University Museum, University of Pennsylvania.

———. 1965a. "Artifacts of the Maya Lowlands." In *Archaeology of Southern Mesoamerica, Pt. 2*, edited by Gordon Willey, 594–602. Handbook of the Middle American Indians 3. Austin: University of Texas Press.

———. 1965b. "Tikal, Guatemala, and Emergent Maya Civilization." *Science* 147 (36654): 1401–1419.

———. 1988. *Tikal: A Handbook of the Ancient Maya Ruins*. Philadelphia: University Museum, University of Pennsylvania.

———. 1990. *Excavations in the Great Plaza, North Terrace and North Acropolis*. Vol. 1. Tikal Report 14. Philadelphia: University Museum, University of Pennsylvania.

Coggins, Clemency. 1975. "Painting and Drawing Styles at Tikal: An Historical and Iconographic Reconstruction." PhD diss., Harvard University.

Coggins, Clemency, and John Ladd. 1992. *Artifacts from the Cenote of Sacrifice, Chichen Itza, Yucatan*. Cambridge, MA: Peabody Museum of Archaeology and Ethnology, Harvard University.

Coggins, Clemency, and Orrin C. Shane III, eds. 1984. *Cenote of Sacrifice: Maya Treasures from the Sacred Well at Chichén Itza*. Austin: University of Texas Press.

Cohodas, Marvin. 1991. "Ballgame Imagery of the Maya Lowlands. History and Iconography." In *The Mesoamerican Ballgame*, edited by Vernon L. Scarborough and David R. Wilcox, 251–288. Tucson: University of Arizona Press.

Colas, Pierre R. 2006. "The Hunting Scenes in the Madrid Codex: Planner for Hunting Rituals." In *Sacred Books, Sacred Languages: Two Thousand Years of Ritual and Religious Maya Literature*, 81–92. Acta Mesoamericana. Markt Schwaben, Germany: Verlag Anton Saurwein.

Colop, Sam. 1999. *Popol Wuj: Versión poética K'iche'*. Guatemala City: Cholsamaj.

———. 2008. *Popol Wuj: Traducción al español y notas*. Guatemala City: Cholsamaj.

Cordry, Donald, and Dorothy Cordry. 1968. *Mexican Indian Costumes*. Austin: University of Texas Press.

Corson, Christopher. 1973. "Iconographic Survey of some Principal Figurine Subjects from the Mortuary Complex of Jaina, Campeche." In *Studies in Ancient Mesoamerica*, edited by John Graham, 51–75. Contributions of the University of California Archaeological Research Facility, no. 18. Berkeley: University of California.

———. 1976. *Maya Anthropomorphic Figurines from Jaina Island, Campeche*. Ballena Press Studies in Mesoamerican Art, Archaeology and Ethnohistory, no. 1. Ramona, CA: Ballena.

Craik, Jennifer. 1994. *The Face of Fashion: Cultural Studies in Fashion*. London: Routledge.

Culbert, T. Patrick, ed. 1991. *Classic Maya Political History: Hieroglyphic and Archaeological Evidence*. Cambridge: Cambridge University Press.

———. 1993. *The Ceramics of Tikal: Vessels from the Burials, Caches and Problematical Deposits*. Tikal Report 25A. Philadelphia: University Museum and University of Pennsylvania.

Dacus, Chelsea. 2005. "Weaving the Past: An Examination of Bones Buried with an Elite Maya Woman." Master's thesis, Southern Methodist University.

Damer, Bruce, and Randy Hinrichs. 2014. "The Virtuality and Reality of Avatar Cyberspace." In *The Oxford Handbook of Virtuality*, edited by Mark Grimshaw, 17–41. Oxford: Oxford University Press.

Day, Jane Stevenson. 2001. "Performing on the Court." In *The Sport of Life and Death: The Mesoamerican Ballgame*, edited by E. Michael Whittington and Douglas E. Bradley, 65–77. Charlotte, NC: Mint Museum of Art with Thames and Hudson.

Deegan, Ann Cordy. 1998. "Prehistoric Puebloan Footwear." In *Prehistoric Sandals from Northeastern Arizona: The Earl H. Morris and Ann Axtell Morris Research*, edited by Kelley Ann Hays-Gilpin, Ann Cordy Deegan, and Elizabeth Ann Morris, 37–50. Tucson: University of Arizona Press.

de Vega, Hortensia, Emiliano R. Melgar, and M. de Lourdes Gallardo. 2010. "The Maya Nacreous Shell Garment of Oxtankah (Quintana Roo, México)." *Munibe* 31: 226–235.

Díaz del Castillo, Bernal. 2012. *The True History of the Conquest of New Spain*. Translated and edited by J. Burke and T. Humphrey. Indianapolis: Hackett.

Domenici, Davide, and Gloria Martha Sánchez Valenzuela. 2016. "Classic Textiles from Cueva del Lazo (Chiapas, Mexico): Archaeological Context and Conservation Issues. Paper presented at the Pre-Columbian Textiles Conference, May 31–June 3, 2016, Centre of Textile Research at the Saxo Institute, University of Copenhagen.

Doniger, Wendy. 2017. *The Ring of Truth and Other Myths of Sex and Jewelry*. Oxford: Oxford University Press.

Douglas, Mary. 1970. *Natural Symbols*. New York: Pantheon.

Doyle, James A. 2010. "Carving of a Frog." In *Fiery Pool: The Maya and the Mythic Sea*, edited by Daniel Finamore and Stephen D. Houston, 132–133. New Haven, CT: Yale University Press.

———. 2012. "A Paleographic Approach to Political Change Using Classic Maya Day Sign Variants." In *Contributions in New World Archaeology*, vol. 4, edited by Jaroslaw Źrałka, Wieslaw Koszkul, and Beata Golińska, 125–137. Kraków: Jagiellonian University and the Polish Academy of Arts and Sciences.

Duncan, William N., and Charles Andrew Hofling. 2011. "Why the Head? Cranial Modification as Protection and Ensoulment among the Maya." *Ancient Mesoamerica* 22: 199–210.

Dunham, Peter S. 1996. "Resource Exploitation and Exchange among Classic Maya: Some Initial Findings of the Maya Mountains Archaeological Project." In *The Managed Mosaic: Ancient Maya Agriculture and Resource Use*, edited by Scott L. Fedick, 313–334. Salt Lake City: University of Utah Press.

Eberl, Marcus, and Takeshi Inomata. 2001. "Maya Royal Headband (Sak Hunal) from Aguateca." *Mexicon* 23 (6): 134–135.

Ekholm, Susanna M. 1979. "The Lagartero Figurines." In *Maya Archaeology and Ethnology*, edited by Norman Hammond and Gordon R. Willey, 172–186. Austin: University of Texas Press.

———. 1985. "The Lagartero Ceramic 'Pendants.'" In *Fourth Palenque Round Table, 1980*, edited by Elizabeth P. Benson, 211–219. Palenque Round Table Series. San Francisco: PARI.

———. 1991. "Ceramic Figurines and the Mesoamerican Ballgame." In *The Mesoamerican Ballgame*, edited by Vernon L. Scarborough and David R. Wilcox, 241–249. Tucson: University of Arizona Press.

Elias, Norbert. 1978. *The Civilizing Process*. Vol. 1, *The History of Manners*. New York: Pantheon Books.

———. 1983. *The Court Society*. New York: Pantheon Books.

Elliott, Charlene. 2008. "Purple Pasts: Color Codification in the Ancient World." *Law and Social Inquiry* 33 (1): 173–194.

El Perú-Waka' Archaeological Project. 2012. "The Queen of El Perú-Waka': New Discoveries in an Ancient Maya Temple." Electronic document. http://media.cleveland.com/science_impact/other/The%20 Queen%20of%20El%20Peru%20Waka,%20Guatemala.pdf.

Escobedo, Héctor L., and Stephen D. Houston. 1997. "Síntesis de la primera temporada de campo del Proyecto Arqueológico Piedras Negras." In *Proyecto Arqueológico Piedras Negras Informe Preliminar No. 1: Primera Temporada, 1997*, edited by Hector L. Escobedo and Stephen Houston, 219–230. Informe preliminar entregado al Instituto de Antropología e Historia. Guatemala City: Brigham Young University/ Universidad del Valle de Guatemala.

Estrada-Belli, Francisco. 2011. *The First Maya Civilization*. New York: Routledge.

Estrada-Belli, Francisco, Alexandre Tokovinine, Jennifer M. Foley, Heather Hurst, Gene A. Ware, David Stuart, and Nikolai Grube. 2009. "A Maya Palace at Holmul, Peten, Guatemala and the Teotihuacan 'Entrada': Evidence from Murals 7 and 9." *Latin American Antiquity* 20 (1): 228–259.

Fash, Barbara. 2011. *The Copan Sculpture Museum: Ancient Maya Artistry in Stucco and Stone*. Cambridge, MA: Peabody Museum of Archaeology and Ethnology, Harvard University.

Fash, William, Barbara Fash, and Karla Davis-Salazar. 2004. "Setting the Stage: Origins of the Hieroglyphic Stairway Plaza on the Great Period Ending." In *Understanding Early Classic Copan*, edited by Ellen Bell, Marcello Canuto, and Robert Sharer, 65–84. Philadelphia: University of Pennsylvania Museum of Archaeology and Anthropology.

Fasquelle, Ricardo Agurcia, and William L. Fash. 1991. "Maya Artistry Unearthed." *National Geographic* 190 (3): 94–105.

Fields, Virginia M. 1991. "The Iconographic Heritage of the Maya Jester God." In *Sixth Palenque Round Table, 1986*, edited by Merle Greene Robertson and Virginia M. Fields. Norman: University of Oklahoma Press.

———. 2012. "Plaque Pendant." In *Ancient Maya Art at Dumbarton Oaks*, edited by Joanne Pillsbury, Miriam Doutriaux, Reiko Ishihara-Brito, and Alexandre Tokovinine, 251–252. Pre-Columbian Art at Dumbarton Oaks. Washington, DC: Dumbarton Oaks.

Fields, Virginia M., and Dorie Reents-Budet. 2005. "Earflare Inlay." In *Lords of Creation: The Origins of Sacred Maya Kingship*, edited by Virginia M. Fields and Dorie Reents-Budet, 184. Los Angeles: Los Angeles County Museum of Art.

Fields, Virginia M., and Dorie Reents-Budet, eds. 2005. *Lords of Creation: The Origins of Sacred Maya Kingship*. Los Angeles: Los Angeles County Museum of Art.

Finamore, Daniel, and Stephen D. Houston, eds. 2010. *Fiery Pool: The Maya and the Mythic Sea*. New Haven, CT: Yale University Press.

Fitzsimmons, James L. 2009. *Death and the Classic Maya Kings*. Austin: University of Texas Press.

Follensbee, Billie J. 2006. "The Child and the Childlike in Olmec Art and Archaeology." In *The Social Experience of Childhood in Mesoamerica*, edited by Traci Ardren and Scott R. Hutson, 249–280. Boulder: University Press of Colorado.

———. 2008. "Fiber Technology and Weaving in Formative-Period Gulf Coast Cultures." *Ancient Mesoamerica* 19: 87–110.

Foncerrada de Molina, Marta, and Sonia Lombardo de Ruiz. 1979. *Vasijas pintadas mayas en contexto arqueológico*. Estudios y fuentes del arte en México. Mexico, DF: Universidad Nacional Autónoma de México.

Foshag, William F., and Robert Leslie. 1955. "Jadeite from Manzanal, Guatemala." *American Antiquity* 21 (1): 81–83.

Foucault, Michel. 1995. *Discipline and Punish: The Birth of the Prison*. New York: Vintage.

Fox, John Gerard. 1996. "Playing with Power: Ballcourts and Political Ritual in Southern Mesoamerica." *Current Anthropology* 37 (3): 483–509.

Freidel, David A., Kathryn Reese-Taylor, and David Mora-Marin. 2002. "The Origins of Maya Civilization: The Old Shell Game, Commodity, Treasure, and Kingship." In *Ancient Maya Political Economies*, edited by Marilyn A. Masson and David A. Freidel, 41–86. Walnut Creek, CA: Altamira.

Freidel, David, Michelle Rich, and F. Kent Reilly III. 2010. "Resurrecting the Maize King." *Archaeology* 63 (5): 42–45.

Freidel, David, and Linda Schele. 1988. "Kingship in the Late Preclassic Maya Lowlands: The Instruments and Places of Ritual Power." *American Anthropologist* 90 (2): 547–567.

Freidel, David A., Linda Schele, and Joy Parker. 1993. *The Path of Life: Three Thousand Years on the Shaman's Path*. New York: William Morrow.

Fritzler, Marlene J. 2005. "Late Classic Maya Warrior Queens: Profiling a New Gender Role." Master's thesis, University of Calgary.

Fussell, Paul. 2002. *Uniforms: Why We Are What We Wear*. Boston: Houghton Mifflin.

Gann, Thomas. 1900. "Mounds in Northern Honduras." In *19th Annual Report, Bureau of American Ethnology*, edited by J. W. Powell, 655–692. Washington, DC: Bureau of American Ethnology.

García Hernández, Abraham, Santiago Yac Sam, and David Henne Pontious. 1980. *Diccionario quiche-espanol*. Guatemala: Instituto Linguístico de Verano.

García Moll, Roberto, Daniel Juárez, Mario Pérez, A. Kaneko, Federico Solís, R. Gallegos, and B. Oliver. 1990. *La exposición de la civilización maya*. Exhibition catalog. Tokyo: Mainichi Shinbunsha.

García Moreno, Renata, David Strivay, and Bernard Gilbert. 2008. "Maya Blue-Green Pigments Found in Calakmul, Mexico: A Study by Raman and UV-visible Spectroscopy." *Journal of Raman Spectroscopy* 39 (8): 1050–1056.

Gerhard, Peter. 1964. "Emperors' Dye of the Mixtecs." *Natural History* 73 (1): 26–31.

Gillespie, Susan D. 1991. "Ballgames and Boundaries." In *The Mesoamerican Ballgame*, edited by Vernon L. Scarborough and David R. Wilcox, 317–345. Tucson: University of Arizona Press.

———. 2008. "Embodied Persons and Heroic Kings in Late Classic Maya Imagery." In *Past Bodies: Body-Centred Research in Archaeology*, edited by Dusan Borić and John Robb, 125–134. Oxford: Oxbow.

Gillespie, Susan D., and Rosemary Joyce. 1998. "Deity Relationships in Mesoamerican Cosmologies: The Case of the Maya God L." *Ancient Mesoamerica* 9 (2): 279–296.

González Cruz, Arnoldo. 2000. "The Red Queen." Mesoweb Palenque Feature Resource. Electronic document. www.mesoweb.com/palenque/features/red_queen/01.html.

———. 2011. *La reina roja: Una tumba real de Palenque*. México, DF: Consejo Nacional para la Cultura y las Artes, Instituto Nacional de Antropolgía e Historia.

Gordon, G. Byron. 1925. *Examples of Maya Pottery in the Museum and Other Collections*. Vol. 1. Philadelphia: University of Pennsylvania Museum.

Graham, Elizabeth. 1991. "Women and Gender in Maya Prehistory." In *The Archaeology of Gender: Proceedings of the Twenty-Second Annual Conference of the Archaeological Association of the University of Calgary*, edited by Dale Walde and Noreen D. Willows, 470–478. Alberta: University of Calgary.

———. 2002. "Perspectives on Economy and Theory." In *Ancient Maya Political Economies*, edited by Marilyn A. Masson and David A. Freidel, 398–418. Walnut Creek, CA: AltaMira.

Graham, Ian. 1967. *Archaeological Explorations in El Peten, Guatemala*. Middle American Research Institute Publication. New Orleans: Middle American Research Institute, Tulane University.

———. 1977. *Corpus of Maya Hieroglyphic Inscriptions*. Vol. 3, pt. 1, *Yaxchilan*. Cambridge, MA: Peabody Museum of Archaeology and Ethnology, Harvard University.

———. 1978. *Corpus of Maya Hieroglyphic Inscriptions*. Vol. 2, pt. 2, *Naranjo, Chunhuitz, Xunantunich*. Cambridge, MA: Peabody Museum of Archaeology and Ethnology, Harvard University.

———. 1979. *Corpus of Maya Hieroglyphic Inscriptions*. Vol. 3, pt. 2, *Yaxchilan*. Cambridge, MA: Peabody Museum of Archaeology and Ethnology, Harvard University.

———. 1980. *Corpus of Maya Hieroglyphic Inscriptions*. Vol. 2, pt. 3, *Ixkun, Ucanal, Ixtutz, Naranjo*. Cambridge, MA: Peabody Museum of Archaeology and Ethnology, Harvard University.

———. 1982. *Corpus of Maya Hieroglyphic Inscriptions*. Vol. 3, pt. 3, *Yaxchilan*. Cambridge, MA: Peabody Museum of Archaeology and Ethnology, Harvard University.

———. 1986. *Corpus of Maya Hieroglyphic Inscriptions*. Vol. 5, pt. 3, *Uaxactun*. Cambridge, MA: Peabody Museum of Archaeology and Ethnology, Harvard University.

———. 1992. *Corpus of Maya Hieroglyphic Inscriptions*. Vol. 4, pt. 2, *Uxmal*. Cambridge, MA: Peabody Museum of Archaeology and Ethnology, Harvard University.

———. 1996. *Corpus of Maya Hieroglyphic Inscriptions*. Vol. 7, pt. 1, *Seibal*. Cambridge, MA: Peabody Museum of Archaeology and Ethnology, Harvard University.

Graham, Ian, and Peter Mathews. 1996. *Corpus of Maya Hieroglyphic Inscriptions*. Vol. 6, pt. 2, *Tonina*. Cambridge, MA: Peabody Museum of Archaeology and Ethnology, Harvard University.

Graham, Ian, David Stuart, Peter Mathews, and Lucia R. Henderson. 2006. *Corpus of Maya Hieroglyphic Inscriptions*. Vol. 9, pt. 2, *Tonina*. Cambridge, MA: Peabody Museum of Archaeology and Ethnology, Harvard University.

Graham, Ian, and Eric von Euw. 1975. *Corpus of Maya Hieroglyphic Inscriptions*. Vol. 2, pt. 1, *Naranjo*. Cambridge, MA: Peabody Museum of Archaeology and Ethnology, Harvard University.

———. 1977. *Corpus of Maya Hieroglyphic Inscriptions*. Vol. 3, pt. 1, *Yaxchilan*. Cambridge, MA: Peabody Museum of Archaeology and Ethnology, Harvard University.

———. 1992. *Corpus of Maya Hieroglyphic Inscriptions*. Vol. 4, pt. 3, *Uxmal, Xcalumkin*. Cambridge, MA: Peabody Museum of Archaeology and Ethnology, Harvard University.

———. 1997. *Corpus of Maya Hieroglyphic Inscriptions*. Vol. 8, pt. 1, *Coba*. Cambridge, MA: Peabody Museum of Archaeology and Ethnology, Harvard University.

Grey, Melissa, Anne-Marie Blais, Bob Hunt, and Amanda C. J. Vincent. 2006. "The USA's International Trade in Fish Leather, from a Conservation Perspective." *Environmental Conservation* 33 (2): 100–108.

Grube, Nikolai. 1990. *Die Entwicklung der Mayaschrift: Grundlagen zur Erforschung des Wandels der Mayaschrift von der Protoklassik bis zur spanischen Eroberung*. Acta Mesoamericana 3. Berlin: Karl-Friedrich von Flemming.

———. 1992. "Classic Maya Dance: Evidence from Hieroglyphs and Iconography." *Ancient Mesoamerica* 3 (2): 201–218.

———. 1994. "Epigraphic Research at Caracol, Belize." In *Studies in the Archaeology of Caracol, Belize*, edited by Diane Chase and Arlen Chase, 83–122. Pre-Columbian Art Research Institute Monograph 7. San Francisco: PARI.

———. 2004. "The Orthographic Distinction between Velar and Glottal Spirants in Maya Hieroglyphic Writing." In *The Linguistics of Maya Writing*, edited by Søren Wichmann, 61–81. Salt Lake City: University of Utah Press.

———. 2014. "Drama von Tod und Auferstehung: Das Ballspiel der Maya." In *Fußball. Macht. Politik: Interdiziplinäre Perspektiven auf Fußball und Gesellschaft*, edited by Jonas Bens, Susanne Kleinfeld, and Karoline Noack, 165–186. Bielefeld, Germany: Transcript Verlag.

Grube, Nikolai, Kai Delvendahl, Nicolaus Seefeld, and Beniamino Volta. 2012. "Under the Rule of the Snake Kings: Uxul in the 7th and 8th Centuries." *Estudios de Cultura Maya* 40: 11–49.

Guderjan, Thomas H. 2007. *The Nature of an Ancient Maya City.* Tuscaloosa: University of Alabama Press.

Guenter, Stanley. 2007. "The Tomb of K'inich Janaab Pakal: The Temple of the Inscriptions at Palenque." Electronic document. www.mesoweb.com/articles/guenter/TI.pdf.

Guernsey, Julia. 1992. "A Thematic Survey of Women on Maya Late Classic Ceramic Vessels." Master's thesis, University of Wisconsin.

————. 2006. *Ritual and Power in Stone.* Austin: University of Texas Press.

Guthrie, Jill, and Elizabeth P. Benson. 1995. *The Olmec World: Ritual and Rulership.* Princeton, NJ: Art Museum, Princeton University.

Hagen, Victor W. von. 1944. *The Aztec and Maya Papermakers.* New York: J. J. Augustin.

Halperin, Christina T. 2008. "Classic Maya Textile Production: Insights from Motul de San José, Peten, Guatemala." *Ancient Mesoamerica* 19: 111–125.

————. 2014. *Maya Figurines: Intersections between State and Household.* Austin: University of Texas Press.

————. 2016. "Textile Techné: Classic Maya Translucent Cloth and the Making of Value." In *Making Value, Making Meaning: Techné in the Pre-Columbian World,* edited by Cathy L. Costin, 433–468. Washington, DC: Dumbarton Oaks.

Halperin, Christina T., Zachary X. Hruby, and Ryan Mongelluzzo. 2018. "The Weight of Ritual: Classic Maya Jade Head Pendants in the Round." *Antiquity* 92 (363): 758–771.

Hammond, Norman, ed. 1991. *Cuello: An Early Maya Community in Belize.* New York: Cambridge University Press.

Hammond, Norman, and Sheena Howarth. 1999. Addendum to *The Discovery, Exploration, and Monuments of Nim Li Punit, Belize.* In Research Reports on Ancient Maya Writing 40a. Washington, DC: Center for Maya Research.

Hammond, Norman, Sheena Howarth, and Richard R. Wilk. 1999. *The Discovery, Exploration, and Monuments of Nim Li Punit.* Research Reports on Ancient Maya Writing 40. Washington, DC: Center for Maya Research.

Hansen, Karen T. 2004. "The World in Dress: Anthropological Perspectives on Clothing, Fashion, and Culture." *Annual Review of Anthropology* 33: 369–392.

Harlow, George E. 1993. "Middle American Jade: Geologic and Petrologic Perspectives on Variability and Source." In *Precolumbian Jade: New Geological and Cultural Interpretations,* edited by Frederick W. Lange, 9–29. Salt Lake City: University of Utah Press.

Hassig, Ross. 1992. *War and Society in Ancient Mesoamerica.* Berkeley: University of California Press.

Haviland, William A. 1997. "The Rise and Fall of Sexual Inequality: Death and Gender at Tikal, Guatemala." *Ancient Mesoamerica* 8 (1): 1–12.

Hayward, Maria. 2009. *Rich Apparel: Clothing and the Law in Henry VIII's England.* London: Routledge.

Healy, Paul F., Jaime J. Awe, and Hermann Helmuth. 2004. "Defining Royal Maya Burials: A Case from Pacbitun." In *The Ancient Maya of the Belize Valley: Half a Century of Archaeological Research,* edited by James F. Garber, 228–237. Gainesville: University Press of Florida.

Healy, Paul F., and Marc G. Blainey. 2011. "Ancient Maya Mosaic Mirrors: Function, Symbolism, and Meaning." *Ancient Mesoamerica* 22 (2): 229–244.

Heim, Michael R. 2014. "The Paradox of Virtuality." In *The Oxford Handbook of Virtuality,* edited by Mark Grimshaw, 110–125. Oxford: Oxford University Press.

Hellmuth, Nicholas M. 1987. *Ballgame Iconography and Playing Gear: Late Classic Maya Polychrome Vases and Stone Sculpture of Peten, Guatemala.* Culver City, CA: Foundation for Latin American Anthropological Research.

————. 1996. *Headdresses and Skirts Shared by Deer Hunters and Ballplayers.* Cocoa, FL: Foundation for Latin American Anthropological Research.

Henderson, Lucia. 2013. "Bodies Politic, Bodies in Stone: Imagery of the Human and the Divine in the Sculpture of Late Preclassic Kaminaljuyú, Guatemala." PhD diss., University of Texas.

Hendon, Julia A. 1997. "Women's Work, Women's Space, and Women's Status among the Classic-Period Maya Elite of the Copan Valley." In *Women in Prehistory: North America and Mesoamerica,* edited by Cheryl Claassen and Rosemary Joyce, 33–46. Philadelphia: University of Pennsylvania Press.

————. 2006. "Textile Production as Craft in Mesoamerica: Time, Labor and Knowledge." *Journal of Social Archaeology* 6 (3): 354–378.

Hernández, Francisco. 1959. *Historia Natural de Nueva España.* Vol. 1. Mexico, DF: Universidad Nacional de México.

Heyden, Doris, and Fernando Horcasitas. 1964. *The Aztecs: The History of the Indies of New Spain.* New York: Orion Press.

Hirth, Kenneth, ed. 2009. *Housework: Specialization, Risk, and Domestic Craft Production in Mesoamerica.* Archaeological Papers, 19. Washington, DC: American Anthropological Association.

Hopkins, Nicholas A., J. Kathryn Josserand, and Ausencio Cruz Guzmán. 2011. "A Historical Dictionary of Chol (Mayan): The Lexical Sources from 1789 to 1935." Tallahassee: Jaguar Tours. Electronic document. www.famsi.org/mayawriting/dictionary/hopkins/CholDictionary2010.pdf.

Hoskins, Janet. 1998. *Biographical Objects: How Things Tell the Stories of People's Lives.* London: Routledge.

Hosler, Dorothy, Sandra L. Burkett, and Michael J. Tarkanian. 1999. "Prehistoric Polymers: Rubber Processing in Ancient Mesoamerica." *Science* 284 (5422): 1988–1991.

Houston, Stephen D. 1984. "A Quetzal Feather Dance at Bonampak, Chiapas, Mexico." *Journal de la Société des Américanistes* 70 (1): 127–137.

————. 1992. "A Name Glyph for Classic Maya Dwarfs." In *The Maya Vase Book: A Corpus of Rollout Photographs of Maya Vases,* edited by Justin Kerr, 3:526–531. New York: Kerr Associates.

————. 1993. *Hieroglyphs and History at Dos Pilas: Dynastic Politics of the Classic Maya.* Austin: University of Texas Press.

————. 1998. "Classic Maya Depictions of the Built Environment." In *Function and Meaning in Classic Maya Architecture,* edited by Stephen D. Houston, 333–372. Washington, DC: Dumbarton Oaks Research Library and Collection.

————. 2001. "Decorous Bodies and Disordered Passions: Representations of Emotion among the Classic Maya." *World Archaeology* 33 (2): 206–219.

————. 2006. "Impersonation, Dance, and the Problem of Spectacle." In *Archaeology of Performance: Theaters of Power, Community, and Politics,* edited by Takeshi Inomata and Lawrence S. Coben, 135–155. Lanham, MD: Altamira Press.

————. 2008a. "A Classic Maya Bailiff?" Entry in *Maya Decipherment,* edited by David Stuart. Electronic document. https://decipherment.wordpress.com/2008/03/10/a-classic-maya-bailiff/.

———. 2008b. "The Epigraphy of El Zotz." Electronic document. www
.mesoweb.com/zotz/articles/ZotzEpigraphy.pdf.

———. 2009. "A Splendid Predicament: Young Men in Classic Maya Society." *Cambridge Archaeological Journal* 19 (2): 149–178.

———. 2010. "Maya Musk." Entry in *Maya Decipherment*, edited by David Stuart. Electronic document. https://decipherment.wordpress.com
/2010/06/17/maya-musk/.

———. 2011. "All Things Must Change: Maya Writing over Time and
Space." In *Their Way of Writing: Scripts, Signs, and Pictographies in Pre-
Columbian America*, edited by Elizabeth Hill Boone and Gary Urton,
21–42. Washington, DC: Dumbarton Oaks.

———. 2012a. "Diadems in the Rough." Entry in *Maya Decipherment*,
edited by David Stuart. Electronic document. http://decipherment
.wordpress.com/.

———. 2012b. "Painted Vessel, Plate 56." In *Ancient Maya Art at Dumbarton Oaks, Pre-Columbian Art at Dumbarton Oaks*, no. 4, edited by
Joanne Pillsbury, Miriam Doutriaux, Reiko Ishihara-Brito, and Alexandre Tokovinine, 314–321. Washington, DC: Dumbarton Oaks.

———. 2012c. "Pendant." In *Ancient Maya Art at Dumbarton Oaks*, edited by Joanne Pillsbury, Miriam Doutriaux, Reiko Ishihara-Brito,
and Alexandre Tokovinine, 444–450. Washington, DC: Dumbarton Oaks.

———. 2014a. "Deathly Sport." Entry in *Maya Decipherment*, edited by
David Stuart. Electronic document. https://decipherment.wordpress
.com/2014/07/29/deathly-sport/.

———. 2014b. *The Life Within: Classic Maya and the Matter of Permanence*. New Haven, CT: Yale University Press.

———. 2017. "Crafting Credit: Authorship among Classic Maya Painters
and Sculptors." In *Making Value, Making Meaning: Techné in the Pre-
Columbian World*, edited by Cathy L. Costin, 391–431. Washington,
DC: Dumbarton Oaks.

———. 2018a. *The Gifted Passage: Young Men in Classic Maya Art and
Text*. New Haven, CT: Yale University Press.

———. 2018b. "What Writing Looks Like." Entry in *Maya Decipherment*,
edited by David Stuart. Electronic document. https://decipherment
.wordpress.com/2018/06/28/what-writing-looks-like/.

———. 2019. "Watery War." Entry in *Maya Decipherment*, edited by David Stuart. Electronic document. https://mayadecipherment.com
/2019/06/17/watery-war/.

Houston, Stephen D., Claudia Brittenham, Cassandra Mesick, Alexandre
Tokovinine, and Christina Warinner. 2009. *Veiled Brightness: A History of Ancient Maya Color*. Austin: University of Texas Press.

Houston, Stephen D., James Doyle, David Stuart, and Karl A. Taube.
2017. "A Universe in a Maya Lintel IV: Seasonal Gods and Cosmic
Kings." Entry in *Maya Decipherment*, edited by David Stuart. Electronic document. https://decipherment.wordpress.com/2017/09/04
/a-universe-in-a-maya-lintel-iv-seasonal-gods-and-cosmic-kings/.

Houston, Stephen D., Thomas G. Garrison, and Edwin Román. 2018.
"A Fortress in Heaven: Researching the Long Term at El Zotz, Guatemala." In *An Inconstant Landscape: The Maya Kingdom of El Zotz,
Guatemala*, edited by Thomas G. Garrison and Stephen Houston,
3–45. Louisville: University Press of Colorado.

Houston, Stephen D., and Takeshi Inomata. 2009. *The Classic Maya*.
Cambridge: Cambridge University Press.

Houston, Stephen D., and Simon Martin. 2012. "Mythic Prototypes and
Maya Writing." Entry in *Maya Decipherment*, edited by David Stuart.
Electronic document. https://mayadecipherment.com/2012/01/04
/mythic-prototypes-and-maya-writing/.

Houston, Stephen D., Simon Martin, and Karl Taube. 2016. "Xenopho-
bia and Grotesque Fun." Entry in *Maya Decipherment: Ideas on Ancient
Maya Writing and Iconography*. Electronic document. https://maya
decipherment.com/2016/03/29/xenophobia-and-grotesque-fun.

Houston, Stephen, Sarah Newman, Edwin Román, and Thomas Garrison. 2015. *Temple of the Night Sun: A Royal Tomb at El Diablo, Guatemala*. San Francisco: Precolumbia Mesoweb Press.

Houston, Stephen D., and David Stuart. 1996. "Of Gods, Glyphs, and
Kings: Divinity and Rulership among the Classic Maya." *Antiquity* 70:
289–312.

———. 2001. "Peopling the Classic Maya Court." In *Royal Courts of the
Ancient Maya*. Vol. 1, *Theory, Comparison, and Synthesis*, edited by
Takeshi Inomata and Stephen D. Houston, 54–83. Boulder, CO:
Westview.

Houston, Stephen, John Robertson, and David Stuart. 2000. "The Language of the Classic Maya Inscriptions." *Current Anthropology* 41 (3):
321–356.

———. 2001. *Quality and Quantity in Glyphic Nouns and Adjectives*. Research Reports on Ancient Maya Writing 47. Washington, DC: Center for Maya Research.

Houston, Stephen, David Stuart, and John Robertson. 1998. "Dishar-
mony in Maya Hieroglyphic Writing: Linguistic Change and Continuity in Classic Society." In *Anatomía de una Civilización: Aproximaciones
Interdisciplinarias a la Cultura Maya*, edited by Andrés Ciudad Real,
María Yolanda Fernández Marquínez, Jose Miguel García Campillo,
María Josefa Iglesia Ponce de León, Alfonso Lacadena García-Gallo,
and Luis Tomás Sanz Castro, 275–296. Madrid: Sociedad Española
de Estudios Mayas.

Houston, Stephen, David Stuart, and Karl Taube. 2006. *The Memory of
Bones: Body, Being, and Experience among the Classic Maya*. Austin:
University of Texas Press.

Hruby, Zachary. 2007. "Ritualized Chipped-Stone Production at Piedras
Negras, Guatemala." In *Rethinking Craft Specialization in Complex Societies: Archaeological Analyses of the Social Meaning of Production*, edited by Zachary Hruby and Rowan Flad, 68–87. Archaeological
Papers of the American Anthropological Association, no. 17. Washington, DC: American Anthropological Association.

Hull, Kerry. 2005. "An Abbreviated Dictionary of Ch'orti' Maya." Foundation for the Advancement of Mesoamerican Studies, Incorporated.
Electronic document. www.famsi.org/reports/03031/03031.pdf.

Hunt, Alan. 1996. *Governance of the Consuming Passions: A History of
Sumptuary Law*. New York: St. Martin's.

Inomata, Takeshi. 2001. "The Power and Ideology of Artistic Creation:
Elite Craft Specialists in Classic Maya Society." *Current Anthropology*
42 (3): 321–349.

———. 2006a. "Plazas, Performers, and Spectators: Political Theaters of
the Classic Maya." *Current Anthropology* 47 (5): 805–842.

———. 2006b. "Politics and Theatricality in Mayan Society." In *Archaeology of Performance: Theaters of Power, Community, and Politics*, edited
by Takeshi Inomata and Lawrence S. Coben, 187–221. Lanham, MD:
Altamira Press.

Inomata, Takeshi, and Markus Eberl. 2014. "Stone Ornaments and Other
Stone Artifacts." In *Life and Politics at the Royal Court of Aguateca: Artifacts, Analytical Data, and Synthesis*, edited by Takeshi Inomata and
Daniela Triadan, 84–117. Monographs of the Aguateca Archaeological Project First Phase, vol. 3. Salt Lake City: University of Utah Press.

Inomata, Takeshi, and Kitty Emery. 2014. "Bone and Shell Artifacts."
In *Life and Politics at the Royal Court of Aguateca: Artifacts, Analytical

Data, and Synthesis, edited by Takeshi Inomata and Daniela Triadan, 127–157. Salt Lake City: University of Utah Press.

Inomata, Takeshi, Erick Ponciano, Richard E. Terry, Estela Pinto, Daniela Triadan, and Harriet F. Beaubien. 2001. "In the Palace of the Fallen King: The Excavation of the Royal Residential Complex at the Classic Maya Center of Aguateca, Guatemala." *Journal of Field Archaeology* 28 (3–4): 287–306.

Inomata, Takeshi, and Daniela Triadan, eds. 2014. *Life and Politics at the Royal Court of Aguateca: Artifacts, Analytical Data, and Synthesis.* Salt Lake City: University of Utah Press.

Inomata, Takeshi, Daniela Triadan, Erick Ponciano, Estela Pinto, Richard E. Terry, and Markus Eberl. 2002. "Domestic and Political Lives of Classic Maya Elites: The Excavation of Rapidly Abandoned Structures at Aguateca, Guatemala." *Latin American Antiquity* 13 (3): 305–330.

Ishihara-Brito, Reiko, and Karl A. Taube. 2012. "Carved Bells." In *Ancient Maya Art at Dumbarton Oaks*, edited by Joanne Pillsbury, Miriam Doutriaux, Reiko Ishihara-Brito, and Alexandre Tokovinine, 458–463. Pre-Columbian Art at Dumbarton Oaks. Washington, DC: Dumbarton Oaks Research Library and Collection.

Jackson, Sarah E. 2013. *Politics of the Maya Court: Hierarchy and Change in the Late Classic Period.* Norman: University of Oklahoma Press.

Johnson, Irmgard Weitlaner. 1954. "Chiptic Cave Textiles from Chiapas, Mexico." *Journal de la Société des Américanistes* 43: 137–148.

Jones, Christopher. 1985. "The Rubber Ball Game: A Universal Mesoamerican Sport." *Expedition: The Magazine of the University of Pennsylvania* 27 (2): 44–52.

Jones, Christopher, and Linton Satterthwaite. 1982. *The Monuments and Inscriptions of Tikal: The Carved Monuments.* Tikal Report 33A. Philadelphia: University Museum and University of Pennsylvania.

Joralemon, Peter David. 1981. "The Old Woman and the Child: Themes in the Iconography of Preclassic Mesoamerica." In *The Olmec and Their Neighbors: Essays in Memory of Matthew W. Stirling*, edited by Elizabeth P. Benson, 163–180. Washington, DC: Dumbarton Oaks Research Library and Collection.

Joyce, Rosemary A. 1992. "Images of Gender and Labor Organization in Classic Maya Society." In *Exploring Gender through Archaeology: Selected Papers from the 1991 Boone Conference*, edited by Cheryl Claessen, 63–70. Monographs in World Archaeology, no. 11. Madison, WI: Prehistory Press.

———. 1996. "The Construction of Gender in Classic Maya Monuments." In *Gender and Archaeology*, edited by Rita P. Wright, 167–195. Philadelphia: University of Pennsylvania Press.

———. 2000a. *Gender and Power in Prehispanic Mesoamerica.* Austin: University of Texas Press.

———. 2000b. "Girling the Girl and Boying the Boy: The Production of Adulthood in Ancient Mesoamerica." *World Archaeology* 31 (3): 473–483.

———. 2000c. "Heirlooms and Houses: Materiality and Social Memory." In *Beyond Kinship: Social and Material Reproduction in House Societies*, edited by Rosemary A. Joyce and Susan D. Gillespie, 189–212. Philadelphia: University of Pennsylvania Press.

———. 2001. "Negotiating Sex and Gender in Classic Maya Society." In *Gender in Pre-Hispanic America*, edited by Cecilia F. Klein and Jeffrey Quilter, 109–141. Washington, DC: Dumbarton Oaks.

———. 2002. "Beauty, Sexuality, Body Ornamentation, and Gender in Ancient Mesoamerica." In *Pursuit of Gender: Worldwide Archaeological Approaches*, edited by Sarah M. Nelson and Myriam Rosen-Ayalon, 81–91. Walnut Creek: Altamira.

———. 2008. *Ancient Bodies, Ancient Lives: Sex, Gender, and Archaeology.* New York: Thames and Hudson.

———. 2014. "Ties That Bind: Cloth, Clothing, and Embodiment in Formative Honduras." In *Wearing Culture: Dress and Regalia in Early Mesoamerica and Central America*, edited by Heather Orr and Matthew G. Looper, 61–78. Boulder: University Press of Colorado.

Joyce, Thomas A. 1933. "The Pottery Whistle-Figurines of Lubaantun." *Journal of the Royal Anthropological Institute of Great Britain and Ireland* 63: 15–25.

Just, Bryan. 2012. *Dancing into Dreams: Maya Vase Painting of the Ik' Kingdom.* New Haven, CT: Yale University Press.

Justeson, John S. 1984. "Appendix B: Interpretations of Mayan Hieroglyphs." In *Phoneticism in Mayan Hieroglyphic Writing*, edited by John S. Justeson and Lyle Campbell, 315–362. Institute for Mesoamerican Studies, Publication 9. Albany: State University of New York.

Kaeppler, Adrienne L. 2011. "The Hands and Arms Tell the Story: Movement through Time in Eighteenth-century Dance Depictions from Polynesia." In *Imaging Dance: Visual Representations of Dancers and Dancing*, edited by Barbara Sparti and Judy Van Zile, 87–102. Hildesheim, Germany: Georg Olms Verlag.

Kaufman, Terrence. 1990. "Algunos rasgos estructurales de los idiomas Mayances con referencia especial al K'iche'." In *Lecturas sobre la lingüística maya*, edited by Nora C. England and Stephen R. Elliott, 59–114. Guatemala City: CIRMA.

———. 2003. "A Preliminary Mayan Etymological Dictionary." With the assistance of John Justeson. Report submitted to the Foundation for the Advancement of Mesoamerican Studies, Incorporated. Electronic document. www.famsi.org/reports/01051/pmed.pdf.

Kaufman, Terrence, and William M. Norman. 1984. "An Outline of Proto-Cholan Phonology, Morphology, and Vocabulary." In *Phoneticism in Mayan Hieroglyphic Writing*, edited by John S. Justeson and Lyle Campbell, 77–166. Institute for Mesoamerican Studies, Publication 9. Albany: State University of New York.

Kelemen, Pál. 1969. *Medieval American Art: Masterpieces of the New World before Columbus.* 3rd ed. New York: Dover.

Keller, Kathryn C., and Plácido Luciano G. 1997. *Diccionario de Chontal de Tabasco (Mayense).* Vocabulario Indígenas 36. Tucson, AZ: Instituto Lingüístico de Verano.

Kennedy, Raymond. 1934. "Bark-Cloth in Indonesia." *Journal of Polynesian Society* 43 (4): 229–243.

Kerr, Justin. 1989. "A Maya Vase from the Ik Site." *Record of the Art Museum, Princeton University* 48 (2): 32–36.

———. 1992. "The Myth of the Popol Vuh as an Instrument of Power." In *New Theories on the Ancient Maya*, edited by Elin C. Danien and Robert J. Sharer, 109–121. Philadelphia: University Museum and University of Pennsylvania.

Kettunen, Harri. 2005. *Nasal Motifs in Maya Iconography.* Helsinki: Helsinki University Printing House.

Kettunen, Harri, and Christophe Helmke. 2014. *Introduction to Maya Hieroglyphs.* 14th ed. Workbook for the Nineteenth European Maya Conference, Bratislava. Electronic document. www.wayeb.org/download/resources/wh2014english.pdf.

Kidder, Alfred V. 1947. *Artifacts of Uaxactun, Guatemala.* Carnegie Institution of Washington Publication 576. Washington, DC: Carnegie Institution of Washington.

Kidder, Alfred V., Jesse D. Jennings, and Edwin M. Shook. 1946. *Excavations at Kaminaljuyu, Guatemala.* Carnegie Institution of Washington Publication 561. Washington, DC: Carnegie Institution of Washington

Knub, Julie N. 2014. "How the Other Half Lives: The Role and Function of Body Paint at Maya Courts." In *Palaces and Courtly Culture in Ancient Mesoamerica*, edited by J. Nehammer Knub, Cristophe Helmke, and Jesper Nielsen, 77–89. Archaeopress Pre-Columbian Archaeology 4. Oxford: Archaeopress.

Ko, Dorothy. 2007. *Cinderella's Sisters: A Revisionist History of Footbinding*. Berkeley: University of California Press.

Kovacevich, Brigitte. 2007. "Ritual, Crafting, and Agency at the Classic Maya Kingdom of Cancuen." In *Mesoamerican Ritual Economy: Archaeological and Ethnological Perspectives*, edited by E. Christian Wells and Karla Davis-Salazar, 67–114. Boulder: University Press of Colorado.

———. 2011. "The Organization of Jade Production at Cancuen, Guatemala." In *The Technology of Maya Civilization: Political Economy and Beyond in Lithic Studies*, edited by Zachary X. Hruby, Oswaldo Chinchilla, and Geoffrey Braswell, 149–161. London: Equinox.

———. 2016. "Pyrite Mirror Production at Cancuen, Guatemala." In *Manufactured Light: Mirrors in the Mesoamerican Realm*, edited by Emiliano Gallaga and Mark Blainey, 73–106. Boulder: University Press of Colorado.

———. 2017. "The Value of Labor: How the Production Process Added Value to Pre-Columbian Maya Jade." In *The Value of Things: Commodities in the Maya Region from Prehistoric to Contemporary*, edited by Thomas Guderjan and Jennifer Matthews, 7–29. Tucson: University of Arizona Press.

Kowalski, Jeff K. 2007. "What's 'Toltec' at Uxmal and Chichén Itzá? Merging Maya and Mesoamerican Worldviews and World Systems in Terminal Classic to Early Postclassic Yucatan." In *Twin Tollans: Chichén Itzá, Tula, and the Epiclassic to Early Postclassic Mesoamerican World*, edited by Jeff K. Kowalski, and Cynthia Kristan-Graham, 251–313. Washington, DC: Dumbarton Oaks.

Kunow, Marianna A. 2003. *Maya Medicine: Traditional Healing in Yucatan*. Albuquerque: University of New Mexico Press.

Lacadena Garcia-Gallo, Alfonso. 1996. "A New Proposal for the Transcription of the a-k'u-na/a-k'u-HUN-na Title." *Mayab* 10: 46–49.

Lakhani, Nina. 2017. "Mexico's Ancient City Guards Its Secrets but Excavation Reveals New Mysteries." *Guardian*, April 24. www.theguardian.com/science/2017/apr/24/mexicos-ancient-city-guards-its-secrets-but-excavation-reveals-new-mysteries.

Landa, Diego de. 1941. *Landa's Relación de las cosas de Yucatan: A Translation*. Translated and edited by Alfred M. Tozzer. Cambridge, MA: Peabody Museum of Archaeology and Ethnology, Harvard University.

———. 1978. *Yucatan before and after the Conquest*. Translated and edited by William Gates. New York: Dover.

Lechuga, Ruth D. 1982. *El traje indígena de México*. Mexico, DF: Panorama Editorial.

Lee, David, and Jennifer Piehl. 2014. "Ritual and Remembrance at the Northwest Palace Complex, El Peru-Waka." In *Ancient Maya Performances of Ritual, Memory and Power*, edited by Olivia C. Navarro Farr and Michelle Rich, 85–101. Tucson: University of Arizona Press.

Lee, Thomas A., Jr. 1969. *The Artifacts of Chiapa de Corzo, Chiapas, Mexico*. Papers of the New World Archaeological Foundation, no. 26. Provo, UT: Brigham Young University.

Leona, Marco, Francesca Casadio, Mauro Bacci, and Marcello Picollo. 2004. "Identification of the Pre-Columbian Pigment Maya Blue on Works of Art by Non-Invasive UV-vis and Raman Spectroscopic Techniques." *Journal of the American Institute for Conservation* 43: 39–54.

Leurquin, Anne. 2003. *A World of Necklaces: Africa, Asia, Oceania, America from the Ghysels Collection*. Milan: Skira.

Leyenaar, Ted J. J. 2001. "The Modern Ballgames of Sinaloa: A Survival of the Aztec Ullamaliztli." In *The Sport of Life and Death: The Mesoamerican Ballgame*, edited by E. Michael Whittington and Douglas E. Bradley, 122–129. Charlotte, NC: Mint Museum of Art with Thames and Hudson.

Lohse, Jon C. 2010. "Archaic Origins of the Lowland Maya." *Latin American Antiquity* 21 (3): 312–352.

Looper, Matthew G. 1991. "The Name of Copán and of a Dance at Yaxchilán." *Copán Note* 95.

———. 2002. "Women-Men (and Men-Women): Classic Maya Rulers and the Third Gender." In *Ancient Maya Women*, edited by T. Ardren, 171–202. Walnut Creek, CA: Altamira.

———. 2003. *Lightning Warrior: Maya Art and Kingship at Quirigua*. Austin: University of Texas Press.

———. 2009. *To Be Like Gods: Dance in Ancient Maya Civilization*. Austin: University of Texas Press.

———. 2010. "Ancient Maya." In *Encyclopedia of World Dress and Fashion*, vol. 2, *Latin America and the Caribbean*, edited by Margot B. Schevill, 34–42. New York: Oxford University Press.

———. 2012. "Ritual Dance and Music in Ancient Maya Society." *Flower World—Mundo Florido* 1.

———. 2014. "Early Maya Dress and Adornment." In *Wearing Culture: Dress and Regalia in Early Mesoamerica and Central America*, edited by Heather Orr and Matthew G. Looper, 411–446. Boulder: University Press of Colorado.

López de Cogolludo, Fray Diego. 1957 [1688]. *Historia de Yucatán*. Coleción de Grandes Crónicas Mexicanas 3. Mexico, DF: Editorial Academia Literaria.

Lothrop, Joy M. 1992. "Textiles." In *Artifacts from the Cenote of Sacrifice, Chichen Itza, Yucatan*, edited by Clemency C. Coggins, 33–90. Memoirs of the Peabody Museum of Archaeology and Ethnology 10:3. Cambridge, MA: Harvard University.

Lothrop, Samuel K. 1936. *Zacualpa: A Study of Ancient Quiché Artifacts*. Washington, DC: Carnegie Institution of Washington.

———. 1952. *Metals from the Cenote of Sacrifice, Chichen Itza, Yucatan*. Memoirs of the Peabody Museum of Archaeology and Ethnology, Harvard University, 2. Cambridge, MA: Peabody Museum, Harvard University.

MacLeod, Barbara. 1987. *An Epigrapher's Annotated Index to Cholan and Yucatec Verb Morphology*. University of Missouri Monographs in Anthropology, no. 9. Columbia: University of Missouri.

MacLeod, Barbara, and Andrea Stone. 1995. "The Hieroglyphic Inscriptions of Naj Tunich." In *Images from the Underworld: Naj Tunich and the Tradition of Maya Cave Painting*, edited Andrea Stone, 155–184. Austin: University of Texas Press.

Macri, Martha J., and Matthew G. Looper. 2003. *The New Catalog of Maya Hieroglyphs: The Classic Period Inscriptions*. Civilization of the American Indian Series. Norman: University of Oklahoma Press.

Mahler, Joy. 1965. "Garments and Textiles of the Maya Lowlands." In *Handbook of Middle American Indians*, vol. 3, *Archaeology of Southern Mesoamerica*, pt. 2, edited by Gordon R. Willey, 581–593. Austin: University of Texas Press.

Mansel, Philip. 2005. *Dressed to Rule: Royal and Court Costume from Louis XIV to Elizabeth II*. New Haven, CT: Yale University Press.

Marcus, Joyce. 1987. *The Inscriptions of Calakmul: Royal Marriage at a Maya City in Campeche, Mexico.* Ann Arbor: Museum of Anthropology, University of Michigan.

Martin, Phyllis M. 1994. "Contesting Clothes in Colonial Brazzaville." *Journal of African History* 35 (3): 401–426.

Martin, Simon. 1999. "The Queen of Middle Classic Tikal." PARI Online Publications. Electronic document. www.mesoweb.com/pari/publications/news_archive/27/lady/tikal.html.

———. 2004. "Preguntas epigráficas acerca de los escalones de Dzibanché." In *Los cautivos de Dzibanché,* edited by Enrique Nalda, 104–115. Mexico City: Consejo Nacional para la Cultura y las Artes, Instituto Nacional de Antropología e Historia.

———. 2012. "Hieroglyphs from the Painted Pyramid: The Epigraphy of Chiik Nahb Structure Sub1–4, Calakmul, Mexico." In *Maya Archaeology 2,* edited by Charles Golden, Stephen Houston, and Joel Skidmore, 60–81. San Francisco: Precolumbia Mesoweb Press.

———. 2015. "The Old Man of the Maya Universe: A Unitary Dimension to Ancient Maya Religion." In *Maya Archaeology 3,* edited by Charles Golden, Stephen Houston, and Joel Skidmore, 186–227. San Francisco: Precolumbia Mesoweb Press.

Martin, Simon, and Nikolai Grube. 2008. *Chronicle of the Maya Kings and Queens: Deciphering the Dynasties of the Ancient Maya.* 2nd ed. London: Thames and Hudson.

Martin, Toby F., and Rosie Weetch, eds. 2017. *Dress and Society: Contributions from Archaeology.* Oxford: Oxbow.

Mascetti, Daniela, and Amanda Triossi. 1997. *The Necklace: From Antiquity to the Present.* New York: Abrams.

Mason, J. Alden. 1943. *Examples of Maya Pottery in the Museum and Other Collections.* Vol. 3. Philadelphia: University of Pennsylvania Museum.

Masson, Marilyn A., and David A. Freidel. 2012. "An Argument for Classic Era Maya Market Exchange." *Journal of Anthropological Archaeology* 31: 455–484.

Mathews, Peter. 1998. "Una lectura de un nuevo monumento de El Cayo, Chiapas, y sus implicaciones políticas." In *Modelos de entidades políticas mayas: Primer Seminario de las Mesas Redondas de Palenque,* edited by Silvia Trejo, 113–139. Mexico, DF: Instituto Nacional de Antropología e Historia.

Mauss, Marcel. 1973. "Techniques of the Body." *Economy and Society* 2 (1): 70–88.

Maxwell, Judith M., and Robert M. Hill. 2006. *Kaqchikel Chronicles: The Definitive Edition.* Austin: University of Texas Press.

Mayer, Karl H. 1981. "Facial Decoration among the Pre-Columbian Mayas." *Organorama* 18 (2): 16–20.

McAnany, Patricia A. 2013. "Artisans, *Ikatz,* and Statecraft: Provisioning Classic Maya Royal Courts." In *Merchants, Markets, and Exchange in the Pre-Columbian World,* edited by Kenneth G. Hirth and Joanne Pillsbury, 229–253. Washington, DC: Dumbarton Oaks.

McAnany, Patricia, and Justin P. Ebersole. 2004. "Ground and Polished Stone Tools." In *K'axob: Ritual, Work and Family in an Ancient Maya Village,* edited by Patricia McAnany, 317–330. Monumenta Archaeologica 22. Los Angeles: Cotsen Institute of Archaeology at UCLA.

McCafferty, Sharisse D., and Geoffrey G. McCafferty. 1991. "Spinning and Weaving as Female Gender Identity in Post-Classic Mexico." In *Textile Traditions of Mesoamerica and the Andes: An Anthology,* edited by Margot B. Schevill, Janet C. Berlo, and Edward B. Dwyer, 19–44. New York: Garland.

———. 2000. "Textile Production in Postclassic Cholula, Mexico." *Ancient Mesoamerica* 11 (1): 39–54.

McDowell, Felice. 2015. "'Old' Glossies and 'New' Histories: Fashion, Dress and Historical Space." *Fashion Theory* 20 (3): 297–316.

McGee, R. Jon. 1990. *Life, Ritual, and Religion Among the Lacandon Maya.* Wadsworth Modern Anthropology Library. Belmont, CA: Wadsworth.

McKillop, Heather. 2004. *The Ancient Maya: New Perspectives.* Santa Barbara, CA: ABC-CLIO.

McNiven, Timothy J. 2000. "Behaving Like an Other: Telltale Gestures in Athenian Vase Painting." In *Not the Classical Ideal: Athens and the Construction of the Other in Greek Art,* edited by Beth Cohen, 71–97. Leiden, the Netherlands: Brill.

Mesick, Cassandra. 2010. "Pectoral Assemblage with an Engraved Ik' Symbol, 1300–1500(?), and Torso with an Ik' Pectoral, 600–800." In *Fiery Pool: The Maya and the Mythic Sea,* edited by Daniel Finamore and Stephen D. Houston, 122–123. New Haven, CT: Yale University Press.

Michel-Morfín, Jesús Emilio, Ernesto A. Chávez, and Lourdes González. 2002. "Population Structure, Effort and Dye Yielding of the Snail *Plicopurpura pansa* (Gould, 1853) in the Mexican Pacific." *Ciencias Marinas* 28 (4): 357–368.

Miller, Mary E. 1988. "The Boys in the Bonampak Band." In *Maya Iconography,* edited by Elizabeth P. Benson and Gillett G. Griffin, 318–330. Princeton, NJ: Princeton University Press.

———. 2009. "Extreme Makeover: How Painted Bodies, Flattened Foreheads, and Filed Teeth Made the Maya Beautiful." *Archaeology* 62 (1): 36–42.

———. 2018. "What Happened on Jaina?" Paper presented at the Eighth Annual Maya at the Lago Conference, April 26–29, Davidson, NC.

Miller, Mary E., and Claudia Brittenham. 2013. *The Spectacle of the Late Maya Court: Reflections on the Murals of Bonampak.* Austin: University of Texas Press.

Miller, Mary E., and Stephen D. Houston. 1987. "The Classic Maya Ballgame and Its Architectural Setting: A Study of Relations between Text and Image." *RES: Anthropology and Aesthetics* 14: 46–65.

Miller, Mary E., and Simon Martin. 2004. *Courtly Art of the Ancient Maya.* London: Thames and Hudson.

Miller, Virginia E. 1981. "Pose and Gesture in Classic Maya Monumental Sculpture." PhD diss., University of Texas.

———. 1983. "A Reexamination of Maya Gestures of Submission." *Journal of Latin American Lore* 9 (1): 17–38.

———. 1985. "The Dwarf Motif in Classic Maya Art." In *Fourth Palenque Round Table, 1980,* edited by Elizabeth P. Benson, 141–153. San Francisco: Pre-Columbian Art Research Institute.

———. 2018. "The Representation of Hair in the Art of Chichén Itzá." In *Social Skins of the Head: Body Beliefs and Ritual in Ancient Mesoamerica and the Andes,* edited by Vera Tiesler and María Cecilia Lozada, 129–141. Albuquerque: University of New Mexico Press.

Moholy-Nagy, Hattula. 1989. "Formed Shell Beads from Tikal, Guatemala." In *Proceedings of the 1986 Shell Bead Conference,* edited by Charles F. Hayes III, 139–156. Research Records, no. 20. New York: Research Division of the Rochester Museum of Science Center.

———. 1994. "Tikal Material Culture: Artifacts and Social Structure at a Classic Lowland Maya City." PhD diss., University of Michigan.

———. 2003. *The Artifacts of Tikal: Utilitarian Artifacts and Unworked Material.* Tikal Report 27B. Philadelphia: University of Pennsylvania Museum of Archaeology and Anthropology.

———. 2008. *The Artifacts of Tikal: Ornamental and Ceremonial Artifacts* and *Unworked Material*. Tikal Report 27, pt. A. Philadelphia: University of Pennsylvania Museum of Archaeology and Anthropology.

Moholy-Nagy, Hattula, and John M. Ladd. 1992. "Miscellaneous: Palm Nut Artifacts, Decorated Gourds, Leather, and Stucco." In *Artifacts from the Cenote of Sacrifice, Chichen Itza, Yucatan*, edited by Clemency Coggins, 359–368. Memoirs of the Peabody Museum of Archaeology and Ethnology, Harvard University, vol. 10, no. 3. Cambridge, MA: Peabody Museum, Harvard University.

Morehart, Christopher T., Jaime J. Awe, Michael J. Mirro, Vanessa A. Owen, and Christophe G. Helmke. 2004. "Ancient Textile Remains from Barton Creek Cave, Cayo District, Belize." *Mexicon* 26: 50–56.

Morley, Sylvanus Griswold. 1937. *The Inscriptions of Peten*. Vol. 5, pt. 1, *Plates*. Carnegie Institution of Washington Publication 437. Washington, DC: Carnegie Institution of Washington.

Morris, Earl H., Jean Charlot, and Ann Axtell Morris. 1931. *The Temple of the Warriors at Chichen Itza, Yucatan*. Carnegie Institution of Washington Publication 406. Washington, DC: Carnegie Institution of Washington.

Morris, Walter F. 1985. "Fall Fashions: Lagartero Figurine Costume at the End of the Classic Period." In *Fifth Palenque Round Table, 1983*, edited by Virginia M. Fields, 245–254. San Francisco: Pre-Columbian Art Research Institute.

Newman, Sarah, Stephen Houston, Thomas Garrison, and Edwin Román. 2015. "Outfitting a King." In *Temple of the Night Sun: A Royal Tomb at El Diablo, Guatemala*, edited by Stephen Houston, Sarah Newman, Edwin Román, and Thomas Garrison, 84–179. San Francisco: Precolumbia Mesoweb Press.

Olko, Justyna. 2005. *Turquoise Diadems and Staffs of Office: Elite Costume and Insignia of Power in Aztec and Early Colonial Mexico*. Polish Society for Latin American Studies and Centre for Studies on the Classical Tradition. Warsaw: University of Warsaw.

———. 2014. *Insignia of Rank in the Nahua World: From the Fifteenth to the Seventeenth Century*. Boulder: University Press of Colorado.

Olson, Kelly. 2009. "Cosmetics in Roman Antiquity: Substance, Remedy, Poison." *Classical World* 102 (3): 291–310.

Ordoñez, Margaret T. 2015. "Appendix V: Textiles." In *Temple of the Night Sun: A Royal Tomb at El Diablo, Guatemala*, edited by Stephen Houston, Sarah Newman, Edwin Román, and Thomas Garrison, 259–263. San Francisco: Precolumbia Mesoweb Press.

Orejel, Jorge L. 1990. *The "Axe/Comb" Glyph as ch'ak*." Research Reports on Ancient Maya Writing 31. Washington, DC: Center for Maya Research.

Orr, Heather S., and Matthew G. Looper. 2014. Preface to *Wearing Culture: Dress and Regalia in Early Mesoamerica and Central America*, edited by Heather S. Orr and Matthew G. Looper, xxi–xlv. Boulder: University Press of Colorado.

Ortíz, Ponciano, and María del Carmen Rodríguez. 1999. "Olmec Ritual Behavior at El Manatí: A Sacred Space." In *Social Patterns in Pre-Classic Mesoamerica*, edited by David C. Grove, and Rosemary Joyce, 225–254. Dumbarton Oaks Pre-Columbian Symposia and Colloquia. Washington, DC: Dumbarton Oaks.

Pancake, Cherri. 1991. "Communicative Imagery in Guatemalan Indian Dress." In *Textile Traditions of Mesoamerica and the Andes: An Anthology*, edited by Margot Blum Schevill, Janet Catherine Berlo, and Edward B. Dwyer, 45–62. New York: Garland.

Parsons, Lee Allen. 1986. *The Origins of Maya Art: Monumental Stone Sculpture at Kaminaljuyu, Guatemala, and the Southern Pacific Coast*. Washington, DC: Dumbarton Oaks.

Parsons, Jeffrey R. 2001. "Agave." In *Archaeology of Ancient Mexico and Central America: An Encyclopedia*, edited by Susan T. Evans and David L. Webster, 4–7. New York: Garland.

Patch, Robert W. 1993. *Maya and Spaniard in Yucatán, 1648–1812*. Stanford, CA: Stanford University Press.

Peiss, Kathy. 1998. *Hope in a Jar: The Making of America's Beauty Culture*. New York: Metropolitan Books.

Pendergast, David M. 1966. "The Actun Balam Vase." *Archaeology* 19 (3): 154–161.

———. 1968. "Four Maya Pottery Vessels from British Honduras." *American Antiquity* 33 (3): 379–382.

———. 1969. *Altun Ha, British Honduras (Belize): The Sun God's Tomb*. Art and Archaeology Occasional Paper 19. Toronto: Royal Ontario Museum.

———. 1979. *Excavations at Altun Ha, Belize, 1964–1970*. Vol. 1. Toronto: Royal Ontario Museum.

———. 1982. *Excavations at Altun Ha, Belize, 1964–1970*. Royal Ontario Museum Publications in Archaeology 2. Toronto: Royal Ontario Museum.

———. 1990. *Excavations at Altun Ha, Belize, 1964–1970*. Royal Ontario Museum Publications in Archaeology 3. Toronto: Royal Ontario Museum.

Pérez Martínez, Vitalino, Federico García, Felipe Martínez, and Jeremias López. 1996. *Diccionario Ch'orti'*. Antigua, Guatemala: Proyecto Lingüístico Francisco Marroquín.

Pérez Robles, Griselda. 2010. "Una corte real: La restauración de 23 figurillas encontradas en el Entierro 39 del Perú." In *Proyecto Arqueológico El Perú-Waka': Informe No. 8, Temporada 2010*, edited by Mary Jane Acuña, 5–59. Guatemala City: Fundación de Investigación Arqueológica Waka'.

Pfeiler, Barbara. 2003. "Early Acquisition of the Verbal Complex in Yucatec Maya." In *Development of Verb Inflection in First Language Acquisition: A Cross-linguistic Perspective*, edited by Dagmar Bittner, Wolfgang U. Dressler, and Marianne Kilani-Schoch, 379–399. New York: Mouton de Gruyter.

Pillsbury, Joanne, Timothy Potts, and Kim N. Richter, eds. 2017. *Golden Kingdoms: Luxury Arts in the Ancient Americas*. Los Angeles: J. Paul Getty Museum and Getty Research Institute.

Pohl, Mary. 1981. "Ritual Continuity and Transformation in Mesoamerica: Reconstructing the Ancient Maya 'Cuch' Ritual." *American Antiquity* 46: 513–529.

———. 1983. "Maya Ritual Faunas: Vertebrate Remains from Burial, Caches, Caves and Cenotes in the Maya Lowlands." In *Civilization in the Ancient Americas*, edited by Richard M. Levanthal and Alan L. Kolata, 55–103. Albuquerque: University of New Mexico Press.

Prager, Christian M. 2018. "The Lexeme *Potz* 'to Wrap, Cover' in Classic Maya Hieroglyphic Texts." *Mexicon* 40 (1): 4–7.

Prager, Christian M., and Geoffrey E. Braswell. 2016. "Maya Politics and Ritual: An Important New Hieroglyphic Text on a Carved Jade from Belize." *Ancient Mesoamerica* 27 (2): 267–278.

Prechtel, Martin, and Robert S. Carlsen. 1988. "Weaving and Cosmos among the Tzutujil Maya of Guatemala." *RES: Anthropology and Aesthetics* 15: 122–132.

Proskouriakoff, Tatiana. 1950. *A Study of Classic Maya Sculpture*. Washington, DC: Carnegie Institution.

———. 1961. "Portraits of Women in Maya Art." In *Essays in Precolumbian Art and Archaeology*, edited by Samuel K. Lothrop, 81–99. Cambridge, MA: Harvard University Press.

———. 1968. "The Job and the Jaguar Signs in Maya Writing." *American Antiquity* 33 (2): 247–251.

———. 1974. *Jades from the Cenote of Sacrifice, Chichen Itza, Yucatan.* Cambridge, MA: Peabody Museum of Archaeology and Ethnology, Harvard University.

Quezada, Sergio. 2001. "Tributos, limosnas, y mantas en Yucatán, siglo XVI." *Ancient Mesoamerica* 12: 73–78.

Quirarte, Jacinto. 1979. "The Representation of Underworld Processions in Maya Vase Painting: An Iconographic Study." In *Maya Archaeology and Ethnohistory*, edited by Norman Hammond and Gordon R. Willey, 116–148. Austin: University of Texas Press.

Recinos, Adrián. 1947. *Popol Vuh, las antiguas historias del quiché.* Mexico City: Fondo de Cultura Económica.

Reed, Fran. 2005. "The Poor Man's Raincoat: Alaskan Fish Skin Garments." In *Arctic Clothing of North America: Alaska, Canada, Greenland*, edited by Jonathan C. H. King, Birgit Pauksztat, and Robert Storrie, 48–52. Montreal: McGill-Queens University Press.

Reese-Taylor, Kathryn, Peter Mathews, Julia Guernsey, and Marlene Fritzler. 2009. "Warrior Queens among the Classic Maya." In *Blood and Beauty: Organized Violence in the Art and Archaeology of Mesoamerica and Central America*, edited by Heather S. Orr and Rex Koontz, 39–72. Los Angeles: Cotsen Institute of Archaeology.

Reischer, Erica, and Kathryn S. Koo. 2004. "The Body Beautiful: Symbolism and Agency in the Social World." *Annual Review of Anthropology* 33: 297–317.

Rice, Prudence M. 1987. *Macanché Island, El Petén, Guatemala: Excavations, Pottery, and Artifacts.* Gainesville: University Press of Florida.

Ricketson, Oliver G., and Edith B. Ricketson. 1937. *Uaxactun, Guatemala, Group E: 1926–1931.* Washington, DC: Carnegie Institution of Washington.

Ringle, William. 2009. "The Art of War: Imagery of the Upper Temple of the Jaguars, Chichen Itza." *Ancient Mesoamerica* 20: 15–44.

Robertson, Catriona M. 2010. "Mortuary Behaviour of the Ancient Maya at Pacbitun, Belize." Master's thesis, Trent University, Peterborough, ON.

Robertson, John, Stephen Houston, Marc Zender, and David Stuart. 2007. *Universals and the Logic of the Material Implication: A Case Study from Maya Hieroglyphic Writing.* Research Reports on Ancient Maya Writing 62. Washington, DC: Center for Maya Research.

Robertson, Merle Greene. 1983. *The Sculpture of Palenque.* Vol. 1, *The Temple of the Inscriptions.* Princeton, NJ: Princeton University Press.

———. 1985a. "'57 Varieties': The Palenque Beauty Salon." In *Fourth Palenque Round Table 1980*, edited by Merle Green Robertson, and Elizabeth P. Benson, 29–44. San Francisco: Precolumbian Art Research Institute.

———. 1985b. *The Sculpture of Palenque.* Vol. 3, *The Late Buildings of the Palace.* Princeton, NJ: Princeton University Press.

———. 1991. *The Sculpture of Palenque.* Vol. 4, *The Cross Group, the North Group, the Olvidado, and Other Pieces.* Princeton, NJ: Princeton University Press.

Robicsek, Francis. 1978. *The Smoking Gods: Tobacco in Maya Art, History, and Religion.* Norman: University of Oklahoma Press.

———. 1981. *The Maya Book of the Dead: The Ceramic Codex: The Corpus of Codex Style Ceramics of the Late Classic Period.* Charlottesville: University of Virginia Art Museum.

Romero, Javier. 1970. "Dental Mutilation, Trephination, and Cranial Deformation." In *Handbook of Middle American Indians*, vol. 9, *Physical Anthropology*, edited by T. Dale Stewart, 50–67. Austin: University of Texas Press.

Rossi, Franco D. 2015. "The Brothers *Taaj*: Civil-Religious Orders and the Politics of Expertise in Late Maya Statecraft." PhD diss., Boston University.

———. 2019. "Murals and the Archaeological Inquiry into Ancient Maya Education." In *Murals of the Americas*, edited by V. Lyall, 41–64. Denver: Denver Art Museum.

Rossi, Franco D., William Saturno, and Heather Hurst. 2015. "Maya Codex Book Production and the Politics of Expertise: Archaeology of a Classic Period Household at Xultun, Guatemala." *American Anthropologist* 117 (1): 116–132.

Rovner, Irwin, and Suzanne M. Lewenstein. 1997. *Maya Stone Tools of Dzibilchaltún, Yucatán, and Becán and Chicanná, Campeche.* New Orleans: Middle American Research Institute.

Roys, Ralph L. 1931. *The Ethno-Botany of the Maya.* Middle American Research Series Publication no. 2. New Orleans: Department of Middle American Research, Tulane University.

———. 1943. *The Indian Background of Colonial Yucatan.* Carnegie Institution of Washington, Publication 548. Washington, DC: Carnegie Institution of Washington.

———. 1972. *The Indian Background of Colonial Yucatan.* Norman: University of Oklahoma Press.

Rubin, James H. 2003. "Realism." Grove Art Online, Oxford University Press. http://doi.org/10.1093/gao/9781884446054.article.T070996.

Ruz Lhuillier, Alberto. 1992. *El templo de las inscripciones Palenque.* 2nd ed. Mexico, DF: Fondo de Cultura Económica.

Sabloff, Jeremy A. 1975. "Number 2: Ceramics." In *Excavations at Seibal: Department of Peten, Guatemala*, edited by Gordon R. Willey. Memoirs of the Peabody Museum of Archaeology and Ethnology, Harvard University, vol. 13. Cambridge, MA: Peabody Museum of Archaeology and Ethnology, Harvard University.

Sahagún, Fray Bernardino de. 1959. *Florentine Codex: General History of the Things of New Spain.* Book 9, *The Merchants.* Translated by Charles Dibble and Arthur J. O. Anderson. Santa Fe, NM: School of American Research.

———. 1961. *Florentine Codex: General History of the Things of New Spain.* Book 10, *The People.* Translated by Charles E. Dibble and Arthur J. O. Anderson. Monographs of the School of American Research, no. 14, pt. 11. Santa Fe: School of American Research and University of Utah.

———. 1969. *Florentine Codex: General History of the Things of New Spain.* Book 6, *Rhetoric and Moral Philosophy.* Translated by Charles E. Dibble and Arthur J. O. Anderson. Monographs of the School of American Research. Santa Fe: School of American Research and University of Utah.

Santana Sandoval, Andrés, Sergio de la L. Vergara Verdejo, and Rosalba Delgadillo Torres. 1990. "Cacaxtla, su arquitectura y pintura mural: Nuevos elementos para análisis." In *La epoca clásica: Nuevos hallazgos, nuevas ideas*, edited by Amalia Cardos de Mendez, 329–350. Mexico, DF: Museo Nacional de Antropología, Instituto Nacional de Antropología e Historia.

Santasilia, Catharina Eleonora. 2013. "Investigations of a Late Classic Elite Burial at the Summit of Structure B1 at the Site of Cahal Pech, Belize." Master's thesis, University of Copenhagen.

Saturno, William. 2009. "High Resolution Documentation of the Murals of San Bartolo, Guatemala." In *Maya Archaeology 1*, edited by Charles Golden, Stephen Houston, and Joel Skidmore, 8–27. San Francisco: Precolumbia Mesoweb Press.

Saturno, William A., Boris Beltrán, Elisa Mencos, Paulo Medina, Asia Alsgaard, Timothy Foarde, and Adam Vitale. 2014. "Excavaciones en el conjunto Los Árboles, Operación XUL 12F19." In *Informe de Resultados de Investigaciones, Temporada de Campo, Año 2014*, edited by Patricia Rivera Castillo and William A. Saturno, 211–296. Guatemala City: Instituto de Antropología e Historia.

Saturno, William A., Heather Hurst, Franco D. Rossi, and David Stuart. 2015. "To Set before the King: Residential Mural Painting at Xultun, Guatemala." *Antiquity* 89 (343): 122–136.

Saturno, William A., Franco Rossi, David Stuart, and Heather Hurst. 2017. "A Maya *Curia Regis*: Evidence for a Hierarchical Specialist Order at Xultun, Guatemala." *Ancient Mesoamerica* 28 (2): 423–440.

Saturno, William A., Karl A. Taube, and David Stuart. 2005. *The Murals of San Bartolo, El Petén, Guatemala*. Pt. 1, *The North Wall*. Ancient America no. 7. Barnardsville, NC: Boundary End Center for Ancient American Studies.

Sault, Nicole L., ed. 1994. *Many Mirrors: Body Image and Social Relations*. New Brunswick, NJ: Rutgers University Press.

Saunders, Nicholas J. 1988. "Anthropological Reflections on Archaeological Mirrors." In *Recent Studies in Pre-Columbian Archaeology*, edited by Nicholas J. Saunders and Oliver de Montmollin, 1–39. BAR International Series 421. Oxford: British Archaeological Reports.

Schele, Linda. 1985. "The Hauberg Stela: Bloodletting and the Mythos of Maya Rulership." In *Fifth Palenque Round Table, 1983*, edited Merle Greene Robertson and Virginia M. Fields, 135–150. San Francisco: PARI.

Schele, Linda, and David A. Freidel. 1990. *A Forest of Kings: The Untold Story of the Ancient Maya*. New York: William Morrow.

———. 1991. "The Courts of Creation: Ballcourts, Ballgames, and Portals to the Maya Otherworld." In *The Mesoamerican Ballgame*, edited by Vernon L. Scarborough and David R. Wilcox, 289–315. Tucson: University of Arizona Press.

Schele, Linda, and Nikolai Grube. *Notebook for the XVIIIth Maya Hieroglyphic Workshop, March 12–13, 1994*. Austin: University of Texas.

———. 1994b. *The Proceedings of the Maya Hieroglyphic Workshop (Tlaloc-Venus Warfare), March 12–13, 1994*. Austin: University of Texas.

Schele, Linda, and Matthew G. Looper. 1996. *Workbook for the XXth Maya Hieroglyphic Forum*. Austin: University of Texas.

Schele, Linda, and Peter Mathews. 1999. *The Code of Kings: The Language of Seven Sacred Maya Temples and Tombs*. New York: Touchstone.

Schele, Linda, and Jeffrey Miller. 1983. *The Mirror, the Rabbit, and the Bundle: "Accession" Expressions from the Classic Maya Inscriptions*. Studies in Pre-Columbian Art and Archaeology, 25. Washington, DC: Dumbarton Oaks.

Schele, Linda, and Mary E. Miller. 1986. *The Blood of Kings: Dynasty and Ritual in Maya Art*. Fort Worth, TX: Kimbell Art Museum.

Scherer, Andrew K. 2015. *Mortuary Landscapes of the Classic Maya: Rituals of Body and Soul*. Austin: University of Texas Press.

Schmidt, Peter J., Mercedes de la Garza, and Enrique Nalda, eds. 1998. *Maya*. New York: Rizzoli.

Sears, Erin L. 2016. "A Reflection of Maya Representation, Distribution, and Interaction: Ceramic Figurines from the Late Classic Site of Cancuén, Petén Department, Guatemala." PhD diss., University of Kentucky.

Seelenfreund, D., A. C. Clarke, N. Oyanedel, R. Piña, S. Lobos, E. A. Matisoo-Smith, and A. Seelenfreund. 2010. "Paper Mulberry (Broussonetia papyrifera) as a Commensal Model for Human Mobil-

ity in Oceania: Anthropology, Botanical, and Genetic Considerations." *New Zealand Journal of Botany* 48 (3–4): 231–247.

Seitz, Russell, George E. Harlow, Virginia B. Sisson, and Karl E. Taube. 2001. "'Olmec Blue' and Formative Jade Sources: New Discoveries in Guatemala." *Antiquity* 75: 687–688.

Sharer, Robert J. 2006. *The Ancient Maya*. 6th ed. Stanford, CA: Stanford University Press.

Sheets, Payson. 1983. "Artifacts." In *The Prehistory of Chalchuapa, El Salvador*, vol. 2, edited by Robert J. Sharer, 1–131. Philadelphia: University of Pennsylvania Press.

Shively, Donald H. 1964–1965. "Sumptuary Regulation and Status in Early Tokugawa Japan." *Harvard Journal of Asiatic Studies* 25: 123–164.

Shook, Edwin M., and Elayne Marquis. 1996. *Secrets in Stone: Yokes, Hachas and Palmas from Southern Mesoamerica*. Memoirs of the American Philosophical Society, 217. Philadelphia: American Philosophical Society.

Simmel, Georg. 1957. "Fashion." *American Journal of Sociology* 62 (6): 541–558.

Skidmore, Joel. 2011. "Earliest Jester God Found at K'o, Guatemala." *Mesoweb Reports* 1–7.

Skinner, H. D. 1966. "Fragments of 'Stone' Tapa-Beaters from Vava'u, Tonga." *Journal of Polynesian Society* 75 (2): 229–230.

Smith, A. Ledyard. 1950. *Uaxactun, Guatemala: Excavations of 1931–1937*. Carnegie Institute of Washington Publication no. 588. Washington, DC: Carnegie Institute of Washington.

———. 1972. *Excavations at Altar de Sacrificios: Architecture, Settlement, Burials, and Caches*. Papers of the Peabody Museum of Archaeology and Ethnography, vol. 62, no. 2. Cambridge, MA: Peabody Museum of Archaeology and Ethnology, Harvard University.

———. 1982. "Major Architecture and Caches." In *Excavations at Seibal, Department of Peten, Guatemala*, edited by Gordon R. Willey, 1–263. Memoirs of the Peabody Museum of Archaeology and Ethnology, vol. 15, no. 1. Cambridge, MA: Peabody Museum of Archaeology and Ethnology, Harvard University.

Smith, A. Ledyard, and Alfred V. Kidder. 1943. *Explorations in the Motagua Valley, Guatemala*. Carnegie Institution of Washington Publication no. 546. Washington, DC: Carnegie Institution of Washington.

Smith, C. Earle, and Stanley G. Stephens. 1971. "Critical Identification of Mexican Archaeological Cotton Remains." *Economic Botany* 25: 160–168.

Smith, Michael E. 2003. "Information Networks in Postclassic Mesoamerica." In *The Postclassic Mesoamerican World*, edited by Michael E. Smith and Frances F. Berdan, 186–193. Salt Lake City: University of Utah Press.

Smith, Robert E. 1962. *The Pottery of Mayapan: Including Studies of Ceramic Material from Uxmal, Kabah, and Chichén Itzá*. Vol. 1. Cambridge, MA: Peabody Museum of Archaeology and Ethnology, Harvard University.

———. 1971. *The Pottery of Mayapan*. Papers of the Peabody Museum of Archaeology and Ethnology 66. Cambridge, MA: Peabody Museum of Archaeology and Ethnology, Harvard University.

Spinden, Herbert J. 1913. *A Study of Maya Art, Its Subject Matter and Historical Development*. Memoirs of the Peabody Museum of Archaeology and Ethnology, Harvard University, vol. 6. Cambridge, MA: Peabody Museum.

Staller, John Edward, and Michael Carrasco. 2010. "Pre-Columbian Foodways in Mesoamerica." In *Pre-Columbian Foodways: Interdisciplinary Approaches to Food, Culture, and Markets in Ancient Mesoamerica*, edited by John Edward Staller and Michael Carrasco, 1–20. New York: Springer.

Stanchly, Norbert. 2014. "Preclassic Maya Animal Resource Utilization." Paper presented at the Fourth Annual Maya at the Lago Conference, April 13, Davidson, NC.

Stone, Andrea. 1995. *Images from the Underworld: Naj Tunich and the Tradition of Maya Cave Painting*. Austin: University of Texas Pres.

———. 2011. "Keeping Abreast of the Maya: A Study of the Female Body in Maya Art." *Ancient Mesoamerica* 22: 167–183.

Stone, Andrea, and Marc Zender. 2011. *Reading Maya Art: A Hieroglyphic Guide to Ancient Maya Painting and Sculpture*. London: Thames and Hudson.

Storey, Rebecca, and Patricia A. McAnany. 2006. "Children of K'axob: Premature Death in a Formative Maya Village." In *The Social Experience of Childhood in Mesoamerica*, edited by Traci Ardren and Scott R. Hutson, 53–72. Boulder: University Press of Colorado.

Strathern, Marilyn. 1979. "The Self in Self-Decoration." *Oceania* 49 (4): 241–257.

Stuart, David. 1985. "The 'Count of Captives' Epithet in Classic Maya Writing." In *Fifth Palenque Round Table, 1983*, edited by Virginia M. Fields, 97–290. San Francisco: Pre-Columbian Art Research Institute.

———. 1996. "Kings of Stone: A Consideration of Stelae in Ancient Maya Ritual and Representations." *RES: Art and Aesthetics* 29–30: 147–171.

———. 1998. "'The Fire Enters His House': Architecture and Ritual in Classic Maya Texts." In *Function and Meaning in Classic Maya Architecture*, edited by Stephen D. Houston, 373–426. Washington, DC: Dumbarton Oaks.

———. 2000. "'The Arrival of Strangers': Teotihuacan and Tollan in Classic Maya History." In *Mesoamerica's Classic Heritage: From Teotihuacan to the Aztecs*, edited by David Carrasco, Lindsay Jones, and Scott Sessions, 465–513. Boulder: University Press of Colorado.

———. 2004. "The Beginnings of the Copan Dynasty: A Review of the Hieroglyphic and Historical Evidence." In *Understanding Early Classic Copan*, edited by Ellen E. Bell, Marcello A. Canuto, and Robert J. Sharer, 215–248. Philadelphia: University of Pennsylvania Museum of Archaeology and Anthropology.

———. 2005. *The Inscriptions from Temple XIX at Palenque: A Commentary*. San Francisco: Pre-Columbian Art Research Institute.

———. 2006. "Jade and Chocolate: Bundles of Wealth in Classic Maya Economics and Ritual." In *Sacred Bundles: Ritual Acts of Wrapping and Binding in Mesoamerica*, edited by Julia Guernsey and Frank K. Reilly III, 127–144. Barnardsville, NC: Boundary End Archaeology Research Center.

———. 2007. "Old Notes on the Possible ITZAM Sign." Entry in *Maya Decipherment*, edited by David Stuart. Electronic document. https://decipherment.wordpress.com/2007/09/29/old-notes-on-the-possible-itzam-sign/.

———. 2008. "A Childhood Ritual on the Hauberg Stela." Entry in *Maya Decipherment*, edited by David Stuart. Electronic document. https://decipherment.wordpress.com/2008/03/27/a-childhood-ritual-on-the-hauberg-stela/.

———. 2010. "Shining Stones: Observations on the Ritual Meaning of Early Maya Stelae." In *The Place of Stone Monuments: Context, Use, and Meaning in Mesoamerica's Preclassic Tradition*, edited by Julia Guernsey, John E. Clark, and Barbara Arroyo, 283–298. Washington, DC: Dumbarton Oaks.

———. 2012a. "The Name of Paper: The Mythology of Crowning and Royal Nomenclature on Palenque's Palace Tablet." In *Maya Archaeology 2*, edited by Charles Golden, Stephen Houston, and Joel Skidmore, 116–142. San Francisco: Precolumbia Mesoweb Press.

———. 2012b. "On Effigies of Ancestors and Gods." Entry in *Maya Decipherment*, edited by David Stuart. Electronic document. https://mayadecipherment.com/2012/01/20/on-effigies-of-ancestors-and-gods/.

———. 2012c. "The Verb *Bix*, 'Go, Go Away.'" Entry in *Maya Decipherment*, edited by David Stuart. Electronic document. https://decipherment.wordpress.com/2012/01/23/the-verb-bix-go-go-away/.

———. 2015. "The Royal Headband: A Pan-Mesoamerican Hieroglyph." Entry in *Maya Decipherment*, edited by David Stuart. Electronic document. https://decipherment.wordpress.com/2015/01/26/the-royal-headband-a-pan-mesoamerican-hieroglyph-for-ruler/.

———. 2019. "A Captive's Story: Xub Chahk of Ucanal." Entry in *Maya Decipherment*, edited by David Stuart. Electronic document. https://mayadecipherment.com/2019/06/23/a-captives-story-xub-chahk-of-ucanal/.

Stuart, David, Marcello A. Canuto, and Tomás Barrientos Q. 2015. "The Nomenclature of La Corona Sculpture." *La Corona Notes* 1 (2). Electronic document. www.mesoweb.com/LaCorona/LaCoronaNotes02.pdf.

Stuart, David, and Ian Graham. 2003. *Corpus of Maya Hieroglyphic Inscriptions*. Vol. 9, pt. 1, *Piedras Negras*. Cambridge, MA: Peabody Museum of Archaeology and Ethnology, Harvard University.

Stuart, David, and Nikolai Grube. 2000. *A New Inscription from Nim Li Punit, Belize/Una nueva inscripción de Nim Li Punit, Belice*. Research Reports on Ancient Maya Writing 45. Washington, DC: Center for Maya Research.

Stuart, David, and Stephen Houston. 1994. *Classic Maya Place Names*. Studies in Pre-Columbian Art and Archaeology no. 33. Washington, DC: Dumbarton Oaks.

Stuart, David, and George Stuart. 2008. *Palenque: Eternal City of the Maya*. London: Thames and Hudson.

Taack, George Henry. 1973. "An Iconographic Study of Deer Hunting Scenes in Maya Painting: Codex Madrid and Vases from Calcehtok and Altun Ha." Master's thesis, University of New Mexico.

Taladoire, Eric. 1990. "Artefacts mineur et objets de parure en pierre polie, céramique, os et coquilles." In *Tonina, une cité maya du Chiapas (Mexique)*, vol. 4, edited by Pierre Becquelin and Eric Taladoire, 1805–1827. Mexico City: Mission Archaéologique et Ethnologique Française au Mexique.

———. 2001. "The Architectural Background of the Pre-Hispanic Ballgame—an Evolutionary Perspective." In *The Sport of Life and Death: The Mesoamerican Ballgame*, edited by E. Michael Whittington, 96–115. London: Thames and Hudson.

Taschek, Jennifer. 1994. *The Artifacts of Dzibilchaltun, Yucatan, Mexico: Shell, Polished Stone, Bone, Wood, and Ceramics*. Middle American Research Institute Publication 50. New Orleans: Tulane University.

Tate, Carolyn E. 1992. *Yaxchilan: The Design of a Maya Ceremonial City*. Austin: University of Texas Press.

Taube, Karl A. 1988. "A Study of Classic Maya Scaffold Sacrifice." In *Maya Iconography*, edited by Elizabeth P. Benson and Gillett G. Griffin, 330–351. Princeton, NJ: Princeton University Press.

———. 1989. "Ritual Humor in Classic Maya Religion." In *Word and Image in Maya Culture*, edited by William F. Hanks and Don S. Rice, 351–382. Salt Lake City: University of Utah Press.

———. 1992a. "The Iconography of Mirrors at Teotihuacan." In *Art, Ideology, and the City of Teotihuacan: A Symposium at Dumbarton Oaks*, edited by Janet Catherine Berlo, 169–204. Washington, DC: Dumbarton Oaks.

———. 1992b. *The Major Gods of Ancient Yucatan.* Studies in Pre-Columbian Art and Archaeology, no. 32. Washington, DC: Dumbarton Oaks.

———. 1994. "The Birth Vase: Natal Imagery in Ancient Maya Myth and Ritual." In *The Maya Vase Book: A Corpus of Rollout Photographs of Maya Vases,* vol. 4, edited by B. Kerr and J. Kerr, 650–685. New York: Kerr Associates.

———. 1995. "The Rainmakers: The Olmec and Their Contribution to Mesoamerican Belief and Ritual." In *The Olmec World: Ritual and Rulership,* edited by Jill Guthrie and Elizabeth P. Benson, 83–103. Princeton, NJ: Princeton University Art Museum.

———. 2000. "The Turquoise Hearth: Fire, Self-Sacrifice, and the Central Mexican Cult of War." In *Mesoamerica's Classic Heritage: From Teotihuacan to the Great Aztec Temple,* edited by Davíd Carrasco, Lindsay Jones, and Scott Sessions, 269–340. Boulder: University Press of Colorado.

———. 2003. "Ancient and Contemporary Maya Conceptions about Field and Forest." In *The Lowland Maya Area: Three Millennia at the Human-Wildland Interface,* edited by Arturo Gómez-Pompa, Michael F. Allen, Scott L. Fedick, and Juan J. Jiménez-Osornio, 461–492. Binghamton, NY: Food Products Press.

———. 2003. "Maws of Heaven and Hell: The Symbolism of the Centipede and the Serpent in Classic Maya Religion." In *Antropología de la Eternidad: La Muerte en la Cultura Maya,* edited by Andrés Ciudad Ruiz, Mario Humberto Ruz, and María Josefa Iglesias Ponece de León, 405–442. Madrid: Sociedad Española de Estudio Mayas.

———. 2004. "Flower Mountain: Concepts of Life, Beauty, and Paradise among the Classic Maya." *RES: Art and Aesthetics* 45: 69–98.

———. 2005. "The Symbolism of Jade in Classic Maya Religion." *Ancient Mesoamerica* 16: 23–50.

———. 2009. "The Maya Maize God and the Mythic Origins of Dance." In *The Maya and Their Sacred Narratives: Text and Context in Maya Mythologies; Proceedings of the 12th European Maya Conference, Geneva, December 7–8, 2007,* edited by Geneviève Le Fort, 41–52. Markt Schwaben, Germany: Verlag Anton Saurwein.

———. 2010a. "At Dawn's Edge: Tulúm, Santa Rita, and Floral Symbolism in the International Style of Postclassic Mesoamerica." In *Astronomers, Scribes, and Priests: Intellectual Interchange between the Northern Maya Lowlands and Highland Mexico in the Late Postclassic Period,* edited by Gabrielle Vail and Christine Hernandez, 145–191. Washington, DC: Dumbarton Oaks.

———. 2010b. "Cache Vessel with Directional Shells and Jades, 500–600, Copan, Honduras." In *Fiery Pool: The Maya and the Mythic Sea,* edited by Daniel Finamore and Stephen D. Houston, 266–267. New Haven, CT: Yale University Press.

Taube, Karl A., and Stephen D. Houston. 2010. "Lidded Bowl with the Iguana-Jaguar Eviscerating Humans, circa AD 500." In *Fiery Pool: The Maya and the Mythic Sea,* edited by Daniel Finamore and Stephen D. Houston, 250–253. New Haven, CT: Yale University Press.

Taube, Karl A., and Reiko Ishiara-Brito. 2012. "From Stone to Jewel: Jade in Ancient Maya Religion and Rulership." In *Ancient Maya Art at Dumbarton Oaks,* edited by Joanne Pillsbury, Miriam Doutriaux, Reiko Ishihara-Brito, and Alexandre Tokovinine, 134–153. Pre-Columbian Art at Dumbarton Oaks, no. 4. Washington, DC: Dumbarton Oaks Research Library and Collection.

Taube, Karl A., William A. Saturno, David Stuart, and Heather Hurst. 2010. *The Murals of San Bartolo, El Petén, Guatemala.* Pt. 2, *The West Wall.* Ancient America 10. Barnardsville, NC: Boundary End Archaeology Research Center.

Taube, Karl A., and Marc Zender. 2009. "American Gladiators." In *Blood and Beauty: Organized Violence in the Art and Archaeology of Mesoamerica and Central America,* edited by Heather Orr and Rex Koontz, 161–220. Los Angeles: Cotsen Institute of Archaeology Press.

Taube, Rhonda, and Karl Taube. 2009. "The Beautiful, the Bad, and the Ugly." In *Mesoamerican Figurines: Small-Scale Indices of Large-Scale Social Phenomena,* edited by Christina T. Halperin, Katherine A. Faust, Rhonda Taube, and Aurore Giguet, 236–258. Gainesville: University Press of Florida.

Taylor, Dicey. 1982. "Problems in the Study of Narrative Scenes on Classic Maya Vases." In *Falsifications and Misreconstructions of Pre-Columbian Art,* edited by Elizabeth H. Boone, 107–124. Washington, DC: Dumbarton Oaks.

———. 1983. "Classic Maya Costume: Regional Types of Dress." PhD diss., Yale University.

Tedlock, Dennis. 1996. *Popol Vuh: The Definitive Edition of the Mayan Book of the Dawn of Life and the Glories of Gods and Kings.* Rev. ed. New York: Touchstone.

Thomas, Cyrus. 1882. *A Study of the Manuscript Troano.* Contributions to North American Ethnology 5. Washington, DC: Government Printing Office.

Thomas, Nicholas. 2014. *Body Arts.* London: Thames and Hudson.

Thompson, J. Eric S. 1930. *Ethnology of the Mayas of Southern and Central British Honduras.* Vol. 2. Anthropological Series, 17. Chicago: Field Museum of Natural History.

———. 1939. *Excavations at San Jose, British Honduras.* Carnegie Institution of Washington, Publication 506. Washington, DC: Carnegie Institution of Washington.

———. 1946. "Tattooing and Scarification among the Maya." *Notes on Middle American Archaeology and Ethnology* 3 (63): 18–25.

———. 1962. *A Catalog of Maya Hieroglyphs.* Norman: University of Oklahoma Press.

Tiesler, Vera. 2011. "Becoming Maya: Infancy and Upbringing Through the Lens of Pre-Hispanic Head Shaping." *Childhood in the Past* 4: 117–132.

———. 2014. *The Bioarchaeology of Artificial Cranial Modifications: New Approaches to Head Shaping and Its Meanings in Pre-Columbian Mesoamerica and Beyond.* New York: Springer.

Tokovinine, Alexandre. 2002. "Divine Patrons of the Maya Ballgame." Mesoweb. Electronic article. www.mesoweb.com/features/tokovinine/ballgame.pdf.

———. 2008. "The Power of Place: Political Landscape and Identity in Classic Maya Inscriptions, Imagery, and Architecture." PhD diss., Harvard University.

Tokovinine, Alexandre, and Dmitri Beliaev. 2013. "People of the Road: Traders and Travelers in Ancient Maya Words and Images." In *Merchants, Markets, and Exchange in the Pre-Columbian World,* edited by Kenneth Hirth and Joanne Pillsbury, 169–200. Washington, DC: Dumbarton Oaks.

Tomasic, John J. 2012. "Donut Stones as Thigh-Supported Spindle Whorls: Evidence of Ancient Maya Household Yarn and Cordage Production." *Latin American Antiquity* 23 (2): 215–228.

Tozzer, Alfred M. 1907. *A Comparative Study of the Mayas and the Lacandones.* Archaeological Institute of America, Report of the Fellow in American Archaeology, 1902–1905. New York: Macmillan.

———. 1957. *Chichen Itza and Its Cenote of Sacrifice: A Comparative Study of Contemporaneous Maya and Toltec.* Memoirs of the Peabody Museum of Archaeology and Ethnology, Harvard University. Cambridge, MA: Peabody Museum of Archaeology and Ethnology, Harvard University.

———. 1966 [1941]. *Landa's Relación de las Cosas de Yucatán: A Translation.* Papers of the Peabody Museum of American Archaeology and Ethnology, 18. Cambridge, MA: Peabody Museum of Archaeology and Ethnology, Harvard University.

Tozzer, Alfred M., and Glover M. Allen. 1910. *Animal Figures in the Maya Codices.* Papers of the Peabody Museum of American Archaeology and Ethnology, vol. 4, no. 3. Cambridge, MA: Peabody Museum of American Archaeology and Ethnology, Harvard University.

Trachman, Rissa M., and Fred Valdez Jr. 2006. "Identifying Childhood among the Ancient Maya: Evidence toward Social Reproduction at the Dancer Household Group in Northwestern Belize." In *The Social Experience of Childhood in Mesoamerica*, edited by Traci Ardren and Scott R. Hutson, 73–100. Boulder: University Press of Colorado.

Tremain, Cara G. 2014. "Pre-Columbian 'Jade': Towards an Improved Identification of Green-Colored Stone in Mesoamerica." *Lithic Technology* 39 (3): 137–150.

———. 2016. "Birds of a Feather: Exploring the Acquisition of Resplendent Quetzal (*Pharomachrus mocinno*) Tail Coverts in Pre-Columbian Mesoamerica." *Human Ecology* 44 (4): 399–408.

———. 2017. "A Study of Dress and Identity in the Late Classic Maya Court." PhD diss., University of Calgary.

Triadan, Daniela. 2007. "Warriors, Nobles, Commoners and Beasts: Figurines from Elite Buildings at Aguateca, Guatemala." *Latin American Antiquity* 18 (3): 269–293.

———. 2014. "Figurines." In *Life and Politics at the Royal Court of Aguateca: Artifacts, Analytical Data, and Synthesis*, edited by Takeshi Inomata and Daniela Triadan, 9–38. Monographs of the Aguateca Archaeological Project First Phase, vol. 3. Salt Lake City: University of Utah Press.

Trik, Aubrey S. 1963. "The Splendid Tomb of Temple I at Tikal, Guatemala." *Expedition* 6: 2–18.

Turner, Terence S. 2012. "The Social Skin." *Hau: Journal of Ethnographic Theory* 2 (2): 486–504.

Twigg, Julia. 2007. "Clothing, Age and the Body: A Critical Review." *Ageing & Society* 27: 285–305.

Vail, Gabrielle. 1997. "The Deer-Trapping Almanacs in the Madrid Codex." In *Papers on the Madrid Codex*, edited by Victoria R. Bricker and Gabrielle Vail, 73–110. New Orleans: Middle American Research Institute.

Vail, Gabrielle, and Christine Hernández, eds. 2010. *Astronomers, Scribes, and Priests: Intellectual Interchange between the Northern Maya Lowlands and Highland Mexico in the Late Postclassic Period.* Washington, DC: Dumbarton Oaks.

Vázquez de Ágredos Pascual, María Luisa, and Cristina Vidal Lorenzo. 2017. "Fragrances and Body Paint in the Courtly Life of the Maya." In *Constructing Power and Place in Mesoamerica: Pre-Hispanic Paintings from Three Regions*, edited by Merideth Paxton and Leticia Staines Cicero, 155–169. Albuquerque: University of New Mexico Press.

Velásquez García, Erik. 2005. "The Captives of Dzibanche." *PARI Journal* 6 (2): 1–4.

Velázquez Castro, Adrián. 2017. "Luxuries from the Sea: The Use of Shells in the Ancient Americas." In *Golden Kingdoms: Luxury Arts in the Ancient Americas*, edited by Joanne Pillsbury, Timothy Potts, and

Kim N. Richter, 91–97. Los Angeles: J. Paul Getty Museum and Getty Research Institute.

Ventura, Carol. 2003. *Maya Hair Sashes Backstrap Woven in Jacaltenango, Guatemala / Cintas Mayas Tejidas Con El Telar de Cintura en Jacaltenango, Guatemala.* English and Spanish ed. Richmond, TX: Ergodebooks.

Viel, René H. 1999. "The Pectorals of Altar Q and Structure 11: An Interpretation of the Political Organization at Copan, Honduras." *Latin American Antiquity* 10 (4): 377–399.

Villacorta, C. J. Antonio, and Carlos A. Villacorta. 1993. *Códices Mayas.* Guatemala City: Tipografía Nacional.

Villa Rojas, Alfonso. 1985. *Estudios Etnológicos: Los Mayas.* Mexico, DF: Universidad Nacional Autónoma de México.

Villela, Khristaan D., and Rex Koontz. 1993. "A Nose Piercing Ceremony in the North Temple of the Great Ballcourt at Chichén Itzá." *Texas Notes on Precolumbian Art, Writing, and Culture* 41.

Vogt, Evon. 1969. *Zinacantan: A Maya Community in the Highlands of Chiapas.* Cambridge, MA: Belknap.

von Euw, Eric. 1977. *Corpus of Maya Hieroglyphic Inscriptions.* Vol. 4, pt. 1, *Itzimte, Pixoy, Tzum.* Cambridge, MA: Peabody Museum of Archaeology and Ethnology, Harvard University.

———. 1978. *Corpus of Maya Hieroglyphic Inscriptions.* Vol. 5, pt. 1, *Xultun.* Cambridge, MA: Peabody Museum of Archaeology and Ethnology, Harvard University.

von Euw, Eric, and Ian Graham. 1984. *Corpus of Maya Hieroglyphic Inscriptions.* Vol. 5, pt. 2, *Xultun, La Honradez, Uaxactún.* Cambridge, MA: Peabody Museum of Archaeology and Ethnology, Harvard University.

von Hagen, Victor W. 1944. *The Aztec and Maya Papermakers.* New York: J. J. Augustin.

von Nagy, Christopher L. 1997. "Some Comments on the Madrid Deer-Hunting Almanacs." In *Papers on the Madrid Codex*, edited by Victoria R. Bricker and Gabrielle Vail, 27–72. New Orleans: Middle American Research Institute.

Voss, Alexander, and H. Jürgen Kremer. 1998. "La estela de Tabi: Un monumento a la cacería." *Mexicon* 20 (4): 74–79.

Wanyerka, Phil. 1996. "A Fresh Look at a Maya Masterpiece." *Cleveland Studies in the History of Art* 1: 72–97.

Welch, Evelyn. 2017. *Fashioning the Early Modern: Dress, Textiles, and Innovation in Europe, 1500–1800.* Oxford: Oxford University Press.

Welsh, William B. M. 1988. *An Analysis of Classic Lowland Maya Burias.* BAR International Series 409. Oxford: British Archaeological Reports.

Whittington, E. Michael. 2001. "Everything Old Is New Again: The Enduring Legacy of the Ancient Games." In *The Sport of Life and Death: The Mesoamerican Ballgame*, edited by E. Michael Whittington and Douglas E. Bradley, 131–135. Charlotte, NC: Mint Museum of Art with Thames and Hudson.

Whittington, E. Michael, and Douglas E. Bradley, eds. 2001. *The Sport of Life and Death: The Mesoamerican Ballgame.* Charlotte, NC: Mint Museum of Art with Thames and Hudson.

Wiessner, Polly. 1985. "Style or Isochrestic Variation? A Reply to Sackett." *American Antiquity* 50: 160–166.

Willey, Gordon R. 1965. "Artifacts." In *Prehistoric Maya Settlements in the Belize Valley*, 391–449. Papers of the Peabody Museum of Archaeology and Ethnology, vol. 54. Cambridge, MA: Peabody Museum of Archaeology and Ethnology, Harvard University.

———. 1972. *The Artifacts of Altar de Sacrificios.* Papers of the Peabody Museum of Archaeology and Ethnology, vol. 64, no. 1. Cambridge, MA: Peabody Museum of Archaeology and Ethnology, Harvard University.

———. 1978. *Excavations at Seibal. No. 1, Artifacts.* Memoirs of the Peabody Museum of Archaeology and Ethnology, vol. 14, no. 1. Cambridge, MA: Harvard University.

Willey, Gordon R., Richard M. Leventhal, Arthur A. Demarest, and William L. Fash Jr. 1994. *Ceramics and Artifacts from Excavations in The Copán Residential Zone.* Papers of the Peabody Museum of Archaeology and Ethnology, vol. 80. Cambridge, MA: Peabody Museum of Archaeology and Ethnology, Harvard University.

Williams, Jocelyn S., and Christine D. White. 2006. "Dental Modification in the Postclassic Population from Lamanai, Belize." *Ancient Mesoamerica* 17 (1): 139–151.

Wisdom, Charles. 1940. *The Ch'orti' Indians of Guatemala.* Chicago: University of Chicago Press.

———. 1950a. *Ch'orti' Dictionary.* Austin: University of Texas Press.

———. 1950b. *Materials on the Chorti Language.* Microfilm Collection of Manuscripts of Cultural Anthropology 28. Chicago: University of Chicago Library.

Wiseman, Frederick M. 1983. "Subsistence and Complex Societies: The Case of the Maya." *Advances in Archaeological Method and Theory* 6: 143–189.

Woodbury, Richard B. 1965. "Artifacts of the Guatemala HIghlands." In *Handbook of the Middle American Indians,* vol. 2, *Archaeology of Southern Mesoamerica,* pt. 1, edited by Gordon Willey, 163–180. Austin: University of Texas Press.

Yadeun, Juan. 1993. *Toniná.* Mexico, DF: El Equibrilista.

Yaeger, Jason, M. Kathryn Brown, Christophe Helmke, Marc Zender, Bernadette Cap, Christie Kokel Rodriquez, and Sylvia Batty. 2015. "Two Early Classic Elite Burials from Buenavista del Cayo, Belize." *Research Reports in Belizean Archaeology* 12: 181–191.

Zender, Marc U. 2004a. "Glyphs for 'Handspan' and 'Strike' in Classic Maya Ballgame Texts." *PARI Journal* 4 (4): 1–9.

———. 2004b. "Sport, Spectacle and Political Theater: New Views of the Classic Maya Ballgame." *PARI Journal* 4 (4): 10–12.

———. 2004c. "A Study of Classic Maya Priesthood." PhD diss., University of Calgary.

———. 2004d. "On the Morphology of Intimate Possession in Mayan Languages and Classic Mayan Glyphis Nouns." In *The Linguistics of Maya Writing,* edited by Søren Wichmann, 195–209. Salt Lake City: University of Utah Press.

———. 2016a. "The Crown Was Held above Him: Revisiting a Classic Maya Coronation Ceremony." Paper presented at the 2016 Maya Meetings, January 15–16, 2016, University of Texas.

———. 2016b. "The Syllabic Sign *we* and an Apologia for Delayed Decipherment." *PARI Journal* 17 (2): 35–56.

———. 2017. "Theory and Method in Maya Decipherment." *PARI Journal* 18 (2): 1–48.

Źrałka, Jarosław. 2014. *Pre-Columbian Maya Graffiti: Context, Dating, and Function.* Kraków: Wydawnicto Alter.

Źrałka, Jarosław, Bernard Hermes, and Wiesław Koszkul. 2018. "The Maya 'Protoclassic' from the Perspective of Recent Research at Nakum, Peten, Guatemala." *Journal of Field Archaeology* 43 (3): 236–256.

Źrałka, Jarosław, Wiesław Koszkul, Bernard Hermes, and Simon Martin. 2012. "Excavations of Nakum Structure 15: Discovery of Royal Burials and Accompanying Offerings." *PARI Journal* 12 (3): 1–20.

Źrałka, Jarosław, Wiesław Koszkul, Simon Martin, and Bernard Hermes. 2011. "In the Path of the Maize God: A Royal Tomb at Nakum, Petén, Guatemala." *Antiquity* 85: 890–908.

Index